THE GREAT WALL OF CHINA

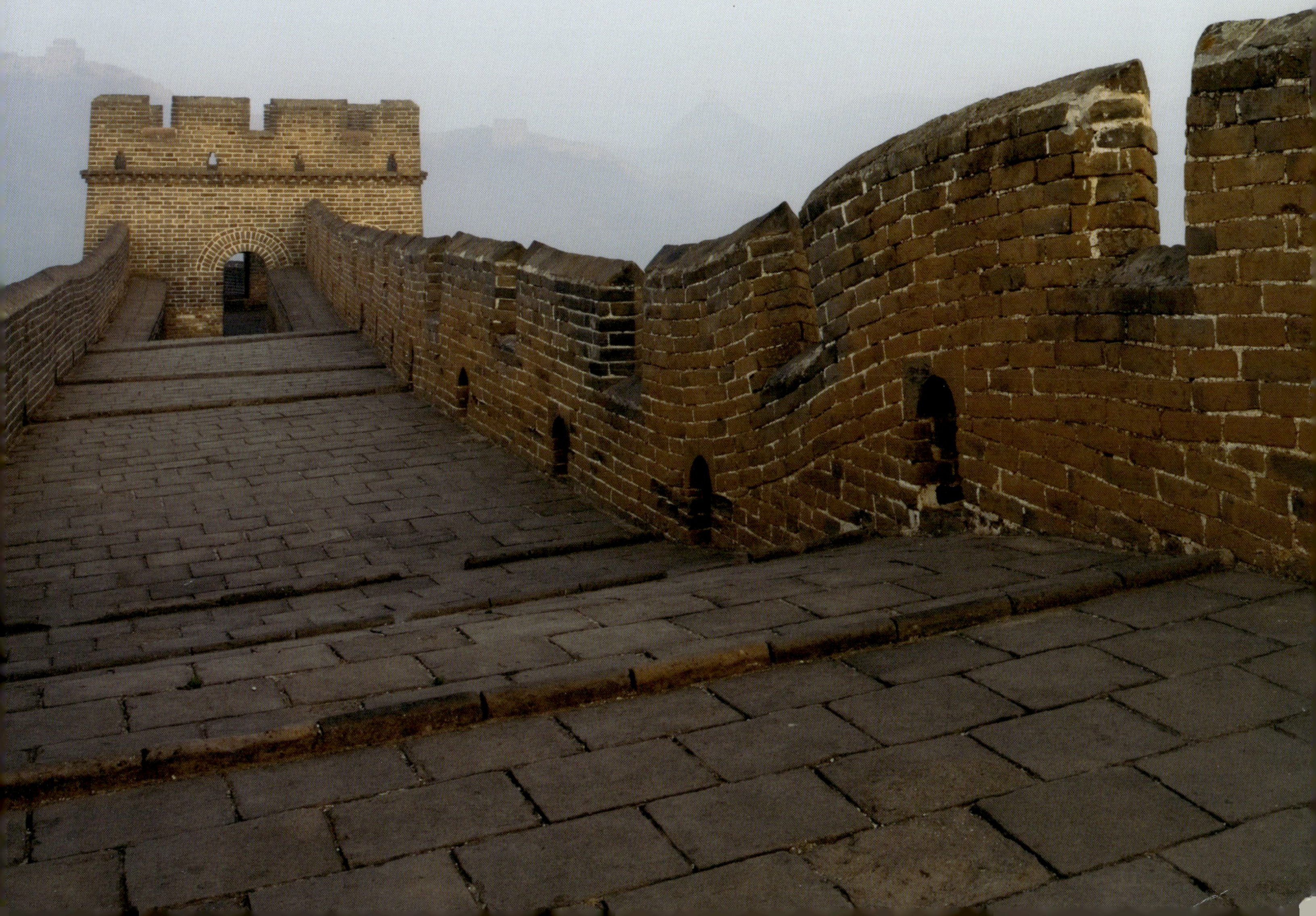

Sponsor's preface

The Beijing Badaling Cablecar Company is proud to support *The Great Wall of China: dynasties, dragons and warriors* exhibition. The cable car, which started operating in 1991, is the first to serve the Great Wall. Our facilities have enabled many millions of people, Chinese and international visitors alike, to enjoy and marvel at this incredible historic structure.

I first came to Australia as a secondary school student in the 1960s. Over the subsequent decades I have developed close personal and business ties in both Australia and China. I regard this exhibition as a wonderful way of fostering Australia-China relations.

As you will read in this handsome book, walls have figured prominently in Chinese people's minds over the centuries. As well as defining spaces, walls encourage people to live within their own realms and thereby to co-exist peacefully. This is the root of Chinese culture — harmony. This reality remains as true today as it was in times past.

As a lover of the Great Wall, I sincerely hope everyone who visits *The Great Wall of China: dynasties, dragons and warriors* or reads this book will feel some of the excitement and awe that one experiences at the Wall itself.

Mr William Chiu
Founder and Chairman
Beijing Badaling Cablecar Company Limited

PRINCIPAL SPONSOR

**BADALING
CABLECAR
COMPANY**

NATIONAL SPONSORS

NOVOTEL   ibis   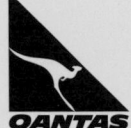 QANTAS   SHARP

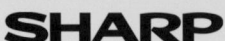

 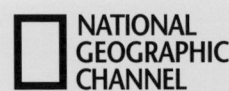 NATIONAL GEOGRAPHIC CHANNEL   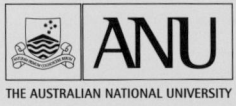 ANU
THE AUSTRALIAN NATIONAL UNIVERSITY

The Great Wall of China: dynasties, dragons and warriors exhibition is a joint project of the National Museum of China, Beijing and the Powerhouse Museum, Sydney, in association with the Palace Museum, Gansu Provincial Museum, Gansu Provincial Research Institute of Archaeology, the Municipal Museum of Dunhuang and Shanhaiguan Great Wall Museum.

THE GREAT WALL OF CHINA

EDITED BY CLAIRE ROBERTS AND GEREMIE R BARMÉ

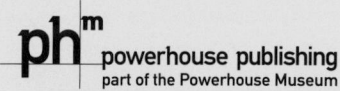
powerhouse publishing
part of the Powerhouse Museum

IN ASSOCIATION WITH
The China Heritage Project,
ANU College of Asia and the Pacific,
The Australian National University

The Great Wall of China is a joint project
of the National Museum of China, Beijing
and the Powerhouse Museum, Sydney

First published in 2006 by
Powerhouse Publishing, Sydney
PO Box K346 Haymarket NSW 1238
Australia
www.powerhousemuseum.com/publications

in association with
The China Heritage Project, ANU College of Asia and the Pacific, The Australian National University
http://rspas.anu.edu.au/pah/chinaheritageproject

Powerhouse Publishing is part of the Museum of Applied Arts and Sciences a statutory authority of,
and principally funded by, the NSW state government.

National Library of Australia CIP
The Great Wall of China.
Bibliography.
Includes index.
ISBN 9781863171212 (pbk)
ISBN 1 86317 121 5 (pbk)
1. Great Wall of China (China). 2. Military architecture - China. 3. China - History -
Ming dynasty, 1368-1644 - Antiquities. I. Roberts, Claire, 1959- . II. Barmé, Geremie. III. Powerhouse Museum.
951.026

The Great Wall of China
© 2006 Powerhouse Museum, Sydney
Essays and translations © the relevant authors or institution
Object illustrations © the relevant museum or institution

Publishing manager and project management: Julie Donaldson, PHM
Text editing: Mary Trewby
Design: 2birds Design Group
Picture research: Linda Brainwood
Rights & permissions: Linda Brainwood and Iwona Hetherington, PHM
Image scanning: Spitting Image (objects) and Ryan Hernandez, PHM
Image pre-press: PictureThis
Index: Jo Rudd
Printing: Hyde Park Press, Adelaide

Published in conjunction with *The Great Wall of China: dragon, dynasties
and warriors* exhibition
Powerhouse Museum 28 September 2006 – 25 February 2007
Melbourne Museum 23 March – 22 July 2007

The Great Wall of China: dynasties, dragons and warriors exhibition is a joint project
of the National Museum of China, Beijing and the Powerhouse Museum, Sydney,
in association with the Palace Museum, Gansu Provincial Museum, Gansu Provincial Research
Institute of Archaeology, the Municipal Museum of Dunhuang and Shanhaiguan Great Wall Museum.

Distributed in Australia and New Zealand by Bookwise International
Distributed in all other territories by Lund Humphries part of Ashgate Publishing, London

Editors' note
Some paintings/calligraphy are to
be read from right to left, a small
arrow indicates the direction.
Hanyu pinyin romanisation has been
used throughout the book except
for some proper names and
bibliographical references.

Abbreviations
PHM—Powerhouse Museum,
Sydney
NMC—National Museum of China,
Beijing
ANU—The Australian National
University

Cover image: designed by
Deuce Design, photo of the Ming
dynasty Great Wall at Jinshanling
by Jean-Francois Lanzarone

All contemporary photos are by
Jean-Francois Lanzarone for
the Powerhouse Museum, 2006,
unless noted otherwise.

CONTENTS

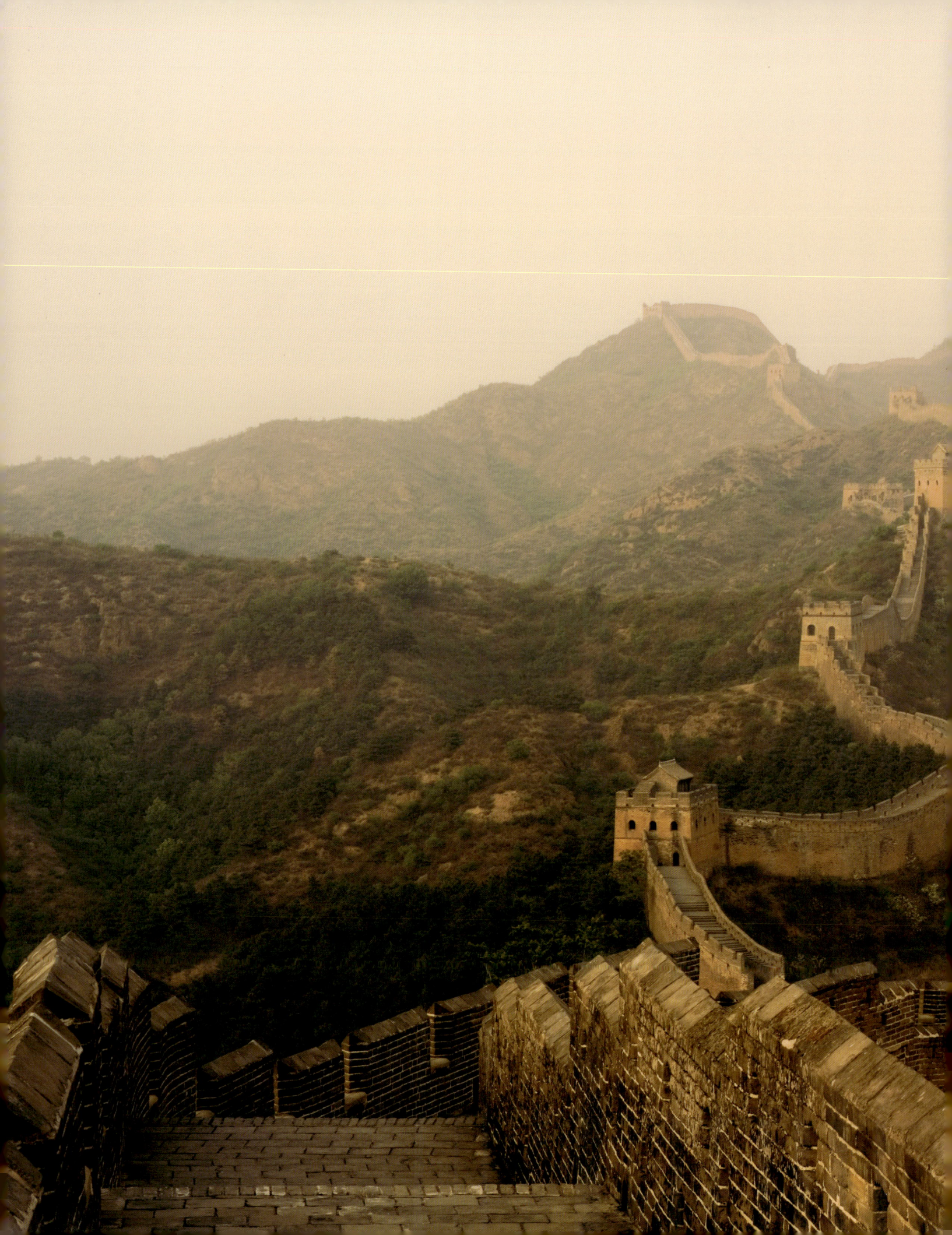

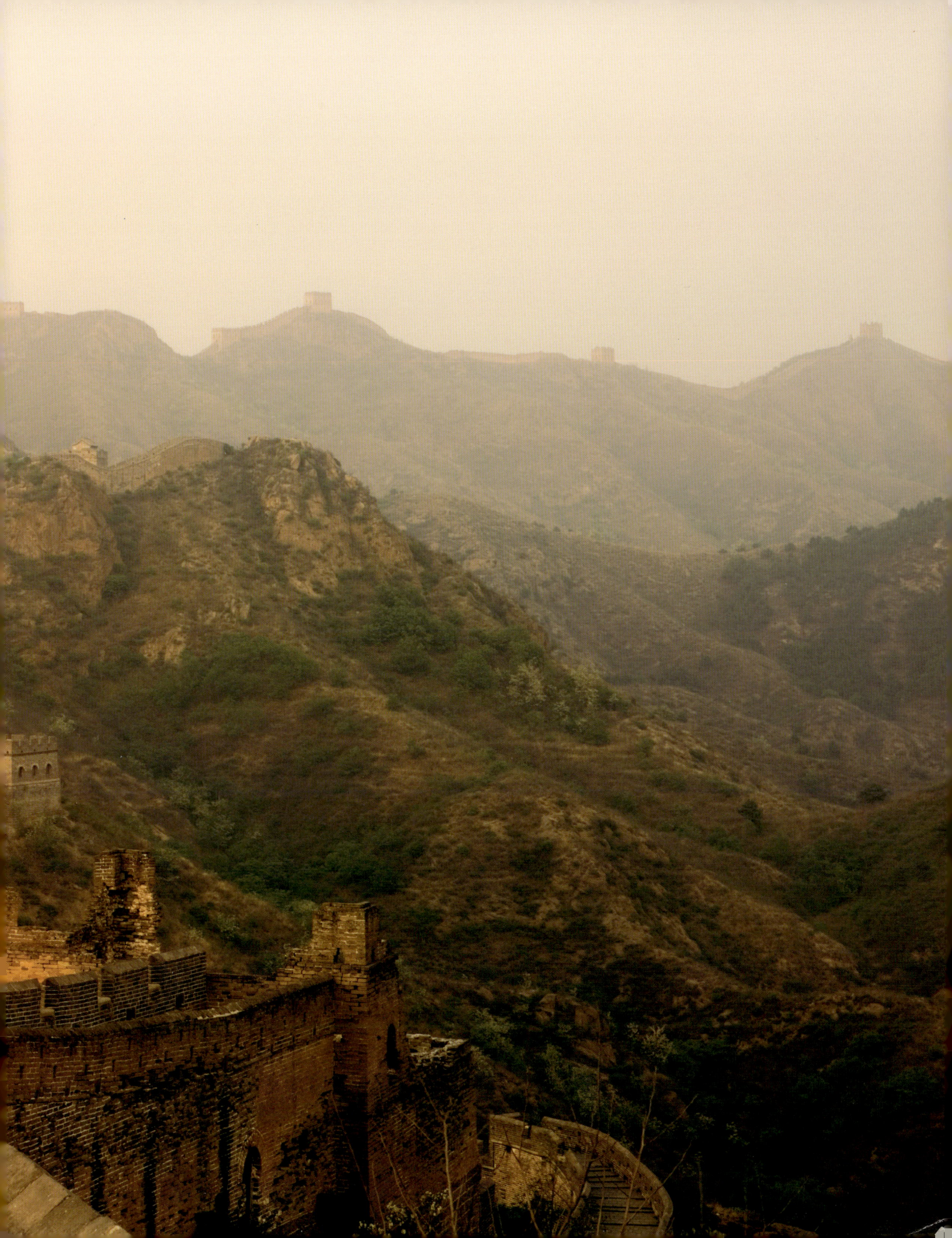

If you were to open an atlas of China you would very soon discover a distinctive line that marks a wall running from Gansu province in the north-west to Liaoning province in the north-east. The line that traverses half of the land mass of China is none other than the Ming dynasty Great Wall. While sections of the Great Wall were built much earlier, the Ming dynasty walls are the most complete and well preserved of all China's walls.

Construction of the Great Wall began in the Warring States period (475–221 BCE) before China was unified by Emperor Qin Shihuang in 221 BCE. During this period, walls were built by the various states as a defence against each other, and to guard against invasions from nomads of the north. Beacon towers and small castellated fortresses to house soldiers were constructed along the borders of states; later walls were built to link the towers and fortresses. These became the first manifestations of the Great Wall. From the beginning, therefore, the history and development of the Great Wall was inextricably linked to the development of China as a multi-ethnic nation.

In China's long history, a variety of ethnic groups including the Xiongnu, Xianbei, Dangxiang, Khitan, Mongols and Jurchen have at different times stepped onto the stage of history. Exchanges and interflows between these peoples and the majority Han population have been common in each period of history. This was particularly the case in regions controlled by ethnic groups located in close proximity to the Great Wall, who, after having adopted the agricultural practices of the Han Chinese, built on to the existing walls as a means of guarding against other nomadic groups encroaching on their lands.

The building and rebuilding of the Great Wall spanned many centuries and involved a tremendous amount of manpower. It was built as a military defence system during the age of 'cold weaponry' warfare and served an indispensable defensive function.

In ancient times the Great Wall separated people of different ethnicities working in disparate economic and cultural zones and allowed each to develop in a stable and secure environment, helping promote the economies of the various regions. Fair and equal communication and exchange among nationalities provided opportunities to enhance good relations, allowing for cultural exchange and the trade of goods which could be beneficial to all parties. These mutually influencing exchanges in the fields of economics, culture and lifestyle laid the foundation for the melding of ethnic cultures in China. Thus, the Great Wall can be seen as both a defensive barrier and an open pass. The various passes or gates constructed along the Wall were closed during times of war and opened in peacetime to allow for trade and other kinds of exchange. An example of this is the ancient wall in the west of China which protected the trade routes known as the Silk Road.

The Great Wall, symbolic of the industriousness, courageousness and intelligence of the Chinese people, is a treasure shared by all of China's nationalities. In 1987, the Great Wall was inscribed on the UNESCO World Heritage List.

The Great Wall of China: dynasties, dragons and warriors exhibition has been jointly developed by the National Museum of China, Beijing, and the Powerhouse Museum, Sydney, and is the first major international exhibition to take the Great Wall as its subject. The exhibition and this associated book include antiquities related to the Great Wall from different dynasties as well as objects from regions in proximity to the Great Wall.

It is my hope that the exhibition will help visitors to better understand the Great Wall of China. I wish the exhibition every success.

PAN ZHENZHOU
SECRETARY-GENERAL, NATIONAL MUSEUM OF CHINA

Previous pages: The Ming dynasty Great Wall at Jinshanling, Luanping, Hebei.
Photo: Jean-Francois Lanzarone

I first went to China to attend the opening of the Powerhouse Museum's exhibition of photographs by Hedda Morrison in May 2002. During that trip I also visited the Great Wall of China. My guide quoted to me the famous line by Mao Zedong: 'You're not a hero if you don't get to the Great Wall.' That evening I mentioned to my Chinese hosts that the Great Wall would make a perfect subject for a Powerhouse Museum exhibition — combining design and architecture with decorative arts and social history. To my surprise they said there had never been a major international touring exhibition about the Great Wall. The idea was still in my head when, a few months later, I welcomed to Sydney a senior delegation from the National Museum of China. They responded enthusiastically to the suggestion that our two museums might jointly work on such a project. It is thus a source of special pride to me to see this idea realised.

The Great Wall of China: dynasties, dragons and warriors exhibition is a truly collaborative undertaking between our two great museums, involving many staff and over 150 superb objects, majestic images and interactive experiences — all underpinned by a strong storyline. Whether it be the story of wall-building in China across the millennia or the recent transformation of the Wall from military structure into one of China's most visited tourist destinations, the Great Wall of China surely is one of the world's foremost structures.

On behalf of the Powerhouse Museum, I wish to thank the Chinese Ministry of Culture and the State Administration for Cultural Heritage, and our colleagues at the National Museum of China, the Palace Museum, Gansu Provincial Museum, Gansu Provincial Research Institute of Archaeology, the Municipal Museum of Dunhuang and Shanhaiguan Great Wall Museum for lending objects to the exhibition tour.

I also wish to acknowledge and thank our national corporate partners: Beijing Badaling Cablecar Company Limited, Channel 7, Accor Asia Pacific, Sharp, Qantas, National Geographic Channel and The Australian National University, without whose help an international project of this scale could not have been realised. I am especially indebted to Mr William Chiu and Mr Robert Ho, who have taken a strong personal interest in our project and assisted us greatly throughout its development.

Finally, I congratulate the editors and authors who have contributed to this very handsome book produced by Powerhouse Publishing in association with The China Heritage Project of The Australian National University to accompany the exhibition. The book is more than a catalogue of the exhibition; rather, it seeks to present multiple contemporary perspectives on the Great Wall of China, from Chinese, Australian and North American scholars, reflecting on the Walls' history and modern-day transformation.

I trust audiences who visit the exhibition in Sydney and Melbourne and readers of this book around the globe can share something of the majesty of the Great Wall, this great human achievement.

DR KEVIN FEWSTER AM
DIRECTOR, POWERHOUSE MUSEUM

Introduction

CLAIRE ROBERTS AND GEREMIE R BARMÉ

The Great Wall of China is the world's largest heritage structure. During the course of its history the Great Wall — or rather the many long walls that constitute what we call the Great Wall — has undergone a remarkable transformation, evolving from a military barrier, built by successive dynasties over more than 2000 years, into a national icon and one of China's most visited tourist attractions.

Known in China as the 'Ten-thousand *li* Great Wall' (*wanli changcheng* — one *li* is approximately 0.5 kilometre) and often referred to in the West as 'The Eighth Wonder of the World', the Great Wall has inspired and fascinated people for centuries.

In 1961, the Great Wall was listed by the State Council of China as a grade-one national cultural heritage site, and in 1987 it was inscribed on the UNESCO World Heritage List. Today, in the lead-up to the 2008 Beijing Olympic Games, there are almost daily news items relating to the Great Wall: to mapping, conserving and rebuilding projects, as well as reports on tourist developments, events, stunts and product launches that use the Wall as a spectacular and media-friendly backdrop.

There is, however, a tension between the needs of tourism and heritage. As well as the Chinese government, there are a number of grass-roots organisations that are active in promoting the value and heritage significance of the Great Wall. Notable among these is the Great Wall Society founded in 1987 with an impressive array of members drawn from all echelons of Chinese society. The society established the Great Wall Museum at Badaling, north-west of Beijing, and it is currently working with the State Bureau of Surveying and Mapping on a major project to measure the length of the Great Wall. More recent groups include A *small site on the Great Wall* (Changcheng xiao zhan, www.thegreatwall.com.cn), which initiates activities on the internet to improve understanding and encourage protection of the wall, particularly among those who live in its proximity, and the International Friends of the Great Wall, established by William Lindesay in 1998.

The Great Wall of China entered the Western imagination as both fact and myth at a time of aggressive European trade expansion. Its status continued to grow as China confronted dynastic decline, foreign incursion and the demands of modern nationhood. Franz Kafka called one of his most famous stories about hierarchy and existential angst 'The Great Wall of China' and the Albanian-born Nobel-laureate, Ismail Kadaré, recently published his story about the Great Wall. The international media never tires of using the Great Wall as a ready-to-hand and immediately recognisable metaphor denoting a distant realm cordoned off by an aggressive barrier. In the world of international finance, executives and traders speak of the 'Chinese wall', to indicate sequestered activities within a company, while in the realm of the internet much is made of the virtual 'Great Firewall of China'.

Ironically, the Great Wall became an icon in its own land at a time of national crisis and renewal, and it has often been used by Chinese thinkers, as well as foreigners, as the overarching metaphor for a China that was a world

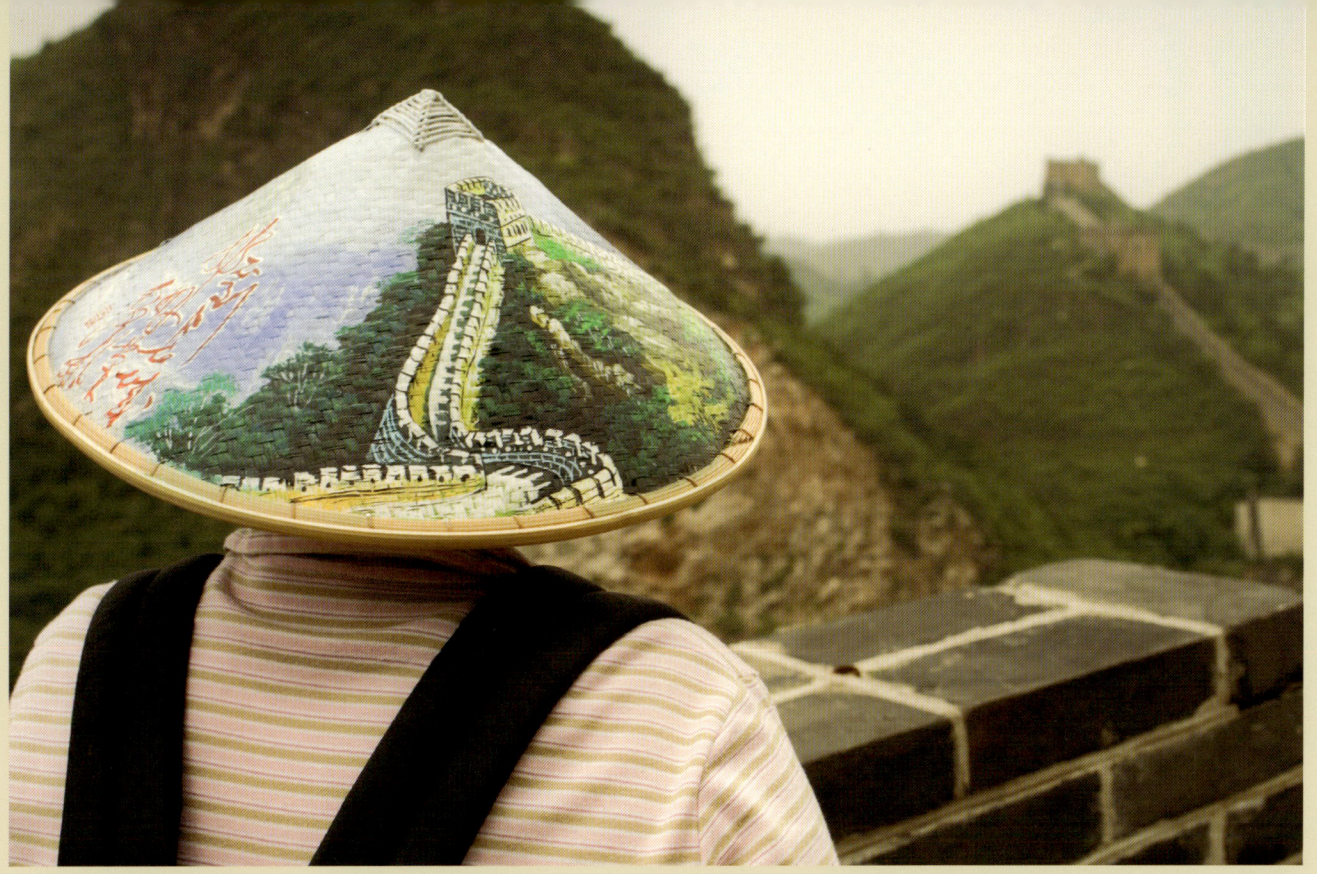

A tourist on the Great Wall north-east of Beijing.
Photo: © Paul Souders/Corbis/APL

unto itself. For many, it has also stood for vainglorious attempts to frustrate movement and exchange. Today, as China becomes an increasingly energetic participant in the global order, the history and status of the Great Wall is being reconsidered.

The most famous quotation relating to the Great Wall in modern China is from 'Liupanshan', a 1935 poem by Mao Zedong: 'We're not real heroes if we don't make it to the Great Wall' (*budao changcheng fei haohan*). Mao composed this poem after the Red Army had crossed the last and final hurdle on its epic Long March. In Mao's poem the Great Wall symbolises the battlelines drawn between patriotic Chinese and the Japanese invaders. The line is the most popular Chinese tourist slogan associated with the wall. Chinese and foreigners alike wear T-shirts emblazoned with the words in Mao's hand, now best translated as: 'You're not a hero if you don't get to the Great Wall'.

In the era of China's hyper-development, the Great Wall remains a powerful, and much imitated, presence. It is sanctified both by politics and by commerce. The first post-Cultural Revolution hotel built in Beijing with foreign capital was the Great Wall Sheraton, opened in 1983; it still boasts a crenellated wall. More recently, at Nanjiecun, a new model communist township in Henan province, a to-scale great wall has been built between the manufacturing end of town and the residential quarter; it has become a tourist attraction in its own right. At various places in China successful business men and women are building replica great walls, large and small, as a sign of both pride and success. In 2002–03, a group of twelve up-coming Asian architects designed Commune by The Great Wall, a series of ultra-modern luxury villas close to the Badaling highway that has now become a boutique hotel.

We are mindful of all these uses and abuses of the Great Wall, its abiding valence and its iconic status. In this book we seek to dispel some of the myths about the wall: after all, it is not a single structure at all — and so we sometimes refer to it as the Great Walls — and it cannot be seen from outer space. Here we offer a history of the Great Walls of China by focusing on their associated textual and material culture. Essays by experts in China, Australia and North America, as well as a specially commissioned series of oral history interviews undertaken along the length of the walls, provide multiple perspectives on the history, construction and military use of China's walls. They also provide readers with new interpretive angles for the appreciation of their significance and heritage value today.

Six themes — fame, form, foundations, forces, frontiers and facades — provide a conceptual structure for the essays and interviews in the book, and they highlight the fact that the subject of the Great Wall crosses many areas of enquiry, including history, engineering, technology, architecture, social history, art history, decorative arts, tourism, heritage and cultural studies.

The National Museum of China has commissioned three essays by the senior research fellows Yang Wenhe, Liu Ruzhong and Wang Yueqian and provided detailed information relating to the museum objects reproduced in this book. The essays focus on the material culture associated with the walls and key objects in the National Museum of China's collection. Other essays commissioned by the editors explore subjects more broadly associated with the Great Wall of China. Luo Zhewen and Xu Pingfang, noted authorities, provide valuable historical and archaeological accounts, Bruce G Doar gives an overview of recent writings by Chinese scholars and explores the concept of Great Wall studies, and Cheng Dalin, who has published widely on the wall and taken many photographs while walking along its many sections, highlights the challenges involved in protecting and preserving this important cultural patrimony. Essays by Jeremy Clarke and Claire Roberts explore the fascination for China, and in particular the walls, expressed by early Jesuit missionaries and by foreign traders, travellers, writers and photographers. Wang Jiapeng and Geremie R Barmé focus on subjects associated with the Manchu-Qing dynasty, a period when the wall, no longer a defensive structure, began its remarkable transformation into becoming a symbol of China.

A human dimension to this extraordinary millennia-long history is provided by the noted scholar Uradyn E Bulag, who tells the story of the beauty Wang Zhaojun, and the oral historian Sang Ye whose interviews with people living along the course of the walls, from Dunhuang in the west to Shanhaiguan Pass in the east, are interspersed throughout the book. These poignant stories are about people whose lives have been marked in different ways by China's Great Walls.

There is a huge body of literature, both popular and scholarly, in Chinese and English related to the Great Wall of China. As Chinese thinkers redefine the modern history of their country and their complex relationships with the peoples of Inner Asia and the West, the Great Wall features once more in their discussions. The wall is a symbolic border, a line of demarcation and a zone of influence against which contemporary China relates to its neighbours and the world. Some key works are referred to in our bibliography but, owing to the limitations of space, this is far from being an exhaustive list. We hope that this book will inspire greater interest in the unfolding history of one of humanity's most remarkable and enduring monuments.

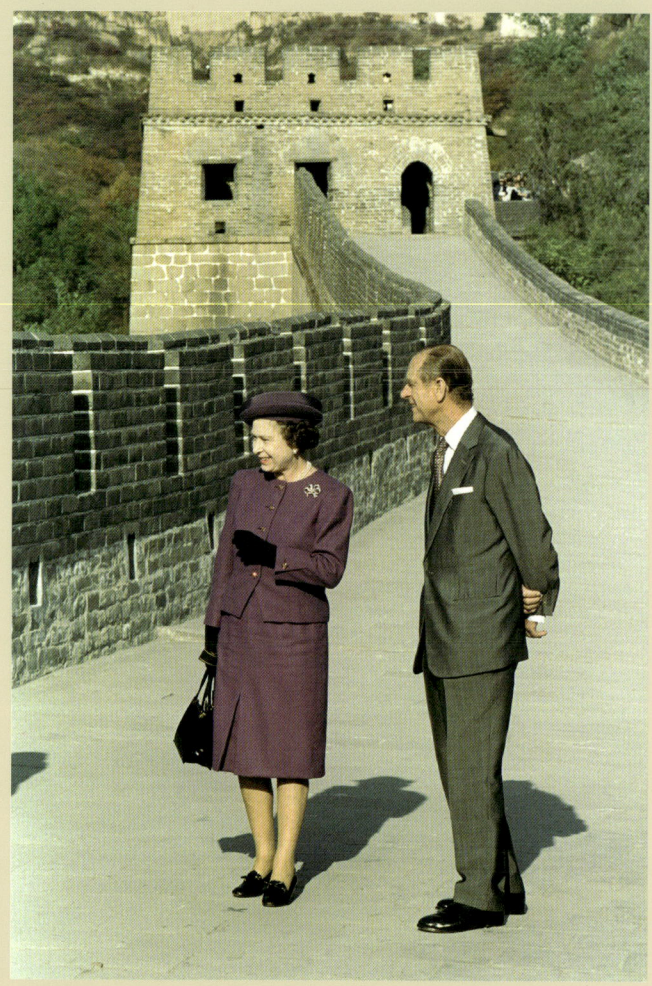

Queen Elizabeth II and Prince Philip sightseeing at the Ming dynasty Great Wall at Badaling, Yanqing, Beijing, in 1986.
Photo: © Tim Graham/Corbis/APL

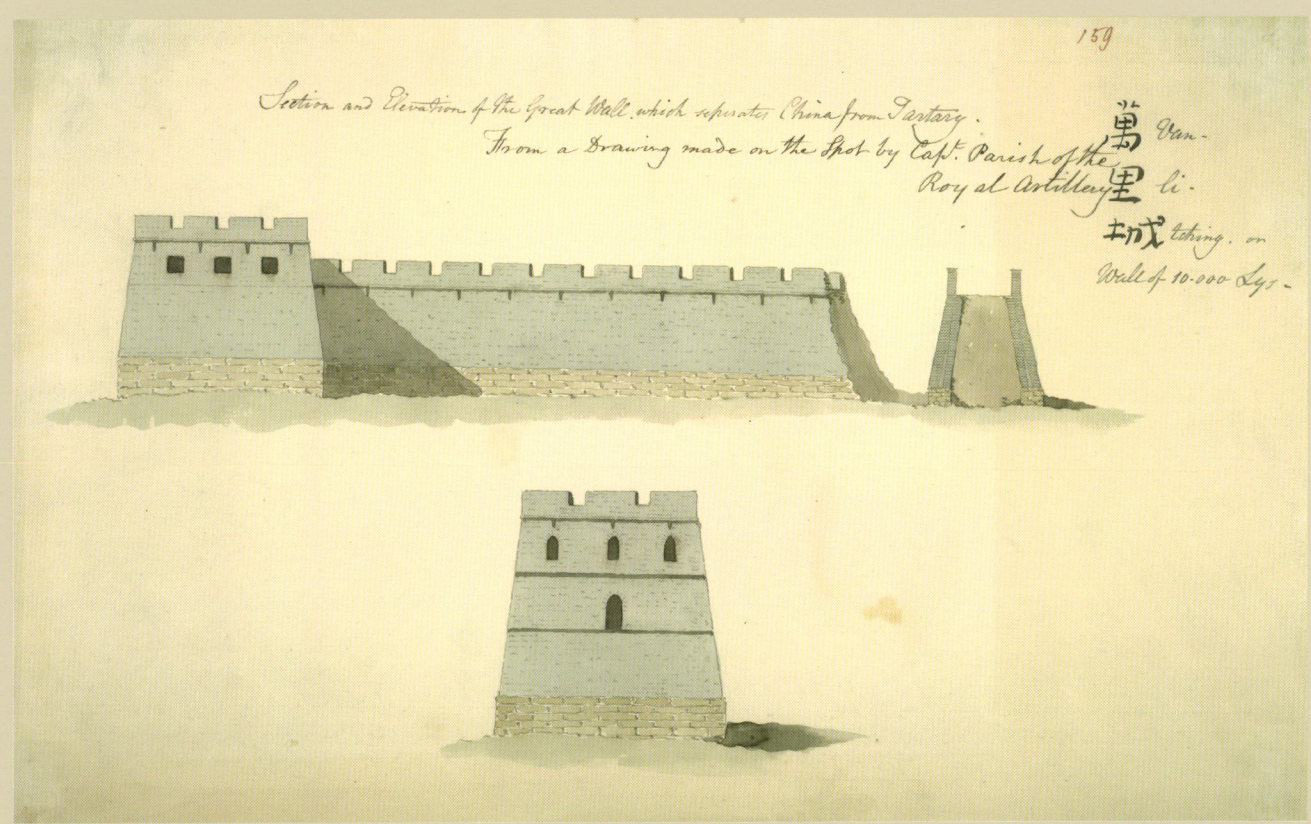

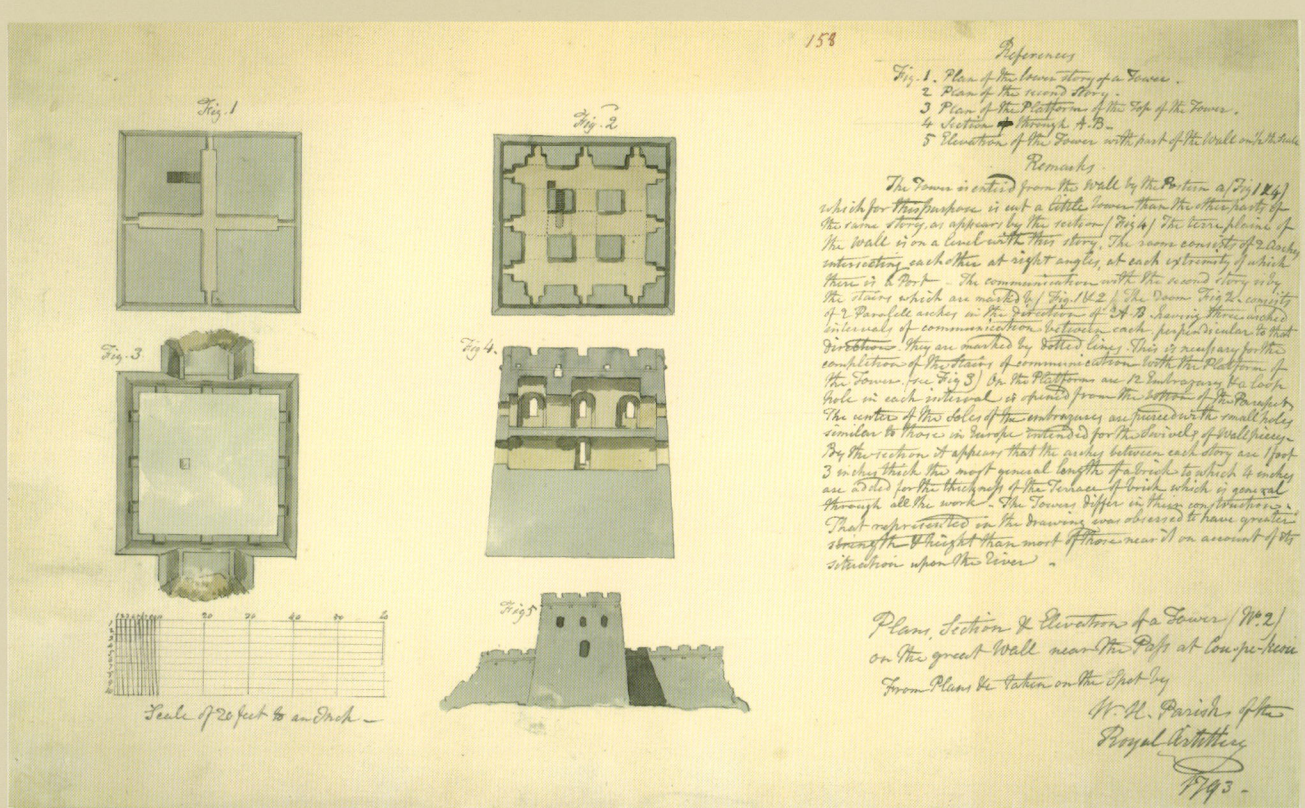

Technical drawings of the Great Wall by Lieutenant Henry William Parish of the British Royal Artillery, 1793. Parish travelled to China with Lord Macartney as part of the first British embassy to the Qing court.

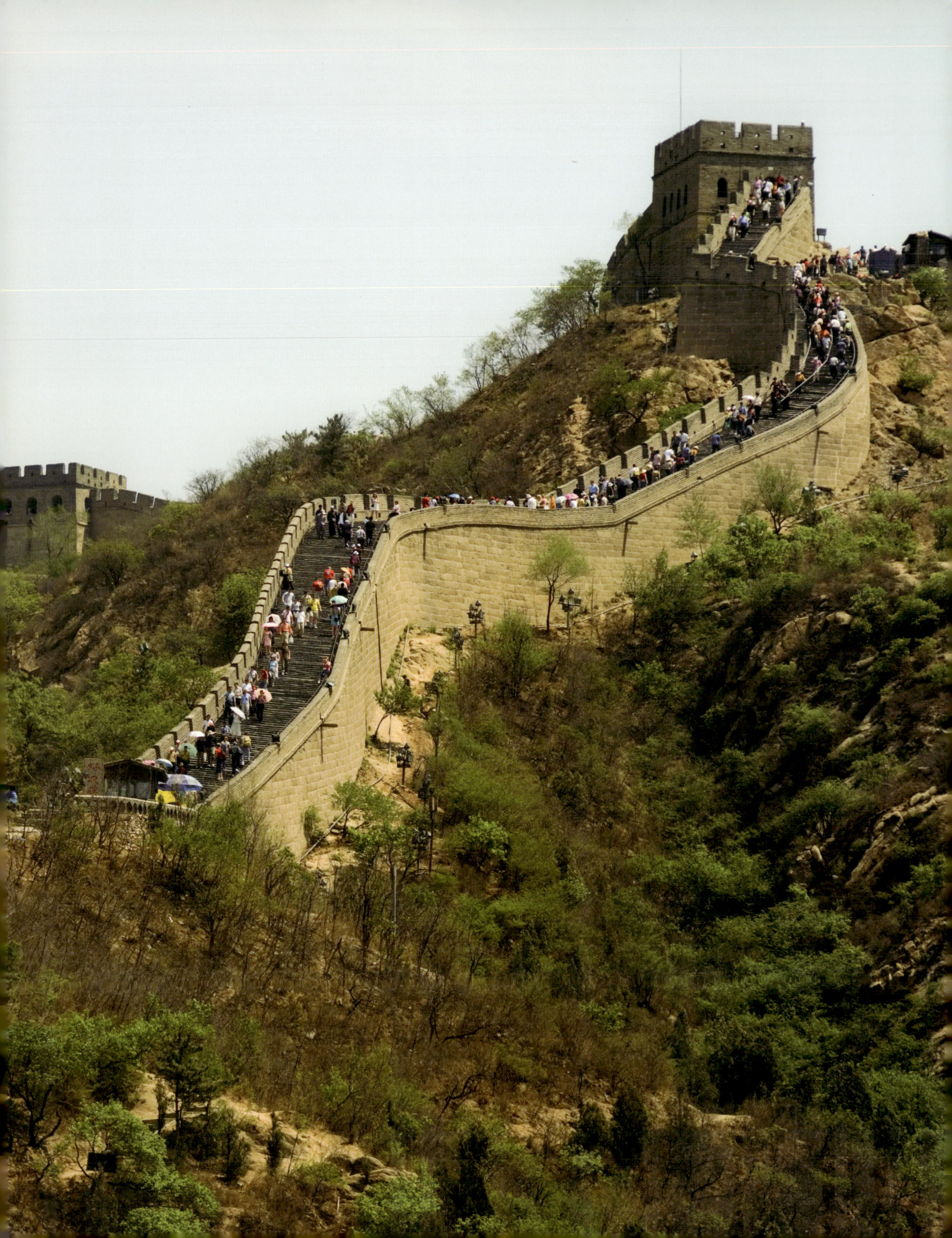

FAME

White Horses by Cao Zhi (192-232)

White horses, all adorned with golden bridles,
On flying hooves go galloping north-west.
Who are the men who are riding these white horses?
They are wandering knights, who come from Yu and Ping.
They left their native towns when they were young,
To make their names on the desert's sandy borders...

They give their bodies to the mercy of point and blade,
Never for a moment do they think of their own lives.
They cannot spare a thought for father and mother,
Still less pay heed to their children or their wives.
Their *fame* is written in the annals of the bold,
For selfish interests have no weight with them.
They die to save their country from its dangers,
And look on death as a sudden journey home.

Excerpt from a translation by J D Frodsham

The Ming dynasty Great Wall at Badaling, Yanqing, Beijing.
Photo: Jean-Francois Lanzarone

China's most famous ruin

CLAIRE ROBERTS

Contrary to popular belief, the Great Wall is not a single wall but a series of walls built by different peoples for defence and offence over more than two millennia. Remarkable, fragmentary and extensive, their physical forms determined by the terrain as well as materials available locally, what started more than two thousand years ago as a series of lines inscribed by successive kings and emperors on notional maps was translated by engineers and labourers into complex concrete structures. Remnants of these walls stretch across the landscape like long arms from west to east, and northwards into present-day Russia and Korea. The walls and watchtowers that remain bear witness to Chinese history — monuments to the builders, soldiers, traders and travellers with whose stories they are inextricably connected.

In fact, the most recent additions to China's long ramparts, the Ming dynasty (1368–1644) walls, faced with stone and fired brick, are chiefly responsible for the images of The Great Wall of China that we carry in our minds.[1] The Ming walls possess the scale and the serpentine majesty of no other heritage structure. No matter whether they are regarded as part of an early and impressive system of integrated military defence, a symbol of containment and oppression or a human folly of extraordinary proportions, the Great Wall of China is a grand idea that has imprinted itself on the minds of people throughout the world.

Walls mean different things to different people. For many Chinese the Great Wall is associated with the foundational but despotic rule of Qin Shihuang (reigned 221–210 BCE), the first emperor of China. It is also associated with the ethnically diverse peoples it was designed to keep out who have historically occupied the strategically important desert area, or Western Region, that connects China to Central Asia and Europe. As early as the sixth century BCE poems were written about the frontier and battles fought between Han Chinese generals and nomadic peoples who were the enemy.

The king has ordered [General] Nan-zhong
To build a fort on the frontier.
To bring out the great concourse of chariots,
With dragon banners and standards so bright.
The Son of Heaven has ordered us
To build a fort on that frontier.
Terrible is Nan-zhong;
The Xian-yun [people] are undone.

Long ago when we started,
The wine-millet and cooking-millet were in flower.
Now that we are on the march again
Snow falls on the mire.

The king's service brings many hardships,
We have no time to rest or bide.
We do indeed long to return;
But we fear the writings on the tablets.[2]

The Western Region is remote for most Han Chinese people and it is associated with exile, hardship and death. In 1906–08, the British explorer and archaeologist Aurel Stein travelled from the border of Afghanistan and India, along the Hindu Kush and Kunlun mountain ranges and

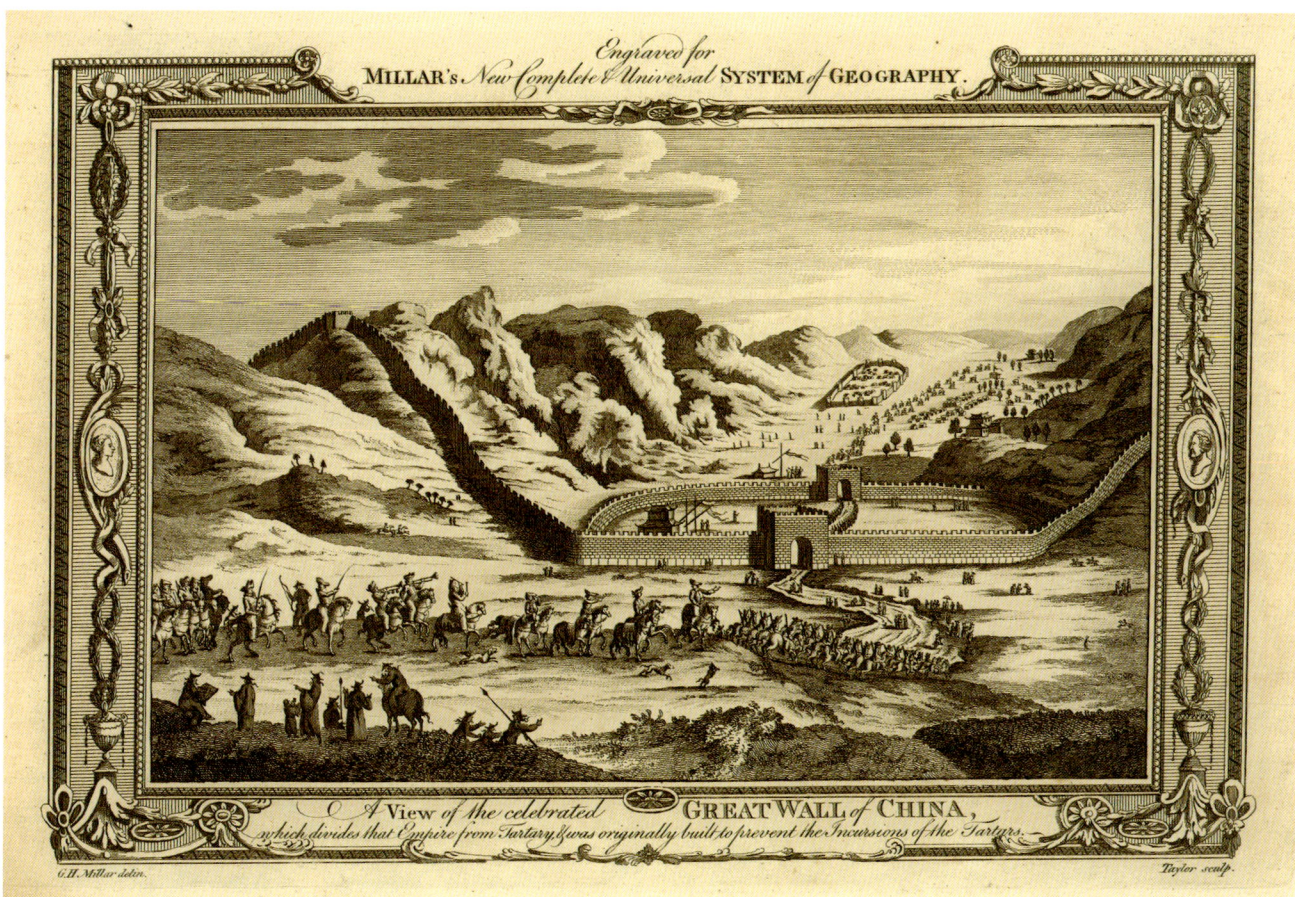

Engraving, 'View of the celebrated Great Wall of China which divides that empire from Tartary and was originally built to prevent the incursions of the Tartars', from *Millar's new complete and universal system of geography*, London, 1782.

across the Taklamakan Desert to the oasis of Dunhuang and beyond. During the course of his expedition he uncovered thousands of archaeological objects from the ruins of watchtowers where troops were garrisoned some 2000 years before. He filled twenty-nine cases with precious manuscripts and paintings from the Mogao Caves at Dunhuang; they are now in the British Museum.[3] Stein observed the sentiment of his Chinese secretary Chiang Ssu-yeh as he approached the Jiayuguan Pass, the westernmost pass of the Chinese empire. 'Ssu-yeh had here said good-bye to true China with tears in his eyes when he passed through seventeen years before. He was sharing now my elation at approaching the famous Gate again.'[4]

Earlier Stein wrote:

It did not need ruins to make me feel the historical importance of the narrow cart track by which we continued our march… I knew that I was now treading the very ground over which all Chinese enterprises towards the 'Western Regions' had moved during more than two thousand years. These terribly barren ridges, furrowed by a maze of narrow ravines, must have frowned down on the very first Chinese missions and expeditions which went forth to conquer Turkestan. How many of those thousands and thousands of soldiers and administrators who have passed by here to the lands of exile in Central Asia, had lived to see the day of their fondly-hoped-for return 'within the Wall'?[5]

For others the Great Wall was a romantic ruin of mythic proportions that came to be regarded as symbolic of China. Lord Macartney saw the wall in 1793–94 when he travelled from Beijing to Chengde (Jehol) as British envoy to the Qianlong emperor. He referred to a section near Gubeikou Pass as 'this celebrated wall which we had heard such wonders of'.[6] His party was fascinated by the wall and examined it at length. Macartney contrasted his own obsession with the apparent disinterest of his guides: 'Wang and Chou, though they had passed it twenty times before, had never visited it but once, and few other attending Mandarins had ever visited it at all.' Macartney commented on the wall's 'ruinous condition' and the 'very little care being taken to preserve it'. By way of explanation he noted astutely that the wall had reached the end of its life as a military barrier: 'For the [Manchu-Qing] Emperor now reigning has extended his territory so far beyond it that I doubt whether his dominions without the wall are inferior to those within.'[7]

In the eighteenth century, China had become a fashionable place to read about and interest in visiting the Great Wall revealed a spirit of wanderlust and curiosity.[8] But many could only dream of visiting it. In 1778, James Boswell observed that his friend Dr Samuel Johnson

expressed a particular enthusiasm with respect to visiting the wall of China. I catched it for the moment, and said I really believed I should go and see the wall of China had I not children, of whom it was my duty to take care. 'Sir' (said he), 'by doing so, you would do what would be of importance in raising your children to eminence. There would be a lustre reflected upon them from your spirit and curiosity. They would be at all times regarded as the children of a man who had gone to view the wall of China. I am serious, Sir.'[9]

Prior to the eighteenth century, the Great Wall of China had featured in Western historic maps and in the accounts of diplomats, missionaries, explorers, intrepid travellers and traders. Writers who referred to the walls include Matteo Ricci (1552–1610), Benedict Goes (1562–1607), Bishop Juan Gonzalez de Mendoza (1550–1620), the Russian diplomat Ivan Petlin (whose report is dated 1619) and E Isbrants Ides (1692).[10] Accounts of China were accompanied by woodblock prints and engravings, including representations of the Great Wall that were often fantastic in their conception. Then, in the mid-to-late nineteenth century, photographs, valued for their authenticity and faithfulness, usurped prints as the favoured medium for image-making of this kind.

Western photographers had begun to document aspects of life in treaty ports where foreigners were permitted to trade. In 1860, Felice Beato (1820s?–1907?) accompanied the British forces to China to record the Second Opium War (1856–60). Beato's photographs of Beijing are the earliest works of that city by an identifiable photographer.[11] His images of the Anglo-French assault on the forts at Dagu (Taku) that protected the approach to the capital and the destructions of the emperor's garden palaces are as memorable as they are shocking. His photographs of Beijing's majestic, intact and fortress-like city walls are of great historical significance. But there is no evidence to suggest that he visited the Great Wall.

Through deluxe books of travel photographs, China was brought gently into the living rooms of Western households with images that were less confronting but no less fascinating. Publications such as the four-volume folio *Illustrations of China and its people* by John Thomson (1837–1921) appeared in 1873–74 and included 200 photographs taken between 1862 and 1872. Thomson's aim was to 'convey an accurate impression of the country I traversed as well as of the arts, usages, and manners which prevail in different provinces of the Empire.' The photographs were arranged in the natural sequence of Thomson's journey, beginning in Hong Kong, then a British colony, continuing to many of the treaty ports that had been forced open to foreign trade following the opium wars, and concluding with photographs of Juyongguan Pass and the Great Wall at Nankou Pass, north of Beijing, now known as Badaling.

Thomson provided an armchair journey through a country that was still exotic and inaccessible for most of his readers. The caption for his photograph of the Great Wall acknowledged it was already established as a symbolic structure: 'My readers doubtless share with me in feeling

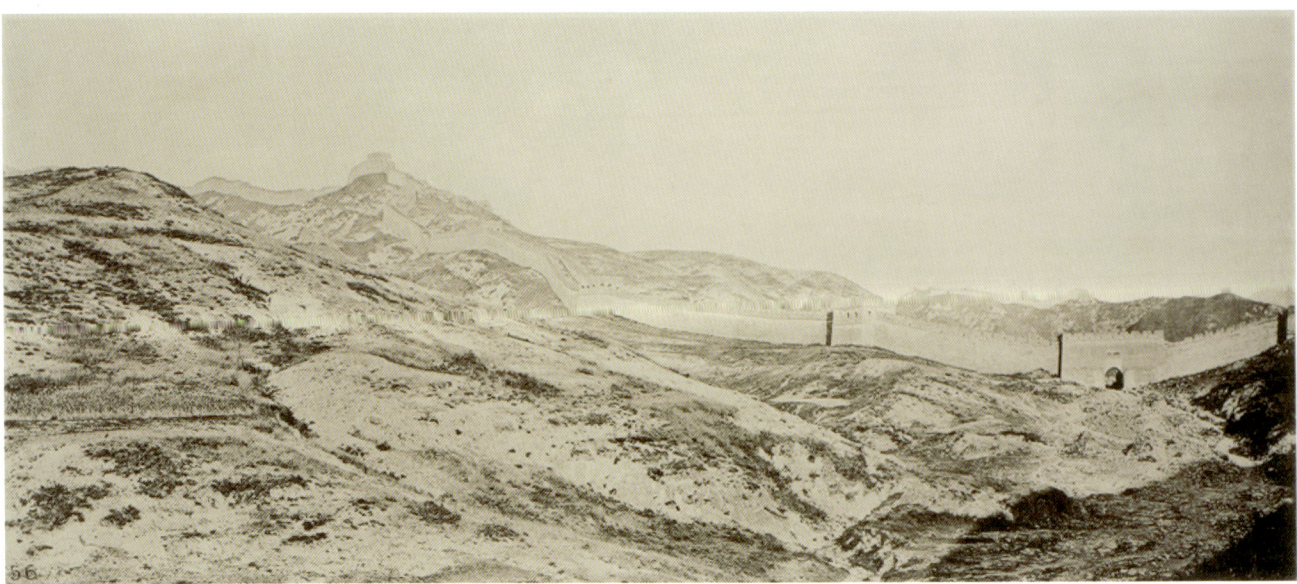

The Great Wall of China, photograph by John Thomson, 1862–72.
Reproduced from *Illustrations of China and its people*, vol 4, plate xxiv, London, 1874

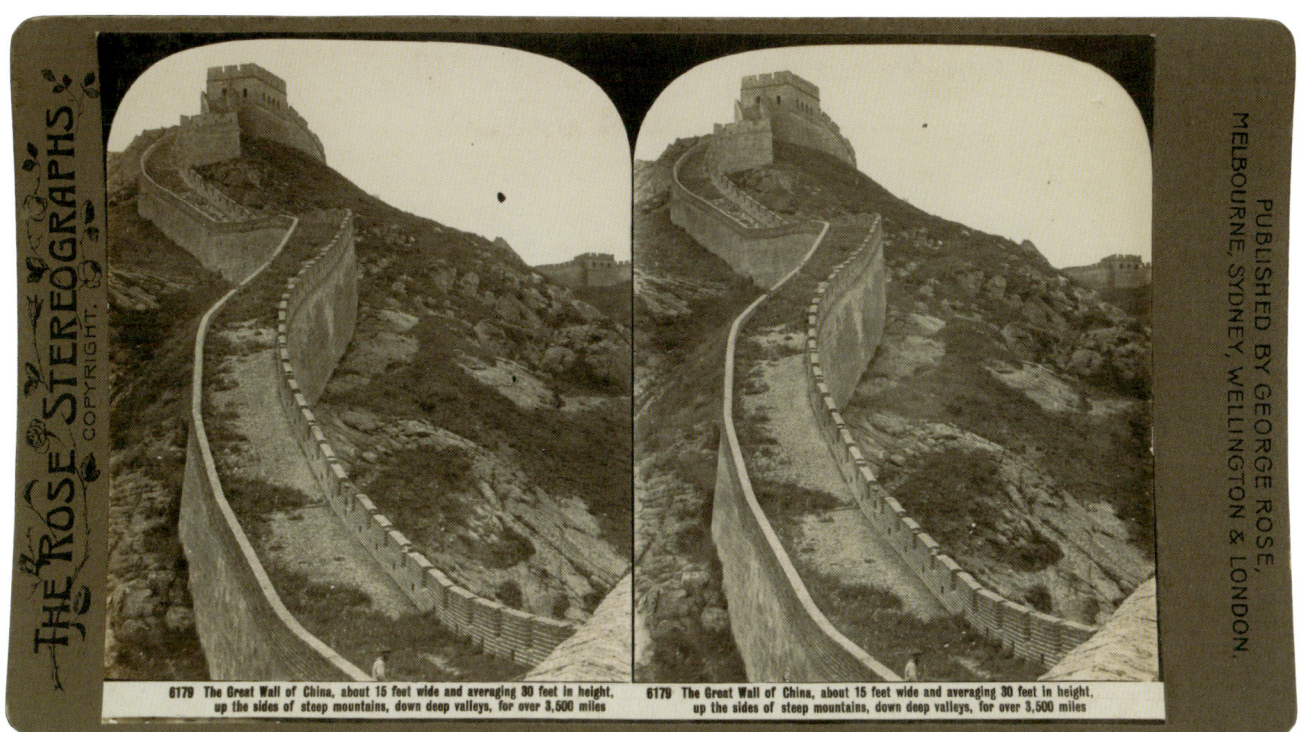

The Great Wall of China, stereograph by George Rose, 1904.
Reproduced courtesy the La Trobe Picture Collection, State Library of Victoria

that no illustrated work on China would be worthy of its name if it did not contain a picture of some portion of the Great Wall.'[12] Thomson travelled to the wall in a 'Pekinese mule-litter … the usual conveyance adopted by the Chinese, if they wish for ease and comfort, when they visit localities outside the great wall'. When he got there he was not impressed. He found it 'neither picturesque nor striking' and called it 'the greatest monument of misdirected human labour to be met with in the whole world.' Thomson's photograph shows a distant section of the Ming dynasty wall at Nankou. It snakes across a bleak and rugged mountain range. Not content with a close-up shot, which might have shown 'its masonry often defective', Thomson chose to convey the wall's length and its integral relationship to the surrounding mountains.

The sections of wall at Nankou Pass, located 60 kilometres north of Beijing, are among the most spectacular. Nankou was of strategic significance because of its mountainous location on the road connecting Mongolia with the markets of China (and the dynastic capital of the Ming). The walls there had prevented many assaults by Mongol and Manchu armies. Owing to their proximity to Beijing these sections of wall were also the most accessible for daytrippers and became favourite sites of tourist pilgrimage. As a consequence, they have also been the most photographed. By 1908, such was the popularity of these sections of wall that the American adventurer William Edgar Geil, who published an account of his

journey from San Francisco to China and along the wall from east to west, described it as the 'Tourists' Great Wall'.[13] When train tracks pierced the wall at Qinglongqiao Bridge in 1909 and a regular rail service was established, the journey was made much easier (see 'Steaming through the Wall', pp 128–29).

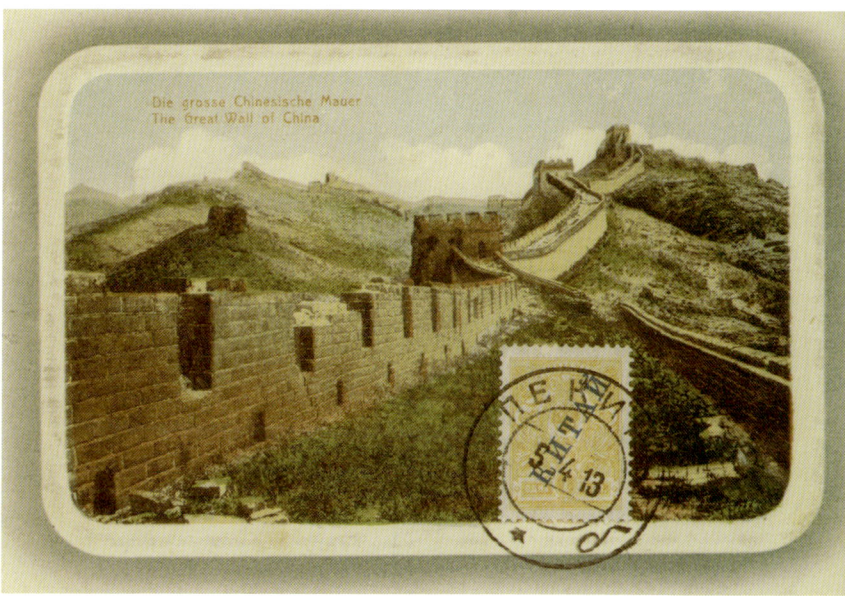

The Great Wall of China, Die Grosse Chinesische Mauer, postcard, about 1905.
Reproduced courtesy Wang Jia'nan and Cai Xiaoli

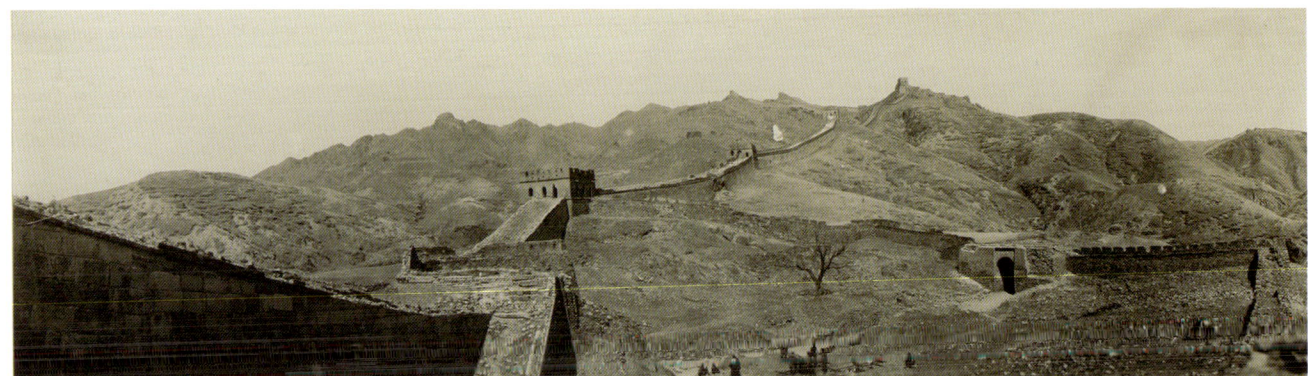

Panorama of Great Wall at Nankow Pass, by H Hartung, about 1922.
National Geographic Image Collection

In the second half of the 1800s, stereographs came into vogue. Stereographs are dual photographs taken side by side and mounted on a card. With the use of a special hand-held or tabletop viewer, known as a stereoscope, the two-dimensional photographs can be transformed into a three-dimensional form. Viewed singly, in themed sets or as part of a 'Tour of the World' with captions or an accompanying guidebook, stereographs became a popular and collectible parlour entertainment. Three-dimensional photographs could transport the viewer from mundane reality into remote and fantastic worlds. The Underwood Brothers were active in America, the largest market, selling stereographs door to door. Negretti and Zambra, based in London, published the first commercial views of China in stereo series in 1859.[14] In 1880, George Rose (1861–1942) established the Rose Stereograph Company in Australia. Rose, born in Clunes, Victoria, travelled extensively in Asia, the Middle East, Europe and North America and became well known for his stereographs of Australia and the Pacific. His 'large wooden glass-plate camera was fitted with two lenses spaced about as far apart as a person's eyes.'[15] In 1904, Rose journeyed to Japan, lured by the photographic prospects of the Russo-Japanese War (1904–05). He did not reach the front-line as he had hoped and travelled on to Korea and China, where he took some fifty stereo views in Weihaiwei, Qufu, Tianjin, Beijing, Shanghai, Canton (Guangzhou) and Hong Kong.[16] Among them is a view taken at Badaling captioned 'The Great Wall of China, about 15 feet wide and averaging 30 feet in height up the sides of steep mountains, down deep valleys for over 3500 miles'. In Rose's dramatic view the Great Wall begins with the masonry in the foreground, ascends steeply, twisting and turning as it climbs, and is punctuated by watchtowers as it recedes into the distance. The tall serpentine form of the wall created a view with clear foreground, middle and background zones and was the perfect subject for the stereograph. Viewed through a stereoscope, the three-dimensional effect was pronounced.[17]

In about 1908, the Rose Company, with offices in Melbourne, Sydney, Wellington and London, shifted its focus to the rapidly developing market for postcards. This Western innovation first appeared in the late 1800s with the emergence of commercial publishers. By the early twentieth century, the postcard industry was booming, driven by the demand of world travellers.[18] Postcards could be printed in large numbers and provided a new application for the work of photographers, even if only a small percentage of photographs taken were deemed suitable. Publishers kept a close eye on the market, catering to a taste for images that were exotic, dramatic and in some cases shocking. The Great Wall of China was a popular subject.

One postcard sent from Beijing shows a crumbling, overgrown, but still majestic ruin of a section of the wall, most probably at Badaling. The caption in German and English indicates the intended tourist market and the Russian stamp and postmark reveal its overland route to Europe. Another card showing the wall at Shanhaiguan Pass in Hebei province sent to Britain in 1905 is inscribed on the front 'Love from Lizzie and Ben'.

Postcards offered a personal, even intimate, way of connecting people and places. In the early 1900s, they were a novel form of time travel. Those particular postcards come from a collection assembled by two Chinese artists, Cai Xiaoli and Wang Jia'nan, who moved from Beijing to London in the late 1980s. Experiencing their own sense of displacement, Cai and Wang were fascinated by the way China was represented on the old postcards they discovered. They were also moved by how the cards had been preserved, treasured by their recipients and handed down through families before eventually being sold.[19] The cards purchased by Cai and Wang in Europe from dealers, auction houses and via the internet have now come full circle: they have recently returned to Beijing with their proud new owners.

S Yamamoto operated a photographic studio in Beijing in the late nineteenth and early twentieth centuries. He was also a publisher of postcards. Yamamoto took many portraits, including one of the renowned Australian journalist George Ernest Morrison (1862–1920) and Sun Tianlu, the manager of Morrison's household, as well as photographs of famous historic sites and scenes of daily life. In 1906, he published a selection of these images in a book titled *Peking*. It was printed in Japan with title page and captions in English and Chinese, suggesting that the primary market was English-speaking residents and tourists in China and Japan. This popular book was reprinted in May 1909. Included in the 100 views of Beijing are four photographs of The Great Wall. The first of these images depicts the Great Wall at Badaling as it zigzags across the bare and rocky mountain range, revealing areas of damage where the wall has been breached. Together these photographs trace Yamamoto's journey up the rampart and along its eroded surface.

A very similar view was accessioned into the photographic archive of the National Geographic Society in Washington DC in 1922. It is captioned *Panorama of Great Wall at Nankow Pass showing passage of road under a loop of the wall* and was taken by H Hartung, a German photographer resident in Beijing. Hartung's photographs of the Great Wall, the Forbidden City and the Summer Palace were used as illustrations in Juliet Bredon's classic book about the old capital, *Peking: a historical and intimate description of its chief places of interest*, first published in 1919. Bredon advised her readers that 'The classical excursion from Peking [Beijing] which no tourist, however hurried,

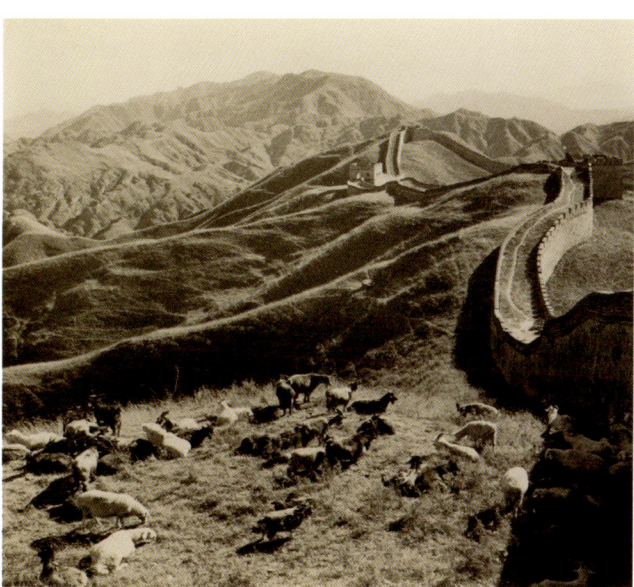

The Great Wall at Nankow, by Hedda Hammer (Morrison), early 1940s.
Collection of the Powerhouse Museum, Sydney

should omit, is to the Great Wall of China via the Nankou Pass … no where is the ancient fortification in better preservation, no where grander.' She described the crumbling towers and the wall in places 'slipping down into the valleys, stone by stone'.[20] In the minds of most Westerners the wall at Nankou Pass *was* 'The Great Wall of China'. Ranging across the tall and rugged mountains, its eloquently dilapidated appearance accorded with the image of a noble and ancient ruin. Juliet Bredon (Lauru), the daughter of Sir Robert Bredon who worked for the Chinese Imperial Maritime Customs Service, spent most of her life in Beijing.[21] Writing under the pseudonym Adam Warwick, her article 'A thousand miles along the Great Wall of China' was published in the *National Geographic Magazine* in February 1923.[22]

During the first half of the twentieth century, many interesting images of the Great Wall at Nankou were taken — by professional and amateur photographers, travellers, adventurers, missionaries and those who sought to capture China's rich cultural heritage. Alice Schalek (1874–1956), a Viennese travel photographer, journalist and war correspondent, sold images of the Great Wall taken near Nankou Pass to the National Geographic Society in 1922. The American missionary Reverend Claude Leon Pickens (1900–85) who lived in China from 1926 to 1937 and conducted surveys of Muslims in north-west China, north-east Tibet and Inner Mongolia in the 1930s, also photographed the Great Wall.[23] Langdon Warner (1881–1955), curator of Asian art at the Fogg Museum at Harvard University, led expeditions to China in 1923 and 1925. In 1923, he took a number of photographs of the Great Wall at Nankou and travelled to sites in Gansu, including Dunhuang from where he removed many precious artefacts, including the mural paintings from the Thousand Buddha Caves that are now

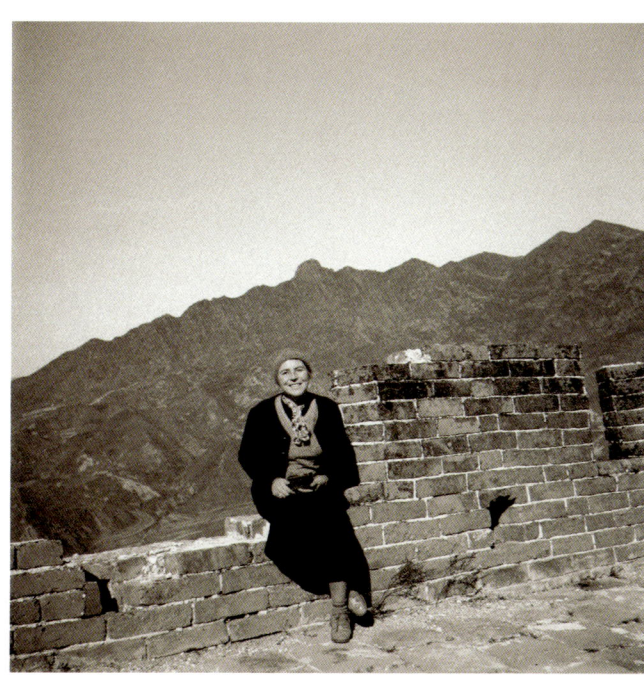

Hedda Hammer (Morrison) at the Great Wall, 1941.
Photo: Alastair Morrison

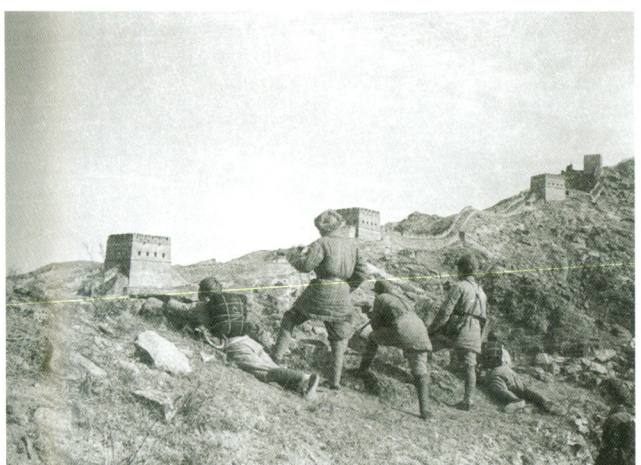

Command site of the Eighth Route Army on Chajian Mountain, Laiyuan, Hebei, Autumn 1937, by Sha Fei.
Reproduced courtesy of Wang Yan

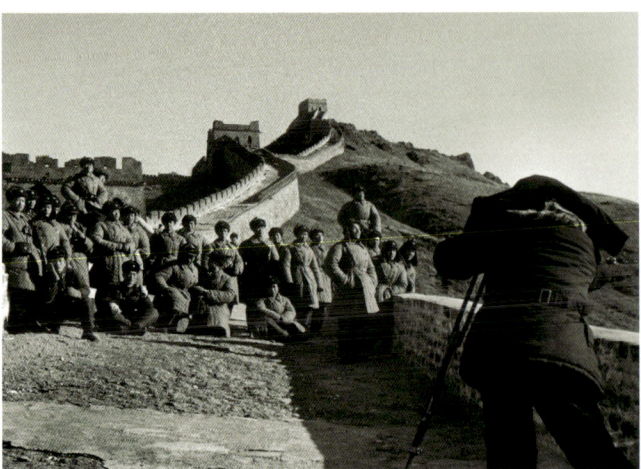

Soldiers of the People's Liberation Army have their photograph taken on the Great Wall outside Beijing in 1957.
Photo: © Marc Riboud/Magnum Photos

displayed in the Arthur M Sackler Museum at Harvard University.[24] Warner's 1923–24 photographs of the Great Wall are a silent reminder of his acquisitive eye and the irreparable damage he inflicted on the great religious monuments near the westernmost extreme of China's mighty wall.

The best known photographer resident in Beijing (called Beiping from 1927 to 1949) during the first half of the twentieth century was Hedda Hammer Morrison (1908–91). Born in Germany, Hedda Hammer arrived in Beiping in 1933 to take up the job of manager at Hartung's Photo Shop, which had been established by H Hartung. The shop was located at East of Legation Street, No 3, inside the Legation Quarter.[25] In 1933, the business employed seventeen Chinese staff, who no doubt included some early photographers of the Great Wall. The business appears to have been successful, judging by the extant photographs and postcards that are identified by the name 'Hartung'. In addition to developing and printing film brought in by customers, many of them expatriates and travellers, Hartung's Photo Shop undertook studio

portraits and commissions, and built up a stock of images that could be sold as souvenir photographs of the old capital or printed as postcards.[26] Hedda worked there until 1938, after which she stayed on in Beiping as a freelance photographer.

Among the more than 10 000 black-and-white photographs that Hedda took during her thirteen-year stint in Beiping there are a number of the Great Wall.[27] In the work titled *The Great Wall at Nankow*, Hedda revisits this famous and much photographed section of the wall. Her photograph is surprising because she presents us with a bucolic image of mountain goats grazing on slopes of spring pasture below the wall. It differs dramatically from most earlier views, which show the wall in a barren and arid landscape. According to her husband, Alastair Morrison, Hedda spent a day at the Great Wall and on arriving at the train station to return to Beiping realised that the roll of film she had taken had been left behind. She hurried back but by the time the missing film had been located the last train had already departed. She decided to spend the night in the open and passed a

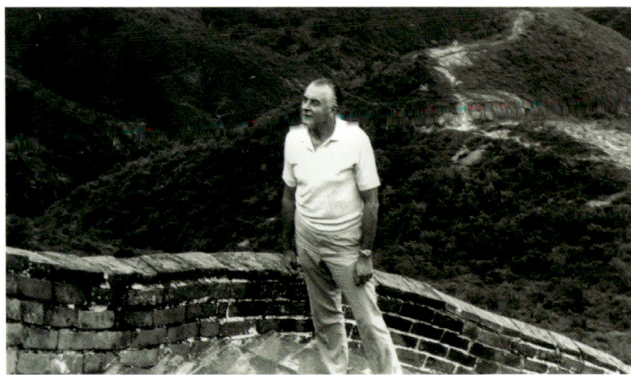

Gough Whitlam, Leader of the Opposition and head of the Australian Labor Party mission to China, at the Ming dynasty Great Wall at Badaling, Yanqing, Beijing, in July 1971.
Photo: © Newspix

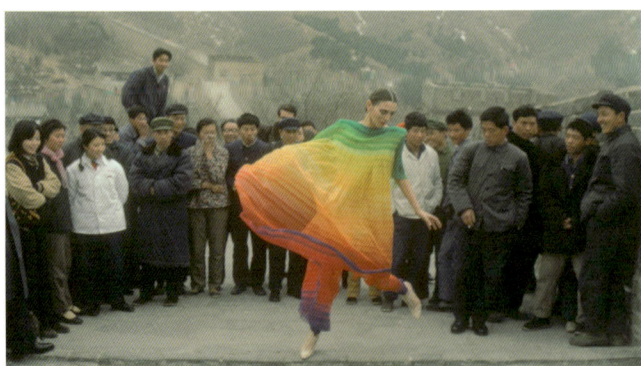

The Pierre Cardin spring/summer 1979 collection at the Great Wall, photographed by Eve Arnold, 1979.
Photo: © Eve Arnold/Magnum Photos

very cold night sleeping by the wall. Perhaps this photograph was taken early the next morning.[28]

The Great Wall at Nankow is one of twenty-one 'Scenes of Beiping' mounted in a silk-covered concertina-style souvenir album of photographs by Hedda Hammer. The captions are written in pencil and the last page is signed. Hedda sold such high-quality albums of photographs to foreign residents and wealthy travellers as mementoes of their sojourn in Beiping. Prospective clients were given the option of making their own selection from themed master albums of numbered images. In this case the thematic focus is architecture and the album also includes photographs of the city walls and gates, the Forbidden City, the Temple of Heaven, Jade Spring Mountain, the Yiheyuan Summer Palace, Chengde (Jehol) Summer Villa and the Great Wall at Shanhaiguan Pass.

A photograph, taken by Alastair Morrison in March 1941, records a trip he and Hedda made to the Great Wall soon after they met. Hedda sits in the winter sun on the edge of a dilapidated section of wall, wearing a cap, layers of woollen jumpers and a cardigan. She nurses her own camera and smiles at the one being operated by Alastair, connecting them with one another and with us, the viewers of the photograph, in that instant. The desire to record a person at a particular place carries with it the exhilaration of the moment. This photograph evokes the dramatic context, the rugged expansive mountains, the bracing spring air and the sense of connection between two people. It is a personal moment that records an impulse that has been repeated by millions of people from all over the world.

In the early twentieth century, the Great Wall was visited by an increasing number of local tourists. A photograph of the architect Lin Huiyin and her father-in-law, the famous thinker and political activist Liang Qichao, and most probably taken by her architect husband Liang Sicheng on an outing at the Great Wall, documents their interest in the historic structure and its emergence as a tourist destination and a national icon.[29]

From a Chinese perspective, the final transformation of the Great Wall from a military barrier into a national symbol began after the Sino-Japanese War (1937–45).[30] Following the Japanese occupation of Manchuria in 1931 and the outbreak of full-scale war in 1937, the Great Wall was once again used as a military base for border defence. This moment in the history of the wall is captured in a series of striking photographs taken at Chajian Mountain in Hebei province by Sha Fei (1912–50), a photographer for the communist Eighth Route Army.[31] But it was not until after the establishment of the People's Republic of China in 1949 that the Great Wall underwent its most fundamental physical and metaphoric transformation. Sections of the wall were restored and its stories were updated and reclaimed. In a photograph taken by the French photographer Marc Riboud (born 1923) during

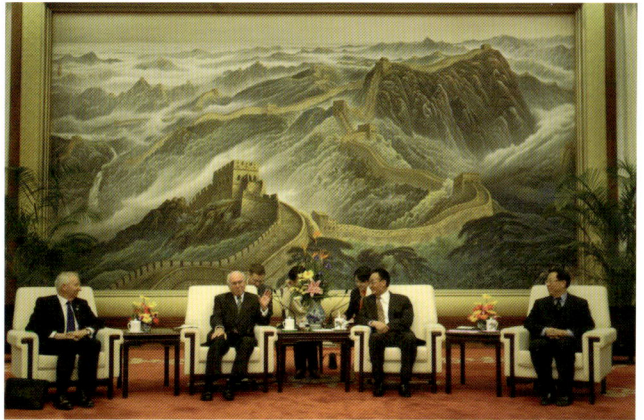

Australian Prime Minister John Howard with the Chairman of the National People's Congress, Wu Bangguo, in the Great Hall of the People in Beijing, 19 April 2005.
Photo: Penny Bradfield/Fairfaxphotos.com

his first visit to China in 1957, a group of off-duty, day-tripping People's Liberation Army soldiers pose for the camera on a section of wall at Badaling. Some strike heroic poses, some seem bemused by the occasion, while others stand on the wall as if to assert their ownership — the Communist Party's — of the historic military structure. The restoration of the wall at Badaling, the section most accessible to the capital, undertaken in 1953 and 1957 as a showpiece for the new China, is clearly visible in this photograph.[32]

As diplomatic recognition of the People's Republic increased in the 1970s, Chinese government leaders began to take important visitors to the Great Wall at Badaling. The Great Wall featured in glossy magazines such as *China Reconstructs* and, despite having suffered depredations during the Cultural Revolution (c 1964–78),[33] was evolving into an icon of which the Chinese leadership was increasingly proud. Gough Whitlam, then Leader of the Opposition in Australia, visited the Great Wall in July 1971 with a delegation from the Australian Labor Party, and American president Richard Nixon was taken there during his ceremonial trip to China in February 1972.

The contrast of old and new featured in the choice of the Great Wall as the backdrop for the launch of Pierre Cardin's spring/summer fashion collection in 1979. The photograph reproduced around the world of a tall, dramatically made-up French model wearing an ethereal rainbow-coloured garment prancing on top of the heavily restored wall at Badaling amid a crowd of bemused onlookers in drab proletarian gear — more appropriate dress for a cold winter's day — marks the beginning of the period when China began to open its doors to the world after the end of the Cultural Revolution.[34] This odd pairing of contemporary international fashion and ancient military structure was an indication of the role

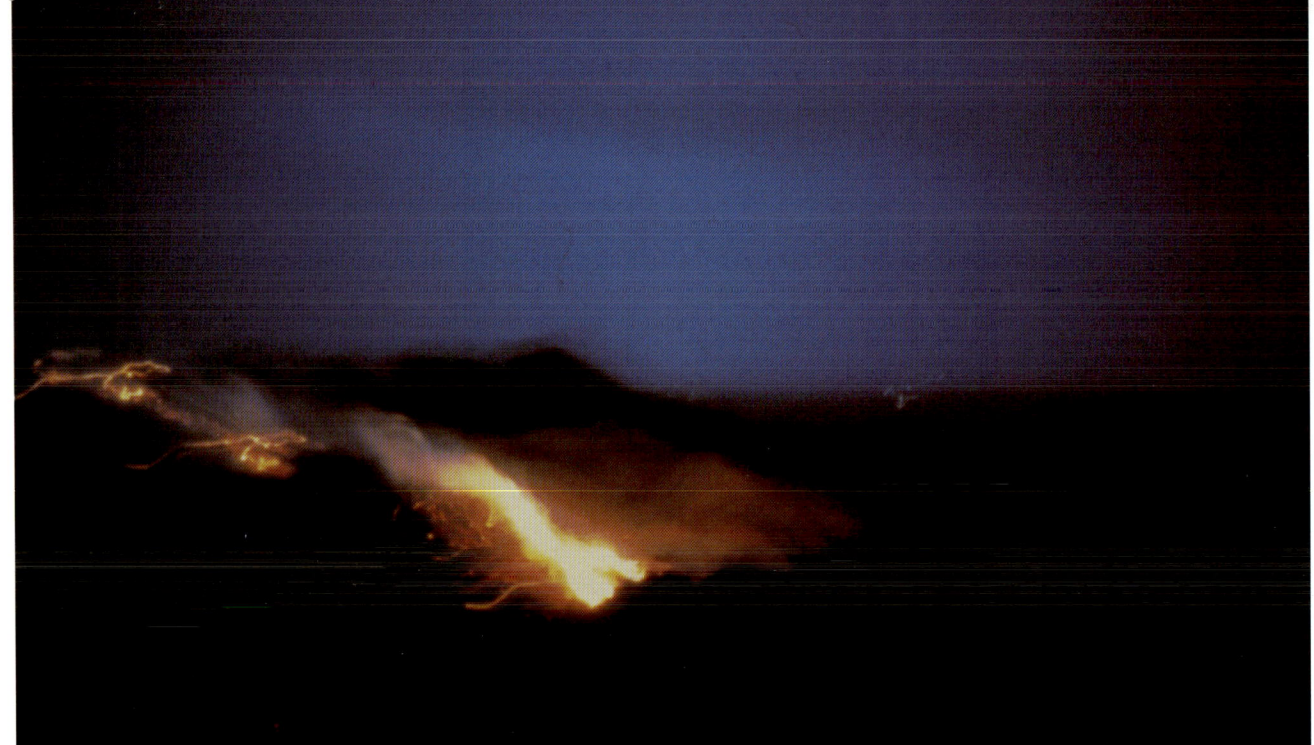

Project for extraterrestrials No 10: project to extend the Great Wall of China by
10 000 metres by Cai Guo Qiang, Jiayuguan Pass, Gansu, 27 February 1993.
Photo: Masanobu Moriyama

the wall would play in years to come. The Great Wall was no longer just a site for tourism, it was also a five-star stage from which to project China to the world.

Since the mid 1980s, contemporary Chinese artists have taken an interest in the Great Wall as an icon and have responded to its complex and multivalent meanings.[35] Many have been inspired by the words of Lu Xun (1881–1936), China's great twentieth-century writer:

> *I have always felt hemmed in on all sides by the Great Wall; that wall of ancient bricks which is constantly being reinforced. The old and the new conspire to confine us all.*
>
> *When will we stop adding new bricks to the Wall?*
>
> *The Great Wall of China: a wonder and a curse.*[36]

Two of the most impressive artworks that take 'The Great Wall' as their subject were made in the 1990s by Xu Bing (born 1955) and Cai Guo Qiang (born 1957).

For Xu Bing the Great Wall represented the meaninglessness of human endeavour on an unparalleled scale. The son of a Peking University history professor, Xu cited the late-Ming dynasty intellectual Gu Yanwu (1613–82), who had remarked on the futility of attempting to close China off from the rest of the world. Xu had made a small rubbing of a section of wall in 1987 while he was a student at the Central Academy of Fine Arts in Beijing, but it was not until May 1990 that he embarked on a monumental project to make a rubbing of a section of the Great Wall, including a watchtower. Xu chose a site at Jinshanling, to the north of Beijing, because the wall there was in good condition and had not been recently restored. He worked with fifteen people and took one month to complete the rubbing, using 300 bottles of ink

and 1300 sheets of paper in the process. The work was pieced together and mounted over a four-month period when Xu was artist-in-residence at the University of Wisconsin-Madison in America.[37] It was first displayed in the Elvehjem Museum of Art at the university in 1991 and more recently in the exhibition *The Wall* which opened in Beijing in 2005. Titled *Ghosts pounding the Wall* (*gui da qiang,* an expression that means 'going around in circles', or being lost), Xu Bing's large installation is invested with power because it is a rubbing of the wall. More than a facsimile, it is like a fingerprint that overwhelms the viewer with its inky blackness and massive scale.

Cai Guo Qiang chose to locate his work in relation to the westernmost pass of the Great Wall, at Jiayuguan in the Gobi desert, a region he had travelled to years earlier. For *Project for extraterrestrials No 10: project to extend the Great Wall of China by 10 000 metres* he laid a 10 000-metre length of encased gunpowder from the Great Wall into the desert. At 7.35 pm on 27 February 1993, Cai created one of his signature night-time pyrotechnic displays when he lit the fuse and set off an amazing fast-burning line of gunpowder that darted across the desert mountains like a writhing supernatural dragon igniting a momentary wall of fire and light. Gunpowder, the dragon and the Jiayuguan Pass are potent symbols of Chinese power. Cai's stated aim for *Project for extraterrestrials* was to recapture the soul of the wall by transmitting signals to the universe and establishing dialogue with other planets. By extending the Great Wall 10 000 metres Cai hoped that energy would circulate between real and virtual worlds and simulate the breath of the universe.[38] Perhaps Cai was also indirectly referring to the ancient Chinese myth in which the first emperor of China dreamt that his soul journeyed to the moon, and from that vantage point the idea of constructing a boundary line around his kingdom was born. When Qin Shihuang's soul re-entered his body, the building of the wall began.[39] Playing on the age-old question of whether the Great Wall can be seen from the moon — it can't — and working with potent symbolic forms, Cai encouraged us to marvel at our place in an interconnected universe and at human folly.

Today artistic representations of 'The Great Wall of China' appear in all kinds of places. In the Great Hall of the People a huge painting of the Great Wall dominates the room where Chinese leaders meet with visiting heads of state. The painting acts as a backdrop for official photographs, hanging behind a formal arrangement of chairs where leaders and their interpreters are seated. An even larger oil painting of the Great Wall beckons as you wait for your passport to be stamped at China's border control or immigration barrier at the Beijing international airport. *Spirit of the Chinese race*

(Huaxia shenyun) by Yuan Yunfu depicts the Great Wall of China snaking across verdant mountains and is painted in a style and palette that re-enforces its majesty and mystery. For official taste-makers the Great Walls that lie to the north of Beijing now stand for China, representing the breadth and beauty of the natural terrain, the ingenuity and might of its people and the antiquity of its civilisation.

So, what is 'The Great Wall of China'? For many people it is the section of wall at Badaling that has been photographed and represented in paintings so often over the past hundred years. This 'Tourists' Great Wall', no more than 10 kilometres long, has become 'The Great Wall of China', symbolic of the nation and the myriad historic structures that were built across China's northern borders over more than two millennia. Like the magical supernatural dragon whose form it is said to emulate, 'The Great Wall' has been invested with meanings that resonate with the ongoing transformation of China. It is China's most famous ruin and one of its most visited tourist destinations, a 'Great Wall' that is an awe-inspiring fragment of something much larger, more complex and contradictory.

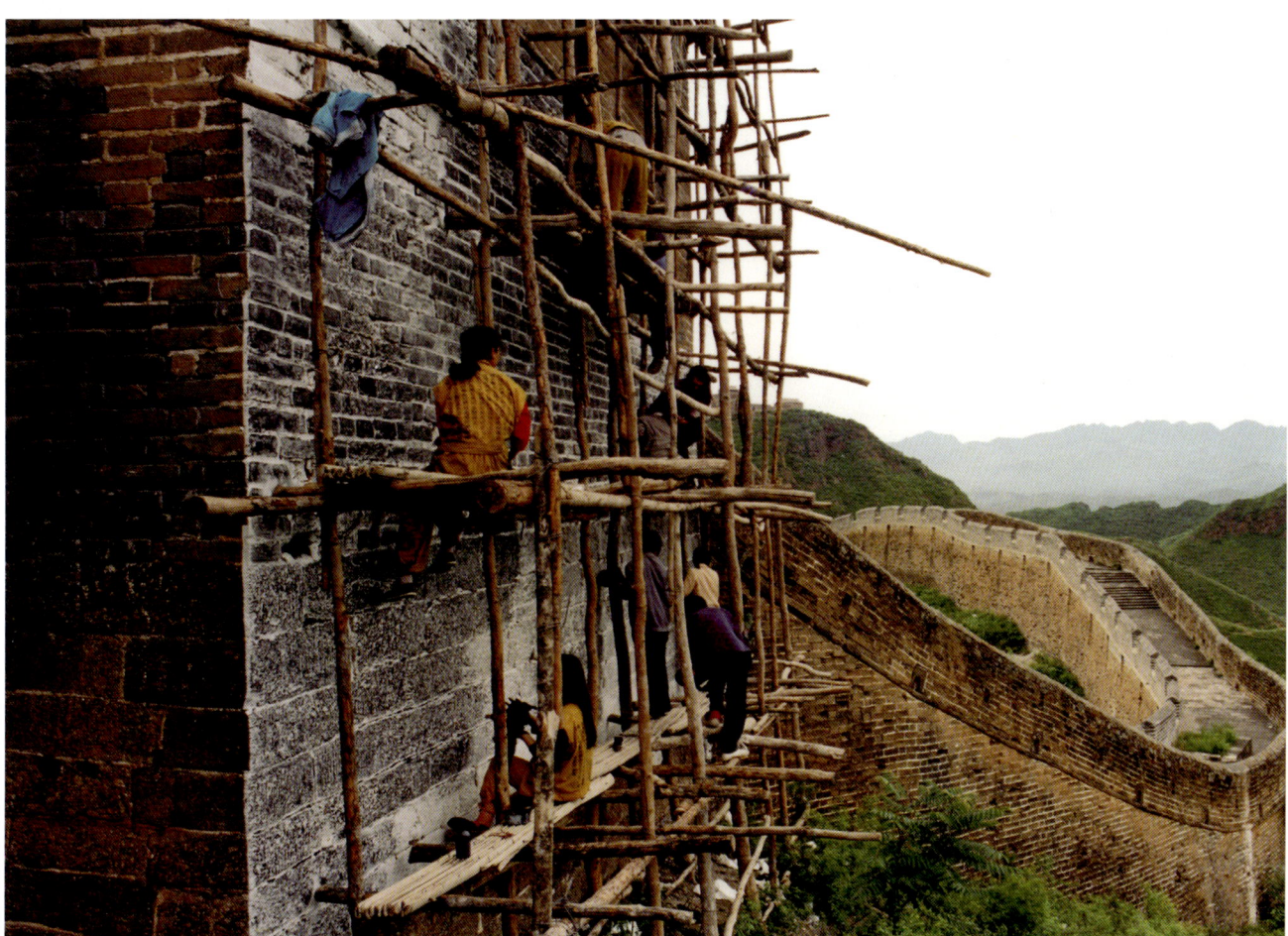

Rubbings being made of the Ming dynasty Great Wall at Jinshanling, Luanping, Heibei, 1990, for Xu Bing's artwork *Ghosts pounding the Wall*.
Photo: Xu Bing

The great tourist icon

CHENG DALIN

The Great Walls of China rank among the world's most impressive architectural achievements, not just as a Chinese cultural treasure but also as part of a shared or global cultural heritage.

For this reason, the preservation, management and study of the Great Walls concern people from all walks of life. In China and abroad, there are many people who are distressed by news reports about the destruction inflicted on the Great Walls by natural and human agents. Both the Chinese general public and specialists have been adamant in demanding better conservation and study of the Great Walls, yet many have expressed extreme dissatisfaction with the current state of affairs. Some international organisations and foreign individuals have also been vocal in their criticism.

The Chinese government encounters real difficulties in tackling the problem of Great Wall conservation. The walls are too extensive simply to be moved into a museum for safekeeping. Sections of what we know as the Great Walls are distributed through eighteen provinces, municipalities and autonomous regions. Their length totals roughly 50 000 kilometres although, because so many different methods have been used at different times to measure these walls, there is no definitive measure of their total extent. A 1985 survey of walls in the area of greater Beijing, which employed remote-sensing equipment, estimated the length of the walls there to be 629 kilometres — a full 446 kilometres longer than the 1980 figure of 183 kilometres arrived at by a team working on foot. But when remote-sensing technology was used between 1990 and 1992 to survey the walls within the Ningxia Hui autonomous region, it revealed 506 kilometres of actual wall structures as opposed to a figure of 1507 kilometres calculated by another survey team

also using remote sensing. The latter was closer to the estimate of 'more than 1500 kilometres', arrived at by a team of Ningxia archaeologists working in the early 1980s. It is not surprising that to the present day no one can state for certain the precise length of the Great Walls of China.

The history of the construction of the Great Walls is also long and complex: archaeological research and reliable historical documents show this history to greatly exceed two millennia. That basic fact is not challenged by any Chinese scholars, but there are sharp differences of opinion as to when particular periods of construction began and ended and which sections of the walls are the oldest.

A delegation of experts who travelled to China in 1987 to assess the Great Walls for UNESCO World Heritage listing was flummoxed by the task, unable to obtain sufficient data to provide a definitive, scientific conclusion regarding the overall length or age of the structures. There is still no strict definition of the Great Walls of China: the debate continues.

It can be said for certain that the walls constitute the world's largest ancient military engineering project with the longest continuous history, that they were constructed by different Chinese multi-ethnic political entities, and that they occupy a special place and significance in Chinese history. The construction of the Great Walls spans almost the entire period of dynastic history, playing a significant role throughout. In their structural forms,

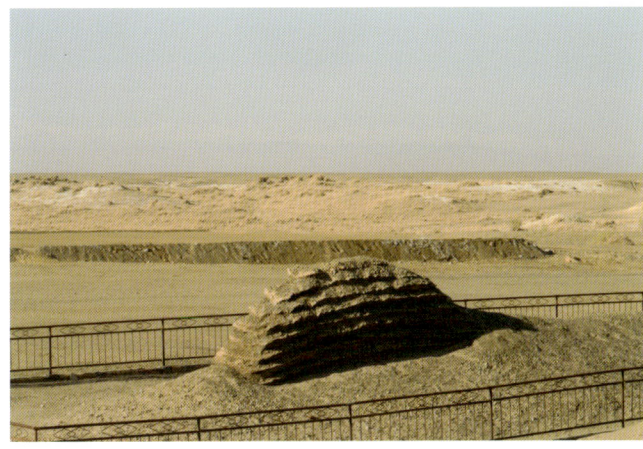
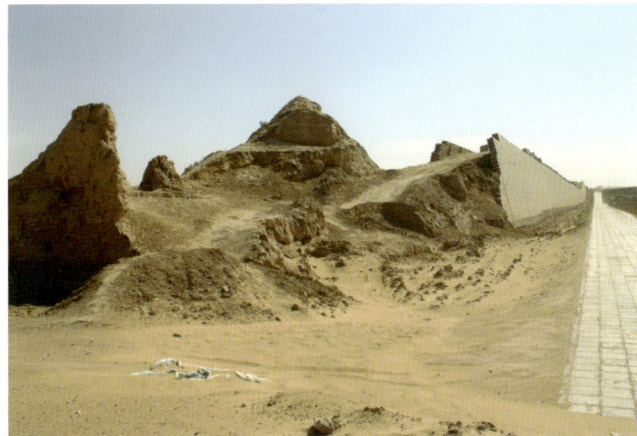
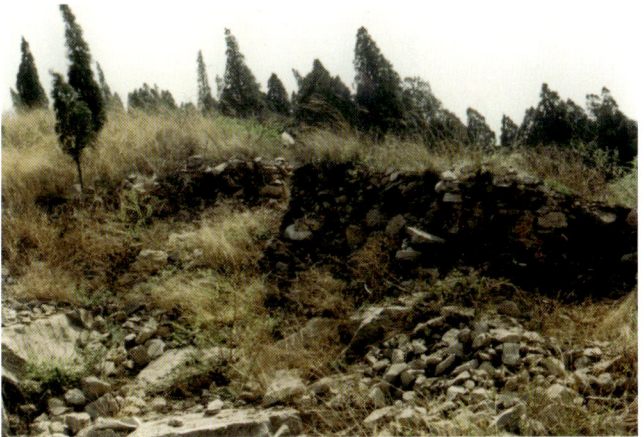
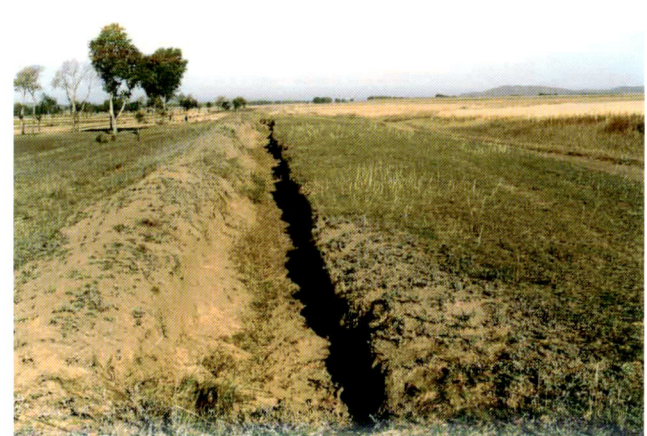

Top left: Remains of Han dynasty Great Wall at Majuanwan, Dunhuang, Gansu.
Photo: Jean-Francois Lanzarone

Top right: A new tourist area being developed at Xiaolongtou in Lingwu, Ningxia.

Bottom left: Remains of walls from the State of Qi, dating from the Warring States period, in the Yuanshan Forest Park in Zibo, Shandong.

Bottom right: Remains of walls from the State of Yan and the Qin dynasty in Guyuan, Hebei. Local farmers have dug a 10-kilometre irrigation canal alongside the walls.
Photos: Cheng Dalin

function and culture, the walls vary according to region and the ethnicity of the surrounding populations. No single definition of the Great Walls could cover the entirety of their unique and complex nature; nor could it do justice to their history, as the walls evolved from concept to perfection, and then to the stage when they finally lost their functional role.

Despite a focus in recent years on conservation and management of the Great Walls, China still has no detailed or accurate data on the present state of their preservation. Surveys in selected provinces and municipalities in 1980 revealed that within Hebei province, for example, 40 per cent of the original walls were 'fairly well preserved', 50 per cent 'seriously damaged', and 10 per cent had 'ceased to exist'. In Inner Mongolia, Shaanxi and Gansu, only about 10 per cent of the walls were 'fairly well preserved'. In Beijing municipality, approximately 50 per cent

of the walls were 'fairly well preserved', but more precise data from a 1985 remote-sensing survey showed that only 10.65 per cent could be considered 'optimally preserved', 8.9 per cent 'well preserved', 18.14 per cent 'moderately well preserved', 15.11 per cent 'poorly preserved' and 46.9 per cent 'in a very bad state of preservation'. A remote-sensing survey conducted of the walls in Ningxia between 1990 and 1992 revealed that 39.5 per cent of the actual wall structures were 'well preserved', 49 per cent only adequately preserved, and 11.5 per cent 'deficient' in their state of preservation. No systematic and comprehensive survey of the state of preservation of the structures has been conducted since 1992, nor has the state of preservation of the pre-Ming dynasty walls ever been specifically surveyed or statistical evidence about them been documented. Present assessments by experts and the media are all based on partial surveys or subjective evaluations. On the basis of the above estimates and my own findings during a field-trip survey of 4500 kilometres of the Great Walls in 2004, however, it is possible to state categorically that the structures have indeed suffered very serious damage.

The 2004 survey revealed that both natural and human factors are causing this damage. Human factors include tourism and construction projects, reconstruction of the walls themselves and the economic activities of local people pursuing their livelihoods. Natural forces causing damage include earthquakes, flooding, sand storms, lightning and acid rain.

It is generally believed that the greatest damage comes from people pursuing their livelihoods in the vicinity of the walls. However, our survey showed that damage created by the tourist industry now leads the field, followed by the destruction caused by building and reconstruction activities and, finally, damage wrought by the natural elements and people doing what they do to earn a living. China's economic reform and open-door policy has been in train for well over two decades, and the economy is booming. The tourist industry has developed apace. All levels of government and people living near them have shown an unprecedented enthusiasm for turning the walls into the world's largest tourist attraction and an important source of revenue. In the course of our 2004 survey — which encompassed all provinces, autonomous regions and municipalities in which the walls are located — we discovered that the governments of about ten of these administrative territories had already developed, or approved the development of, more than 230 tourism companies and tourist zones targeting and focused on the walls. The majority of these were in Beijing municipality and Hebei province, where there were approximately 130 designated tourist areas along the Ming walls. Most of these were run by enterprises developed by government tourism departments together with companies, villagers and private investment. We found that one out of ten enterprises received inadequate supervision by government cultural and cultural relics departments.

In recent years, Hebei has promoted as its goal 'the total preservation of Great Wall cultural relics sites while developing tourism resources in tandem with economic growth.' The province has constructed or repaired 1754 kilometres of roads linking the walls and nearby tourist zones. In villages along these roads large signs proclaim:

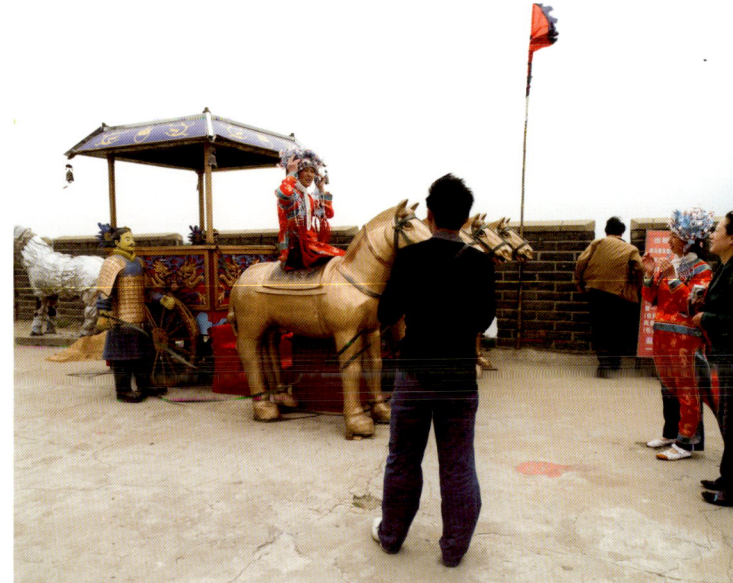
Tourists dress up in Qing dynasty costume with replicas of Qin dynasty warriors and horses on top of the Great Wall at Shanhaiguan Pass, Qinhuangdao, Hebei.
Photo: Jean-Francois Lanzarone

'Let the growth of Great Wall tourism play the leading role in guiding the development of tourism.' The opening up of these roads has spurred economic growth and raised the standard of living in what were once remote mountain areas. And yet none of the projects approved by local governments along these Great Wall roads were ever submitted to the Hebei office of the State Administration of Cultural Heritage for examination and approval. Nor, according to the office, did they incorporate conservation plans or formulate managerial regulations or technical guidelines as prescribed. The result has been a chaotic situation of unsystematic development and ineffective management: not only have the residents and governments in these tourist areas failed to reap the full economic benefits that they had anticipated but the walls themselves have been seriously damaged.

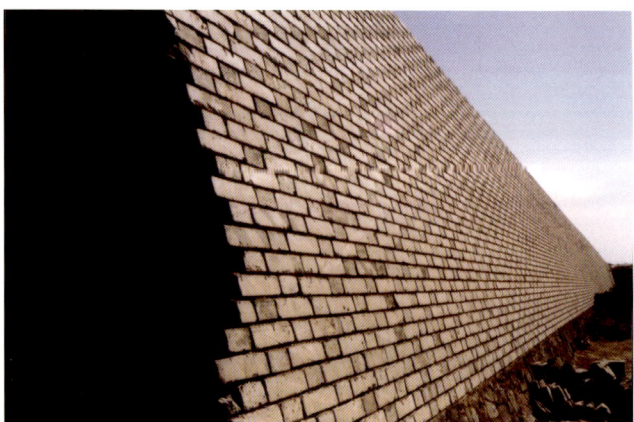
In a new development area bricks cover the original earthen walls at Xiaolongtou in Lingwu, Ningxia.
Photo: Cheng Dalin

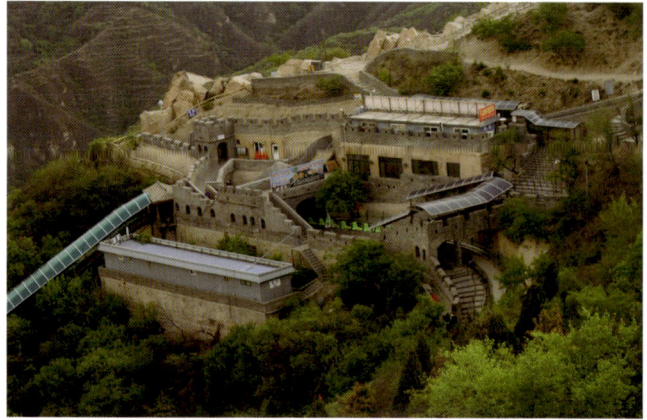
Tourist ride from the northern section of the Great Wall at Badaling, Yanqing, Beijing.
Photo: Jean-Francois Lanzarone

In Shandong and Ningxia, the development of tourism has also had negative consequences — in some places so severe that the walls have been destroyed altogether. For instance, the developers of a major scenic tourist zone in Lingwu, Ningxia, faced the original earthen ramparts of the local walls with stone so that they would resemble the renowned length of the Ming wall at Badaling in Beijing. Other unwarranted and historically baseless reconstruction work has completely transformed the original appearance of 2000-year-old archaeological sites at Yuanshan Park in Zibo and the Qixingtai Resort in Zhangqiu, both in Shandong. Several years ago, Du Xiaofan of the UNESCO China office commented acerbically that parts of China's largest world cultural heritage site resembled geriatrics recovering from radical cosmetic surgery. China's main media service, Xinhua News Agency, recently called this 'the movement to build the Great Wall anew'.

Although many of the management units, companies or individuals running tourist sites proclaim that the development of tourism is instrumental in raising money to protect the walls, this is often mere sloganeering. Most Great Wall tourist areas developed within Beijing municipality are brazen commercial ventures with no takings from ticket sales being used for Great Wall conservation. According to regulations, 80 per cent of the money earmarked for the preservation of world heritage sites within the municipality is to be derived from ticket sales. Although ticket revenues alone would not be sufficient to undertake cultural relics protection work at any one of the sites, a percentage is skimmed off by higher level organisations. For example, 40 per cent of the takings at Badaling is handed over to the Yanqing county government. And 20 per cent of the money from ticket sales at the Ming tombs site, earmarked for the Juyongguan Pass, is appropriated by the Changping county government. Maximising profit is the true goal of most governments and enterprises in these areas and this directly results in indifference towards cultural heritage. After the Jinshanling section of the Great Wall in Hebei came under the management of a business company, its annual income was estimated at 3 to 4 million yuan [$A500–675 000], but it had spent less than 300 000 yuan [$A50 000] over an eight-year period on Great Wall conservation work, and more than 300 000 yuan raised for conservation through public donations had ended up in the company's coffers. Entrepreneurs have built many tourist service facilities in protected areas on or adjacent to the walls, where construction is meant to be controlled. At the popular Great Wall sites at Badaling, Shanhaiguan, Jinshanling and Simatai, developers have constructed cable car lines. There are even entertainment facilities with slides, dodgem cars and shooting galleries, shopping centres, hotels and villas. And since night-time tourism was first developed at Badaling in the mid 1990s, batteries of lights have been installed to illuminate the Jiayuguan and Jinshanling sections of the walls. These activities have resulted in enormous damage to the original environment. Large-scale sporting and cultural events, and even rave parties and banquets, are also organised at Great Wall venues, presenting serious physical threats to the integrity of the structures. A journalist writing for an Argentinian newspaper described the Great Walls as 'the Disneyland of the Orient'.

Economic development has also wrought serious damage. Transport infrastructure projects have been especially destructive to the walls in Shaanxi and Ningxia. When the central government proposes transportation projects for these areas, it must demonstrate that the schemes adopt suitable measures to minimise damage to the walls. Yet when provincial, regional and township governments, local industrial parks and private enterprises are engaged in road building, frequently they ignore legislation designed to protect the Great Walls as well as circumventing the regulations concerned with preserving cultural relics. Road building has resulted in the wilful demolition of whole sections of the walls. In 2003, for example, a road improvement program in Dingbian

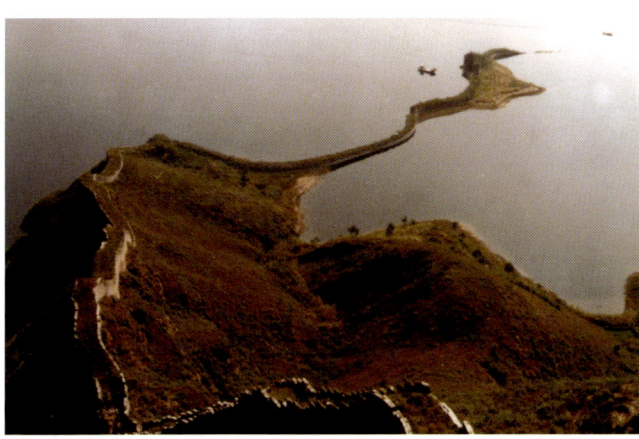

A section of the Ming dynasty Great Wall submerged by the waters of the Panjiakou Dam at Kuancheng, Hebei.
Photo: Cheng Dalin

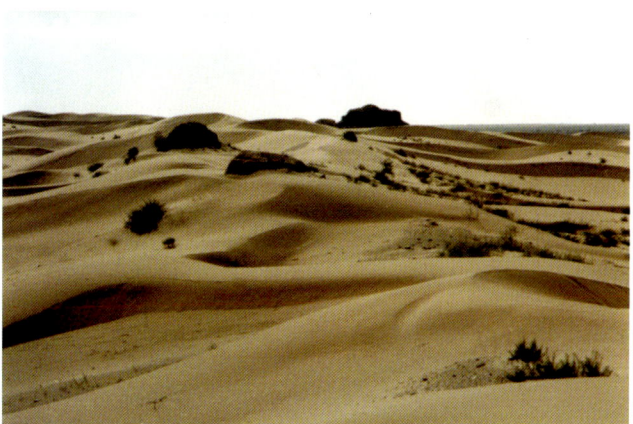

A section of the Ming dynasty Great Wall covered by the encroaching desert at Qingyang Well, Yanchi, Ningxia.
Photo: Cheng Dalin

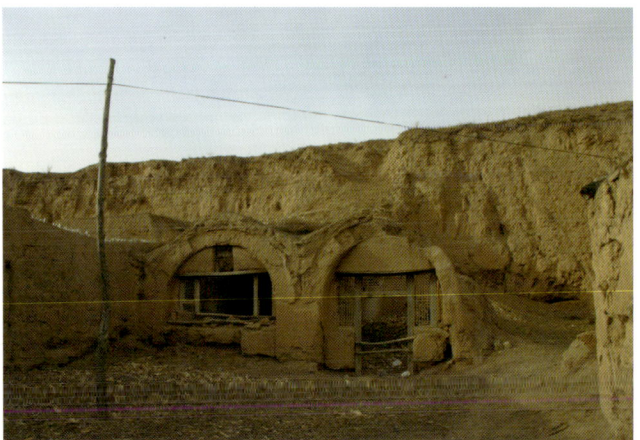

Abandoned houses built next to the Great Wall at Datong in Shanxi.
Photo: Cheng Dalin

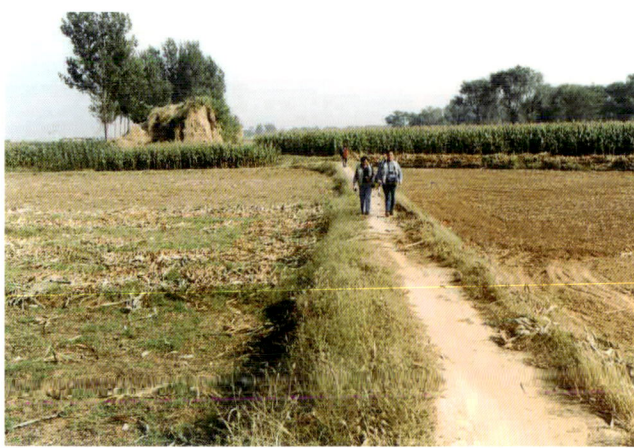

Walls in Xushui, Hebei, originally built by the State of Yan during the Warring States period, which are now used as a raised path by local farmers.
Photo: Cheng Dalin

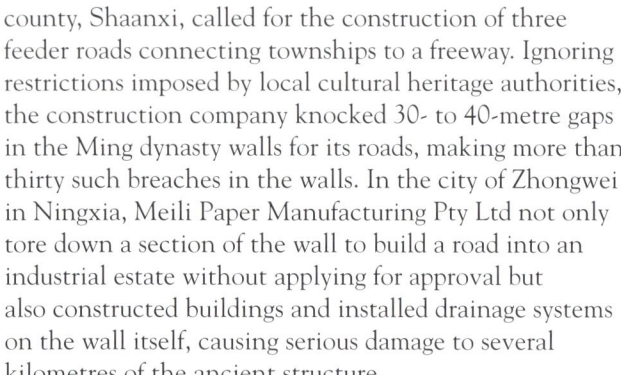

county, Shaanxi, called for the construction of three feeder roads connecting townships to a freeway. Ignoring restrictions imposed by local cultural heritage authorities, the construction company knocked 30- to 40-metre gaps in the Ming dynasty walls for its roads, making more than thirty such breaches in the walls. In the city of Zhongwei in Ningxia, Meili Paper Manufacturing Pty Ltd not only tore down a section of the wall to build a road into an industrial estate without applying for approval but also constructed buildings and installed drainage systems on the wall itself, causing serious damage to several kilometres of the ancient structure.

The provision of electric power, communications and natural gas, as well as irrigation systems for agricultural purposes, mining and forestry projects, and the construction of industrial development zones have all resulted in unchecked building on and in the vicinity of the Great Walls, including the demolition of entire sections. Damage has also been caused by tree planting on the remains of walls or by the construction of canals. Particularly striking are the cases in northern and north-west Hebei. Ten kilometres of the Great Walls were destroyed when a canal was constructed through commercial pastures in Guyuan county. Forestry departments in Xiaochang township levelled a section to provide access for a forestry road and they dug holes on the wall to plant trees. In Laiyuan county, the proprietor of a mine instructed workers to use an industrial excavator to rip up 60 metres of the Great Walls in order to run water pipes into the mining area. In addition, power-line stanchions, high-tension wire pylons and various telecommunications towers, as well as geological and hydrological markers, have been installed at many places along the walls. Reservoirs have been built near many of the ancient passes, submerging parts of the walls: the Panjiakou Reservoir in Hebei, for example, inundated the famous passes at Xifengkou and Panjiakou.

The forces of nature can also be lethal to the Great Walls. Prior to the Ming dynasty, the walls were generally made of tamped loess in the plains and rocks in mountainous areas. Construction using large bricks and large-scale stone masonry for the foundations only began in the fifteenth century, in the mid Ming dynasty, and then only on a large scale along those parts of the walls intended to defend the capital Beijing and the grounds enclosing imperial mausoleums. In other areas masonry was employed at vital mountain passes and forts — the remainder of the walls were still built using loess, which was readily obtainable and easily worked.

During the Ming dynasty the upkeep and repair of the walls was undertaken on an annual basis, with major repairs and rebuilding embarked on every five to ten years. Historical records demonstrate that during this dynastic period the custodians of the walls understood the need to address damage from natural forces at least once a decade. Floods, earthquakes and sandstorms wrought the most damage, followed by lightning and the encroaching root systems of plants. Documents show that in 1482 heavy rains in Changping county outside Beijing caused floods that damaged the forty-nine large drain openings servicing the Juyongguan Pass section of the walls, as well as towers and forts. Earthen ramparts are most prone to damage from extended periods of rain, which can cause these parts of the walls to disappear completely. This threat is particularly acute in Shanxi, Shaanxi, Ningxia and Gansu. Adding to the threat, China is one of the three areas most affected by acid rain worldwide. Acid rain contributes to the fading and erosion of many of the inscriptions on the stones and bricks of the walls, to the point where many are no longer legible.

China is also earthquake prone, and most of the northern walls run through seismically unstable zones. A major earthquake in Jiuquan county, Gansu, in 1609 crushed more than 840 soldiers and civilians to death and toppled 560 kilometres of Great Wall fortifications.

Eighteen years later, in the first two months of the lunar year, earthquakes and tremors shook Great Wall military forts on more than a hundred occasions and caused walls, buildings, side walls and forts to collapse. At Hongguozikou in Shizuishan, Ningxia, one can still see where stones were dislodged from the wall by an earthquake.

In the course of our 2004 survey, we also saw how dust storms had buried and eroded long stretches of the Great Walls in Shaanxi and Ningxia. No specialist study has yet been undertaken on the state of preservation of the buried parts of the walls, but it is clear that wind erosion has wrought immense damage, a situation exacerbated when powerful winds and rain coincide. There are areas where the Great Wall structures of the Han dynasty (206 BCE–220 CE) have been transformed into an eerie landscape of seemingly natural forms.

In the many places where people live and pursue their livelihoods close to both sides of the wall, constant long-term damage results. According to locals, many of the defensive trenches that were once part of the Great Wall complex of fortifications were flattened or removed between 1937 and 1949 during the Japanese invasion and civil war. Refugees fleeing the invasion dug cave dwellings into the structures of the walls or removed stone and brick material from them in order to construct homes and shelters. When cultivating adjacent virgin lands, they also levelled sections of the walls to extend their fields.

After the establishment of the People's Republic of China in 1949, the lives of many of those living along the Great Walls remained impoverished. Unable to afford other building materials, they removed stones from the walls to construct homes, fence in courtyards and build pens for livestock. Some dug cave dwellings or storage caves for vegetables in the earthen ramparts. Activities such as the removal of earth for building purposes or digging in the ramparts for medicinal herbs continue to the present day. During the first thirty years of the People's Republic, the Chinese government mobilised people living along the walls in large-scale agricultural projects for which great quantities of bricks and stones were removed to terrace fields, build canals and construct reservoirs. Some sections of the earthen ramparts were levelled or used as fertiliser.

Responding to successive political campaigns — encouraged by slogans such as those in the Cultural Revolution that called on people to destroy the 'Four Olds' (old thinking, old culture, old customs, old habits) or 'make the past serve the present' — or to over-enthusiastic 'recycling' drives, people have pulled down large sections of the Great Walls and their associated structures. The well-known walls at Gubeikou-Wohushan in Beijing municipality suffered extensive damage as a result of political campaigns and people removing bricks to build houses. It was only after people were injured

and media attention was drawn to this activity that the theft of bricks was halted. Today, this stretch of the Great Wall is being developed as a scenic area.

On the other hand, our 2004 survey revealed that economic development has also greatly reduced some earlier forms of destruction. Since so many younger villagers have gone to the cities to find work, standards of living have improved and farmers now use new bricks and ceramic tiles to build their houses, instead of bricks from the Great Walls. Farmers have pulled down or abandoned many of their old houses, and most of the cave dwellings and storehouses dug into the walls have fallen into disuse. What to do about these abandoned caves has become a new challenge for conservationists.

But the threat to the Great Walls from farming continues. Cultivated fields run through sections of the walls and surround beacon towers and isolated parts of the structures. Farmers regularly encroach on the walls, using them as paths between fields and irrigating farmland at their feet.

Chinese professionals, the general public and the central government have all begun to discuss measures that will correct past errors and prevent future abuses.

In 2002, the newly drafted *Cultural heritage protection law of the People's Republic of China* stated that the policy in cultural relics work should 'prioritise protection and salvage, rationalise usage and strengthen management.' It declared: 'Immovable cultural relics which belong to the nation cannot be exploited. No museum, heritage management site or tourist venue at a protected cultural relic site can be run as a business venture.' Documents issued by the State Council, Ministry of Construction and State Administration of Cultural Heritage have all reiterated this point. In April 2003, seven ministries, including the Ministry of Culture, State Administration of Cultural Heritage and the Ministry of Construction, jointly issued the *Directive calling for further strengthening of the protection and management of the Great Wall*. This document further clarifies the controlling role to be played by cultural relics administrative departments and stresses that it is not permissible for Great Wall management and control to be placed in the hands of enterprises and companies. Where enterprises and companies are already responsible for management and control of sections of the Great Wall, this situation must be corrected within a limited period of time.

Beijing, Shaanxi and Inner Mongolia have also enacted local regulations to protect their sections of the Great Walls. Hebei, Gansu and Beijing have recruited conservationists to conduct regular patrols along the walls in an effort to curb harmful activities. Many social organisations, volunteers and international friends have also participated in Great Wall conservation work, and media organisations have investigated, exposed and

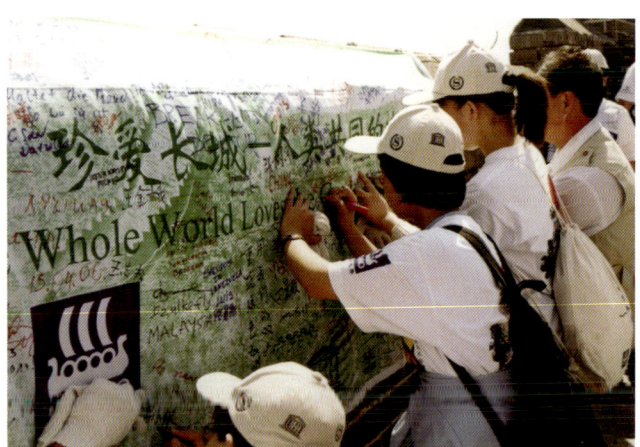

Volunteers sign their names on a poster pledging their respect and support for work to help protect the Great Wall.
Photo: Cheng Dalin

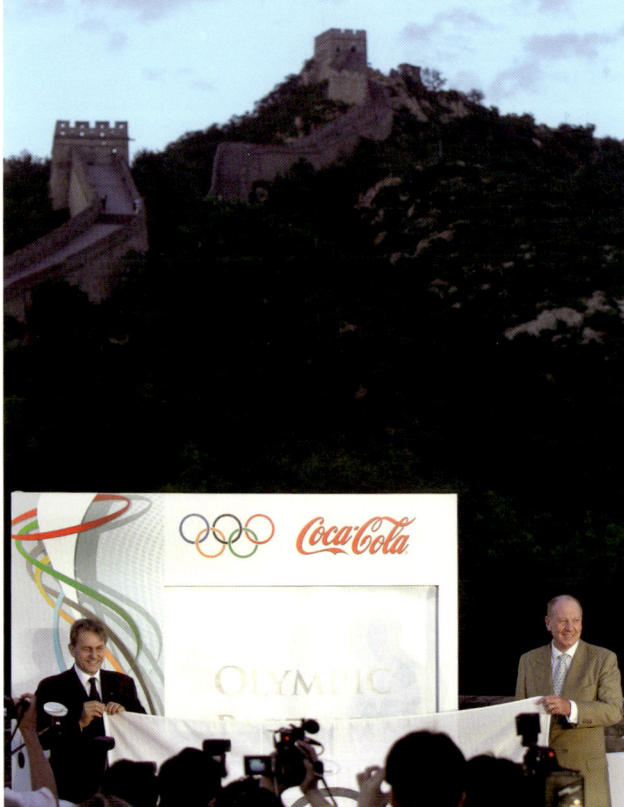

Ceremony at the Great Wall of China to mark the American Coca-Cola Company's partnership with the Olympic Games, 1 August 2005. Neville Isdell (right), the company's chairman and CEO, and the International Olympic Committee President, Jacques Rogge (left).
Photo: courtesy AAP

critiqued incidents of damage. This has led to greater public awareness of the cultural heritage value of the Great Walls and the benefits of conservation.

And yet, because there is still no curtailment of entrepreneurial activity along the Great Walls, the damage continues.

Concerned individuals from all sectors of Chinese society have called on the government to pay greater attention to protecting this great heritage treasure by enacting specific protective legislation, establishing a management body to supervise the entire extent of the Great Walls, strengthening the authority of supervisory departments, and investing more money and personnel in the enterprise. In December 2005, the State Council responded by issuing a *Directive of the State Council on strengthening cultural heritage protection*. In order to stress the importance and urgency of cultural heritage protection in China, the directive declared that, beginning in 2006, the second Saturday in June would be designated Cultural Heritage Day. It also states that cultural heritage protection must be 'a guiding ideology, basic policy and overall goal'.

> *By 2010, the preliminary work of establishing a reasonably comprehensive system of cultural heritage protection will be complete and that there will be a marked improvement in cultural heritage protection work. By 2015, a fairly comprehensive system of cultural heritage protection will have taken shape, and all cultural heritage items of historical, cultural or scientific value will receive full and adequate protection. The protection of cultural heritage will be embraced as a concept and acted upon by society as a whole.*

The State Council has already drafted a set of proposals for conservation management of the Great Walls. The State Administration of Cultural Heritage has also made conservation one of its top priorities, activating a Great Wall conservation project, formulating a plan for preserving the walls and implementing a system of legal inspections of Great Wall preservation work.

Conservationists now have the full attention of the central government. By drawing on the valuable cultural heritage experience of other countries, we can take on the challenge presented by the Great Walls. If the Chinese people remain industrious in this endeavour, then we will be able to bequeath the walls to future generations who will cherish the memory of their ancestors, rather than think of the Great Walls as a ruined inheritance.

TRANSLATED BY BRUCE GORDON DOAR

www.thegreatwall.com.cn

INTERVIEW WITH ZHANG JUN BY SANG YE

Zhang Jun, thirty-two, and his wife are the webmasters of *A small site on the Great Wall* (www.thegreatwall.com.cn). There are many sites devoted to the Great Wall on the internet, be they official or run by professional or amateur groups. There are also sites run by tourism companies.

We've used our internet site to initiate some activities to protect the Great Wall. At the moment we're engaged in a project called *I live with the wall*, which encourages members to visit spots all along the Great Wall and take photographs of the people who live there.[1] They process the photos on the spot so the villagers can keep a copy and they then make larger versions for exhibition.

We hope something like this will make people who live near the Great Wall more conscious of their neighbour and get them to take a greater interest in its protection. The exhibition aims to give city dwellers a better idea about the people who live along the length of the wall. This will raise awareness of the importance of preserving the Great Wall and help more people realise that, in fact, we are all living with it.

The first series of photographs produced in this project is on display at a gallery here in Beijing. Later the exhibition will tour to various universities. Again, we hope more young people become involved with the wall's conservation and protection.

Previously we printed some booklets about protecting the Great Wall. We've asked the participants in the photographic project to hand out copies to the villagers they photograph. We've also asked them to take pens and notebooks as gifts to the kids in the villages so that they don't need to hunt for scorpions on the wall — that's because they use the money they make from selling scorpions to buy pens and paper.

Many villagers living by the Great Wall, or near to it, dig mines, fire bricks, dig canals, build roads and hunt for scorpions in the cracks of the wall — all activities that threaten to destroy it. The aggressive development of tourism is also very detrimental. People do these things for short-term gain, even if it only means a little extra money.

Isn't there a theory that says if a butterfly flaps its wings in the Amazon it might end up creating a hurricane along the Mississippi? That's a warning to people that small actions can have massive, even calamitous, effects. In practical terms, it's not that hard to understand. One of the famous speciality foods sold on the Wangfujing shopping mall in Beijing is fried scorpion. But for every scorpion sold to tourists in Beijing, ten or more bricks have been dug out of the Great Wall in Hebei or Shanxi provinces. That's why we need to use various means to encourage mass participation in protecting the wall, including platforms like the internet — though our aim is to have an effect far beyond the net.

It is glaringly obvious: the Great Wall is already under serious threat. Vast stretches of the wall outside Beijing have been damaged by people wanting to use the bricks for construction, or demolished to make way for roads or other infrastructure. As for the Great Wall north of Beijing, excessive tourism has been the main culprit.

Everyone knows that the Great Wall is one of the greatest engineering marvels in the world, and people are familiar with Mao Zedong's line: 'You're not a hero if you don't

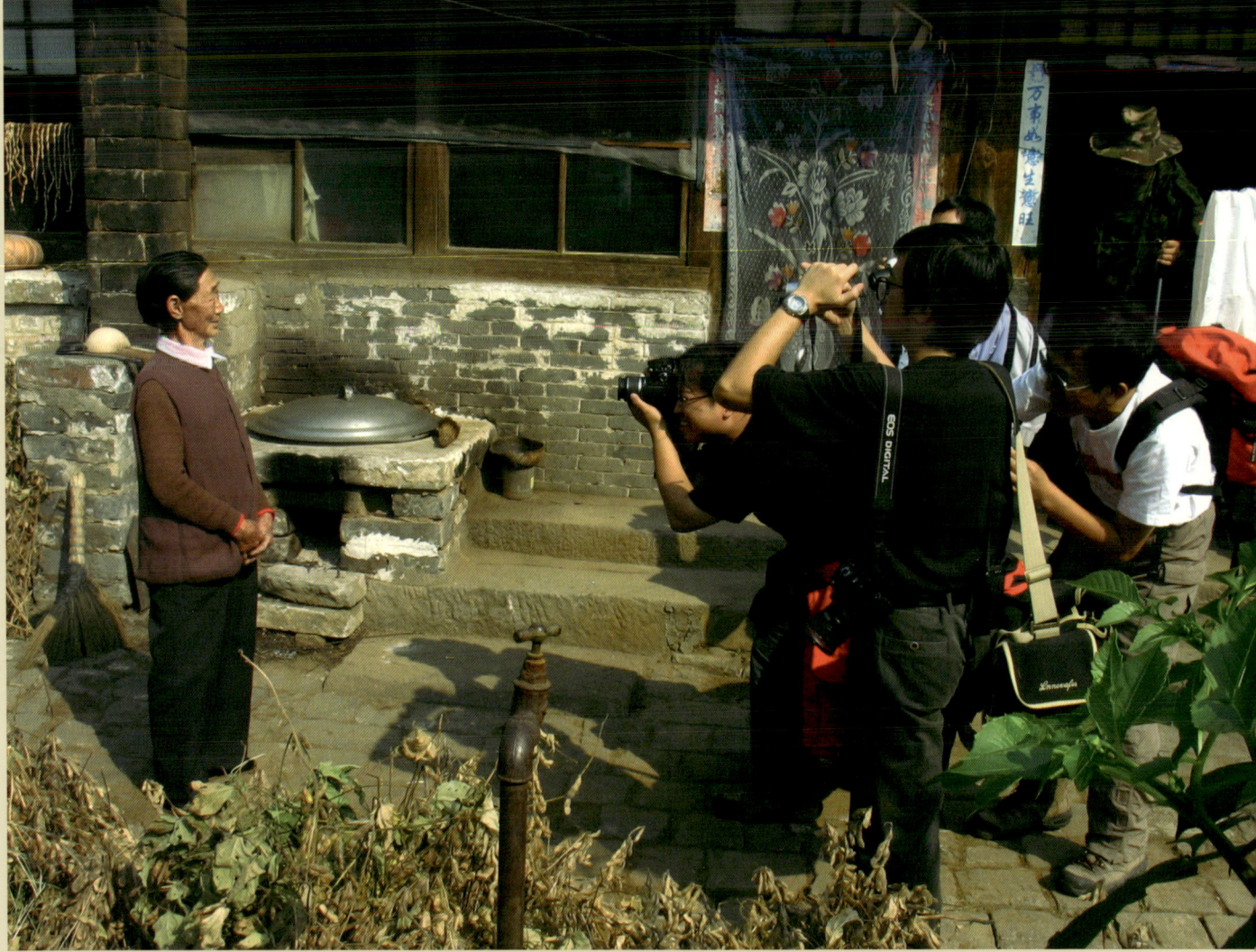

Members of the website *A small site on the Great Wall* photographing Mrs Wang, who is eighty years old. Her courtyard is built with bricks from the Great Wall close to their house, which was still in good condition up until the 1950s. Her son pointed to the distance and said, 'The pass used to be beautiful.' But he was pointing at nothing. He explained, 'We dismantled it. If the pass was still there, we'd be as popular as Badaling. We'd have made a fortune.'

Photo: J Freeman; location: Xixia Pass, Beijing

get to the Great Wall' (*bu dao changcheng fei haohan*). The tourism industry has packaged these things together, putting 'greatness' and the 'wall' in one semiotic bundle to instil in people a monumental desire to subjugate the Great Wall itself. So tourists have a destructive impetus to conquer the wall. Moreover, in the more prosperous areas, or places that want to make money out of their proximity to the wall, people have undertaken restoration projects that are in themselves extremely destructive. Local governments or companies put up the money to build the Great Wall anew, even though such activities clearly destroy the original. Yet they think this will create wealth for future generations.

I'm from Jiaxing near Shanghai, in the south of China. Geographically, it's a long way from the Great Wall. But from my childhood I was aware that the Great Wall was sacred and magnificent, the symbol of the Chinese nation.

When I first came to Beijing for university I rushed out to see the Great Wall at Badaling, but was bitterly disappointed. That Great Wall wasn't sacred or magnificent. It was a noisy bazaar, a theme park. Most people probably have a similar experience: after all the anticipation they get to Badaling and are sorely disillusioned. They feel that life is cruel, and here's the proof for they've been cheated yet again.

Later I saw some photos taken by a friend who'd been to the Great Wall at Simatai and taken pictures of the Pavilion Looking Towards the Capital (*Wangjinglou*). That was before mass tourism had hit and it hadn't been 'restored'. I'll never forget the grandeur and sense of history conveyed by those images. So that's what the Great Wall was really like! I had to go there.

On 1 May 1993, equipped with only a few steamed buns, a blanket and a map, we set off on our bikes.

Simatai was 120 kilometres away, but since we were only poor students we didn't mind. When we reached Simatai we haggled over the entry fee because we didn't have much money. We said that as students we were entitled to half-price entry. They said they didn't have discount tickets, but in the end they had a heart and let us both in for the price of one. Finally I saw the real Great Wall. I also saw what I wanted to do with my life. I began to think about how this history had unfolded and how the Great Wall had come to be built. I began to think about things that weren't discussed in the history books.

I ended up marrying the girl who took me out to Simatai, and she is the one who created *A small site on the Great Wall*. We manage the website together.

Our *Small site* was posted in 1999. Initially we got some sponsorship from a company with absolutely no connection to the Great Wall or the tourism industry. A friend of mine was working there and he arranged to give us some space on the company's server. It grew too quickly and so many people began visiting the site that we could no longer rely on that company — the download times were becoming far too slow. So we started renting space on a commercial provider; they charge an annual fee of 4200 yuan [about $A700]. The server is physically located in the southern suburbs of Beijing, in the opposite part of the city from where we live. Every time we have to go down there to carry out maintenance on the site we have to traverse the whole of the city from north to south. We might be poor, but we can't afford to be daunted by long distances.

We're getting 4000 visitors daily. We have got to know some of the frequent visitors to our forum and communicate with them by phone or over the internet. We also organise some regular and more casual gatherings — sometimes we go out to the wall together. It's a hobby for all of us, although everyone has a different focus. Some are environmentalists, others are just into the Great Wall for itself. There are those interested in the military angle, some are into photography and some just enjoy being with other people who share an interest … As for those who are mainly interested in the Great Wall, each has a particular angle: engineering, culture, folk customs, history, the war of resistance against the Japanese, the environment, and so on. The web friends we go out with often belong to different faith communities or even different nationalities. People might have their political differences and their views on various news events may diverge. When there are clashing views, we stay off the subject; there's no need to get caught up in such things.

Most of our members are young to middle-aged white-collar workers who share a similar outlook on the Great Wall. After all, they've come together because of a common interest so our relationship — be it on the internet or in real life — is pretty relaxed. There's a fairly stable number of core participants, though there are lots of others who come and go, as well as many one-off visitors. All we ask of core participants is that, when they decide to leave the group, they allow us to benefit from their experiences and ideas. You can't expect much else.

We collect subscriptions to pay for the server. We're not very good at raising money — we've tried to learn from other people. We produced some T-shirts but, though we managed to sell some on the open market, it was mostly friends who bought them. We get a bit of money from ads posted on the site too, but there are differences of opinion about what kind of ads we should allow. Some participants have opposed anything pornographic, and we agree — that would be completely out of order. Others are against everything Japanese. That's a little more difficult, especially when people even object to ads for schools that teach Japanese. The ad company we use bundles the ads according to category and they can't ensure that the occasional plug for a Japanese language school doesn't pop up. If we rejected everything related to education we'd have trouble getting any ads at all.

I don't think of the Great Wall as a political icon — it's a historic relic. It is a crucial link for the study and understanding of the history of our multi-ethnic country. To respect both history and the future, to protect this crucial link to our history, we have to research and experiment. For example, we organise volunteers to go to the wall to pick up rubbish. Of course, it's not an original idea, we weren't the first, but we emulate what we think is worthwhile. But we also need to generate our own ideas, like using modern technical means to evaluate the condition of the Great Wall, to use GPS technology to create a database of watchtowers, to search for images of the Great Wall from different periods and to chronicle the destruction of the Great Wall in recent times … In fact, we're working on all of these things, although we're still some way from realising our goals in practice. It's difficult to do everything we want to all at once. But I believe you have to have your own ideas, and you'll be in trouble if you can't come up with any.

Government action is needed to protect the wall, as is popular involvement. I hope that our *A small site on the Great Wall* will gradually evolve into an non-government organisation, an NGO. We'll work closely with the authorities while insuring our independence, both intellectually and in terms of our activities. We want to do practical things to protect the wall. There is a pressing need for it, and only in this way can we achieve sustainable development. Our hope is still just that — an idea, a hope. It's very hard to get permission to register as an NGO.

TRANSLATED BY GEREMIE R BARMÉ

Portraits

CLAIRE ROBERTS AND JEAN-FRANCOIS LANZERONE

In May 2006, photographer Jean-Francois Lanzarone travelled to China with Sang Ye and me to photograph China's Great Walls. We began our project in the Gobi Desert in China's far northwest and ended it at Shanghaiguan Pass on the east coast where the Great Wall meets the sea.

In the course of our travels we were interested not only in the physical remains of the ancient walls, but also in the people whose lives are shaped by them. Many of the people we met are involved, in various ways, in China's booming economy. We were fascinated, for example, by the synergy between ancient towers made from tamped earth — used to light beacon fires and alert troops to enemy advances — and recently erected mobile telephone towers.

Similarly, we noted the many ways in which the Great Wall is used in contemporary society: in political campaigns, tourism promotions and in advertising. For instance, the Great Wall features as the back-drop for posters that can be seen around Beijing which promote the 'eight socialist concepts of honour and disgrace' (abbreviated as *ba rong ba chi* in Chinese) which Hu Jintao, General Secretary of the Chinese Communist Party, announced in March 2006. The Great Wall is also the subject of a striking repoussé copper mural in the entrance foyer of the Beijing Shengshiyuan Hotsprings Hotel in Yanqing, located near Badaling. The mural depicts the nearby Ming dynasty Great Wall and incorporates the famous line by Mao Zedong, 'You're not a hero if you don't get to the Great Wall', in the Chairman's calligraphy. Also of interest to us was a large billboard advertising Great Wall brand wine that was prominently displayed inside a restaurant at the Mogao Caves at Dunhuang, which are famous for their Buddhist murals and carvings.

The Great Wall also provides livelihood for tour guides, particularly in areas north of Beijing and on the east coast at Shanhaiguan Pass. We met Zhang Handan, a young woman who was leading a group of Chinese tourists on a tour of the temple dedicated to Lady Mengjiang (Mengjiang nü). A railing protected the stone — *Wangfushi* — where Lady Mengjiang was said to have gazed out to sea in search of her husband who died working on the Great Wall more than 2500 years ago. The rail was hung with locks, placed there by couples hoping they will never be separated, unlike the tragic Lady Mengjiang and her husband.

We also made friends with the self-styled 'General Liu' who runs a photographic stall for tourists at Badaling. At our request, he modelled the costume of an ancient warrior, one that he had for hire. For a small fee you can dress-up and have your photograph taken in character against the Great Wall with the Beijing Olympic Games slogan 'One World, One Dream' (*Tong yige shijie, tong yige mengxiang*) visible in the distance. The laminated image is an instant souvenir, proof to friends and family that you have made it to China's Great Wall.

The portraits on the following pages are a small selection of Jean-Francois Lanzarone's work. Through branding, marketing and tourism the Great Wall finds a contemporary relevance; and its power continues to resonate with many of the people who live in its proximity.

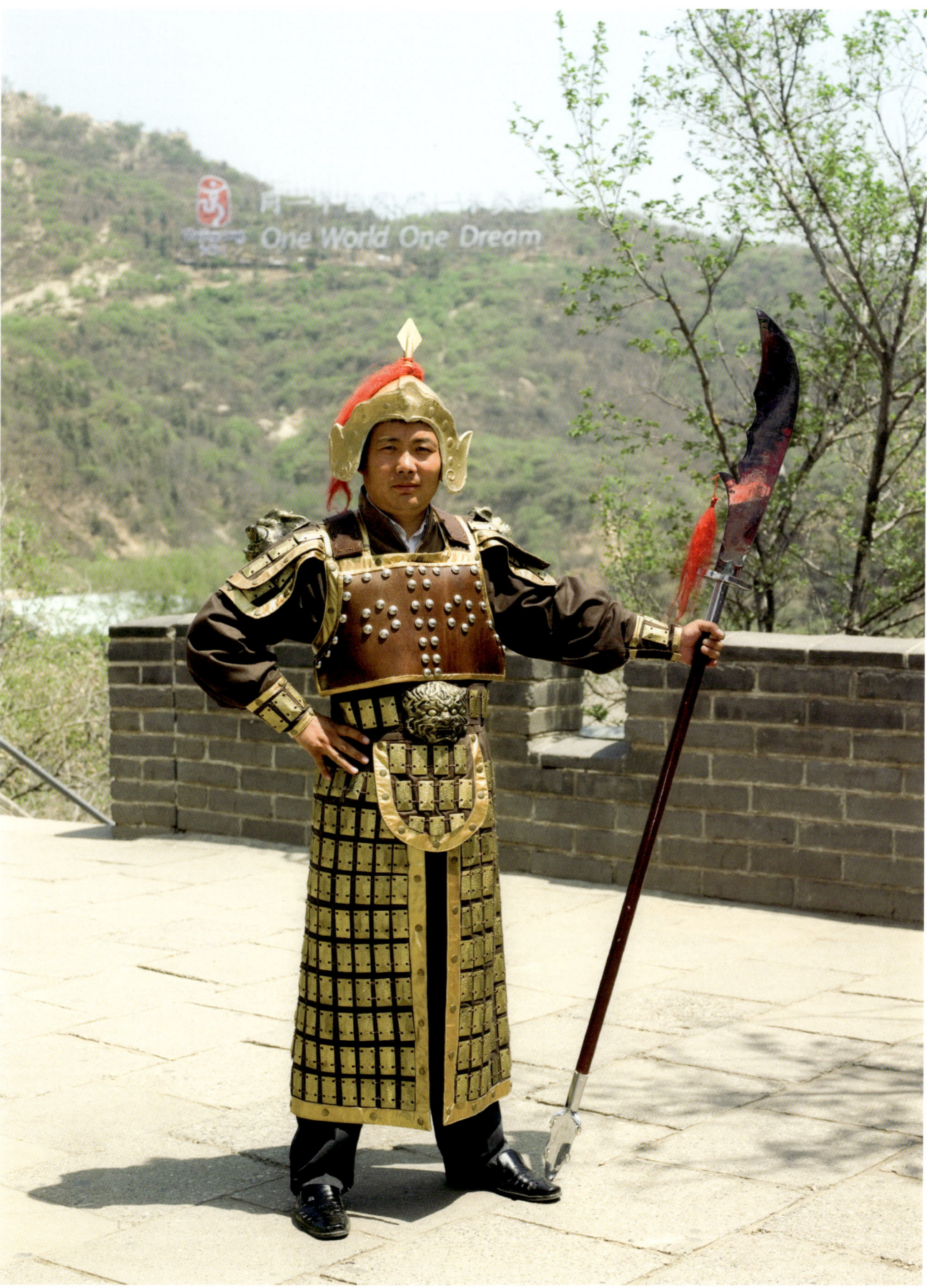

'General Liu', owner of a photographic stall at Badaling, Yanqing, Beijing.

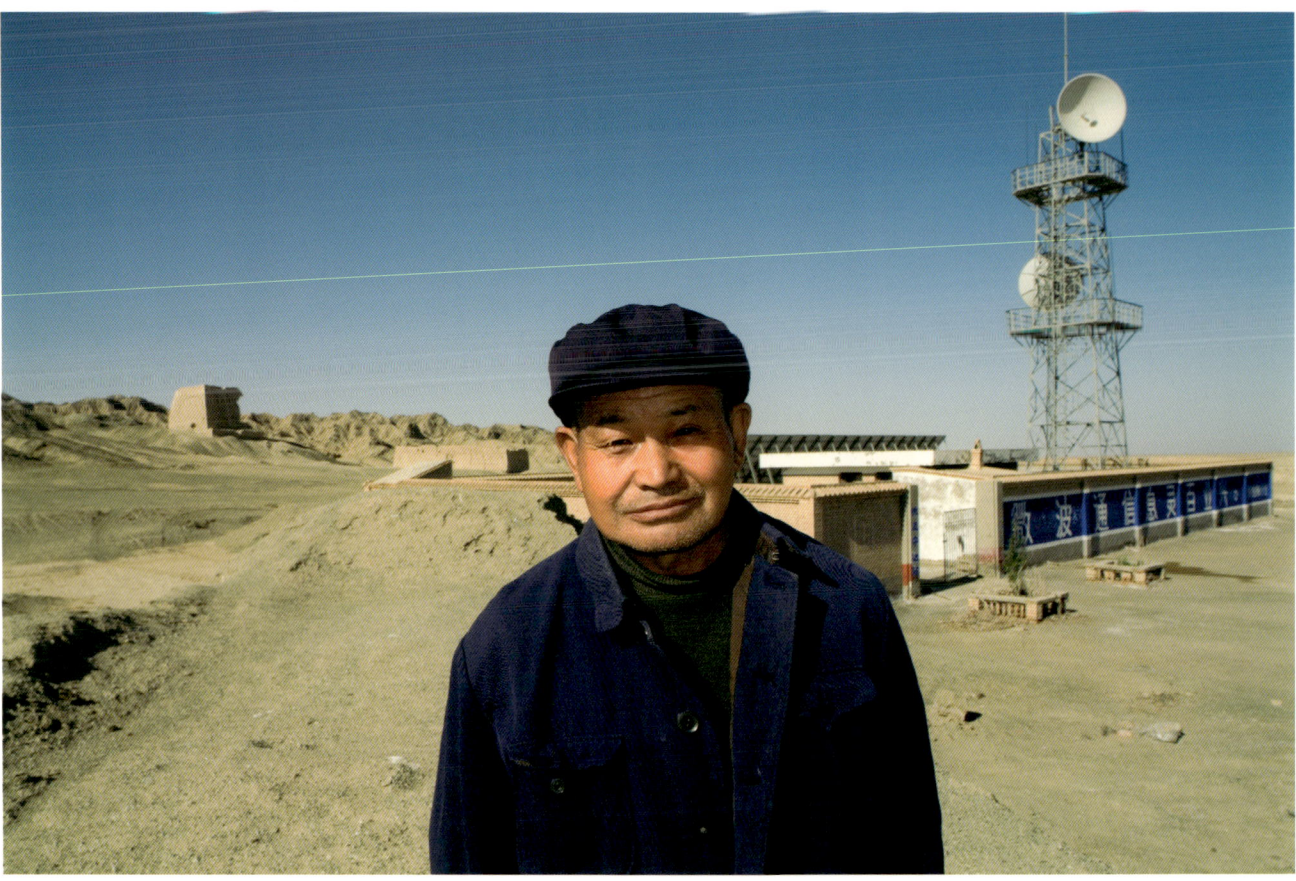

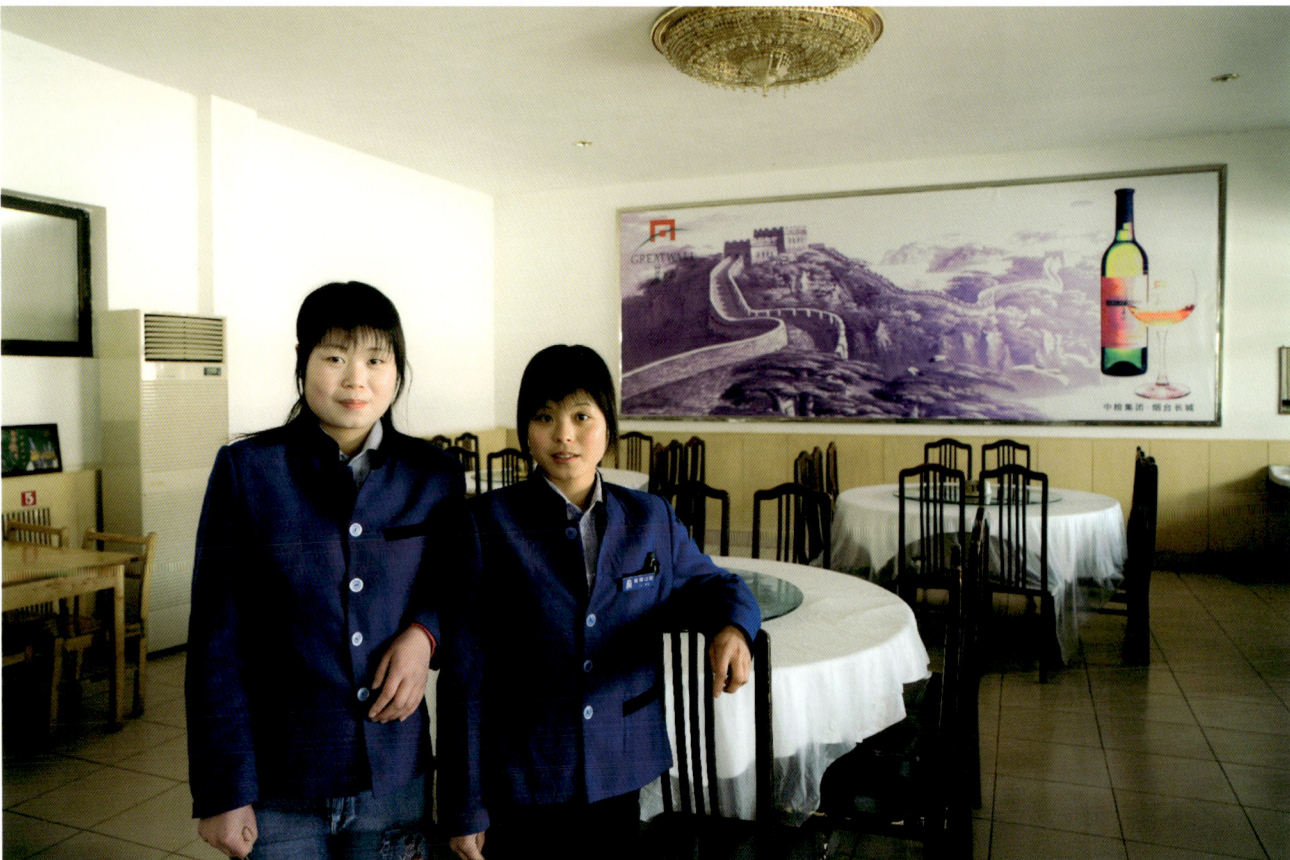

Top: Han Keqing, caretaker of a mobile telephone tower near the ancient Lucaogou beacon tower on the road between Dunhuang and Anxi, Gansu.

Bottom: Waitresses and an advertisement for Great Wall brand wine in a restaurant at the Mogao Caves, Dunhuang, Gansu.

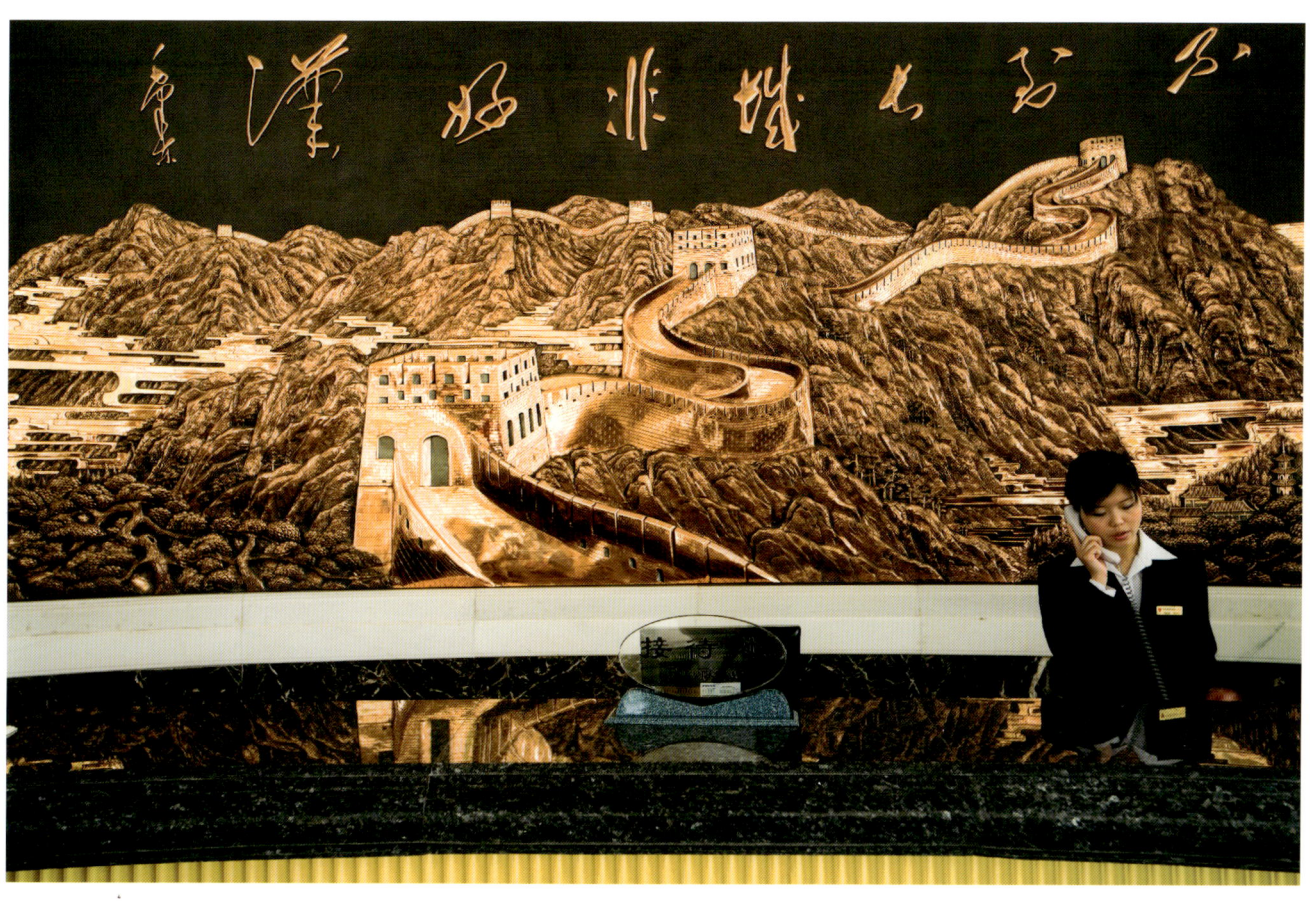

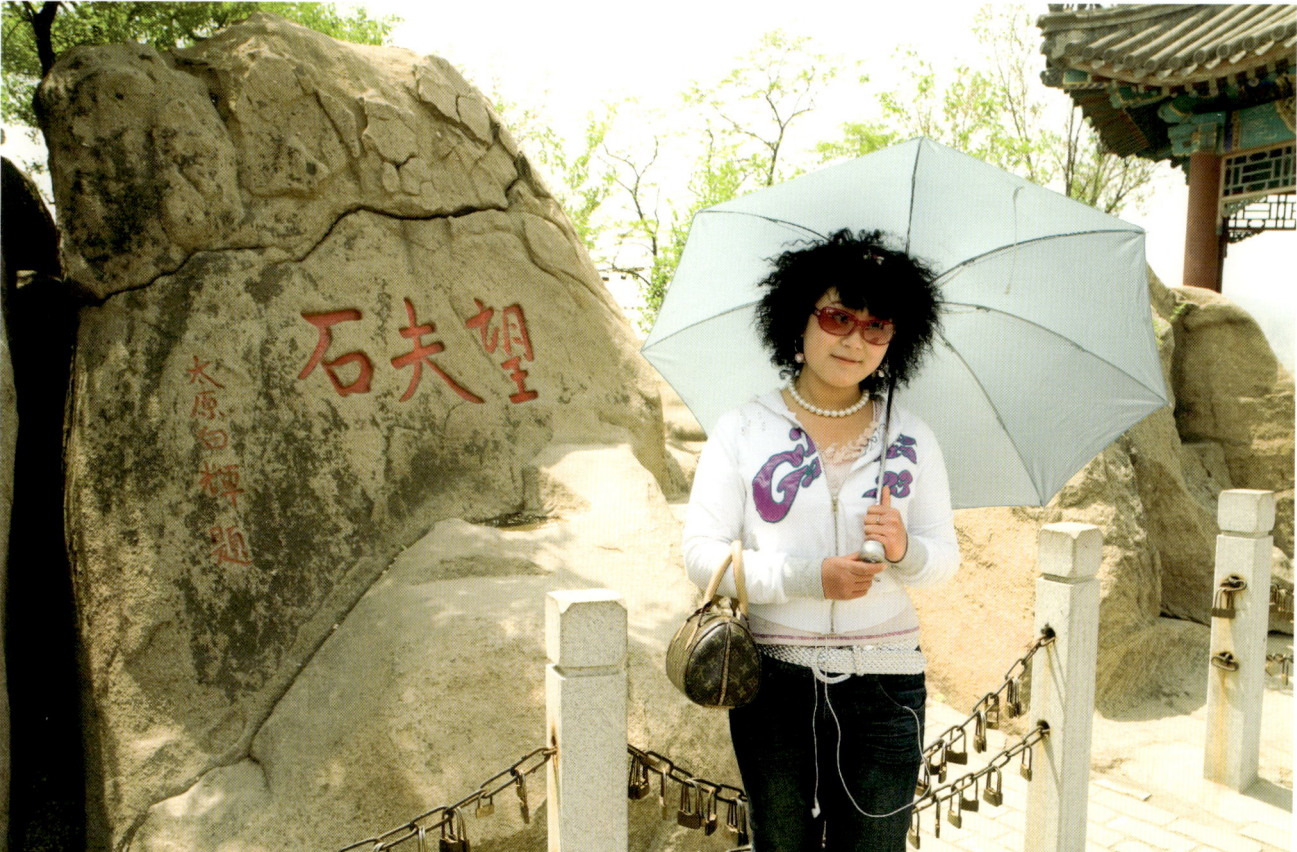

Top: Zhang Handan, receptionist at the Beijing Shengshiyuan Hotsprings Hotel, Yanqing, Beijing.

Bottom: Tour guide, Zhang Dandan, at the stone from which Lady Mengjiang stood looking for her husband, Shanhaiguan, Hebei.

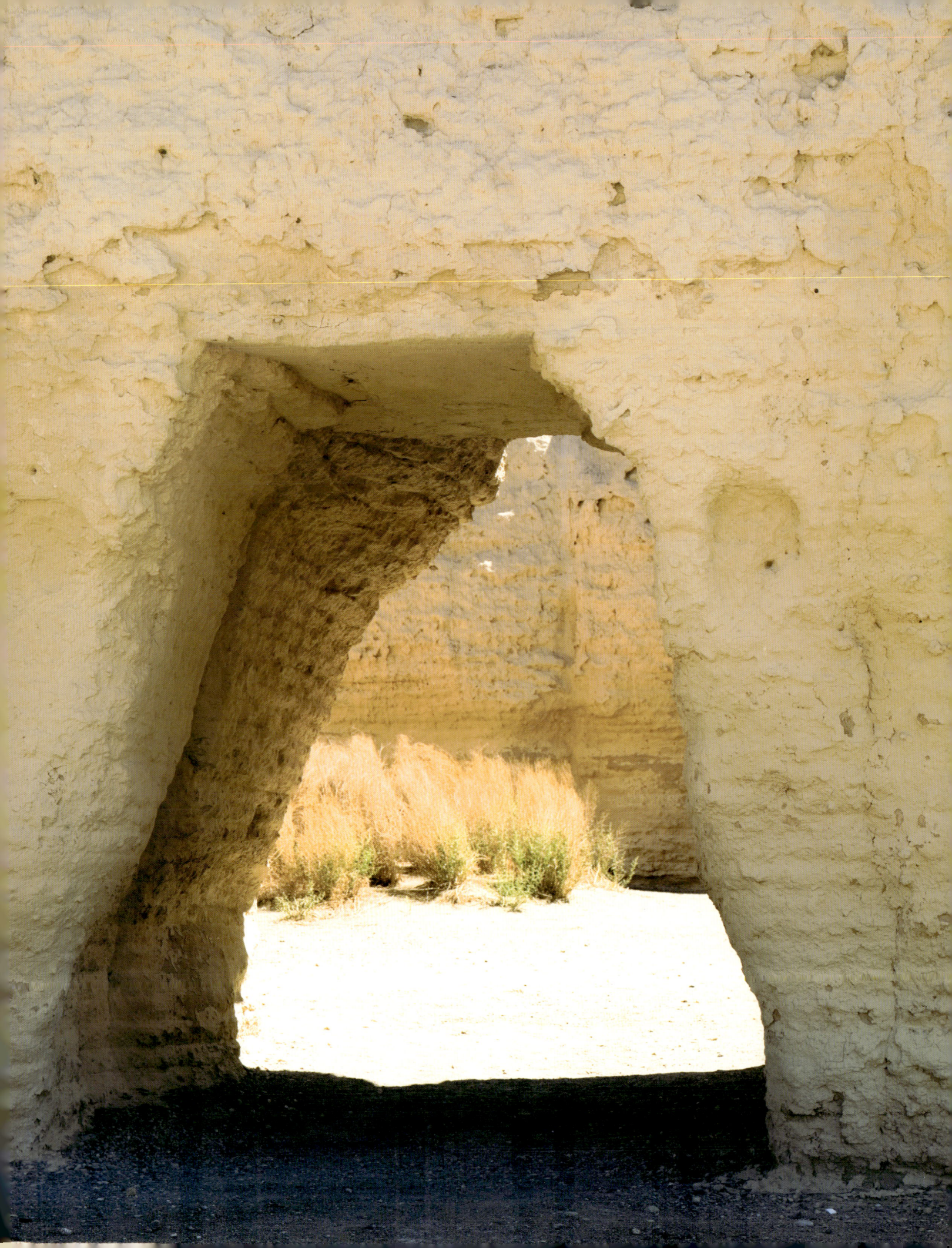

FORM

We Fought South of the City Wall, a ballad from the Western Han dynasty (206 BCE–8 CE)

We fought south of the city wall.
We died north of the ramparts.
In the wilderness we dead lie unburied, fodder for crows.
Tell the crows for us:
"We've always been brave men!
In the wilderness we dead clearly lie unburied.
So how can our rotting flesh flee from you?"
Waters deep, rushing, rushing,
Reeds and rushes, darkening, darkening.
Heroic horsemen fought and died fighting,
Flagging horses whinnied in panic.
Raftered houses we built,
And south, alas! And north;
If grain and millet aren't reaped, what will you eat, Lord?
We longed to be loyal vassals, but how can that be?
I remember you, good vassals,
Good vassals I truly remember:
In the dawn you went out to glory,
At nightfall you did not return.

Translated by Anne Birrell

Detail of Jade Gate Pass, Dunhuang, Gansu.
Photo: Jean-Francois Lanzarone

The Great Walls of China

LUO ZHEWEN

The Great Wall of China straddles fifteen provinces, municipalities and autonomous regions at all points of the Chinese compass. The total length of the various walls built during different historical periods which constitute the Great Wall of China exceeds 50 000 kilometres. In 1961, segments of the Great Wall and the passes at Shanhaiguan, Badaling and Jiayuguan were listed as grade-one national cultural heritage sites and in 1987 the Great Wall was inscribed on the UNESCO World Heritage List.

For more than 2000 years, ruling Chinese dynasties engaged in an almost continual project of constructing the Great Walls of China. Work began during the Spring and Autumn (722–476 BCE) and Warring States (475–221 BCE) periods. Like walled towns and walled fortresses, the Great Walls are an integral part of China's defensive military architecture.

The Great Walls have ancient origins. Archaeologists discovered the remains of city walls dating back 7000 years at the Xishan archaeological site in Zhengzhou, Henan province, and a moat almost 6 metres across and 7 metres deep surrounding the 6000- or 7000-year-old neolithic village at Banpo outside Xi'an in Shaanxi province. These structures belong to the same category of defensive architecture as fortified walls. Trenches or moats were later incorporated into the Great Wall engineering projects of the later Eastern Han (25–220 CE), Liao (916–1125) and Jin (1115–1234) dynasties.

A definition

Like walled towns and fortresses, China's Great Walls were built for defence. But town and fortress walls circle back in on themselves to enclose and protect particular spaces. In the case of the Great Walls, however, the different sections do not join up to create a sealed enclosure. The stretches of wall are also significantly longer than the walls that surround cities or fortified buildings, ranging in length from 300 to 500 kilometres in the case of shorter sections, and between 1000 and 10 000 kilometres for longer ones — hence the expression *changcheng*, that is 'long walls'. In addition to ramparts and gates, the term 'Great Walls' also encompasses gated passes, fortresses, military camps and beacon towers, which are part of the integrated network of defensive structures.

Building the Great Walls

There's a common misperception in China and abroad that the founding emperor of the Qin dynasty (221–206 BCE), Qin Shihuang, was responsible for the construction of the first Great Wall. In fact, construction began more than 500 years before Qin Shihuang's reign. Scholars generally refer to these early walls as the 'pre-Qin Great Walls'.

In the seventh and eighth centuries BCE, well before Qin Shihuang's unification of China, the land was divided into numerous feudatory kingdoms. These kingdoms were constantly at war with one another in a competition for supremacy. Each feudal lord selected defensible, strategic locations within his domain and linked them with long defensive walls from which his forces could retreat or attack. According to historical records, the state of Chu had a wall in the seventh century BCE, the earliest known long wall on record. Later, the states of Qi, Zhongshan, Wei, Zheng, Han, Qin and Yan all constructed their own great or long walls.

The length and dimensions of these walls varied according to the extent of each state's territory and strength. The longest walls, extending for roughly 2000 kilometres, were those constructed by the state of Yan in the area that is now Beijing; the shortest, measuring only about 300 kilometres in length, were those built by the state of Zhongshan in what is now Sichuan province.

Qin Shihuang's walls
Qin Shihuang unified China in 221 BCE, bringing an end to long years of internecine warfare and the resultant social chaos and creating China's first centralised state. To address the needs of this newly unified state and to promote administrative, economic, military and cultural development, Qin Shihuang implemented a system of administrative control over prefectures and counties and unitary systems for the written language, carriage gauges, and weights and measures, as well as a set of ethical principles.

But a nomadic group to the north of the Qin empire, the Xiongnu, remained very powerful. The Xiongnu often launched raids southwards, threatening the security of the Qin empire. For protection, the Qin adopted the method of 'long walls' defence used during the Warring States period, together with a system of stationing troops in defensive garrisons.

According to Sima Qian's (c 145-86 BCE) *Records of the historian (Shi ji)*:

> the Xiongnu were expelled from the north-west. The land occupied from Yuzhong along the eastern side of the Yellow River all the way to Yinshan was then divided into thirty-four counties. In the neighbourhood of the Yellow River, walls were erected and these served as a strategic barricade … [General] Meng Tian was despatched across the Yellow River and he attacked and captured Gaoque, Taoshan and Beijiazhong.

The following passage from this same work, entitled 'The biography of Meng Tian', explains in more detail:

> After Qin had annexed the whole country, Meng Tian was despatched at the head of an army of 300,000 men to drive out the Rong and Di [barbarian tribes] to the north. He annexed Henan [the lands south of the Yellow River] and constructed long walls. In this, he relied on the topography of the land, and built barricades connecting strategic locations. From Lintao in the west to Liaodong in the east, the Great Wall extended for more than 10,000 li.

The idea of the Great Wall of China, which in Chinese is commonly referred to as 'The Ten-thousand *li* Great Wall' (*wanli changcheng*) — the *li* is the traditional Chinese mile, approximately equivalent to half a

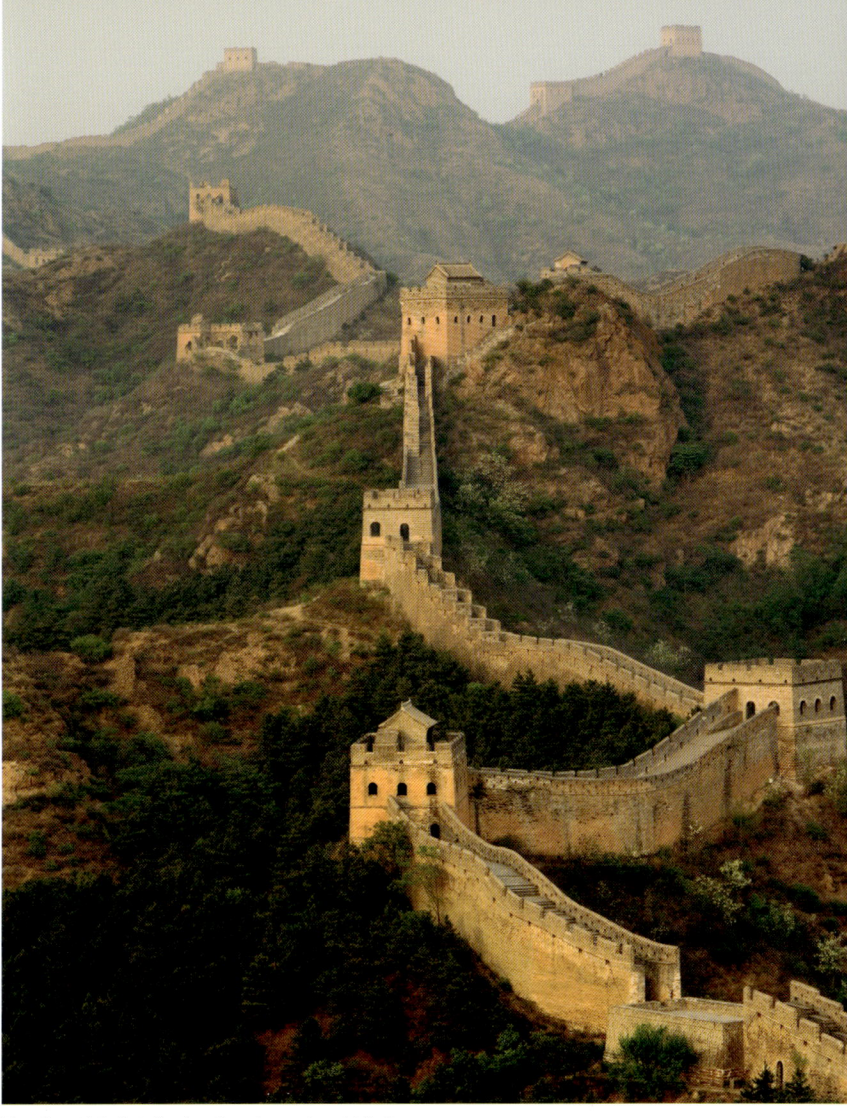

The Great Wall at Jinshanling, Luanping, Hebei.
Photo: Jean-Francois Lanzarone

kilometre — began with Qin Shihuang's enterprise. This has led to the misperception that it was Qin Shihuang who first built the Great Walls.

Qin Shihuang's construction of long walls was a prodigious engineering feat, but an enterprise that caused untold suffering among the countless people who were forced into labouring on it. Their story is one reason why Qin Shihuang is often remembered as a tyrant. According to the classic *Great words from Huainan* (Huainanzi) from the second century BCE, 'Qin despatched five hundred thousand men under Yang Gongyang and Wen Zijiang to build long walls from the desert to the west to the Liao River in the north … and the bodies of those who died along the roads filled trenches.' The famous story of the Lady Mengjiang, who searched in vain for her husband who had died while working on the construction of the walls, symbolised the suffering and sorrow caused by Qin Shihuang's grand project. Many popular ballads and poems fiercely attacked the emperor's obsession with wall-building. For more than 2000 years debate has raged about whether the construction of the Great Walls was a good or a bad thing. In the seventeenth century the Manchu-Qing Kangxi emperor (1662–1722) wrote a poem that contains the couplet:

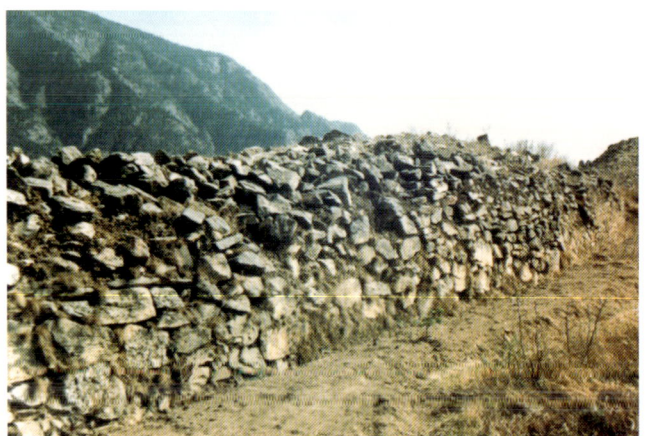

Wall from the State of Qi built using irregular shaped stones,
at Taishan in Shandong.
Photo: Luo Zhewen

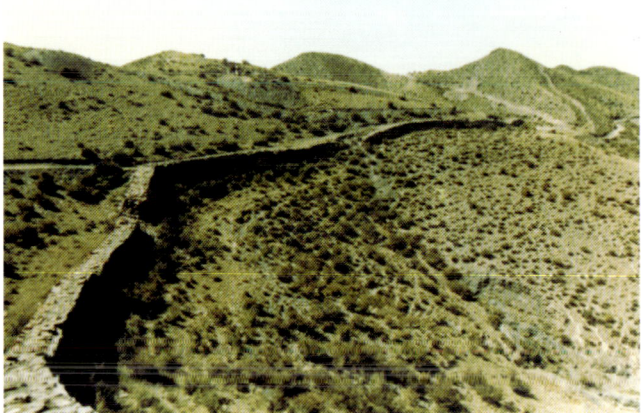

Remains of the Great Wall built during the Qin dynasty, at Guyang,
Inner Mongolia.
Photo: Luo Zhewen

Undone yet by wasteful toil
Does the world now belong to thee?

Despite the high price paid, for more than two millennia
rulers of almost every dynasty continued to expend vast
human resources on an engineering project dictated by
national security concerns.

Sun Yat-sen (1866–1925) who, in the early years of the
twentieth century, led the democratic revolution that
overturned the dynastic system and established a republic,
provided his own assessment:

> *There is nothing in ancient times on a similar scale to the
> Great Wall of China and it is a unique wonder of the
> world … Qin Shihuang heroically dominated a generation
> and conquered the six rival states to unify China … a
> legacy for all time, defended and preserved by his noble
> deed of constructing the Great Wall. Qin Shihuang lacked
> principles, yet his Great Wall was an achievement he
> bequeathed to later generations that can be likened to Yu the
> Great's quelling of the flood waters.*

Sun's view was that, although Qin Shihuang may have
been a tyrant, the Great Wall contributed to the unity of
China for more than two millennia. By comparing their
construction to the achievement of Yu the Great, the
legendary ruler and hydraulic engineer thought to have
lived about 4000 years ago, in stemming the destructive
floods of the Yellow River, Sun was lavishing the highest
praise on this engineering achievement.

After Qin Shihuang
In the two millennia after Qin Shihuang, from the Han
dynasty through the Ming (1368–1644) and Qing (1644–
1911) dynasties, almost every imperial ruler was involved
in the construction of Great Walls. Some projects
continued over long periods and others lasted only a short
time. Historical documents show that after Qin Shihuang,
the Western Han, Eastern Han, Jin, Northern Wei,
Eastern Wei, Western Wei, Northern Qi, Northern Zhou,
Sui, Tang, Song, Liao, Jin, Yuan, Ming and Qing dynasties

all built new walls, augmented or repaired existing walls,
or made use of fortified passes and walls. The Han and
Ming dynasties initiated the largest projects: it is
estimated that the Han walls were over 10 000 kilometres
in length; those of the Ming exceeded 7000 kilometres.
The Northern Qi walls stretched over 1000 kilometres,
and the Liao-Jin walls were five times that length.

In the history of the construction of Great Walls, the Han
dynasty walls are unusual both in their extent and the
length of time over which they were built. They also
demonstrate innovations in defensive capabilities,
building materials and architectural engineering.

After Liu Bang overthrew the Qin in 206 BCE, and
established the Han dynasty with himself as the emperor
— he was known as Emperor Han Gaozu (reigned 206–
195 BCE) — the new state concentrated its resources on
consolidating its internal power and addressing the issue
of continued incursions by the Xiongnu. The Han
emperors Wen (reigned 180–157 BCE) and Jing (reigned
156–141 BCE) adopted a policy of rapprochement and
payments to the Xiongnu, which included the provision
of women in 'diplomatic marriages' (*heqin*).

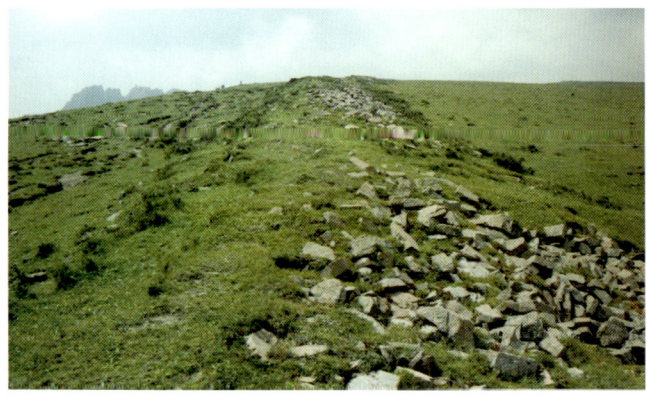

Remains of the Great Wall built during the Northern Qi dynasty,
in Ningwu, Shanxi.
Photo: Luo Zhewen

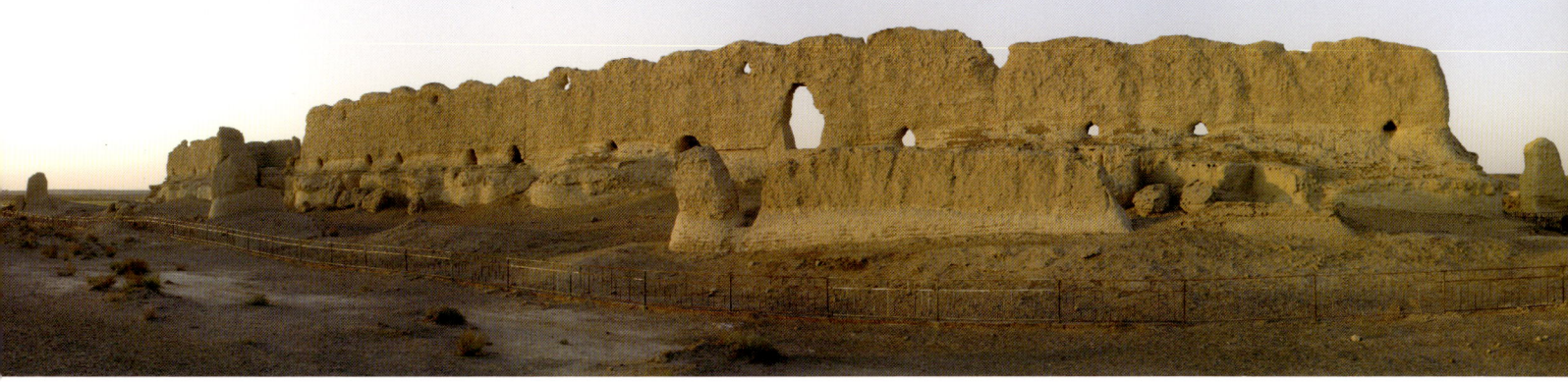

Remains of an ancient grain store built during the Western Han dynasty, at Dafangpan, Dunhuang, Gansu.
Photo: Jean-Francois Lanzarone

In 134 BCE, Emperor Han Wudi (reigned 140–87 BCE) took a more martial approach. He appointed the head of the palace garrison, Li Guang, as general in command of the garrison in the Yunzhong region, and put the head of the capital garrison, Cheng Bushi, in charge of the garrison at Yanmen Pass. The Xiongnu continued to launch attacks against the Liaoxi, Shangjun and Yuyang districts in northern China. Han Wudi ordered his generals Wei Qing and Huo Qubing to lead large armies to crush the invaders. He also initiated the largest construction project of great walls since the time of Qin Shihuang. By 111 BCE, Emperor Wudi had built walls and beacon towers as far west as Dunhuang in present-day Gansu province and had set up fortified post-stations and beacons along what is known as the Silk Road all the way to the west of today's Kashgar in Xinjiang. In the closing years of the Western Han (206 BCE–8 CE), the dynasty was subject to internal rebellion and the Xiongnu threat rose afresh. Following the establishment of the Eastern Han dynasty in 25 CE, Emperor Guangwu (reigned 25–57) initiated another large-scale program of wall construction. By 48 CE, internal dissension among the Xiongnu tribes led them to split into southern and northern groups. The southern Xiongnu became subjects of the Han dynasty and many intermarried with ethnic Han people living in the areas adjacent to the Great Walls, during which time no further walls were seen as necessary.

The Great Walls of the Han dynasty stretched more than 10 000 kilometres in length, and in both function and layout display many unique features. In present-day Xinjiang, for example, where their main function was to provide security for merchant caravans along the Silk Road trade routes, they consist only of fortified post-stations and beacon towers built at fixed intervals with no adjoining walls. The walls and beacon towers served as powerful sentinels that from an early time guarded China's contact with the outside world.

The Ming: the great wall-builders

The Ming Great Walls represent the last era of large-scale wall construction. They are also the most sophisticated, based as they were on some two millennia of wall-building experience.

The founders of the Ming dynasty overthrew the Mongol-Yuan dynasty in 1368. The Yuan represented a period when the northern nomads breached the Great Wall so completely that they could extend their rule over the Central Plains of China. The Yuan rulers, unwilling to concede defeat to the Ming, withdrew to the Mongolian plateau to prepare a counterattack and restoration of their empire. Defence against a Mongol assault naturally remained a major concern of the Ming court. In 1368, the first Ming emperor, Zhu Yuanzhang, despatched General Xu Da to repair and rebuild the Great Walls at Juyongguan Pass, north of present-day Beijing. In 1420, Zhu Yuanzhang's son, Zhu Di (the Yongle emperor, reigned 1403–24) moved the Ming capital from Nanjing in the south of China to Beiping (which he renamed Beijing) in the north in a show of defiance against the Mongols: a capital located near the Great Walls signalled

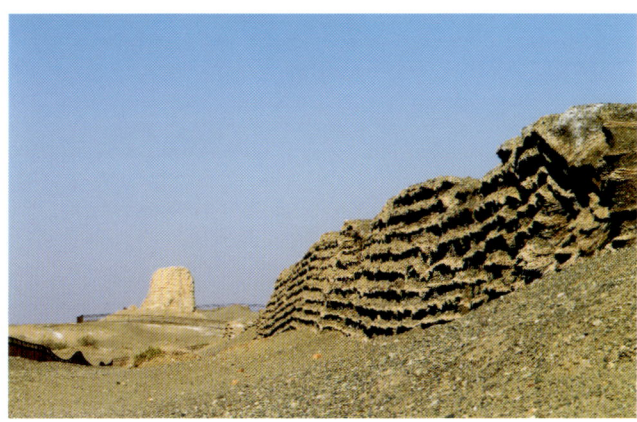

Remains of the Han dynasty Great Wall at Majuanwan, Dunhuang, Gansu.
Photo: Jean-Francois Lanzarone

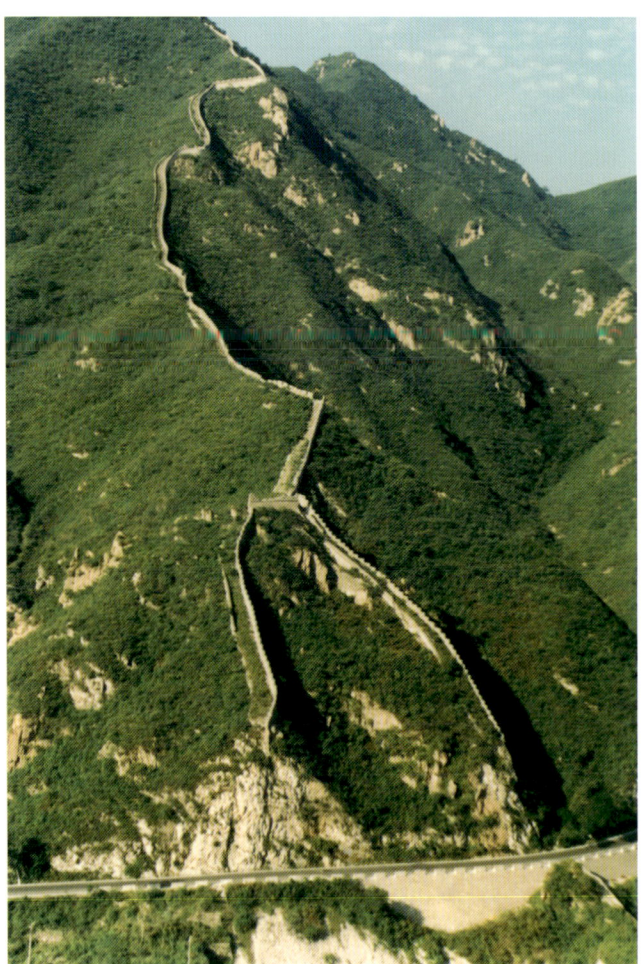

Aerial view of the Great Wall at Juyongguan Pass, Changping, Beijing.
Photo: Luo Zhewen

and its defensive importance. Troop allocations ranged from tens to hundreds of thousands and a military regional commander was appointed to every commandery. In all, more than a million troops guarded the walls at the time of the Ming.

Repair and construction of the walls fell under the jurisdiction of the Board of War (*Bingbu*), equivalent to today's Ministry of Defence. In times of war, the emperor appointed senior ministers from his war cabinet or the chief minister of the Board of War to take direct control of the armies along the walls. On occasion, emperors would even take direct charge of the troops. The military communication systems along the Ming Great Walls were also greatly improved: the relay of military intelligence via beacon towers acquired a scientific precision and speed.

Defensive Great Wall buildings

The most prominent architectural feature of the Great Walls are, of course, the crenellated barriers that can be seen crossing vast stretches of mountains, grassland and desert. The Great Walls also include thousands of passes, and tens of thousands of forts, emplacements, beacon towers and terraces, forming an integrated set of structures. Walls built during different periods are of various heights and thicknesses. They were designed to harmonise with different landforms, topographies and environments: walls constructed along mountain ridges tend to be lower and narrower than the higher sections built on level ground, reflecting defensive requirements and enabling economies in the use of human and material resources. At Badaling, the most popular tourist site today, for example, the walls are comparatively high — approximately 7 metres on average — because Badaling is a major mountain pass. At their base, they are approximately 7 metres thick narrowing to 6 metres at the top. On the outside there are merlons and inside are barrier walls, stairways and corridors. Also constructed

that he was an 'emperor who defended the nation's borders'. Thereafter, construction of walls proceeded apace. The last ruler of the Ming, the Chongzhen emperor, Zhu Youjian (reigned 1628–44), was still constructing the Xiluocheng fortifications at the Shanhaiguan Pass in Hebei when the dynasty collapsed.

The Ming rulers extended and enhanced the Great Walls to create a comprehensive system of fortifications. To better regulate the more than 7000 kilometres of walls as a defensive line and to provide it with a hierarchical line of command, the Great Walls were organised into a number of commanderies, each of which was responsible for the control of a specific section.

Initially nine sections of wall and nine commanderies were established: Liaodong, Jizhou, Xuanfu, Datong, Shanxi [Piantou], Yulin [Yansui], Ningxia, Gansu and Guyuan. The Chang and Zhenbao commanderies were also set up to strengthen the military protection of Beijing and the Shisanling area, where the Ming imperial mausoleums were located. Each commandery oversaw a stretch of the Great Walls; military resources were assigned according to the scope of the section of wall

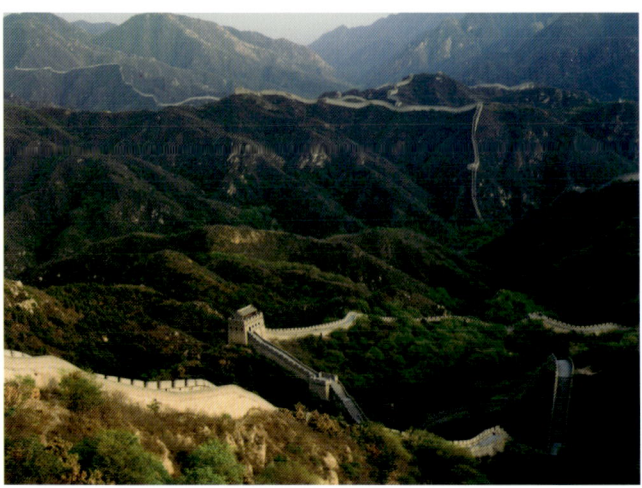

View from the northern section of the Great Wall at Badaling, Yanqing, Beijing.
Photo: Jean-Francois Lanzarone

with reference to topography and defensive requirements, watchtowers and terraces were appropriately spaced to enable infantrymen to patrol and keep watch. At the sections of the Ming wall at Jinshanling and Simatai, banks of barrier walls were also constructed here and there along the tops of the walls for use in battle.

Beacon towers, known in Chinese as *fenghuotai, fengsui* or *yandun*, are an ancient Chinese invention for the relay of military intelligence and other information. A story about how King You of the Zhou dynasty (reigned 782–771 BCE) used beacon fires to play a trick on his feudal lords dates their existence back at least three millennia. For more than 2000 years, beacon towers were an integral component of the Great Wall defensive systems, used to communicate information by smoke signals during the daytime and with burning brands at night. The number of smoke signals or the number of times torches were raised or lowered indicated the numbers of approaching enemy troops. In the Ming dynasty, cannon fire was also used to signal information. A law promulgated in 1466 stated:

> We command the border watch responsible for signals to issue one fire beacon or one cannon shot if between one and approximately one hundred persons are sighted. If approximately five hundred persons are sighted, then two fire signals or two cannon shots should be discharged; sightings of a thousand and more persons require three discharges; sightings of five thousand require four discharges; and sightings of ten thousand or more require five discharges.

As well as the introduction of cannon fire, the Ming added sulphur and saltpetre to the fires, allowing for greater precision and speed in signalling. It is estimated that there were tens of thousands of beacon towers along the Great Wall; thousands survive in some form to the present day. At Jade Gate Pass (Yumenguan) and other places within the Dunhuang district of Gansu, unburnt straw intended for use in signal fires during the Western Han dynasty has been found in a fine state of preservation.

Within the Great Wall system there are many other defensive structures, details of which are recorded in historical documents. These include: garrison towns (*cheng*), fairly large defensive structures; forts (*bao*), the most basic defensive structure; barriers (*zhang*), small walls within mountainous areas; lookout posts (*hou*), structures for maintaining a defensive watch; passes (*guan*), important architectural structures that facilitated transport through the walls and which could be opened or closed; and other types of passes, with special features designed for specific environments (*sai, ai* and *kou*).

Garrison towns differ, depending on their position in the military command and their place in the hierarchy of towns involved with the control and defence of the walls. For example, there were military command towns (*zhencheng*) where the main command garrison was

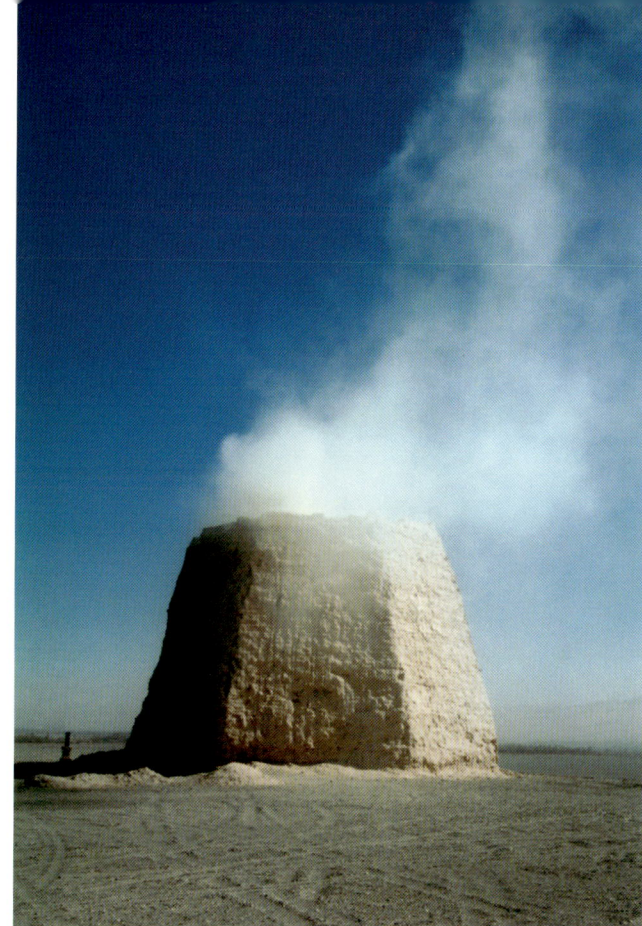

Smoke signals were sent from beacon towers during the day.
Photo: Luo Zhewen

stationed, administrative military circuit towns (*lucheng*), military battalion towns (*yingcheng*), towns at passes (*guancheng*), towns at mountain barriers (*zhangcheng*), and fortress towns (*baocheng*).

Passes are an important architectural feature of the Great Wall. Strategic considerations about secure transport and communications routes often determined the location of the passes. Their strategic nature is illustrated by the ancient Chinese proverb, 'If one man defends a pass, 10 000 cannot enter' (*yi fu dang guan, wan fu mo kai*). More than a thousand passes have been found along the Great Walls and, at the larger passes, many smaller auxiliary passes were also constructed; these were under the control of the military administrative unit called the 'circuit' (*lu*). The circuit of the Shanhaiguan Pass, for example, controlled ten smaller passes in its environs. The passes also had their own attached towns, the size of which were determined by their strategic importance and the number of troops stationed there. The best preserved passes open to the public, which represent some of the finest examples of the Ming walls include: Shanhaiguan, Huangyaguan, Jinshanling, Mutianyu, Simatai, Juyongguan, Badaling, Yanmenguan, Zhenbeitai, Jiayuguan, Yumenguan and Yangguan.

Organising labour at the Great Walls
Today, even a simple climb up the Great Walls at Juyongguan, Badaling, Mutianyu, Simatai, Shanhaiguan or Jiayuguan passes can be physically taxing. It is impossible not to be in awe of the workers who carried

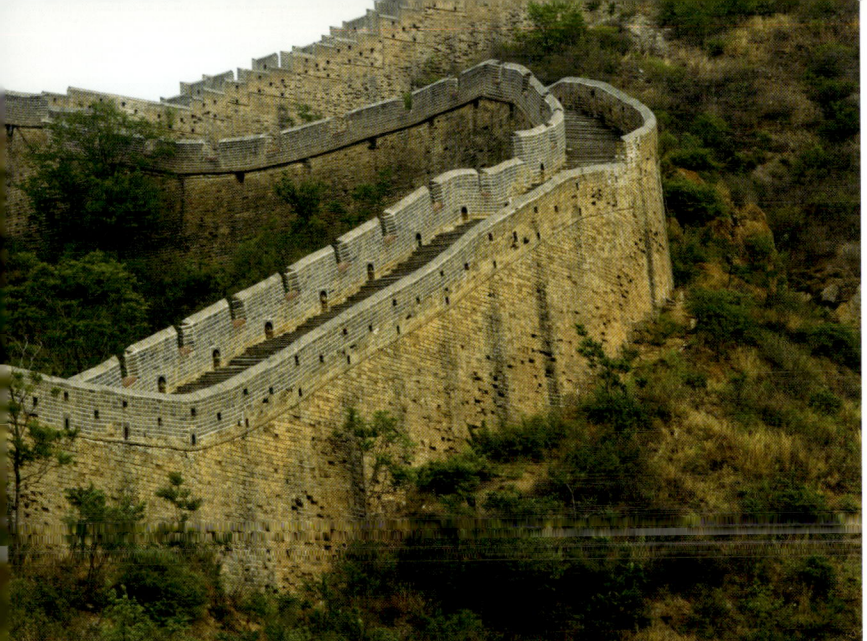

Section of the Ming dynasty Great Wall at Jinshanling, Luanping, Hebei.
Photo: Jean-Francois Lanzarone

the stones to the tops of the ridges on which the walls were constructed. The largest of these stones could weigh 1000 kilograms and even the smallest was over 10 kilograms.

The construction of the walls relied on brute strength, which is why people say that they were built from flesh and blood. It is impossible to calculate the total number of human lives expended in their construction, despite the existence of some vital statistics in historical records. We know, for example, that the main pool of labour used came from the troops assigned to defend the borders. The 300 000 troops Qin Shihuang assigned to border defence constructed walls for more than a decade. The Han dynasty walls were built over a period of more than two centuries, and the Ming assigned more than a million border troops to wall construction and repair. We know that conscripted or corvée labour was used, but we have no statistics documenting the extent of this. Criminal offenders were also pressed into service. Emperor Yangdi (reigned 605–18) of the Sui dynasty (581–618) so exhausted the available male manpower that he eventually conscripted the widows of those who had died building the Great Walls.

Some idea of how such a vast pool of labour was organised can be gleaned from an inscribed stone tablet at the Badaling Great Wall. Dated 1582, the stele records details of repair work carried out at a section of the Juyongguan Pass. It reads:

> The imperially commissioned Shandong Supreme Commander in charge of the Autumn Defence Roster Left Battalion supervised the officers Shou Chun and Lu Wenyuan to fulfil their written instructions and separately oversee the repair of the border walls in the area of Shifosi Temple at the Juyongguan circuit. To the east, support is provided by a battalion of labourers working on the wall

> that extends for 75 zhang and 2 chi [about 0.25 km], and one inner stone gate. Now that the government troops have completed their construction tasks, the names of those who supervised this work are hereby enshrined on this tablet to be erected and stand for eternity.

> Officials in charge of the work:

> Adjutant Commander of the Jinan Defence Forces, Liu Youben

> Company Commander of the Qingzhou Left Defence Forces, Liu Guangqian

> Company Deputy Commander of the Jinan Defence Forces, Zong Jiguang

> Battalion Commander of Grain Supplies of the Feicheng Guard, Zhang Tingyin

> Kiln and Quarry Management Squad Managers: Zhao Congshan, Liu Yanzhi, Song Dian, Bian Yingchun, Zhao Guanghuan

> Erected in the tenth month of the tenth year of the Wanli reign.

From this stone inscription, we know that several thousand government troops participated in the restoration work, that many civilians worked under contract to construct a 250-metre stretch of wall and a gate, and that government troops were brought in from the Jinan, Qingzhou and Feicheng defence guards of Shandong.

Prior to the Ming dynasty most of the Great Walls and also city and township fortifications were made from tamped earth and stone, rarely from brick. Timber and tiles were also used. The required quantities of earth and stone were large, and usually obtained locally

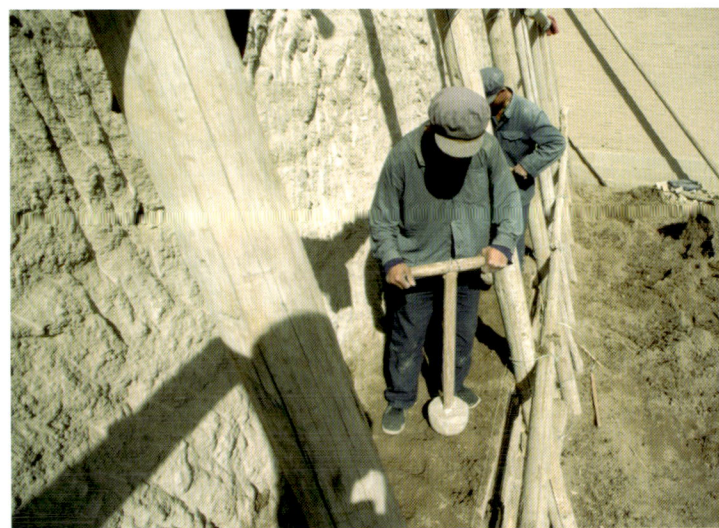

Men repairing the Ming dynasty Great Wall at Jiayuguan Pass, Gansu.
Photo: © John Slater/Corbis/APL

Great Walls sites open to tourists from east to west:

1. **Hushan Great Walls, Dandong** on the banks of the Yalu River in Dandong city, Liaoning province, the easternmost starting point of the Ming Great Walls.

2. **Jiumenkou Great Walls** in Suizhong county, Liaoning province, is an impressive 'water gate' (*shuimen*) of the Ming Great Walls.

3. **Shanhaiguan Pass** in the Shanhaiguan district of Qinhuangdao city, Hebei province, is the largest pass in the eastern section of the Ming Great Walls, and is an impressive sight as it meets the sea.

4. **Huangyaguan Pass** in Jixian county, Hebei province, is one of the important passes of the Ming Great Walls.

5. **Jinshanling** in Luanping county, Hebei province is one of the most spectacular scenic spots of the Ming Great Walls.

6. **Simatai** in Miyun county, Beijing municipality, is one of the most strategic and varied stretches of the Ming dynasty Great Walls.

7. **Mutianyu** in Huairou county, Beijing municipality. This section of the Ming Great Wall has a highly distinctive gate.

8. **Juyongguan Pass** in the Changping county, Beijing municipality, is a major pass located close to the Ming dynasty capital and famous for the Yuan dynasty Cloud Terrace (*Yuntai*).

9. **Badaling** in Yanqing county, Beijing municipality, is perhaps the best known section of the Ming Great Walls, both in China and internationally.

10. **Zijingguan Pass** in Yixian county, Hebei province, is a major pass of the Ming Great Walls known for its unusual layout.

11. **Yanmenguan Pass** in Daixian county, Shanxi province, has been an important pass for more than 2000 years. The present site is part of the Ming Great Wall. The Drum Tower there is the largest adjacent to the Great Wall, and there is also a Shrine to the Generals of the Yang Clan at the site.

12. **Zhenbeitai** in Yulin, Shaanxi province, is the tallest battle terrace (*zhantai*) of the Ming Great Walls.

13. **Jiayuguan Pass** in Jiayuguan, Gansu province, is the end point of the Ming Great Walls.

14. **Jade Gate Pass (Yumenguan)** in Dunhuang, Gansu province, is the site of a Western Han dynasty Great Wall gate dating back to the 2nd millennium BCE. The gate marks a fork in the road where the Silk Road diverges to the north.

15. **Beacon tower at Kuche** in Kuche county, Xinjiang autonomous region, is a beacon tower that was built beside the Silk Road in the Western Han dynasty, near the Kizil Caves.

COMPILED BY LUO ZHEWEN, TRANSLATED BY BRUCE GORDON DOAR

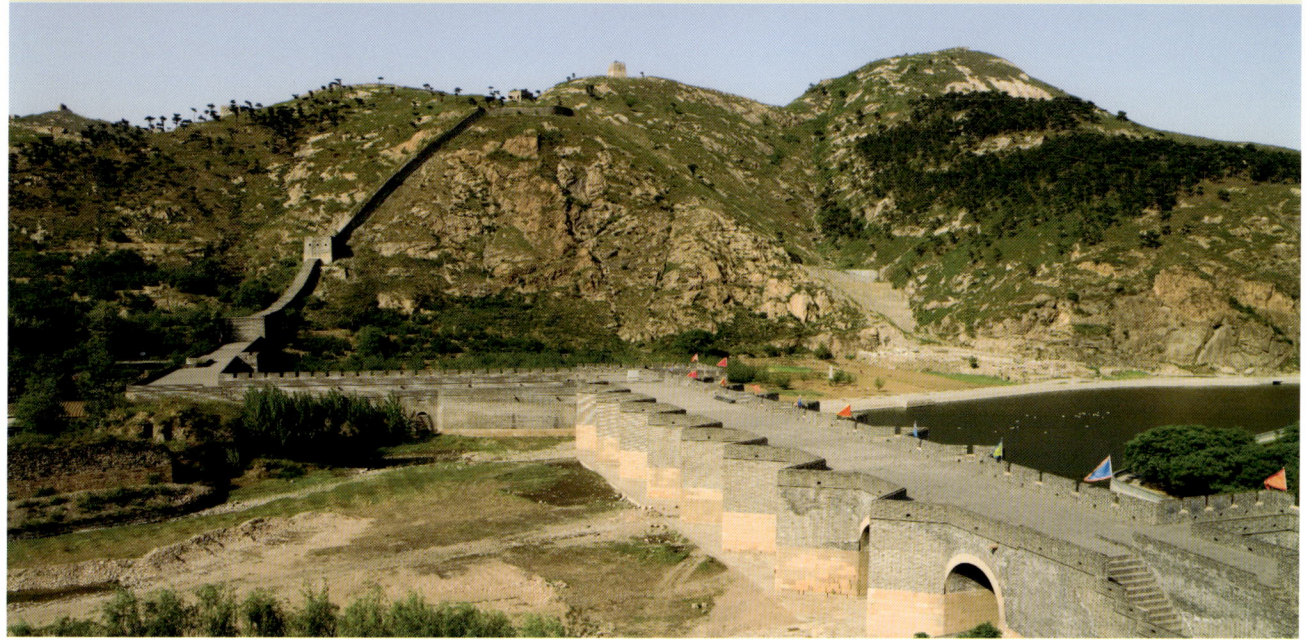

The 'water gate' at Jiumenkou, Suizhong, Liaoning.
Photo: Jean-Francois Lanzarone

at the building site. In mountainous areas, stone was cut from the mountains and worked on site. In plains areas, loess was worked on site by tamping. In the early period of the Ming, rocks were the predominant building material, but bricks gradually came to replace them as the favoured material in Great Wall construction. This was especially the case after Qi Jiguang (1528–87), the general in charge of resistance to Wo pirates attacking coastal areas, was re-assigned from his southern command to take charge of the Jizhou Great Wall commandery. Qi Jiguang oversaw the encasement in brick of the strategically important stretches of the Great Wall and passes in the vicinity of Beijing. (For a discussion of Qi Jiguang, see 'Manning the Wall' by Liu Ruzhong, pp 182–88.)

In desert areas, the construction method entailed laying down reeds (*luwei*) or Chinese tamarisk (*hongliu*) branches in layers — this mode of construction can be seen at well-preserved sections of the Han walls in the Lop Nur district of Xinjiang and at the Jade Gate Pass in Gansu. On top of the reeds or desert tamarisk, a layer of sandy gravel was applied and, above it, another layer of vegetation, and this could be repeated until the walls were 5 or 6 metres in height. The layers of vegetation were approximately 5 to 10 centimetres thick, and the sandy gravel 20 centimetres thick. The construction of a 6-metre high wall would involve up to twenty layers. Oak planks were also used in the construction of the Liaodong Great Walls in China's north-east.

Building the walls that ran through mountainous and desert areas was extremely arduous work. The large bricks that can be seen today at sections of the Great Walls at Juyongguan Pass and Badaling are up to 3 metres long and weigh more than 500 kilograms. Apart from the technological challenges of stone masonry, there was the problem of transporting the materials to the building site. Large quantities of earth, lime, rock and wall bricks had to be moved up mountains. Those who worked on the walls came up with many ingenious solutions.

Manual transportation, the most primitive method, involved carrying bricks, lime and rocks up mountains, either on the back, by hand, in panniers or slung from poles. In some cases labourers formed human chains that spread from the base to the top of a mountain so that bricks or rocks could be passed in relay from hand to hand or in baskets. On narrow mountain trails, this relay method prevented accidents occurring and proved relatively efficient. Use was also made of simple machinery, such as small pushcarts for gradual inclines, although more frequently the carts were used in the construction of towns attached to passes and forts. Labourers also employed wooden rollers and levers as well as capstans to move large rocks weighing more than 500 kilograms. Flying-fox pulley systems transported bricks and lime across narrow ravines. Legend has it that donkeys with panniers of mortar strapped on their backs

and mountain goats with bricks lashed to their horns were driven up the mountains during construction of the Great Wall in the precipitous Badaling area. In winter in areas where there were large bodies of frozen water, materials could be slid or pulled across the ice.

No available method of transportation was overlooked. Each brick, pipe, sod of earth or rock used in the building and maintenance work drew on the ingenuity, sweat and blood of labouring people, who take credit for the grand achievement of Great Wall construction, along with the ancient architects and engineers.

Although they have long since fulfilled their historical mission of defence, the Great Walls remain the largest cultural heritage site in China, and indeed the world. The ancient walls at Juyongguan, Badaling, Shanhaiguan and Jiayuguan are now key tourist destinations that attract millions of visitors each year from China and abroad.

TRANSLATED BY BRUCE GORDON DOAR

Right: Detail of 'Tiger-skin' stone work at the base of a Ming dynasty Wall.
Photo: Jean-Francois Lanzarone

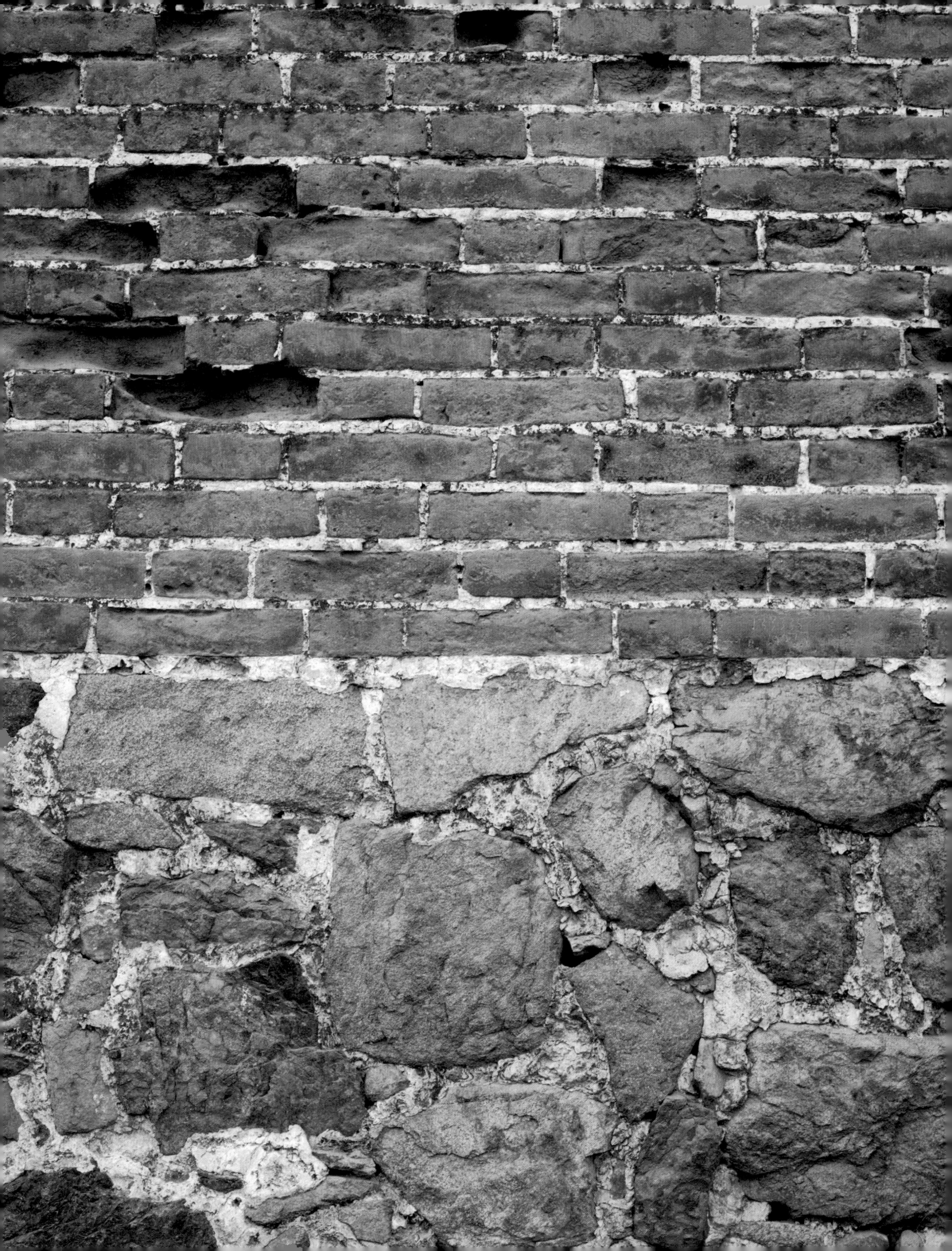

Archaeology of the Walls

XU PINGFANG

The Great Walls of China we see today, which run from Jiayuguan Pass in the west to Shanhaiguan Pass in the east, and include sites near Beijing such as Badaling, Gubeikou and Mutianyu, were mainly built in the early Ming dynasty. Older Great (or long) Walls built more than 2500 years ago during the Warring States period (475–221 BCE), and later by the Qin (221–206 BCE) and Han (206 BCE–220 CE) dynasties have mostly disappeared with the passage of time. Where above-ground structures remain at some older sites, for the most part they are badly damaged. Historical documents only briefly mention the location and types of walls built during those earlier periods. They leave little for later scholars to base their research upon and provide much room for speculation. Since the 1970s, Chinese archaeologists have conducted extensive field surveys of the walls of all periods, from Xinjiang in the west to Liaoning in the east, greatly enriching our knowledge. This essay presents an overview of the remains of the Great Walls as revealed by archaeological research and through reference to historical documents.

The walls of the Warring States

In the first half of the fourth century BCE, the various Warring States — Qi, Chu, Wei, Zhao, Yan, Qin and Zhongshan — began building defensive walls along their borders. With the exception of those of Zhongshan, remains of all of these can still be seen.

The Qi walls, constructed in the mid fourth century BCE, run from Changqing county south of Jinan, in Shandong province, to the coast at Huangdao in the municipal area of Qingdao city, totalling 618.9 kilometres in length. Apart from the walls, there are remains of fortified passes, wall fortresses and beacon platforms. To conserve resources in mountainous areas, builders constructed the walls on the top or southern side of ridges, integrating cliffs and strategic features into the walls themselves. Across level ground, they used local materials: slabs of timber, quarried rock or a mixture of earth and stone. After the demise of Qi, other polities continued to use these walls, which are

the best and most extensively preserved of all the Warring States Great Walls.

The Great Walls of Wei, built in 352 BCE, were intended to protect the state from Qin in the west. The Wei walls run, at their southern end, from Huayin county in Shaanxi province to the western bank of the Yellow River, to the south of the northern Luohe River — a distance of more than 200 kilometres. Remains of isolated sections of these walls can still be seen. Since 1955, they have been surveyed or excavated in a preliminary fashion on three occasions. Made of tamped earth, they vary in thickness, with narrow walls having bases ranging from 5 to 6 metres and wide walls from 16 to 20 metres. The tallest extant section, near Huayin, is 18 metres high.

The Zhao Great Walls were constructed about 333 BCE. According to the relevant passage in Sima Qian's *Records of the historian* (Shi ji), 'Wei was surrounded, but not

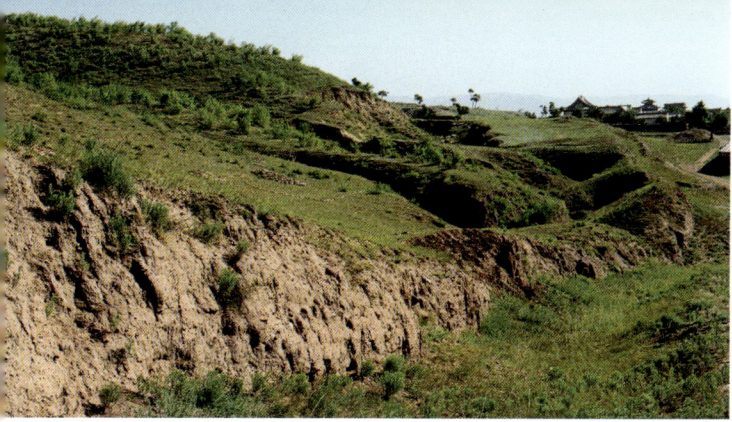

Wall built during the State of Zhao, Warring States period, Hohhot, Inner Mongolia.
Photo: Cheng Dalin

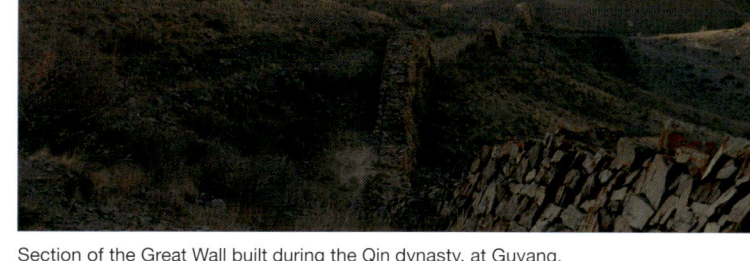

Section of the Great Wall built during the Qin dynasty, at Guyang, Inner Mongolia.
Photo: Remote Sensing and Aero-photographic Archaeology Department, NMC

vanquished, and so constructed the long walls.' These run westwards from north of Yuzhou, on to Lanzhou and then to the north. The state's southern boundary was apparently demarcated by Great Walls running north of the Zhangshui River.

When he established the Qin dynasty (221–206 BCE) and built his Great Walls, Emperor Qin Shihuang (reigned 221–210 BCE) incorporated the northern walls of Zhao that had been constructed by King Wuling (reigned 325–298 BCE), as well as the northern walls of Yan, and those in Longxi, Beidi and Shangjun built by King Zhaoxiang of Qin (reigned 306–250 BCE).

The Qin: extending the defensive line

In 221 BCE, Qin Shihuang vanquished all rival powers and unified China under a Qin empire. In 215 BCE, he ordered General Meng Tian to lead an army of 300 000 to attack the Xiongnu in the north, recover the Ordos (Hetao) region and build *changcheng*, long or great walls.

Archaeologists refer to the walls built by Qin Shihuang as having western, northern and eastern sections.

The western section, stretching from Lintao in Gansu to Zhungar Banner in Inner Mongolia, was built by King Zhaoxiang of Qin. This is described in *Account of the Xiongnu* (Xiongnu liezhuan) of *Records of the historian*: 'Qin built long walls in Longxi, Beidi and Shangjun to resist the Hu people.' Archaeologists have found the remains of walls conforming to the locations outlined in *Records of the historian*. They run northwards from a site in Lintao county in Gansu province to Weiyuan, Longxi, Tongwei and Jingning, on to Xiji and Guyuan in the Ningxia Hui autonomous region, and then back into Gansu through Zhenyuan, Huanxian and Huachi. Another wall continues into Shaanxi, passing Wuqi, Zhidan, Jingbian, Yulin and Shenmu. Finally, it enters the Zhungar Banner of Inner Mongolia and ends at Shi'erliancheng, across the Yellow River from Tokto. After Qin Shihuang unified the empire, he extended this section of the wall westwards. 'The basic annals of Qin Shihuang' (Qin Shihuang benji) in *Records of the historian* describes how the newly extended wall 'ran from Yuzhong [in present-day Lanzhou, Gansu], stopping on the eastern side of the Yellow River in the Yinshan area, and in Sishisi prefecture are the walls above the Yellow River.'

The wall would have run eastwards from Lanzhou to join that built by King Zhaoxiang at Lintao. It would then have followed the Yellow River on its northern banks to the Ordos. There are still Ming dynasty walls in this area, but no Qin dynasty walls have yet been found. Because the 'walls above the Yellow River' connected with the Ordos section of the Great Wall in the north, they would have been of great military importance.

The Ordos section of Qin Shihuang's northern wall runs south from Hanggin Banner to enclose the Ordos region and south from Qog Ondor through Langshan, Shilanji and Urad Banner to Guyang and Wuchuan, after which it enters the Daqingshan Mountains. The second stretch runs north from Baotou through the Daqingshan Mountains to the area north of Hohhot, then turns east to Zhouzi county and Ulan Qab Front Banner. These two sections were built by King Zhaoxiang of Qin and remained in use following Qin Shihuang's unification. The remains of the strategically important place called Gaoque can be found at Shilanji, south of the Langshan Mountains. The third section of the northern Great Walls of Qin Shihuang — constructed after unification — passed through Gusiwang Banner, Shangdu and Huade, and then went on to Baokang in Hebei. From there the walls entered Gutaipusi Banner, Zhenglan Banner and Duolun. They then ran to Fengning and Weichang in Hebei and on to Chifeng in the Ju Ud League in Inner Mongolia. To the south there were still the northern Great Walls of Yan built in the Warring States period. The remains of Qin Shihuang's Great Walls show that, after unifying the empire, he not only relied on existing walls but actively extended this line of defence northwards to serve new strategic requirements.

The eastern section of Qin Shihuang's walls began in Chifeng and ran westwards to join the three sections of the northern stretch, and then turned east to Aohan Banner, entering Fuxin county, Liaoning province. To the south it ran parallel with an existing stretch of the Yan Great Walls in an easterly direction until the two lines met in Fuxin. It then extended through Zhangwu, Faku and Kaiyuan, crossing the Liao River and turning south, passing through Xinbin and going to Kuandian and the present-day Democratic People's Republic of Korea (North Korea).

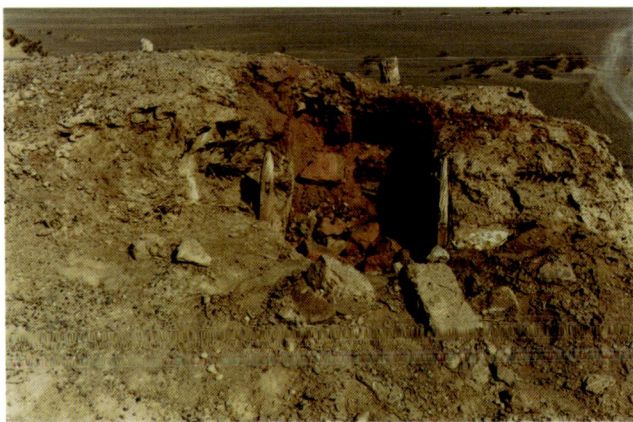

Remains of a Han dynasty watchtower at Jiaqu, Ejina Banner,
Inner Mongolia.
Photo: Remote Sensing and Aero-photographic Archaeology Department, NMC

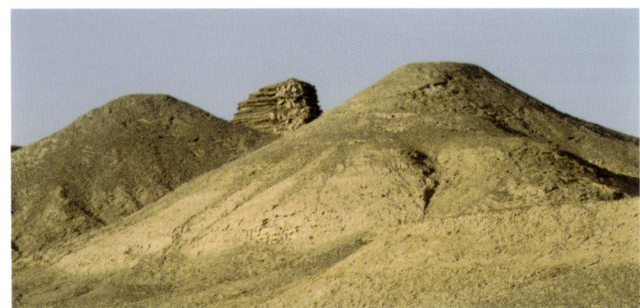

Remains of the Han dynasty Cangting beacon tower near Hecangcheng,
Dunhuang, Gansu.
Photo: Jean-Francois Lanzarone

The Han expansionist policy

The early Han emperors maintained the walls of the Qin.
In 200 BCE, Han armies suffered punishing defeats in
the battles of Pingcheng and Baideng. The northern
defence line shrank dramatically, and the Han began
paying tribute to the Xiongnu, entering into a placatory
diplomatic policy, a central component of which was the
diplomatic marriage of Han women to Xiongnu chieftains.
(For a discussion of this policy, see 'The Great Wall
embodied' by Uradyn E Bulag pp 214–20). In 158 BCE,
the Xiongnu again decimated the Han in the north, in
Shangjun and Yunzhong, and the news of these events,
relayed by beacon fires, created panic in Ganquan and
the Han capital Chang'an (present-day Xi'an). In order
to protect the threatened capital, Emperor Han Wudi
(reigned 140–87 BCE) needed to wrest back control of
the defensive line at Shanggu prefecture in the north-east
and Zaoyang in the north, and concentrate his forces
along the line of defence of the 'territories south of the
Yellow River'. In 127 BCE, he ordered that the walls built
by Meng Tian once again be repaired. Archaeologists
have recently discovered remains of the Han walls in
ancient Yuyang, Youbeiping and Liaoxi prefectures from
before Han Wudi's time. They run from Luanping in
Hebei to Fengning, then cross the Yixun River to
Longhua and Chengde. The walls then enter Inner

Mongolia, run to Ningcheng and Harqin Banner, and
cross the Laohahe River. They re-enter Liaoning and run
to Jianping, Chaoyang, Beipiao and Yixian counties. In
the stretch from Fengning in Luanping county to Zhiyun
in Longhua county the remains of many beacon platforms
can still be seen, and between Zhiyun and Xiaochengzi in
Ningcheng county there are even the ruins of a stone
wall. This stretch of Han walls was built to the south
of the Yan and Qin walls. Relations with the Xiongnu
changed following decisive Han victories in the wars of
121 and 119 BCE. After Han Wudi resolved the Xiongnu
threat, he went on to devote his efforts to opening up
communications with the Western Region, a policy that
included securing the Silk Road trade routes. This strategy
comprised four parts.

The first was the repair of the walls above the Yellow
River between Hanggin in Inner Mongolia and Wuchuan
county originally constructed by Meng Tian.

The second was in 102 BCE, when Han Wudi ordered
the head of the imperial body guard, the Chamberlain
of Attendants Xu Ziwei, to supervise the construction of
the Guanglu walls beyond the Wuyuan walls. Traces of
northern and southern sections of the Guanglu walls have
been discovered by archaeologists. The eastern sections of
these two walls converge at Halaheshao and Halamendu
in Wuchuan county, Inner Mongolia, and there join the
northern section of the Qin walls. The southern end of
the Guanglu walls runs from Wuchuan county through
Damaolianhe Banner, Urad Central Banner and Urad
Rear Banner, entering the territory of present-day
Mongolia. They then turn in a south-westerly direction
and re-enter Inner Mongolia in the territory of Ejina
Banner, where they join with the Han dynasty Juyan
walls. In the north the wall runs from Wuchuan through
the administrative centre of the Damaolianhe League
and on to Sanggin Dalai. From Oljit in Urad Rear Banner,
the wall enters Mongolia and runs to the Altai Mountains.

The third part of the strategy was to open up the Western
Region. To do this Han Wudi established 'the four
prefectures', an administrative move undertaken in
conjunction with his military strategy of building walls
and beacon platforms in Hexi. Historical documents
suggest that the Hexi walls and beacon platforms were
constructed progressively from east to west. The wall from
Lingju to Jiuquan was built between 121 and 119 BCE,
that from Jiuquan to Yumen from 116 to 105 BCE, and
the lookout posts and beacon towers from Dunhuang
to Yanze between 100 and 97 BCE. During the Han
dynasty, Lingju was administered by Jincheng prefecture,
comprising part of present-day Yongdeng county in
Gansu. On the northern bank of the Yellow River at
Hekou in the city of Lanzhou, to the east of the Ming
Great Walls, remains of the Han dynasty walls have
been found. The Ming and Han walls run parallel
through Yongdeng county to Tianzhu, where they

cross the Wuxiaoling Mountains and enter Gulang. From there, they pass the city of Wuwei and go on to Yongchang and Shandan, then follow the northern bank of the Heihe River to Linze and Gaotai. From Jiuquan they then run north along the Ruoshui River and go on to Dingxin, where they join the Juyan walls. From Jiuquan they run west through Jinta and the Jiayuguan Pass, along the banks of the Shule River until they reach Anxi. North of Dunhuang they pass through Halanur, Xiaofangpan and Yushuquan. The ruins of the Han dynasty Jade Gate Pass are in Xiaofangpan and those of the Weiguan Pass are at Nanhu. Between the two passes some beacon terraces remain but no walls can be seen. Likewise, no walls can be seen outside the Jade Gate Pass, only lookout posts and beacon terraces. From the Han dynasty Lingju walls to the Ming dynasty Jade Gate Pass walls, the Hexi walls built during the Han dynasty ran, by and large, westwards either to the east or north of the Ming walls. The Silk Road ran along the southern side of the Hexi walls, which, historically, protected this international route through the Western Region.

The final part of Han Wudi's strategy involved protecting the security of the Hexi Corridor, and preventing the Xiongnu from linking up with the Qiang people. Emperor

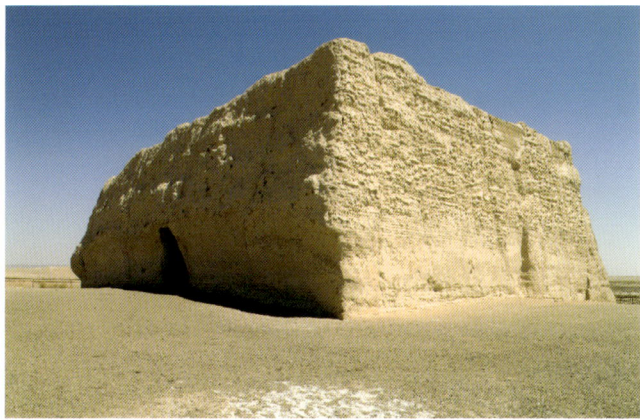

Remains of the Han dynasty Jade Gate Pass, Dunhuang, Gansu.
Photo: Jean-Francois Lanzarone

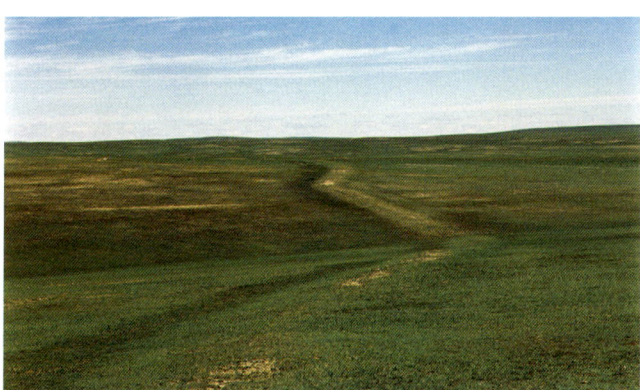

Remains of the Great Wall built during the Northern Wei dynasty, at Damao Banner, Inner Mongolia.
Photo: Cheng Dalin

Han Wudi constructed the Juyan walls in 102 BCE. These walls ran through the commanderies of Juyan and Jianshui in the prefecture of Zhangye. Surveys and excavations carried out since 1930 have been able to paint a fairly clear picture of the trajectory of the Han Juyan walls and their various architectural features. Several tens of thousands of manuscripts and inscribed wooden slips have also been unearthed. The walls run northwards from Dingxin in Jinta, Gansu, in the south, along the Ruoshui River, passing through Ejina Banner in Inner Mongolia, where they connect with the southern end of the Guanglu walls.

Emperors Zhaodi (86–74 BCE) and Xuandi (73–49 BCE) consolidated the northern defences erected by Han Wudi, and completed an entire northern wall defence system running westwards from Liaodong through Liaoxi, Youbeiping, Shanggu, Yunzhong, Wuyuan, Wuwei, Zhangye, Jiuquan and Dunhuang. The Han walls opened up the north-west of China, running well beyond, and enclosing, the western end of the Qin walls, which had lost their defensive function.

Historical texts describe how after the Han dynasty, the Northern Wei, Northern Qi, Northern Zhou and Sui (581–618) dynasties all built walls in the north. Recently, in Inner Mongolia, remains of the Northern Wei walls have been found running from Wuchuan through Damaolianhe Banner to Siziwang Banner, Qahar Right Banner, Qahar Rear Banner and Shangdu. But what remains is an earth rampart less than one metre in height, with no extant towers or fortifications.

The nine commanderies of the Ming dynasty

The Ming dynasty walls extend some 6300 kilometres, from Jiayuguan Pass in the west to the Yalu River in the east, straddling Gansu, Ningxia, Shaanxi, Shanxi, Inner Mongolia, Hebei, and Liaoning, as well as the outer regions of the Beijing and Tianjin municipalities. The remains of these walls are the most complete and imposing of all. For 276 years, the Ming project of building and repairing the walls continued without interruption. At the same time, the Ming implemented a defensive system based around regional Great Wall military commanderies. In the early Ming dynasty the four commanderies of Liaodong, Xuanfu, Datong and Yansui (Yulin) were established, and some time later the three commanderies of Ningxia, Gansu and Jizhou were formed. Together with the Taiyuan commandery, the headquarters of which was in Piantou, and the Sanbian commandery based in Guyuan, the Ming in all set up nine commanderies along the Great Wall.

The Liaodong regional commander was stationed in Liaoyang and later in Beizhen, Liaoning province. His jurisdiction began in Dandong on the banks of the Yalu River in the east, skirted Kaiyuan, and then ran south to Shanhaiguan Pass — a distance of 975 kilometres. Most of this section of the wall was made from rammed earth

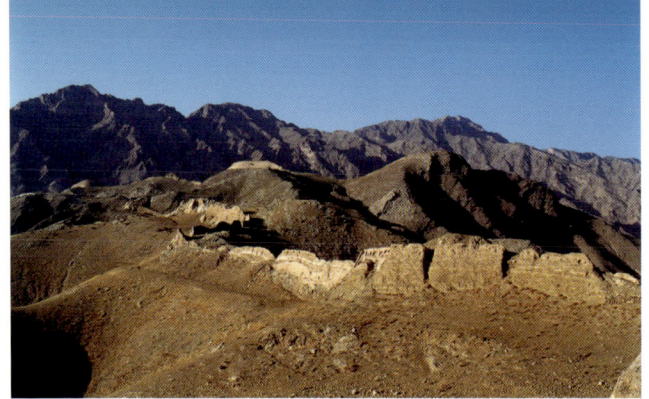

Remains of Ming dynasty Great Wall at Helanshan Mountain, Ningxia.
Photo: Remote Sensing and Aero-photographic Archaeology Department, NMC

and not encased in brick; after the mid-Ming period this part of the wall was rarely repaired, with the result that most of it has disappeared. The walls near Shanhaiguan Pass, however, are fairly well preserved. Those at Jiumenkou, on the border between Suizhong in Liaoning and Hebei provinces, passed through mountainous terrain to straddle the Jiujiang River, which flowed through nine sluice gates in a section called 'the Great Wall on the water'.

The Jizhou commandery had its headquarters in Santunying (present-day Qianxi, Hebei), and its jurisdiction ran from Shanhaiguan Pass west to Huilingkou at Juyongguan Pass, a distance of more than 600 kilometres. This is the best preserved section of the Great Walls today. When Qi Jiguang (1528–87) served as commander of the Jizhou commandery, he built equestrian ramparts and watchtowers, enhancing the defensive capability of the walls. Because this stretch of wall protected the capital, it was kept in good repair.

The Xuanfu commandery was in Xuanhua, Hebei province, and its jurisdiction ran from Juyongguan Pass westwards to the Xihunhe River (in the north-eastern district of present-day Datong, Shanxi province), a total distance of 511.5 kilometres. The strategically important Xuanfu commandery guarded the capital itself. These walls were solid and, in some sections, there were nine banks of walls.

The Datong commandery, in Shanxi, exercised jurisdiction from Zhenkoutai (in north-eastern Tianzhen, Shanxi) westwards to Yajiaoshan (in north-eastern Pianguan county, also in Shanxi), a distance of 335 kilometres.

The Taiyuan commandery, also called the Shanxi commandery, had its headquarters in Pianguan, Shanxi. The stretch of wall south of the Xuanfu and Datong commanderies was called the Ming Inner Great Wall. It ran from Shiti'ai Pass on the eastern bank of the Yellow River in Hequ county, south-west of Pianguan, then from the Laoyingpu fortress at Pianguan it turned towards the south-west, passing through Pinglu and Shenchi as well as Ningwuguan, Yanmenguan and Pingxingguan passes. To the north-east of the latter it joined the Zijingguan Pass in Hebei. From Pingxingguan Pass it ran southwards,

passing via Longquanguan and Guguan passes into Heshun county, Shanxi, a total distance of more than 800 kilometres.

The Yansui commandery, also called the Yulin commandery, had its headquarters in Yulin fortress in present-day Yulin, Shaanxi. Here the Great Wall ran westwards from Qingshuiying (today's Fugu in Shaanxi) to Huamachi (Yanchi), Ningxia Hui autonomous region, a total length of 885 kilometres.

The headquarters of the Ningxia commandery was stationed in Yinchuan. The Great Wall here ran westwards from Lanjing (present-day Gaolan in Gansu and Jingyuan in Shanxi) for a distance of 1000 kilometres.

The Guyuan commander stationed in Guyuan oversaw the stretch of wall between Jingyuan, in the east, and the Great Walls of the Yulin commandery. Another stretch of wall he supervised ran from the southern end of the Ningxia commandery westwards past the Ningxia commandery wall in Jingyuan and Gaolan, towards Lanzhou, forming an 'inner great wall' with a total length of more than 500 kilometres.

The Gansu regional commander was stationed at Zhangye and defended walls in an area bordered on the east by Lanzhou and, on the west, by Jiayuguan Pass, a total length of some 800 kilometres.

The Ming Great Walls had a total length of some 6300 kilometres. This figure is not derived from actual surveys, but is an approximation arrived at from an examination of textual sources. If the double sections of wall are considered, then the total would no doubt greatly exceed this estimated length.

The Great Walls reflect the uniqueness of Chinese architecture and engineering. Prior to the tenth century, most of the walls were made using tamped earth construction that relied on the terrain and locally available materials. Rock was used sparingly, with earth and crushed rock serving as fill. These materials did not hold together well and the walls constructed in this way collapsed easily. In the Gobi Desert region of the north-west, there is little earth and a lot of sand, so construction was even more difficult. Desert willow fronds and reeds were layered with sand to construct ramparts, and, after a process of natural calcification, the walls became quite solid. Walls built during the Ming dynasty were often made from fired bricks held fast by a lime mortar, which created a very solid structure. Ancillary buildings, such as watchtowers, platforms, horse ramps and beacon platforms, were standardised, and sophisticated engineering techniques were used in their construction. The walls and passes are imposing examples of Chinese architecture and can stand proudly with the finest architectural achievements from around the world.

TRANSLATED BY BRUCE GORDON DOAR

Living with the past

INTERVIEW WITH CAO HAI BY SANG YE

During the reign of Liu Che, Emperor Han Wudi (140–87 BCE) of the Western Han dynasty, attempts to mollify the aggressive Xiongnu tribes to the north of Han territory were abandoned in favour of more robust defences and war. The walls built during the Qin dynasty were enlarged and extended. The westernmost point of these long walls was at Jade Gate Pass, or Yumenguan, in what is today Gansu province. Jade Gate Pass, built some 1500 years before the Ming walls, stands, a solitary sentinel, near the ancient oasis of Dunhuang, a key station on the Silk Road, and bordering on modern-day Xinjiang. Much of the Han wall has been obliterated by time and the constant work of erosion. Apart from a slight rise in some places, the once heavily patrolled defences were long ago reduced to ground level. What remains of the walls show that much of their structure was made of friable materials such as Chinese tamarisk and reeds.

Cao Hai is the 52-year-old former head of the Jade Gate Pass Cultural Heritage Protection Office at the remains of the Jade Gate Pass, which is under the jurisdiction of Dunhuang in Gansu province, west China.

Jade Gate Pass is over 2000 years old. After Emperor Han Wudi of the Han dynasty abandoned his peace and conciliation policy towards the Xiongnu tribes, under which he had forged alliances with the barbarians through marriage, the cavalry general Huo Qubing led a victorious western expedition against them. This resulted in the establishment of command posts at Wuwei and Jiuquan in the second year of Yuanshou [121 BCE], and at Zhangye and Dunhuang in the sixth year of Yuanding [111 BCE]. Shortly afterwards, in the third year of Yuanfeng [108 BCE], they extended the Great Wall this far west and built Yangguan Pass and Jade Gate Pass. This represented a massive expansion of the territory ruled over by China.

Over the following two centuries, Yangguan and Jade Gate Pass were the crucial strategic outposts on China's western flank, the gateways linking the inland to west Asia and Europe via the trade routes of the Silk Road. China's silk and porcelain went out through these passes, while various religions, arts and foods — like pepper, grapes and watermelons — came in from the West. During the Han dynasty, the Silk Road split into two routes after leaving Dunhuang: one went west through Yangguan Pass, the other tracked to the north-west via Jade Gate Pass. Back then, this place flourished, with a constant parade of camel trains and merchant caravans. But there would also have been the ceaseless rumble of war chariots and the whinnying of battle horses, and soldiers with bows and quivers on their backs and swords at their waists — for there was always some war to be fought.

Later, from the time of the Wei-Jin [3rd–4th centuries] right through to the Tang dynasty [618–907], there was constant chaos and warfare. During the Hundred Years War, when Anxi and the four garrison districts of Qiuzi, Yueban, Yutian and Shule were embroiled in war, Dunhuang fell on hard times. It became a military

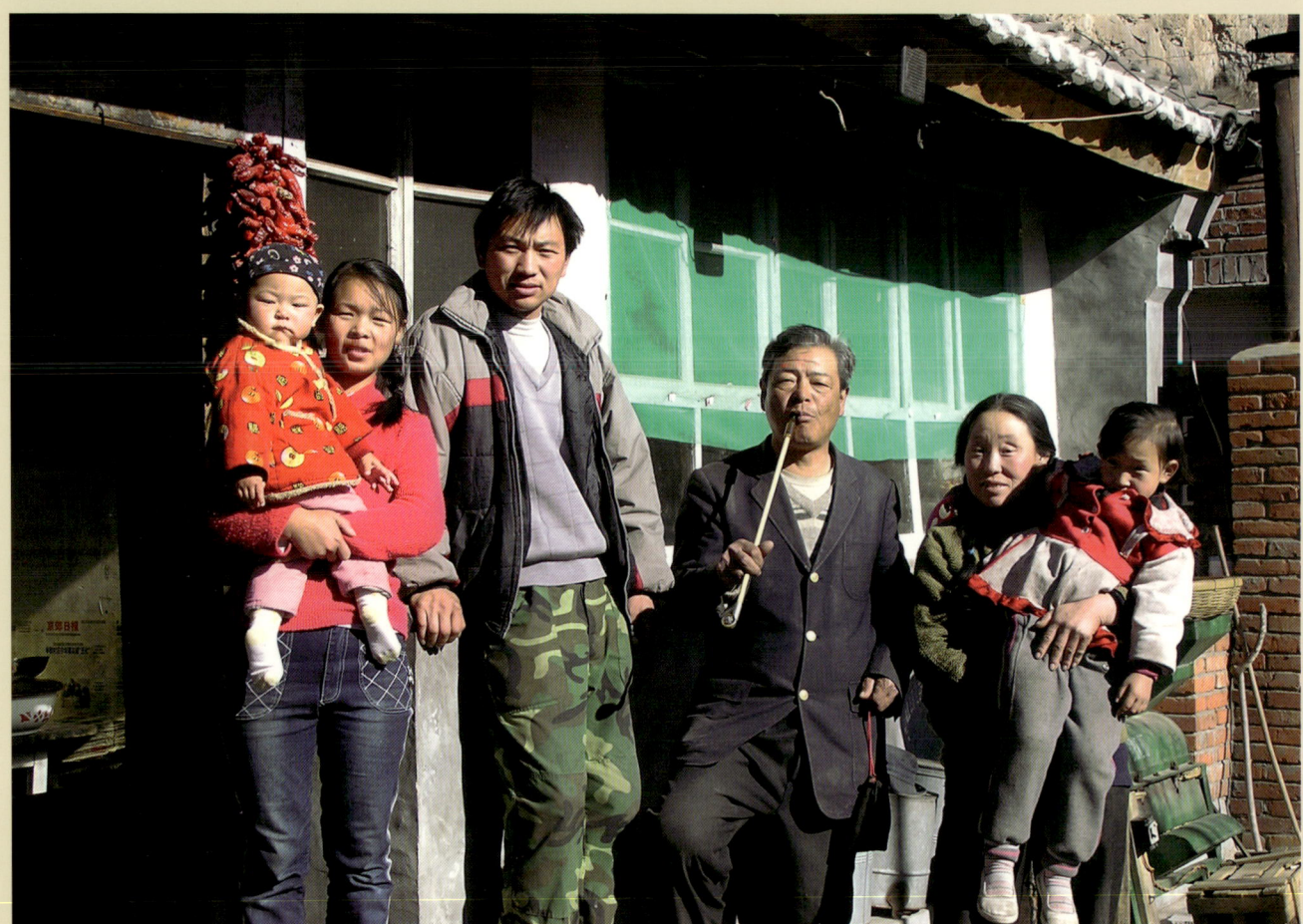

The Wang family, (from left) granddaughter, daughter-in-law, son, Wang Chongfa, Wang's wife and first born granddaughter. The family lives near the Great Wall at Five Tiger's Pass and owns 0.4 hectares of land. In the summer, they run a bed and breakfast for tourists visiting the Great Wall. To protect the already-damaged stone carvings on the pass gate from further ruin, Mr Wang took the carvings home and buried them on his land for safekeeping. He says that when the State Administration of Cultural Heritage comes to repair the pass, he will dig them up and give them back.

Photo: Ji Xuelu; location: Huayuan village, Beijing

outpost as well as a supply depot, and its menfolk were conscripted. What could people do? Life became impossible, so they fled. And Dunhuang went into decline: as the poem says, 'Spring winds never again blew through Jade Gate Pass.'

In the Tang dynasty, the Silk Road followed a new route north, through Anxi on to Hami [in present-day Xinjiang]. And so the Jade Gate Pass of the Han era was abandoned and gradually forgotten, buried over the centuries by the shifting sands of the desert.

In 1907, the Englishman Aurel Stein was the first to undertake an archaeological dig at the remains of the Han dynasty Great Wall here at Dunhuang. He unearthed some Han bamboo slips bearing the words 'Jade Gate Pass Garrison' near Xiaofangpan. In 1944, [the archaeologist] Mr Xia Nai undertook his own research at Xiaofangpan and further to the east at Fengsui, where he found a bamboo slip on which was written 'Jiuquan Jade Gate Pass Garrison'. This settled once and for all the exact location of the Han dynasty Jade Gate Pass. Today, the remaining ramparts at Xiaofangpan are 24.5 metres by 26.4 metres, and you can make out what has been a square walled area, the 'pass'. The highest point is on the north wall, which is 10.05 metres high, 3.7 metres wide and 4.9 metres at the base. In the south-east corner of the walled city there is a horse track that is nearly a metre wide, along which you can go right up onto the wall, which is 1.3 metres wide, with crenellations.

I was born in Dunhuang. My father was a low-level cadre. The Cultural Revolution was still in full swing when I finished high school: everyone was being sent off to the countryside. I was allocated a job in the state forest at Yangguan Pass, about 70 kilometres away. I'd heard of Yangguan from the time I was in primary school.

Our textbooks had a famous line from the Tang poet Wang Wei [701–61] written when farewelling a friend: 'Drink another cup of wine my friend, for you'll find none you know west of Yangguan Pass.' During my days in the state forest, all that was left of the Yangguan Pass was one dilapidated beacon tower. This lonely earthen hillock in the vast Gobi Desert was once known as the 'eyes and ears' of Yangguan. All that remains is a communications tower for sending signals, not a gateway with a proper crenellated defence around it — that has long since disappeared.

I planted trees for over a decade until I was transferred to the Dunhuang forestry station to work as a ranger. Though on paper it was government policy to give city jobs to young people who'd been sent out to labour in the country during the Cultural Revolution, I was still in the Gobi. Out in the desert there are no forests as such, no matter what they say in the books. The only things that survive in the Gobi are a few small creatures and wolves. I was in charge of protecting tamarisk and reeds that grow there, and of keeping an eye on poachers or people who wanted to dig illegal mines, graze their sheep or collect licorice root for use in Chinese medicine. I worked there for nine years, most of that time outdoors. I was completely used to the Gobi and to moving around it.

In 1992, I was transferred to the Cultural Relics Bureau in Dunhuang, though I agreed to be posted out to Jade Gate Pass and not take a desk job in Dunhuang itself. Why? For one thing, it was a way of carrying on in the tradition of solitude associated with guarding Jade Gate Pass. I could just shut myself away here and study the history of Dunhuang and the Great Wall. Secondly, the pay was good — 90 yuan [$A15] a month. Wages and prices in Dunhuang were both pretty low; back then, 90 yuan went a long way. And by then I had a wife and son to look after. The new job gave me security into my old age, unlike the forestry job which was on contract. Working for the Cultural Relics Bureau I became a state employee.

I hadn't done any specialised study in this field, but the leadership told me they needed someone who was stable and reliable and who had experience living in the Gobi. They didn't say what their other reason was for giving me the job, but I knew — it is incredibly desolate and lonely out at Jade Gate Pass. There's no one else within 100 kilometres, and there are no diversions at all. I don't want to big-ticket myself. Although I just said that I was interested in that tradition of solitude, the main reason I accepted the job was that the money was good. Similarly, although the leadership said they needed a reliable person, for them it was even more important to find someone who could cope with the isolation.

The provincial Cultural Relics Bureau allocated three jobs to the new Jade Gate Pass cultural relics preservation station, but they made two of them desk jobs at the bureau in town. The leadership didn't hide this from me. They said we should first get the station set up; if the workload increased in the future they'd find the money to hire an assistant for me. In reality, it would have been very difficult to find any extra funding, so for many years I was a one-man band.

The Cultural Relics Bureau gave me a hunting rifle and a Lucky 250 motorbike. The motorbike is the kind people use to gad about the city, completely unsuited to conditions in the Gobi, but it was cheap. So that's how I set up the Jade Gate Pass preservation station. At first there was no electricity or running water. There wasn't even anywhere to live, and no one else to help out. My first task was to dig a well.

A few years back a photographer turned up and asked me if there were times when I didn't bother washing my face. I told him that apart from the first few days when I was without water, I washed my face every day. 'Why did you bother?,' he asked. I laughed because I couldn't answer. I did it for myself.

My main job was to look after the remains of Jade Gate Pass, to chase off people who came out there to dig up licorice root or treasure hunters come to fossick around. Later on I had to keep an eye on the tourists. Only two types of tourist come out to the Gobi: the type who likes to hoon around in their Hummers and Land Rovers, and feisty backpackers with their minds set on travelling the length of the Great Wall or the Silk Road. Normal traffic only got access to this area from 1999, after they finished laying the gravel road.

Most days you wouldn't see a soul. I only saw about a hundred people the entire first year I was there. Apart from peasants coming to dig up licorice root, they were mostly archaeologists and historians. Those people always came in groups, and only for the day. The only ones who ever stayed overnight were old herders and a few truckers hauling saltpetre.

My days were always crowded with work though. Apart from keeping an eye on Jade Gate Pass, I was responsible for Hecangcheng 13 kilometres to the east and Majuanwan and the Han Great Wall 15 kilometres to the west. They were all in my remit; they form what's called 'The Remains of the Han Great Wall and Beacon Towers'. The State Council in Beijing designated it one of the first groups of protected cultural relics of China. So I was never able to achieve my original aim of researching the history of the Great Wall and Dunhuang. Apart from experiencing the traditional sense of isolation that I was interested in, nothing was as easy as I thought it would be. By day I was always scooting around on my motorbike. And, thanks to the relentless mosquitoes and the lack of electricity, I couldn't read at night. So the first year I was here I gave up on my original aim and focused on my rounds. I also had to clear up all the sheep dung that had collected in the place over many years. Before the station was established, an old herdsman used to bring his sheep over here to shelter from the big sandstorms, so the ancient walled gate compound was filled with sheep shit over half a metre deep. Like an ant gnawing a bone, I cleaned it up bit by bit. Apart from the sheep shit, the old herdsman also left a hut behind, and that's what I moved into. It was halfway between a tent and a shed — just a simple wooden structure covered with plastic and canvas. But it was a 10-metre square area that kept out the rain and the sand. This courtyard you see here today was built in 1999, but for the first seven years I was out here that tent was both my office and home. There wasn't even a place to hang the sign announcing that this was the cultural relics preservation station at Jade Gate Pass. Since I was living in a shepherd's tent, I decided to raise my own flock of sheep for company.

Jade Gate Pass is 92 kilometres from Dunhuang, and 64 from the closest shop at Shazaoyuan. This road was completed in 1999 and, although 60 kilometres is unsealed, it's much better than before. Before, to get here from Dunhuang, you travelled a 30-kilometre stretch of dirt road and then through 60 kilometres of desert. Getting lost was the biggest problem, but that didn't worry me much because I'm very familiar with the Gobi. The other scary thing is the wolves, though I was okay as I had my rifle.

So I lived out here and went into town once a month to pick up my provisions. If I ran out of anything, so be it. I wasn't going to starve as I had several vats of vegetables I'd pickled. From 1996, I had a wind-powered generator too, which meant I could watch satellite TV at night, but only for a short while as it didn't have much storage capacity — two and a half hours tops. Guess that's why my wife divorced me. At first I was pretty upset, but gradually I saw it from her point of view. I lived in the Gobi and she lived in the city: she was married to a guy who never came home. She had other options.

Occasionally people turn up here — they're always only passing through. I welcome them warmly and see them off warmly as well. So long as you don't harm any artefacts or leave any rubbish behind, we can all get on with our own business. Not long after my courtyard was finished the movie director Zhang Yimou turned up. He wanted to make his film *Hero* in this part of the Gobi.

Zhang told me he wanted to rent my courtyard for his film crew to use. Funny that, since some of his people had already moved in on me quite a few days earlier. I refused his offer. I told him that I wasn't interested in making money. Friends could come and stay a few days for free, no problem, but if they hung around too long they'd get in my way, disrupt my work. These past days, I told him, your people have been running around and clambering all over the place. It's not good for the cultural relics. You're already getting in my way, I told him, so I think it's time you went. And that became news. It's probably because people don't usually say no to a big star. There I was, this nobody protector of cultural relics in the middle of the desert, saying no to Zhang Yimou. So it made the news. The principle isn't hard to comprehend: everyone should simply behave appropriately. They make their films, I protect my cultural relics. The real hero is someone who knows how to behave appropriately.

In the years before the road came through I experienced something of the ancient desolation of this place. I was a modern-day Jade Gate Pass commander, guarding the border between history and the present. I found Han bamboo slips, and have had stare-offs with wolves as well, each of us waiting to see who had the most patience. After the road was built things changed completely — anyone who could afford the trip out here and the 30 yuan [$A5] entrance fee could come and wander around.

Some tourists are appalling. They should consider themselves lucky to be able to see what our ancestors from 2000 years ago have left behind for us. But they're not happy just looking, they want to touch as well, and dig, and they want to pull out the reeds and tree branches in this ancient stretch of the Great Wall. These things have existed in perfect harmony for over two millennia, but these visitors want to pull them out for no other reason than to satisfy their idle curiosity. They say they come out here to cultivate and temper their hearts and minds, but then they throw rubbish all over the place. Ever since they built the road we've had 3000 tourists a year. The whole place is strewn with lunch boxes and plastic bags, more than I could possibly pick up. My advice would be not to worry about self-cultivation until you've learned a few basic manners and some sense of civic duty.

Although our organisation was established to protect cultural relics, there's a lot of people who are more interested in press-ganging cultural relics into the service of tourism. Is this appropriate? You won't hear anyone saying otherwise. The mayor says nothing, and the central government itself is silent. If you want my opinion, here it is: I'm in favour of tourism, but it mustn't be allowed to harm cultural relics. It's obvious enough: you can have tourism in a place where there are cultural relics, but you've got to do it so your descendants will be able to travel here and see more than just the souvenirs of your tourism.

Loneliness can give you an inflated sense of self. The isolation made me sensitive to the fact that once the hooves of great armies on horseback had thundered over the very earth on which I was walking. Countless soldiers and horses, endless trains of merchants, had passed through a place that is now a vast emptiness. You become a little disoriented and, like Chairman Mao's poem: 'Brooding over this immensity, / I ask, on this boundless land, / Who rules over man's destiny?' You become delusional, and think that you are king of all you survey, and can do whatever you please.

In this desolate vastness I have heard the sighs of ancient warriors, and the rumble of the chariots of war racing towards me from across the Gobi, banners fluttering in the wind. Everyone knows that science says there are no ghosts, but I really have heard them and seen things.

The stretch of the Great Wall between Jade Gate Pass and Majuanwan is the best preserved because the salinity of the desert here is very high. Over the centuries, this section of the wall has absorbed a lot of that salt, and it's formed a hard crust that protects it from erosion by the wind and rain. I guess I'm a bit like that myself.

If you go on a bit further you'll come across a raised battlement where Han dynasty soldiers had their quarters. From the broken wall of their 2000-year old kitchen you can make out the layers — black, yellow, black, yellow, on and on. Every time cooking smoke blackened the wall, the soldiers would cover it with fresh mud.

Redecorating a kitchen plays no part in fighting a war. There are a number of possible explanations. Maybe older soldiers who were about to be discharged and sent back home wanted to leave behind a clean kitchen for the new recruits. Maybe they'd heard that family members had undertaken the arduous journey to come visit them and didn't want their loved ones to see the poor circumstances in which they lived. Or maybe someone's girlfriend was coming — people back then had girlfriends too — so they decided they'd better get their act together. Or maybe it was for no particular reason at all. Maybe the kitchen was just too dirty and they decided to clean up, just like I wash my face every day, just for my own satisfaction. Regardless of the reason, you get a real sense of humanity from those walls. No one ordered them to do it, but they did, and may even have enjoyed it.

After conditions out here at Jade Gate Pass improved they allocated seven other people to work here during the high season. That's when the leadership began to say I'd done the hard yards and it was time for me to think of going back to the city. At first I didn't agree, so I hung around for another two years until I realised they wanted to move their family members in here. I stopped resisting. It wasn't worth it. The famous general Ban Chao [32–102 CE] spent three decades defending the Western Region for the Han dynasty, convinced he was irreplaceable. He finally wrote a letter to the Han emperor saying that he was old and had achieved nothing, that he only did what was expected of him as a minister of the throne and that he dared not even hope to be assigned to the command post at Jiuquan, but expected to live out his remaining years at Jade Gate Pass. Why should I let things get to that stage? This minister was going back to the city.

I returned to Dunhuang in 2002. The whole system in the city had changed. They'd set up the Dunhuang Museum with a cultural relics department. They made me head of the department, but I didn't have the education or administrative skills for it. I just had this hard, salty crust that had grown on me in the Gobi Desert, just like the Han Great Wall. I was terrible at dealing with people. The leadership could see I just didn't have the knack for administrative work so they looked after me. They gave me a job collecting tickets at the museum entrance. But even that required bookkeeping skills. You also had to write reports and essays on your political thinking. I hadn't done that stuff for years. What could I possibly say?

Within a year I was off sick with a serious eye condition that I was told couldn't be cured. The doctor suggested I be allowed early retirement, but that too was hard. You see, without a high-level position I wouldn't make enough to have a comfortable retirement. They had high-level researchers, curators, accountants and all that, but they couldn't make me any of those. I'd just been looking after Jade Gate Pass, and my high school diploma, my work history and my experience weren't qualification enough. Moreover, it was too late for me to try and pass the exams for a promotion. Eventually they thought of a way around it.

They let me take an advanced driving test and I got the promotion and the wages that went with the position of top-level driver. I retired in 2003 with a pension of over 1000 yuan [$A166] a month. It's ridiculous, I know, but that's the system. Though, if you think about it, my title on retirement really does suit me. The most advanced skills I acquired in my long years of service all had to do with riding across the trackless Gobi on a motorbike.

TRANSLATED BY GEREMIE R BARMÉ

Warring States to Han dynasty

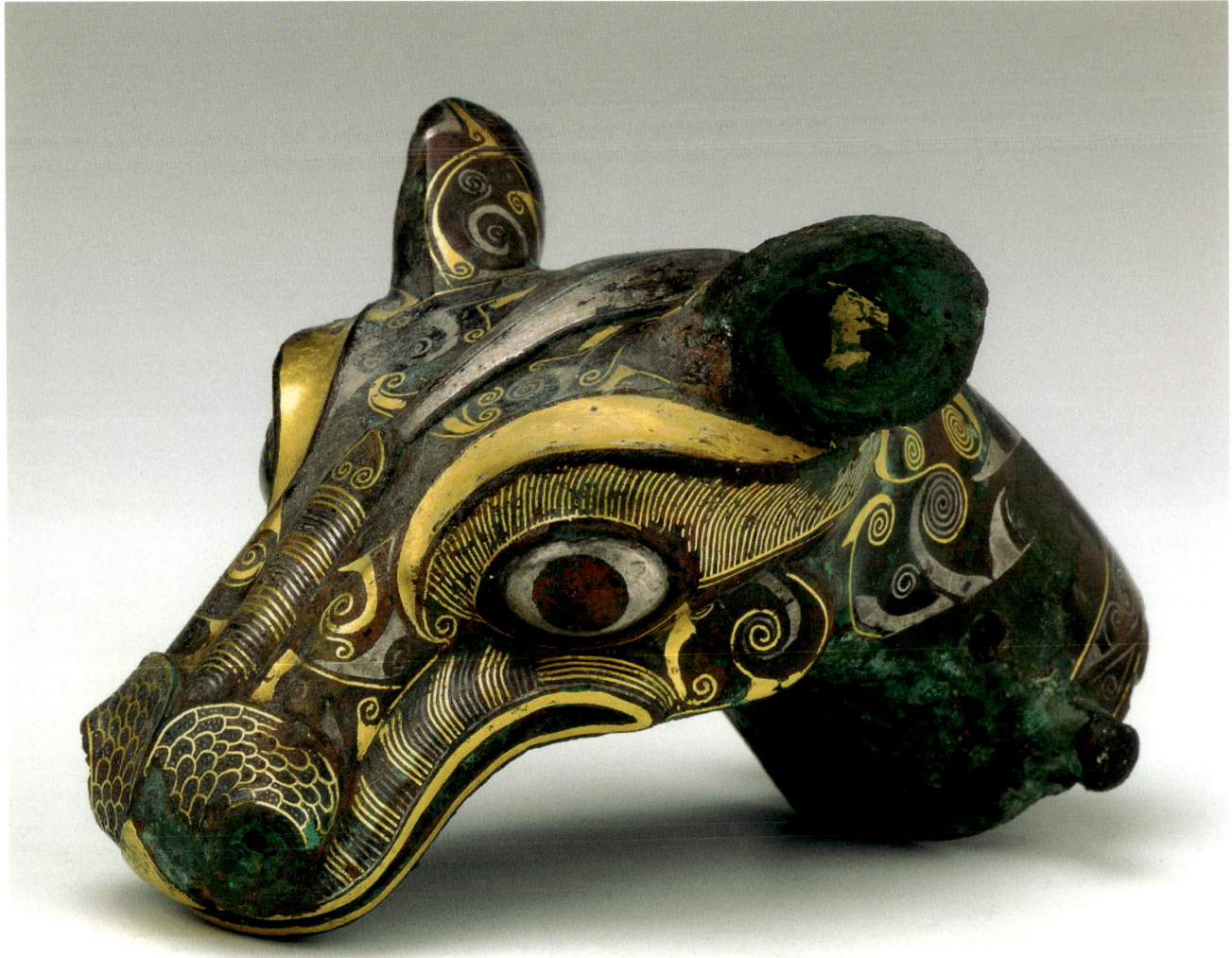

Thill
*Warring States period
(475–221 BCE), State of Wei*
Unearthed in 1951 at Huixian
county, Henan province
Bronze inlaid with gold and silver
8.8 (h) x 13.7 (l) x 4.8 (base diam) cm
Collection of the National
Museum of China (Y96)

This object served to protect and decorate the end of the timber shaft attached to the front of a horse-drawn carriage. The stylised bronze animal head is gilded and inlaid with gold and silver, a technique that dates back to the Spring and Autumn period. Different precious metals delineate the features of the horse's head and create a striking design incorporating whorls, parallel lines and other graphic features.

Wei was a strong state in the Central Plains region. Its territory covered the south-western part of present-day Shanxi and northern Henan, and its capital was first established in Anyi (present-day Xiaxian county, Shanxi province) and later moved to Daliang (Kaifeng, Henan province). The tomb in which this object was found had a large central chamber and two long passages: its ground plan resembled the outline of the Chinese character 中. The tomb was part of a larger cemetery.

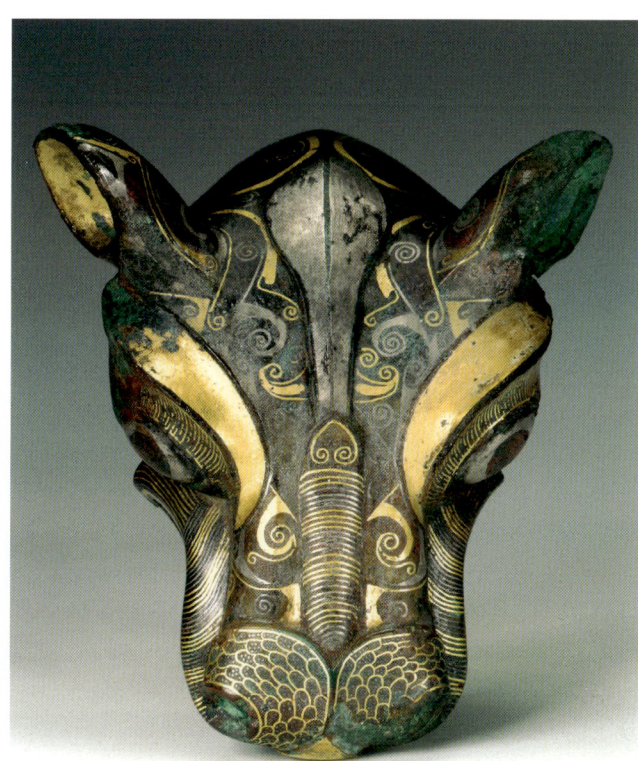

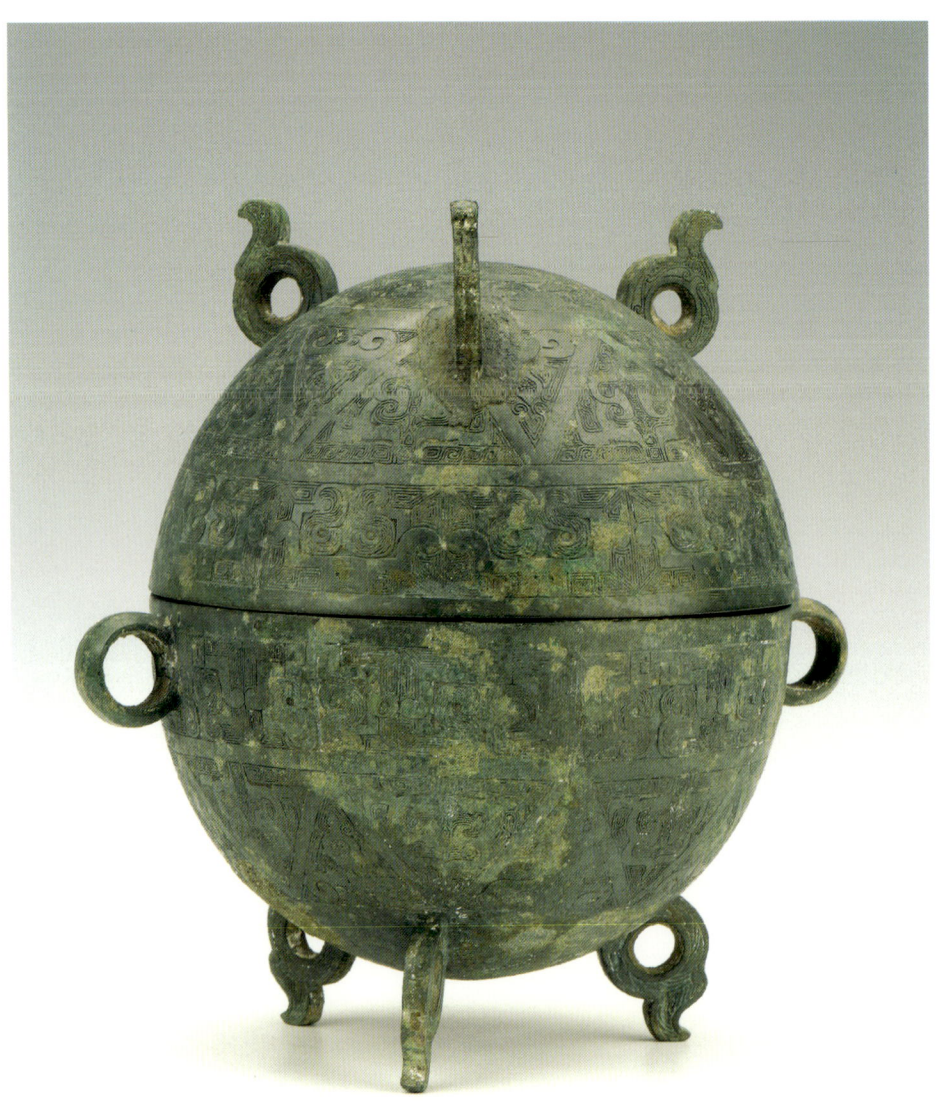

Covered vessel
Warring States period (475–221 BCE), State of Yan
Unearthed in 1952 at Tangshan, Hebei province
Bronze
22 (h) x 14.3 (mouth diam) cm
Collection of the National Museum of China (K6344)

This covered bronze vessel, known as a *dui*, was used to hold grain. It was unearthed from a tomb of the Warring States period in Jiagezhuang village, Tangshan, Hebei province, in 1952. During the Warring States period, the Tangshan area lay within the state of Yan and, in terms of shape and design, this vessel is typical of bronze wares from that state.

The ovoid vessel comprises two parts that join with a double groove. On the top of the lid there are three ring-shaped handles which echo the number and shape of the feet on which the vessel is supported. The lid can be removed, inverted and stood on the upper handles. On the base of the vessel is a pair of undecorated ring-handles positioned below the rim. Each half of the vessel

is ornamented with four different patterned registers separated by plain, wide, horizontal bands. The top of the lid is decorated with a whorl design, as well as cloud and thunder motifs, above a register of twisted rope design. The third register is distinguished by triangles and a modified cicada design, and the final register by a cloud and thunder pattern with double 'S' motifs.

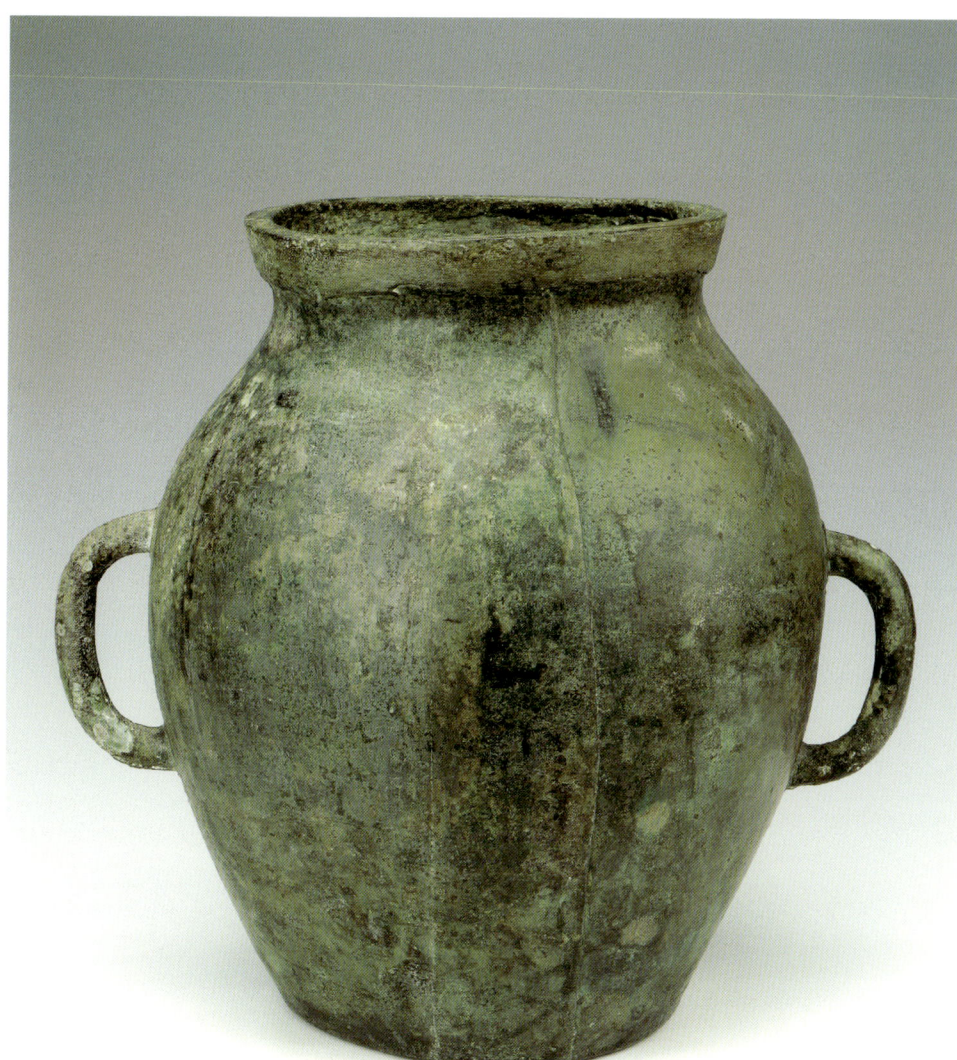

Measuring vessel
*Warring States period
(475–221 BCE), State of Qi*
Said to have been unearthed in
1857 in Lingshanwei, Jiao county,
Shandong province
Bronze
38.5 (h) x 22.3 (mouth diam) x 19
(base diam) cm, 20.46 ltr capacity
Collection of the National
Museum of China (Y204)

This cast bronze vessel, known as a *fu*, was used to measure grain. Reflecting its function, it has a full body, flat bottom and two handles for ease of carrying. The body of the vessel is inscribed with nine lines of Chinese characters which stipulate a strict system for managing the measurement of grain. The text records that Zi Hezi had sent people to tell Chen De that the capacity of the vessel to be used in Zuoguan should be based on that of the state's central granary vessels.

The officials of Zuoguan were forbidden from increasing or decreasing their calculations of amounts of grain, and if they did not follow the rules they would be punished in accordance with the seriousness of their crime. Zi Hezi is the title of the Grand Master Tianhe of the State of Qi, who later became the ruler of Qi. This vessel provides important information relating to the history of economic management and the trade in grains within the State of Qi during the Warring States period.

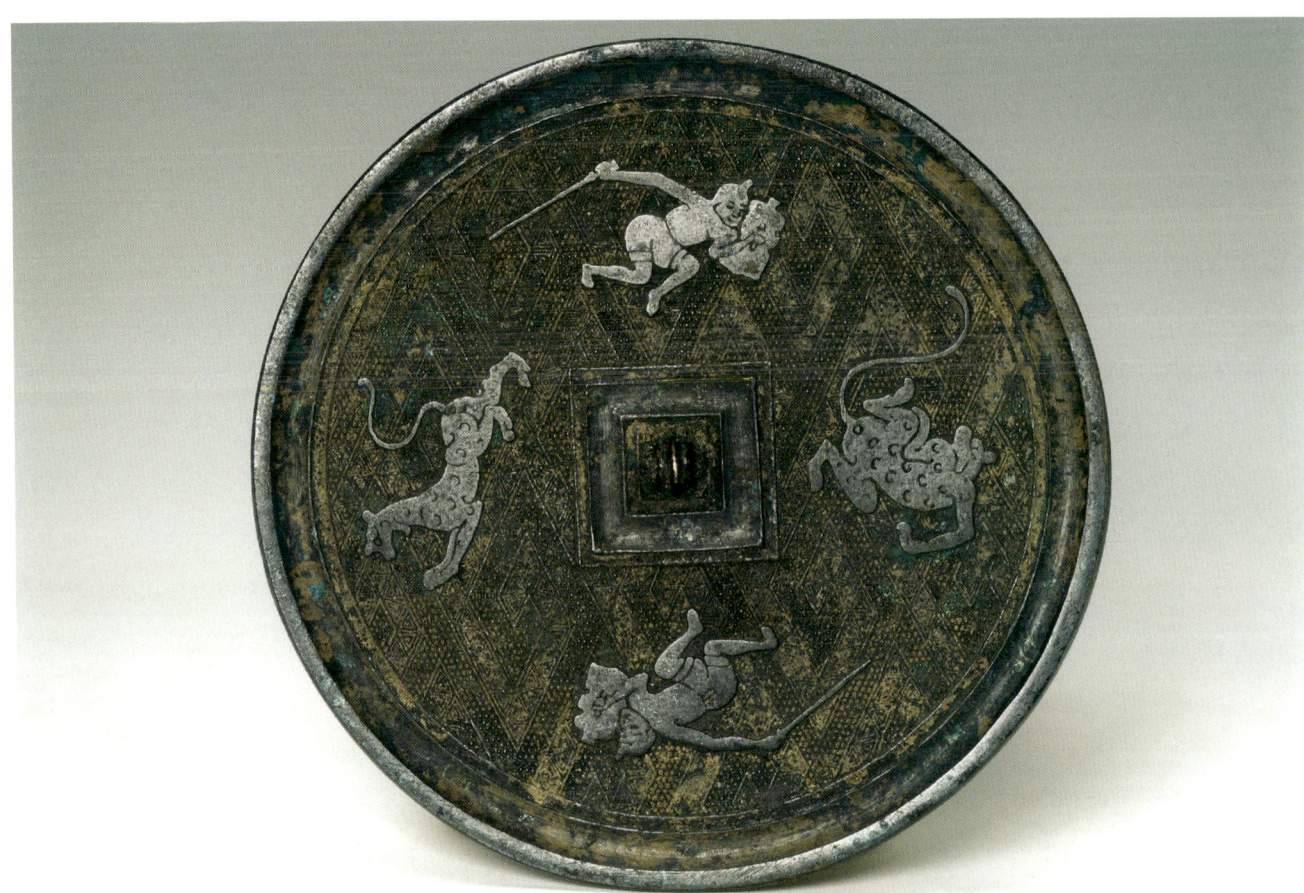

Mirror
Warring States period
(475–221 BCE), State of Qin
Excavated in 1975 from a Qin
tomb in Shuihudi, Yunmeng county,
Hubei province
Bronze
10.4 (diam) x 0.2 (rim thickness) cm
Collection of the National
Museum of China (Y2003)

Bronze mirrors were articles of everyday use. The plain side was highly polished to create a reflective surface. The back of the mirror has a knob at its centre formed by three loops of bronze.

A silk cord would originally have been threaded through the knob for handling. Between the handling knob and the edge of the mirror is a geometric ground pattern and an applied design of semi-naked warriors with bare feet hunting wild animals, which resemble a leopard or tiger. The helmeted warriors hold a shield in one hand and a sword in the other. The motifs reflect the martial spirit of the State of Qin during the Warring States period.

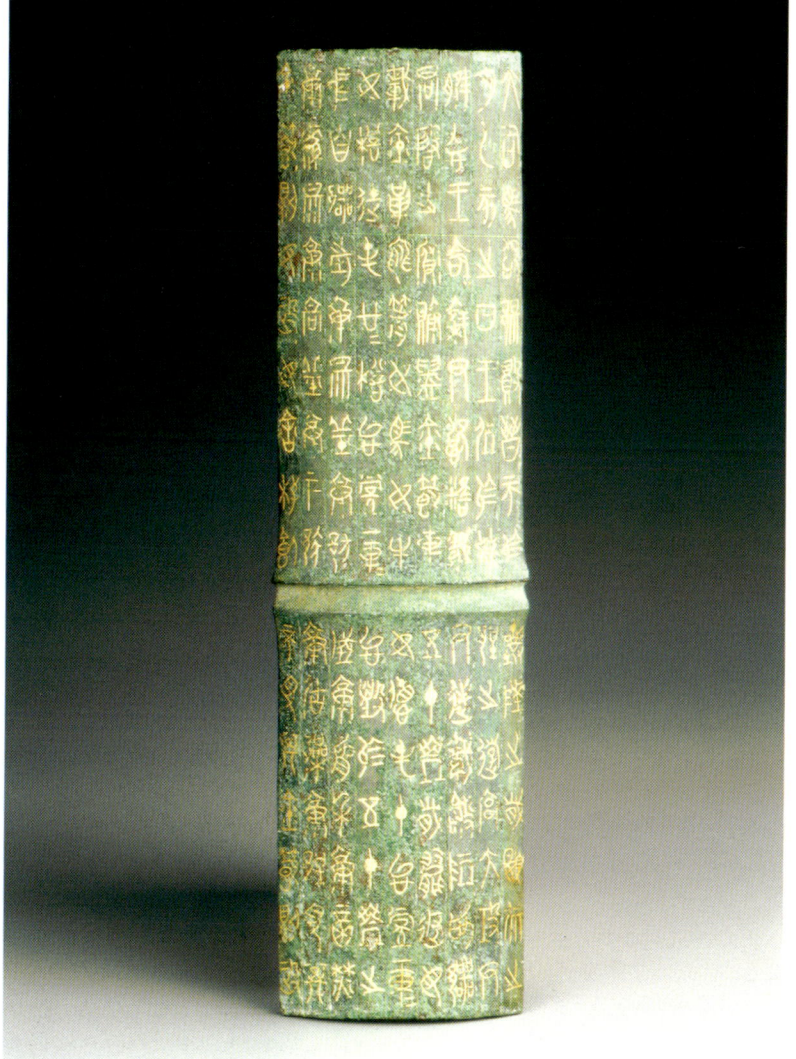

Permit

*Warring States period
(475–221 BCE), State of Chu*
Unearthed in 1957 at Qiujiahuayuan,
Shouxian county, Anhui province
Bronze inlaid with gold
29.4 (h) x 7.3 (w) x 0.7 (d) cm
Collection of the National
Museum of China (Y134)

This fine bronze object, known as a *jie*, is a type of tally issued by a ruler permitting a vassal or subject to travel and transport goods unimpeded and exempt from tolls through frontier toll gates and heavily defended passes. This permit was issued by King Huai of the State of Chu in 323 BCE, the 6th year of his reign, to the Duke of E, exempting him from road tolls and other road taxes.

This example was cast in the form of a bamboo segment. Its surface has been inscribed with seal script characters and inlaid with gold. The text records details of the number of permissible shipments, the routes that could be travelled and the types of goods that could be transported.

The technique of gold inlaying was invented during the Spring and Autumn period. Characters were cast or carved on to the surface of the object, very fine gold wire was inlaid to fill the cavities and the surface was polished.

This object was unearthed with four other permits — authorising land transport, and river transport.

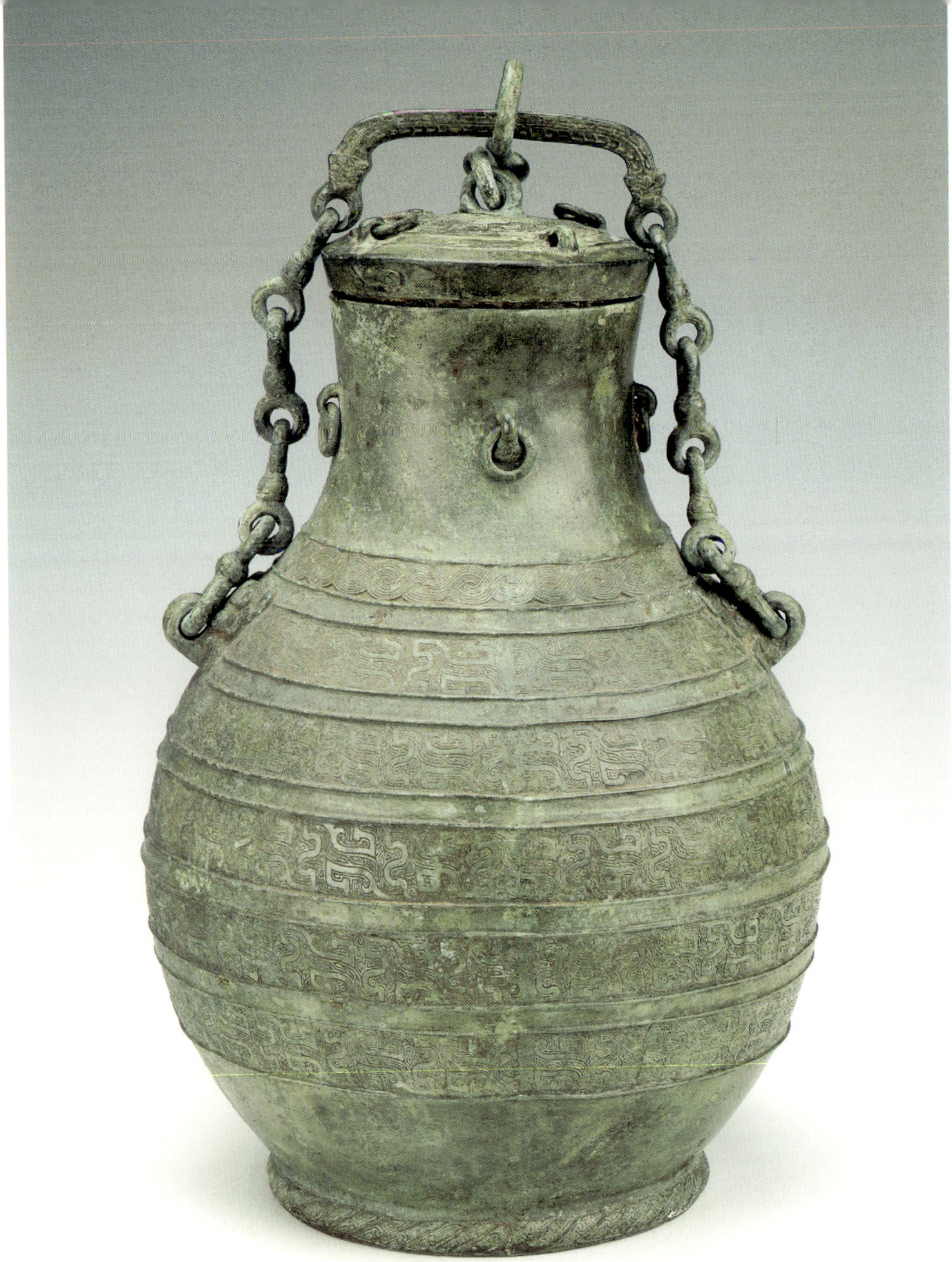

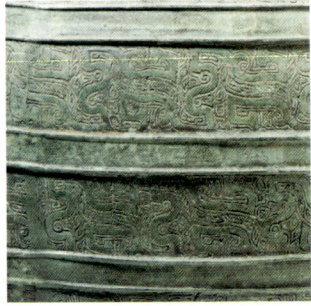

Covered vessel
*Warring States period
(475–221 BCE)*
Unearthed in 1951 at Huixian
county, Henan province
Bronze
37.8 (h) x 10.2 (mouth diam)
x 14.5 (foot diam) cm
Collection of the National
Museum of China (Y140)

This vessel, known as a *hu*, was used as a container for water or wine, and is typical of those used for banquets in the Central Plains area south of the Great Wall during the Warring States period. The shape of the vessel reflects its function. Cast from bronze, it has a relatively narrow, slightly waisted neck and bulging body. Four rings are attached at the neck and there are two applied faces of beasts either side, each holding a ring in its mouth connecting to the linked carrying handle. The cover is slightly rounded and has five attached rings and the central ring is connected to the carrying handle, ensuring that the cover remains attached when removed.

The vessel is richly patterned reflecting its value as an object. The cover and the body of the vessel are decorated with bands containing a modified coiled dragon (*panchi*) pattern, which alternates with plain wide strips with raised edges. The high level of artistic and technical skill displayed in the design of this vessel highlights the advanced nature of bronze technology at this time.

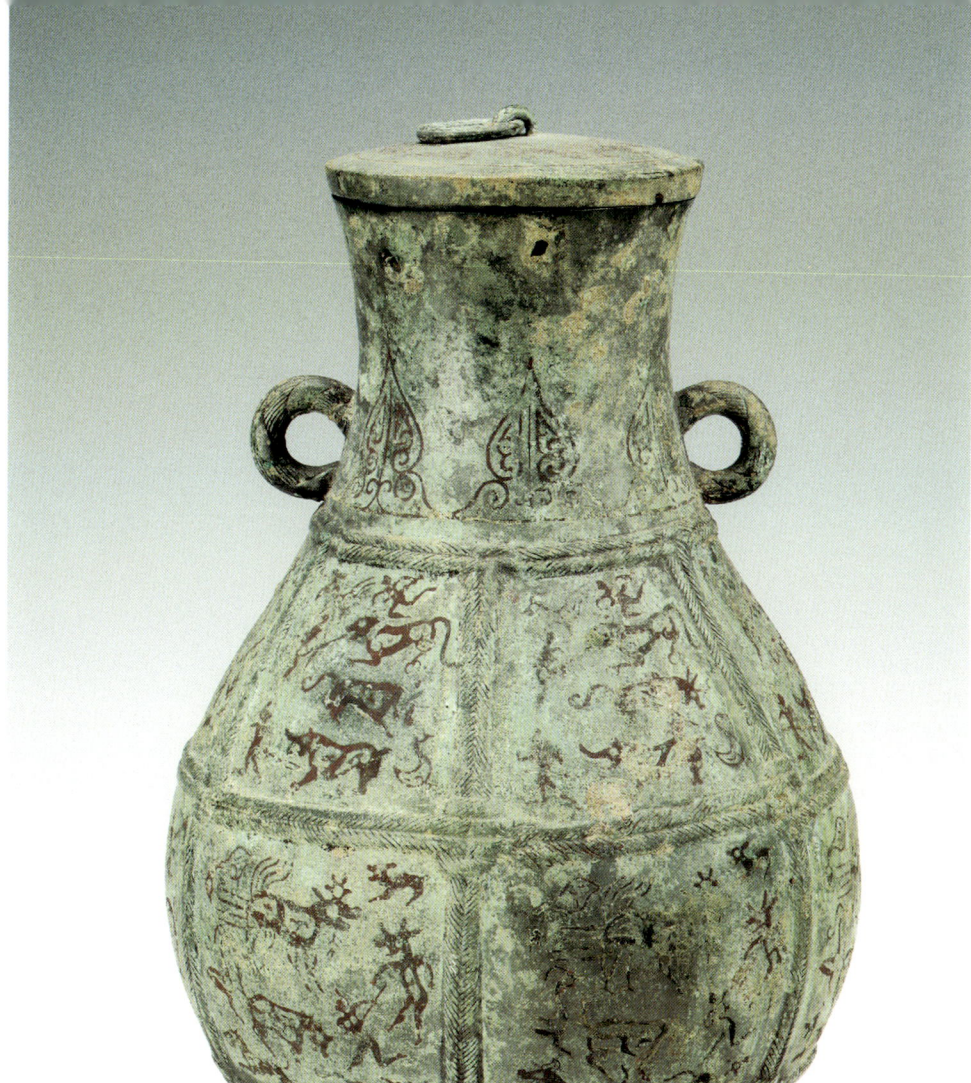

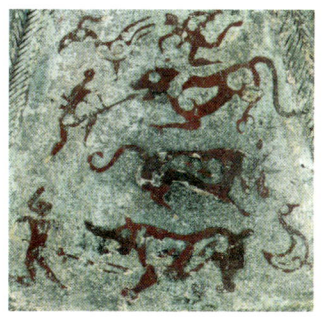

Covered vessel
*Warring States period
(475–221 BCE)*
Unearthed in 1951
at Tangshan, Hebei province
Bronze inlaid with copper
35.2 (h) x 11.5 (foot diam) cm
Collection of the National
Museum of China (Y203)

This cast bronze vessel
(*hu*) was used to store wine
or water. It is decorated with
patterns inlaid with copper.
The body of the vessel is
divided into twelve panels
arranged in two registers,
each framed with a border
simulating two strands of
rope. The panels contain
vivid scenes of hunters
armed with spears and other
weapons engaged in combat
with a variety of wild
animals. The fine quality
of the inlay and the lively
depiction of hunters and
animals reflect life during
the Warring States period.

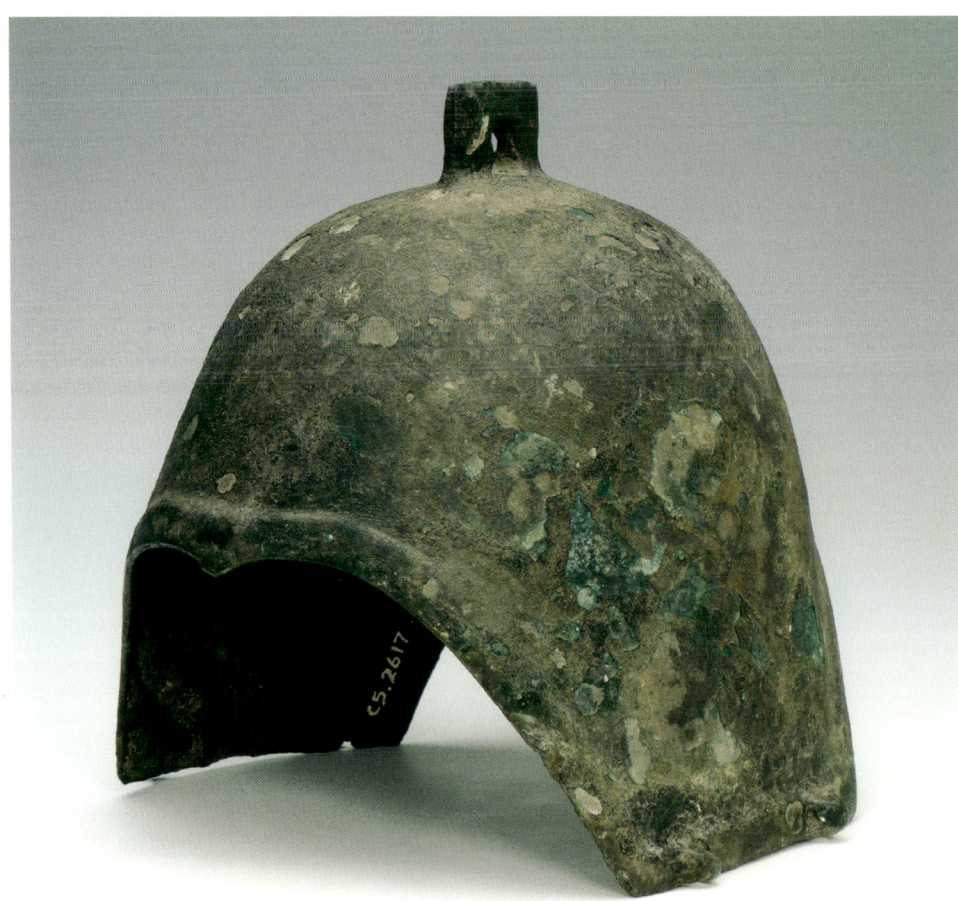

Helmet
*Warring States period
(475–221 BCE)*
Bronze
21(h) cm
Collection of the National
Museum of China (C5.2617)

This is a typical style
of helmet worn by soldiers
during the Warring States
period. It is extremely heavy
and was designed to protect
both the head and neck
in combat. The helmet was
called *mou* in the Warring
States period, *doumou*
in the Qin and Han dynas-
ties and *kui* after
the Song dynasty. With its
round crown and straight
lower edges, this example
resembles a cap (*mao*).
Its front and back are similar
in shape, and the sides
extend to cover the ears.
There are small eyelets near
its lower rear edges, and
a perforated square flange
on its top.

Halberd
*Warring States period
(475–221 BCE)*
Unearthed in 1957 at Houchuan,
Shaanxian county, Henan province
Bronze
8.7 (*ci* l) x 17.5 (*yuan* l)
x 12.2 (*hu* l) x 10.8 (*na* l) cm
Collection of the National
Museum of China (K3759)

The halberd combined the
functions of the spear and
dagger-axe, or of the dagger-
axe and knife, and so could
be used to kill the enemy
either by thrusting or dragging its blades. The earliest
known bronze halberd was
excavated from a Shang
dynasty tomb and
is a composite weapon
integrating the lethal
components of the spear
and dagger-axe. The first
halberds cast as a single
weapon appeared in
the Western Han dynasty.

This example, made in
the early Warring Sates
period, is a composite.

The spike (*ci*) at the top
of this halberd is short
and roughly triangular in
outline. The shaft by which
it is attached to the halberd
is also short. The trailing
edge (*yuan*) of the dagger is
curved like its leading-edge
blade, and the base section
(*hu*) of the dagger-axe
component is perforated.
The rear section (*na*)
is long, and it is bladed at
its diagonal end. The body
has a pronounced green
patina and rust in places.
There is a 3 centimetre-long
wooden dowel wedged
in the cavity of the socket
(*qiong*) on the spike.

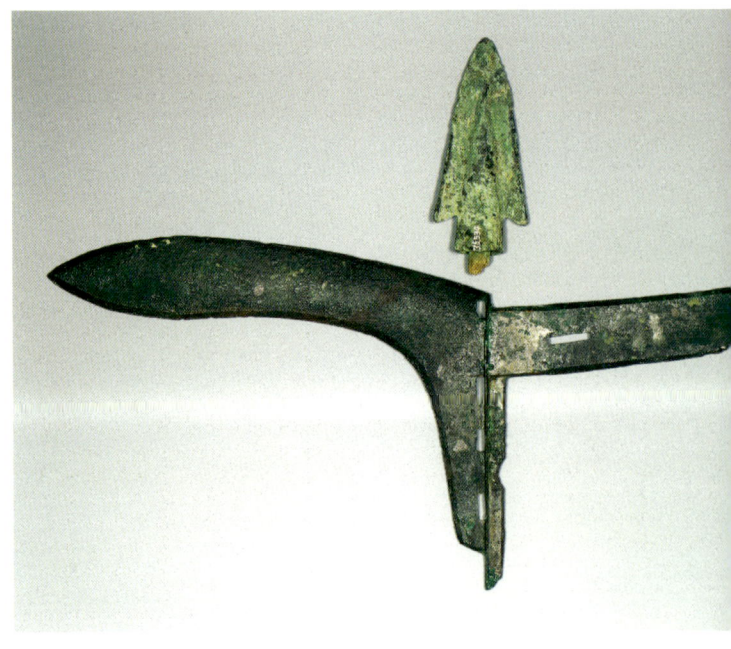

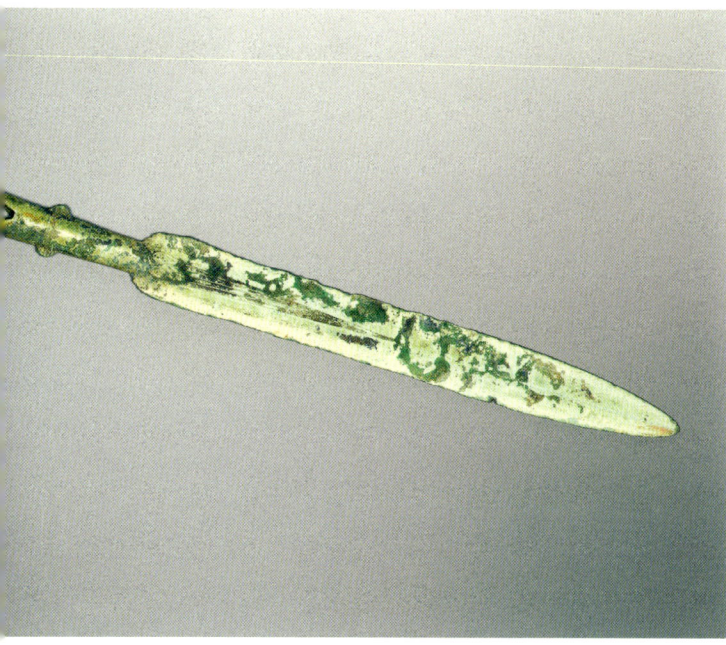

Spearhead
*Warring States period
(475–221 BCE)*
Unearthed in 1975 in Chuwan,
Yunnan province
Bronze
3.6 (w) x 37.4 (l) cm
Collection of the National
Museum of China (K9684)

Spears like this were
commonly used as assault
weapons on ancient
Chinese battlefields.
The spearhead has a fine
double-edged blade with
a sharp tip, similar to
a sword, and a central
section (*jiao*) that encloses
the shaft. An elongated
triangular pattern with
curved ends that follows
the form of the blade is
incised on the central
section of the reverse side
of the spear. The *jiao* has
no ridge, but has two
eyelets in the lower section,
which have since corroded,
and inverted 'V'-shaped
notches at the lower edge.
These features indicate
that the spear was probably
made in Wu or Yue, two
states in south-eastern
China during the Warring
States period.

Arrowheads
*Warring States period
(475–221 BCE)*
Bronze
1. 6.4 (l) cm; 2. 5.5 (l) cm
Collection of the National
Museum of China
(CO5.1711, CO5.1723)

These arrowheads have
two wings with sharp
front edges that meet at
a point. The wings extend
backwards with sharp
trailing edges which embed
the arrowhead in the body
of an animal or person,
making it very painful
and difficult to remove.
The staff, between the rear
edges of the wings, held
the arrowhead in
a timber shaft, typically
about 1 metre in length.
The arrow would have
been shot from a bow,
propelled by the string
when released. Operation
of the compound bows
made in this period required
strength and skill, acquired
during long periods
of training. Bronze
arrowheads can be traced
back to the early bronze-
age period during the
second millennium BCE.
Their shape changed over
time. There are three main
forms of arrowhead: with
double wings, triple wings,
or triple edges.

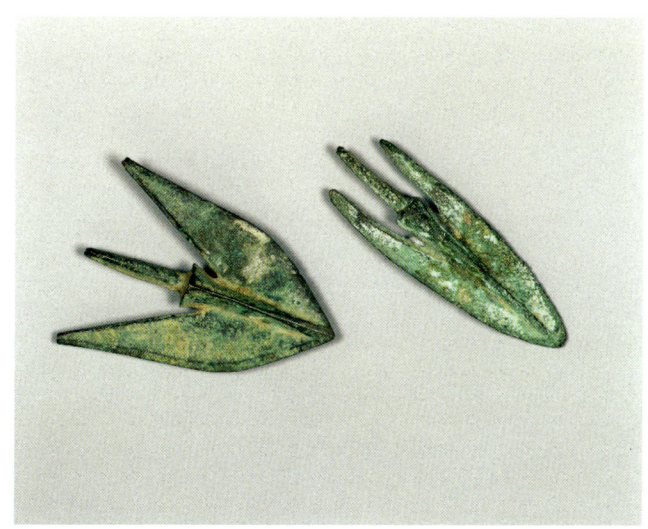

Adze blade
*Warring States period
(475–221 BCE)*
Unearthed at Gangcun,
Zhengzhou, Henan province
Iron
5 (w) x 17 (l) cm
Collection of the National
Museum of China (Yuwen 264)

This iron adze blade
is wedge-shaped in profile,
tapering to a sharp edge.
The edge of the tool shows
some damage. The cavity
for the shaft (*qiong*)
is rectangular and also
tapers, following the form
of the blade. Originally
the iron blade fitted closely
over a shaped section
of wood that was attached
to the handle. Late in
the Warring States period,
iron tools came into
widespread use, reflecting
developments in iron
smelting technology.
This technology brought
lighter, stronger and more
durable tools into
production, and it made
possible much larger
construction projects, such
as the building of long walls.

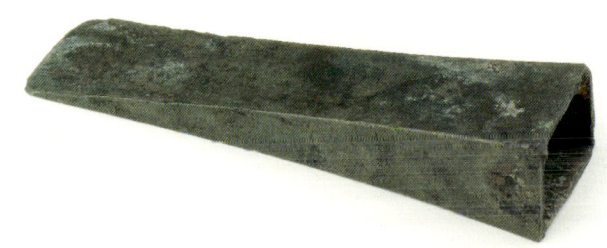

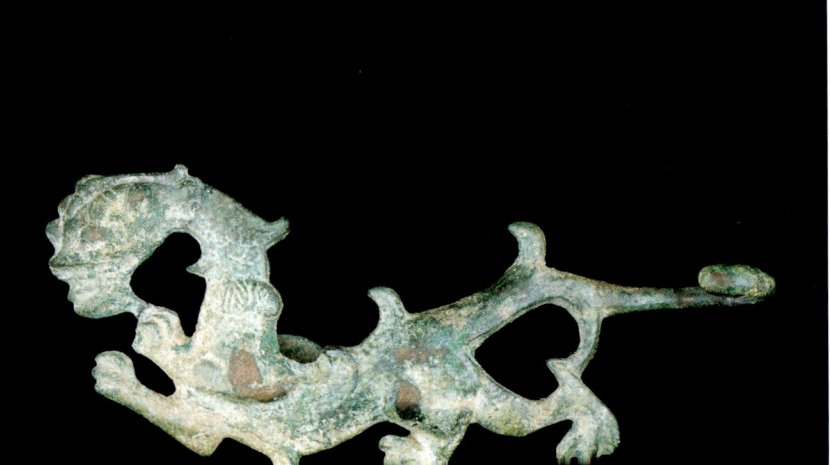

Belt-hook
*Warring States period
(475–221 BCE)*
Unearthed at Zigui, Hubei province
Bronze
13.5 (l) cm
Collection of the National
Museum of China (K9851)

Decorative belt-hooks were
used to secure garments
at the waist and are thought
to have first been used
by nomadic peoples in
northern China. In the
Spring and Autumn period,
the belt-hook was adopted
by the ethnic Han people
and became an integral
element of Chinese dress
until the Han dynasty.
This belt-hook is made
of bronze and takes
the form of a tiger at

the moment of attack.
The true-to-life depiction
of a tiger attests to the skill
and creativity of the artisans
of the Warring States
period. There is a raised
circular knob on the reverse
that is used to secure
the object to the belt, and
the curving tail of the tiger
forms the hook that is used
to fasten the belt. The
object was found at Zigui
in Hubei province and
it is likely that it was used
by a person of the Ba ethnic
group. The belt-hook
attests to the way in which
pastoral cultural influences
could cross the Great
Wall and reach far into
southern China.

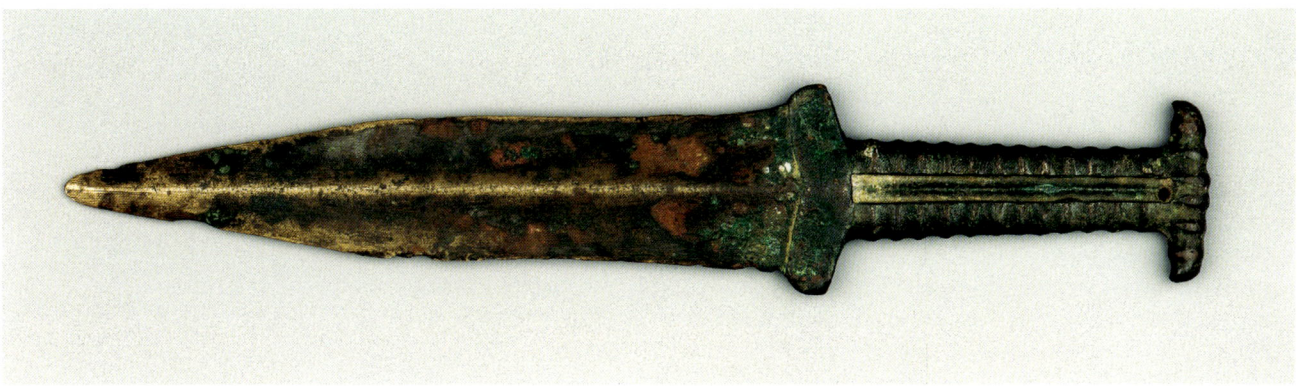

Short sword
*Warring States period
(475–221 BCE)*
Excavated in 1979 at Ih Ju
League, Inner Mongolia
Bronze
26.7 (l) cm
Collection of the National
Museum of China (K10374)

Daggers and short swords were developed as multi-functional weapons for both self-defence and use in battle. They could also demonstrate the social status of their owners. Bronze was the metal commonly used to make daggers and swords in the late Spring and Autumn and early Warring States periods. Iron daggers and swords began to be used in the late Warring States period and became widely used in the Qin and Han dynasties, after which bronze daggers and swords gradually went out of use.

This short sword, which was excavated from a Xiongnu tomb in the Ih Ju League of Inner Mongolia, is dated to the early Warring States period. It has a striated handle and a centrally placed columnar cavity. Bronze short swords such as this were commonly used by Xiongnu warriors.

This frontal guard for a horse, known as a *danglu*, functioned as a talisman and was used by the Donghu people. Its upper part takes the form of a frog supporting itself on its two front legs; the lower body comprises two entwined snakes.

The Donghu people are the earliest northern nomadic tribe recorded in the ancient Chinese histories. During the Warring States period, the Donghu established the first nomadic state in the northern grasslands, neighbouring the Xiongnu in the west and the states of Yan and Zhao to the south. Raids by Donghu mounted warriors posed a great threat to Yan and Zhao, the rulers of which ordered the building of long walls along their northern borders for defence. Invasions by the Donghu resulted in the bold reforms launched by King Wuling of Zhao, who advocated learning the customs of the northern peoples, especially horse-riding and archery. In 206 BCE, Modun, king (*shanyu*) of the Xiongnu, defeated the Donghu and effectively eliminated this people, who had been in existence for many centuries.

Many objects excavated from tombs suggest that the Donghu people used horse harnesses, including a bridle that comprised a gag bit (*mabiao*) and harness frontlet (*jieyue*) with a frontal guard (*danglu*), an ornament that hung down the horse's forehead between the eyes and acted as a charm to protect it from arrow fire.

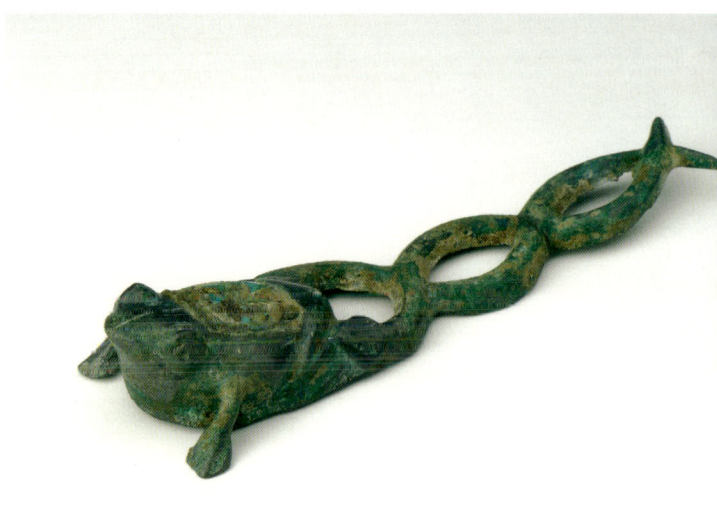

Forehead guard for a horse
Warring States period
(475–221 BCE)
Unearthed in 1976 at Sanguandianzi, Lingyuan, Liaoning province
Bronze
5.7 (w) x 20 (l) cm
Collection of the National Museum of China (K9962, Y2027)

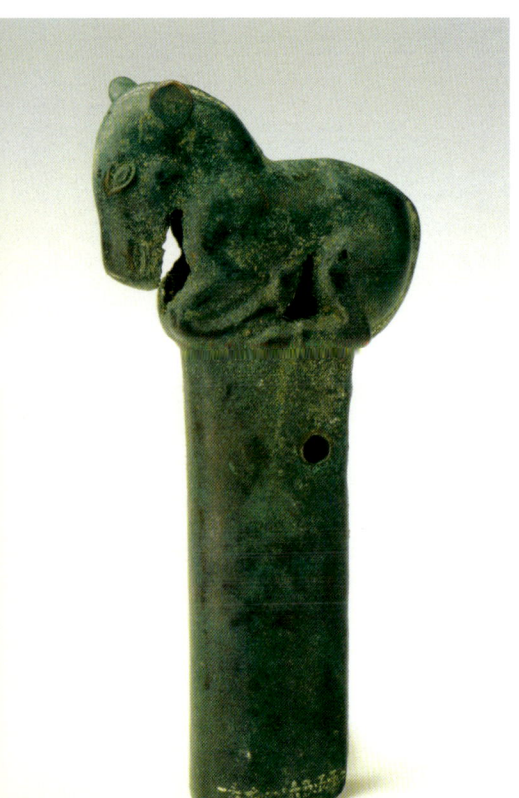

Finial
Warring States period
(475–221 BCE)
Unearthed in 1962 at Ih Ju League, Inner Mongolia
Bronze
16.2 (h) x 7.3 (w) cm
Collection of the National Museum of China (K10371)

Cast using the lost-wax method, this horse-shaped bronze carriage ornament depicts a kneeling pony at rest. The pony has a relatively large head and is not very tall. These are typical features of the Mongolian horse which, though not as tall and handsome as Arabian horses, are known for their great endurance and are well suited to the harsh conditions typical of the Mongolian plateau. For nomadic peoples, horses represent wealth and tribal strength. They are an important investment in the face of climatic and economic uncertainty and are also companions to their owners. Horses are needed for raising livestock, hunting and warfare, and the expression 'peoples on horseback' aptly describes the nomadic peoples of the steppe. The practice of interring live horses with the dead was popular among some nomadic peoples. Horse heads were often buried in Xiongnu tombs as sacrificial offerings, and horses were also sacrificed and buried in early Khitan tombs. The custom of burying horses with the dead only ceased in the Liao dynasty when Emperor Shengzong (reigned 983–1031) ordered his people, the Khitan, to end the practice and preserve horses for war.

Carriage ornament
*Warring States period
(475–221 BCE)*
Unearthed in 1962 at Ih Ju
League, Inner Mongolia
Bronze
17 (h) x 11.9 (l) cm
Collection of the National
Museum of China (K10373)

This carriage ornament, hollow-cast using the lost-wax method, takes the form of an alert stag with its head raised and the tips of its long horns almost level with its haunches. In the Warring States period, deer were commonly seen and hunted on the northern grasslands and across the Eurasian steppe, as is evident from the number of representations of these animals that have been found. Among the carriage ornaments of this kind that have been discovered are standing or crouching does, most of which have been excavated in Ningxia, Gansu and Inner Mongolia and date back to the period from the fifth to the third centuries BCE. Most scholars believe objects such as this were used to decorate the yokes of carriages and would have been used with a number of similar finial ornaments.

Previously, such carriage ornaments were attributed to the Xiongnu people, but archaeological excavations indicate that these objects were popular before their time and gradually disappeared from use after the Xiongnu consolidated their rule over the grasslands.

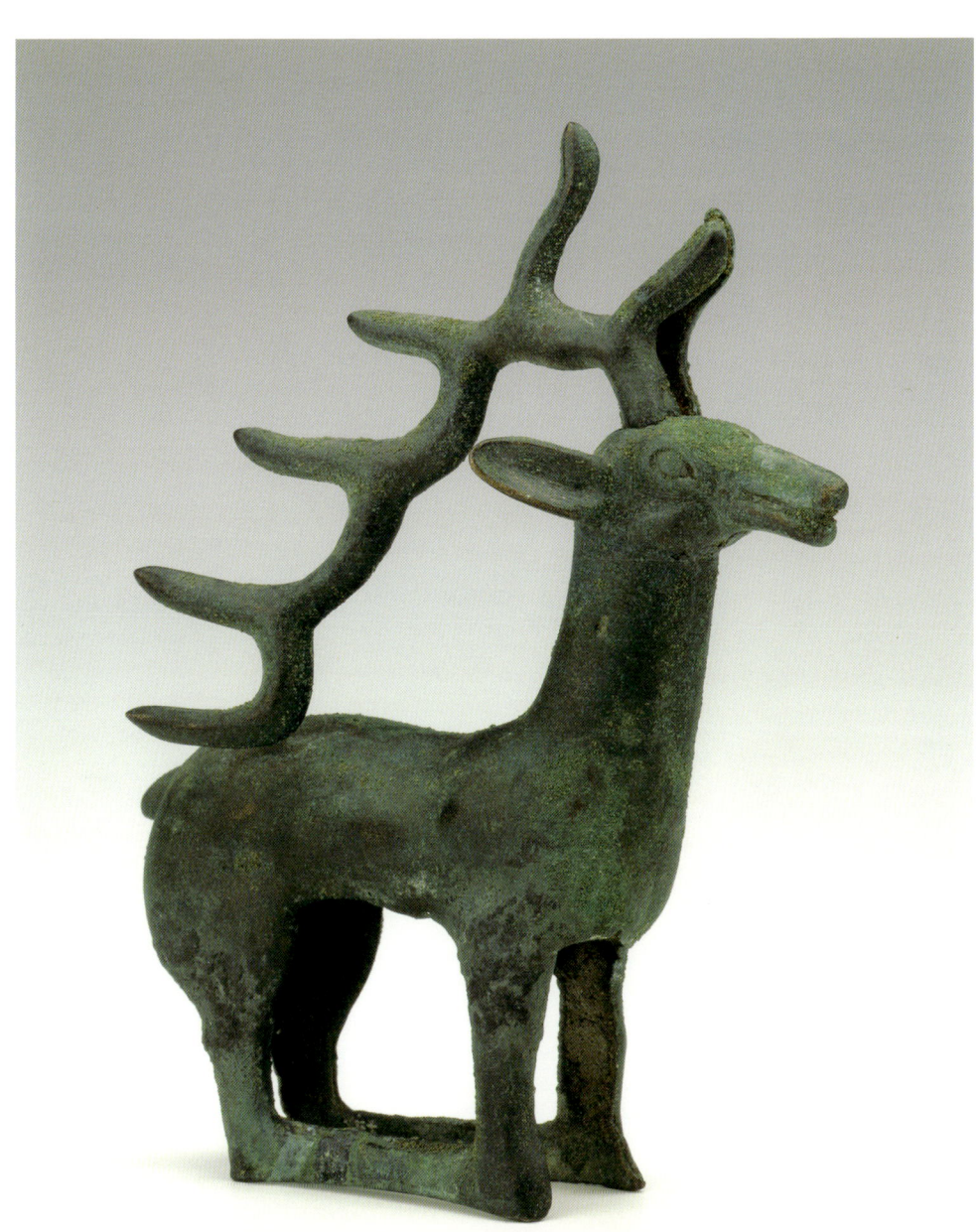

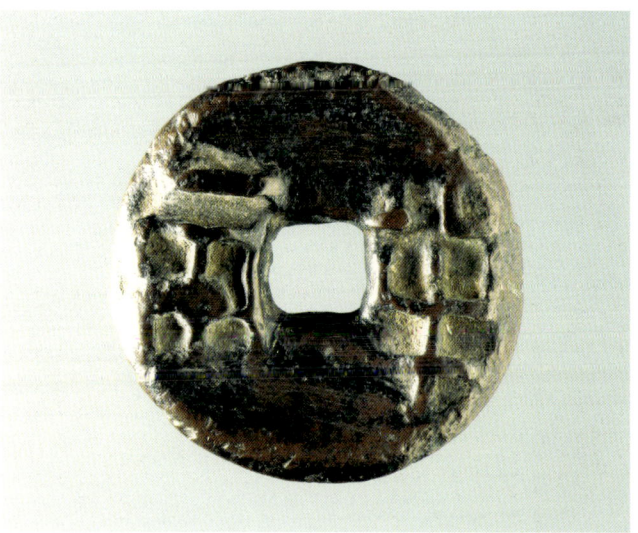

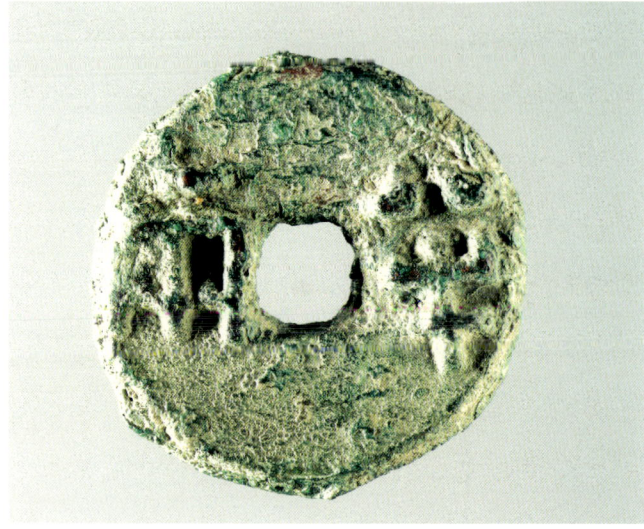

Coins
Qin dynasty (221–206 BCE)
Bronze
1. 3.6 (diam) cm, 20.3 g;
2. 3 (diam) cm, 14.9 g
Collection of the National
Museum of China (H3.357, H3.320)

These two coins are examples of the lowest denomination of currency in the Qin dynasty. On one side of the coins is a raised inscription, reading *'banliang'* (or half a *liang*), in seal script. After Emperor Qin Shihuang unified China, he standardised the currency, defining gold for the highest denominations and bronze for the lowest denominations. Both kinds of coins were circulated throughout the country.

Unlike the hammered coins of the West, Chinese coinage was cast in batches in moulds known as coin 'trees'. After cooling, the coins were removed from the sprue, or 'tree', and skewered, making the characteristic hole, for filing. The square hole stopped the coins from spinning during this cleaning process; it also enabled the coins to be strung, which was one of the features of the standardised specie introduced by Qin

Shihuang. Prior to the Qin dynasty, Chinese currency was irregular in shape, with 'knife'-shaped and other forms of coinage making the handling and circulation of money inconvenient. This type of round coin introduced in the Qin dynasty remained the basic model for Chinese coinage until the twentieth century.

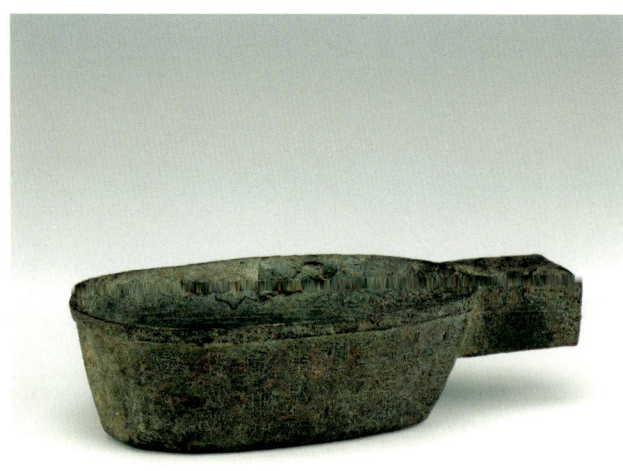

Volume measure
Qin dynasty (221–206 BCE)
Bronze
5.5 (h) x 20.5 (l) cm
Collection of the National
Museum of China (C5.3085)

This bronze object is thought to have been used as a volumetric standard, perhaps for establishing conformity in measuring grain. The body of the object is elliptical with a flat bottom and a short handle. The exterior is inscribed with a forty-character imperial decree issued by Qin Shihuang, who in the twenty-sixth year of his reign, 221 BCE, declared himself

to be first emperor of the Qin dynasty. The decree, significantly, conveys his order that weights and measures be standardised through all the conquered states which previously had their own idiosyncratic measurement systems. The standardisation of weights, measures, coinage and other items, such as the colour of clothing (which determined a person's rank) and the axle widths of carts, indicates the legalistic and bureaucratic nature of the Qin dynasty as it sought to unify the administration of the empire.

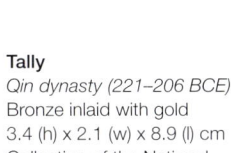

Tally
Qin dynasty (221–206 BCE)
Bronze inlaid with gold
3.4 (h) x 2.1 (w) x 8.9 (l) cm
Collection of the National
Museum of China (Y176)

This tally was issued by Emperor Qin Shihuang to a general stationed at Yangling. It was an imperial authorisation for troop movements within the Qin empire instituted by the emperor following the unification of the separate kingdoms which had existed in the Warring States period. The tally is in the form of a crouching tiger looking forward, with its head raised and tail curled.

The left and right sections of the neck and back of the animal are inscribed with inlaid gold seal-script characters: 'A tally for the armoured forces. The right [half] is with the emperor, the left [half] with Yangling' (*Jia bing zhi fu, you zai huangdi, zuo zai Yangling*).

The tally was divided laterally into two halves, which, when brought together, formed the whole body of the tiger. One half was held by the emperor and the other entrusted to the general stationed in Yangling, located to the east of Xianyang, the Qin imperial capital in what is today's Shaanxi province. When the emperor's half was conveyed to the general by a high-level emissary, the bringing together of the two halves of the tally validated the mobilisation order issued by the emperor.

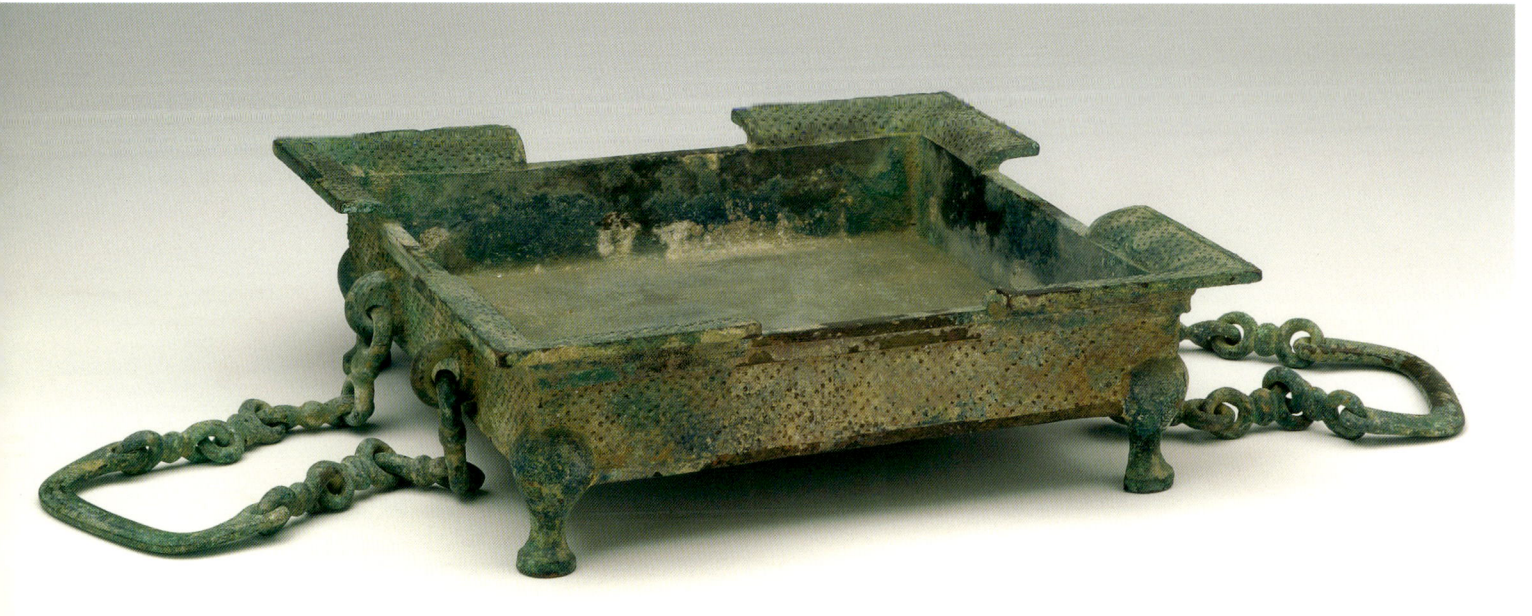

Brazier
Qin dynasty (221–206 BCE)
Unearthed in 1966 at Xianyang,
Shaanxi province
Bronze
8.1 (h) x 23.6 (w) x 24.4 (l) cm
Collection of the National
Museum of China (K7954)

This bronze brazier was used for carrying hot coals and could be suspended to disperse heat. The tray for the coals has an everted or flared rim and it is supported by four horse hoof-shaped feet that are ornamented with the faces of beasts. One foot has been damaged and repaired. Attached to both ends of the tray are chain carrying handles formed from bronze links. The sides of the tray and the flat rim are ornamented with a cast cloud and thunder pattern and a nipple or cleat design. The simple, but pleasing, design of the brazier highlights its role as a practical vessel used for heating in ancient China.

Plate
Qin dynasty (221–206 BCE)
Excavated in 1979 from the tomb
of Liu Xiang, King of Qi, in Zibo,
Shandong province
Gilt silver
5.4 (h) x 37 (mouth diam)
x 21.1 (foot diam) cm
Collection of the National
Museum of China (Jie1757)

This fine gilt silver plate is decorated on both sides with an all-over coiled dragon design that, in stylistic terms, is typical of the Warring States period. On the underside of the rim is an inscription written in Qin seal script which reads 'thirty-third year'.

It is thought that the plate was made in 274 BCE for use in the Xianyang Palace and that, after the demise of the Qin dynasty, it was taken from the palace by Xiang Yu and later came into the possession of Liu Bang, the first emperor of the Han dynasty (reigned 206–195 BCE). After founding the Han dynasty, Liu Bang assigned family members as local lords

across the country and it is likely that he presented this plate to Liu Fei, King of Qi, the capital of which was near Linzi, Shandong province. After Liu Fei's death, his son Liu Xiang became King of Qi. When Liu Xiang died, this plate was buried with him, and it was recovered during archaeological work in Shandong in 1979.

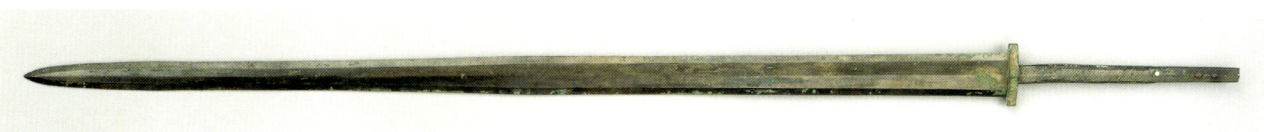

Sword
Qin dynasty (221–206 BCE)
Excavated in 1974 from
the mausoleum site of Emperor
Qin Shihuang, Lintong,
Shaanxi province
Bronze
69 (l) cm
Collection of the National
Museum of China (K8143)

Swords are one of the common bladed weapons of ancient China. The blade of this example is long and narrow with a raised central ridge and sharp double edges now slightly nicked in places. The hilt is flat. The sword guard, the binding on the grip and the wooden scabbard are no longer extant. The sword was most probably a fighting weapon, rather than a ceremonial object. The sword was cast in a mould formed from a model, and finished by burnishing and polishing. Its surface has been analysed and found to have an extremely fine layer of dense oxidation comprising metallic compounds of chromium, zinc, iron, manganese and lead. This layer acted as a protective coating against corrosion and increased the tensile strength of the sword.

Although the sword was buried for 2000 years, it is still in extremely good condition and the double-edge blades remain very sharp. Many other bronze swords made using similar technology have been excavated from the sacrificial burial pits near the tomb of Emperor Qin Shihuang, and indicate the high level of bronze casting technique at that time.

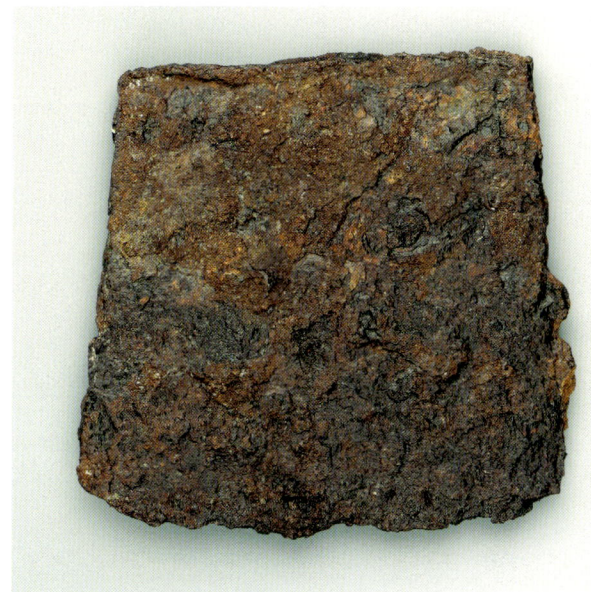

Axe head
Qin dynasty (221–206 BCE)
Unearthed in 1975
at Lintong, Shaanxi province
Iron
9.2 (w) x 9.7 (l) cm
Collection of the National
Museum of China (K7945)

This corroded iron axe head has a trapezoid outline and a curved double-edged blade. Iron axes were common tools, and were sometimes also used as weapons in the late Warring States period and during the Qin dynasty, as more advanced iron casting and iron-working techniques were developed.

Crossbow mechanism
Qin dynasty (221–206 BCE)
Excavated in 1974 from
the mausoleum site
of Emperor Qin Shihuang,
Lintong, Shaanxi province
Bronze
13.5 (l) cm
Collection of the National
Museum of China (K8145)

This trigger mechanism
for a crossbow comprises
separately cast bronze
components: the hook
(*ya*) to hold the bowstring
until released, the sights
(*wangshan*) which function
as the aiming system,
and the trigger (*xuandao*,
literally 'suspending knife')
which, when pulled, moves
the hook allowing it
to release the bowstring
and the bolt or arrow.
The mechanism would
have been held in a timber
body to which the bow
arms were attached.

The cast bronze components
had to be precisely made
and assembled to operate
effectively, requiring
a high level of skill in metal
casting and finishing.

Crossbows came into
use during the Warring
States period and become
more widespread in the
Han and Jin dynasties.
They required less skill
and strength to use than
the composite bow, and
were more powerful,
allowing relatively
untrained infantry to
be more effective when
fighting well-trained
warriors on horseback
using bows. The crossbow
was a formidable weapon
and it is said that it could
fire a bronze bolt a distance
of some 800 metres.

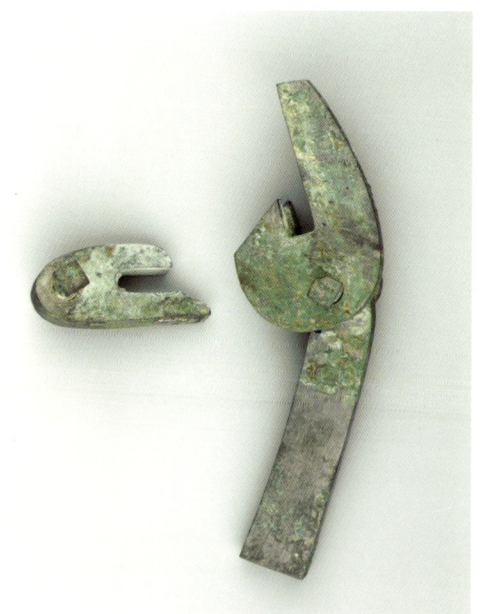

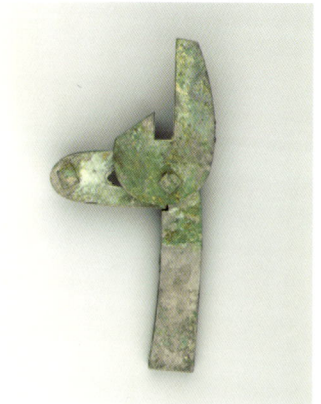

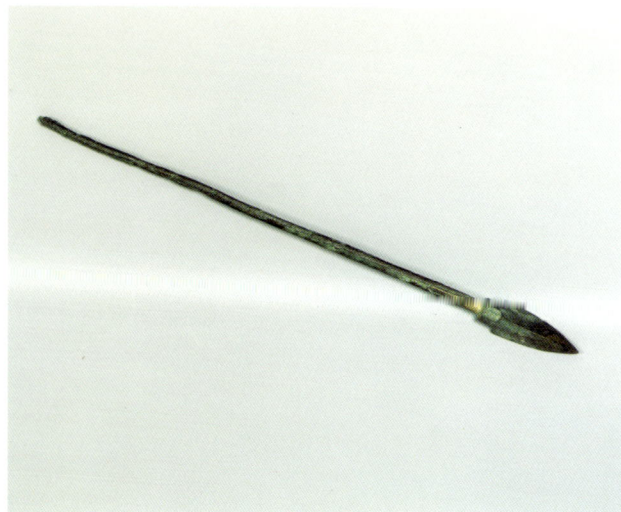

Arrowhead
Qin dynasty (221–206 BCE)
Excavated in 1974 from
the mausoleum site of
the Emperor Qin Shihuang,
Lintong, Shaanxi province
Bronze
16.2 (l) cm
Collection of the National
Museum of China (K8147)

This arrowhead is a
projectile shot from a bow.
The bronze arrowhead, cast
separately from the shaft,
is triangular with a rounded
tapering stem (*ting*) to
which eagle feathers were
originally attached to form
the fletches. The taut string
rested against the groove
(*kuo*) at the end of the arrow
shaft before firing.

This arrowhead is relatively
well preserved with no sign
of corrosion. Spectroscopic
analysis of the head reveals
high levels of lead, as well
as copper and tin compounds
used in making bronze.
The higher than usual
lead content may have
made the arrowhead a more
lethal weapon.

Tens of thousands of weapons
have been excavated from
the sacrificial pits to the east
of Emperor Qin Shihuang's
mausoleum. Bronze bolts
and arrowheads are the most
numerous, indicating the
importance of crossbows and
bows in military conflict in
the Qin dynasty.

Archer
Qin dynasty (221–206 BCE)
Excavated in 1974 from
the mausoleum site of
Emperor Qin Shihuang,
Lintong, Shaanxi province
Terracotta
188.5 (h) cm
Collection of the National
Museum of China (K8159)

The renowned terracotta warriors of Emperor Qin Shihuang's mausoleum were discovered in 1974 in Lintong county outside present-day Xi'an. The vast complex of burial pits in the mausoleum site have been the focus of extensive excavation and documentation ever since. The army of soldiers that was designed to guard the emperor's tomb in the afterlife was cast from clay and fired. The figures are highly realistic and are depicted with individual facial expressions and details of apparel.

This warrior figure, who has a strict frontal pose, is a light infantryman. He is without armour and wears a robe that crosses to the right and is fastened around the waist with a leather belt, short trousers, leg protectors and shoes with laces. The soldier's hair is plaited at the base of his head and tightly coiled into a neat round bun, which is positioned on the right side of the head. A stamp has been affixed to the hair at the base of the head close to the hairline — an artisan's seal. Judging by the stance of the figure, it is possible that he once held a crossbow in his hand. This warrior figure is tall and slender, and has a long and angular face with pronounced features believed to have been typical of Qin people living in the Guanzhong area.

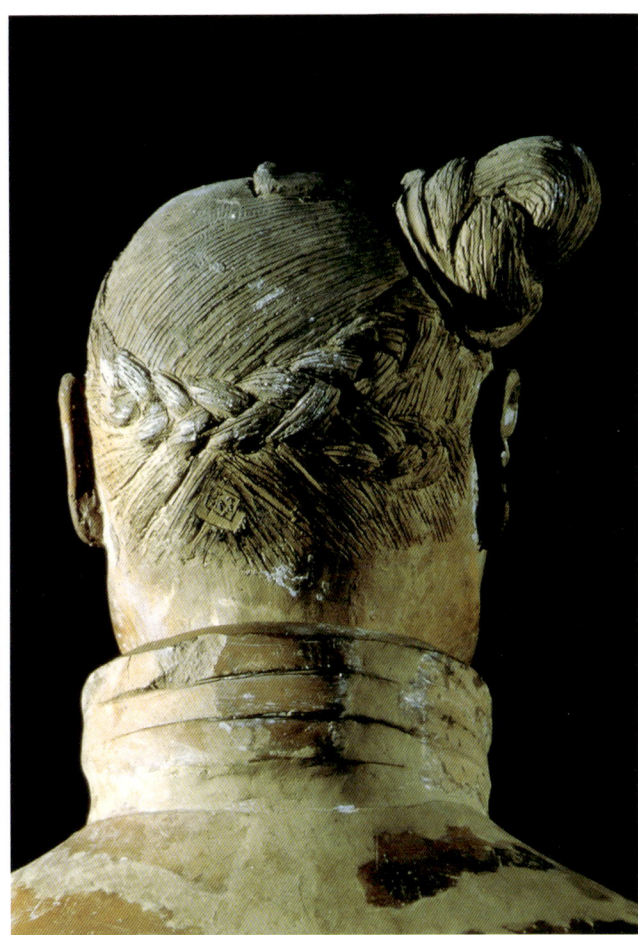

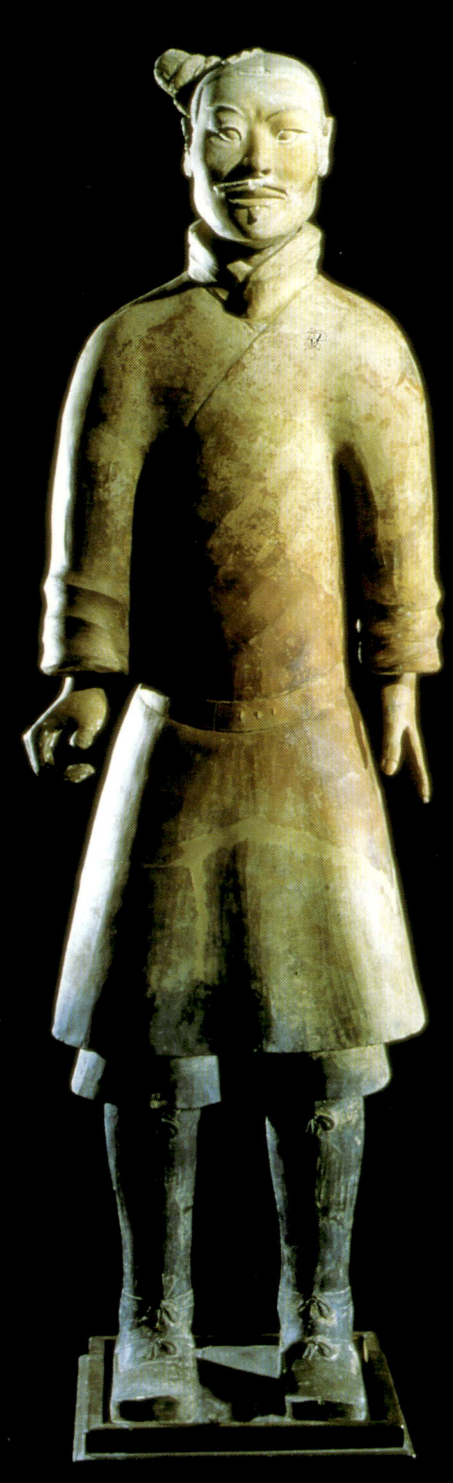

Bowl
*Western Han dynasty
(206 BCE–8 CE)*
Bronze
8.6 (h) x 36.1 (mouth diam) cm
Collection of the National
Museum of China (C5.521)

This round bowl, called a *xi*, was used for washing the face and hands. The well has a cast design of paired fish and bears the inscription, 'May you be blessed with sons and grandsons' (*jun yi zisun*). Both the fish motif and the inscription carry auspicious sentiments typical of China's popular and high cultures. The form of basin or washer first appeared in the late Warring States period and became popular in the Han dynasty.

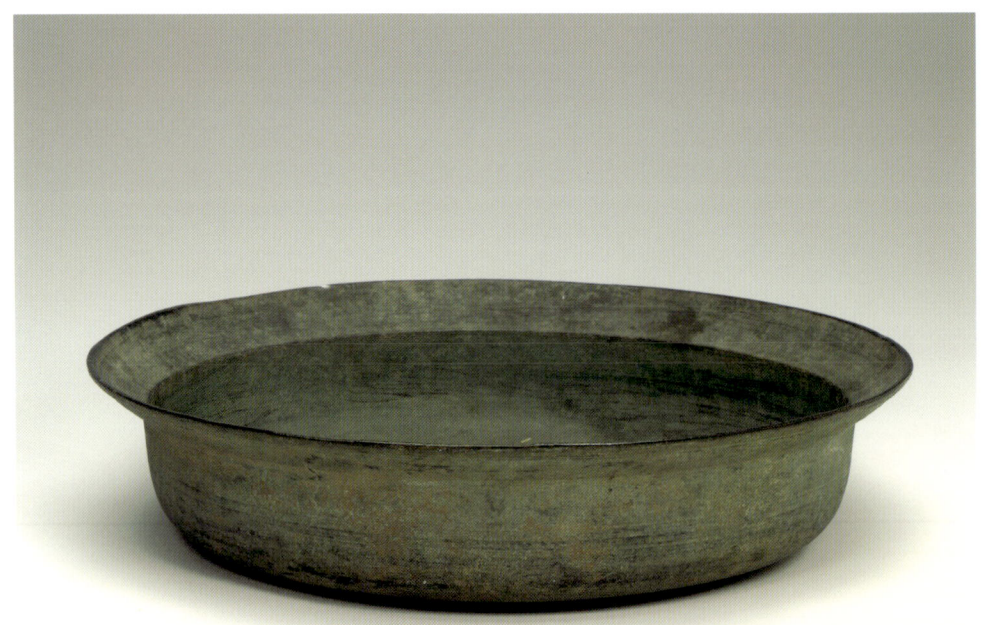

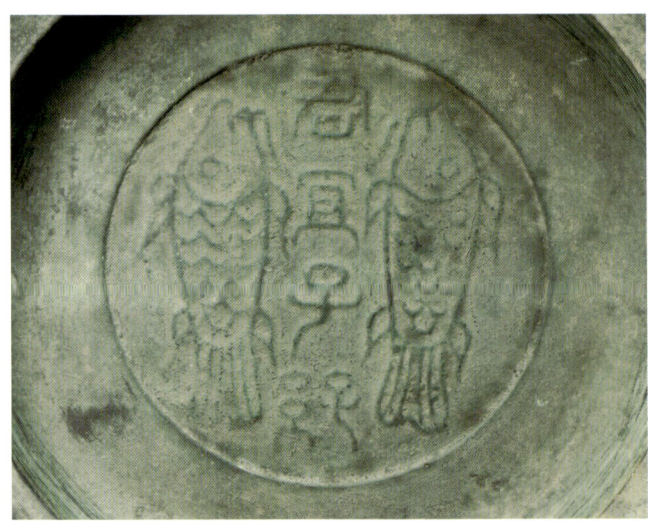

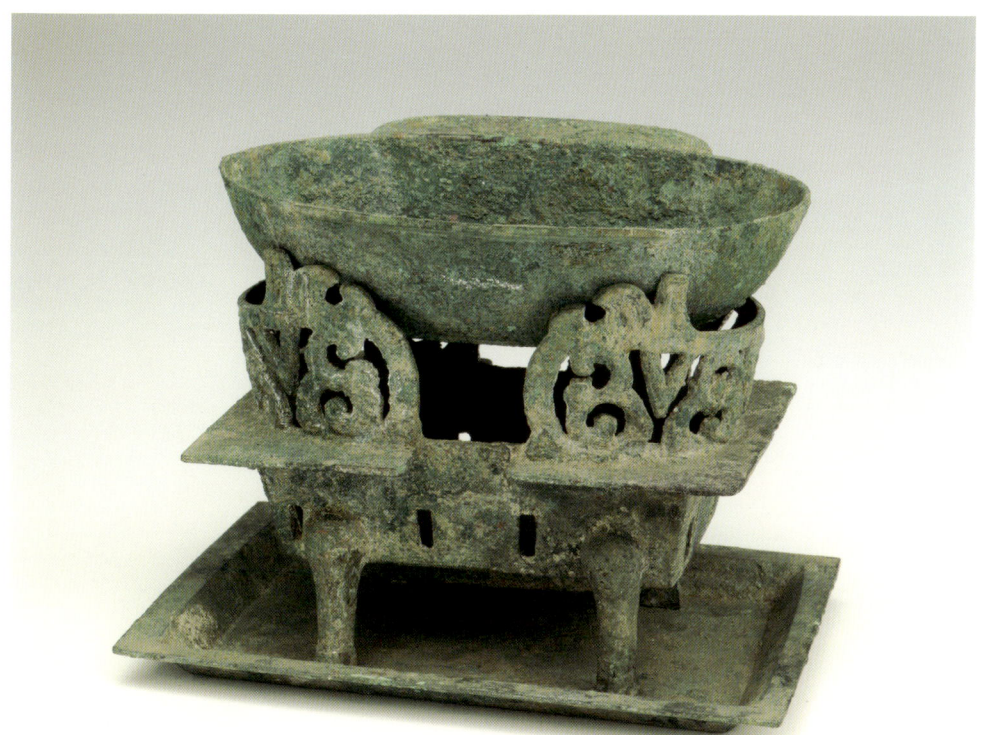

Brazier and bowl
Han dynasty (206 BCE–220 CE)
Unearthed in 1956 at Houchuan,
Shanxian county, Henan province
Bronze
12.4 (h) x 13.3 (w) x 18.5 (l) cm
Collection of the National
Museum of China (K4698)

This bronze vessel comprises a brazier and a bowl. It is thought to have been used to heat ingredients for a hot-pot sauce. Each person would have had their own brazier and dipped meat into the warmed sauce.

The brazier is rectangular in shape and has four hoof-shaped feet which sit on and are attached to a shallow rectangular plate.

There are rectangular holes in the sides of the brazier and in the base, to allow for the circulation of air and also to attach a handle so that the vessel could be moved when hot. The upper section of the brazier was made using an openwork technique and functions as a support for the bowl.

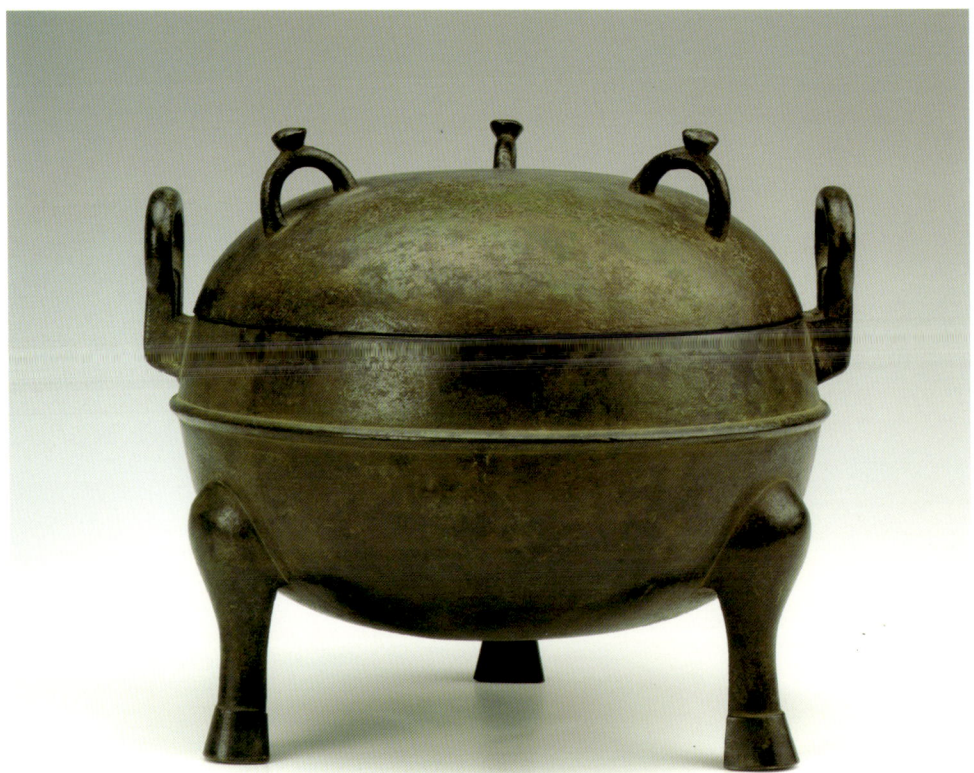

Covered vessel
*Western Han dynasty
(206 BCE–8 CE), dated 23 BCE*
Unearthed in Jinan,
Shandong province
Bronze
22.5 (h) x 20 (mouth diam) cm
Collection of the National
Museum of China (Lubo15)

This ancient Chinese vessel known as a *ding* was either a practical or sacrificial cooking vessel. In style, it is typical of *ding* made from the time of the Warring States period to the Western Han dynasty. The cover, with three ring handles, has been designed to fit tightly on to the body; when removed and upturned, the handles served as feet. The three feet of the body resemble animal legs and allowed the vessel to be heated from below. There are two large rounded carrying handles at each side.

The body and lid of the vessel each bear an inscription. The inscription on the body reads: 'Shanglin bronze *ding* weighing 16.6 *jin* with a capacity of 2 *sheng*, made by Li Jun in the 3rd month of the 2nd year of the Yangshuo reign [23 BCE], number 298 of 500 vessels'. The inscription on the lid reads simply: 'Shanglin number 16'. Shanglin refers to the Shanglin Park, first established during the Qin dynasty and then later extended by Emperor Han Wudi of the Western Han dynasty. The site of this imperial garden, located on the outskirts of Xi'an in Shaanxi province, had a circumfence of 340 *li* [1 *li* equals 500 metres] and grounds containing palaces, parklands and landscaped gardens. This vessel was especially made for use in the palace compound attached to the Shanglin imperial park.

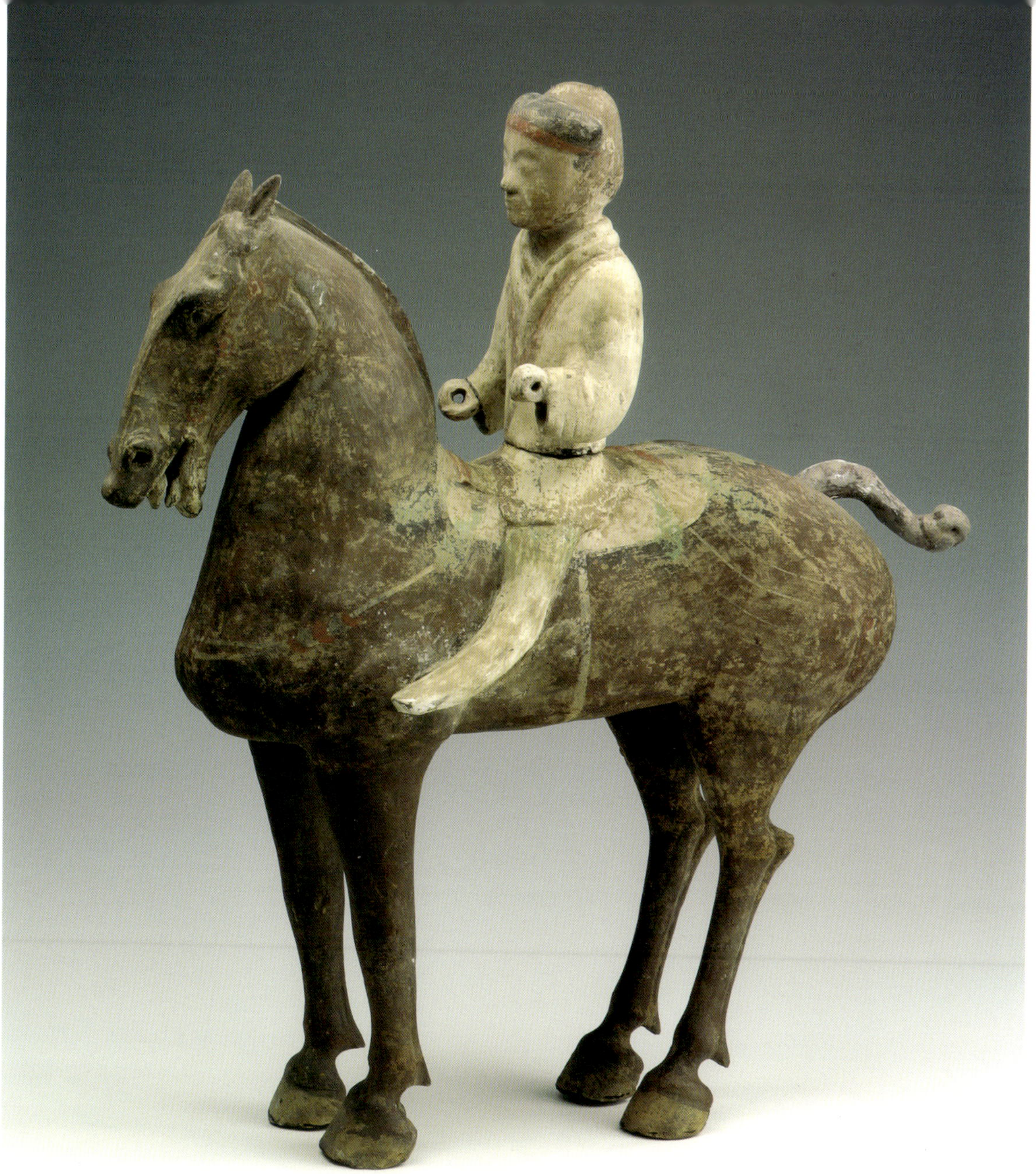

Cavalry officer on horseback
Western Han dynasty (206 BCE–8CE)
Unearthed in 1965 at Yangjiawan, Xianyang, Shaanxi province
Earthenware with pigments
67.7 (h) x 61 (l) cm
Collection of the National Museum of China (Jie 1397)

This mounted cavalry officer is made from grey pottery and has been painted to appear more life-like. The officer wears an ethnic Han Chinese garment that crosses and fastens to the right. The weapon he would have held has perished. The sturdy horse stands erect with its eyes wide open, and its ears pricked and alert.

This figurine is part of a cavalry procession comprising 3000 pottery warriors and horses excavated in 1965 from a sacrificial pit of Changling, the mausoleum of Emperor Jingdi (reigned 156 BCE-141BCE) of the Han dynasty, in Yangjiawan, Xianyang, Shaanxi province. The excavation of these warriors and horses has provided important information for research into equestrian culture, weaponry and sculpture of the Han dynasty.

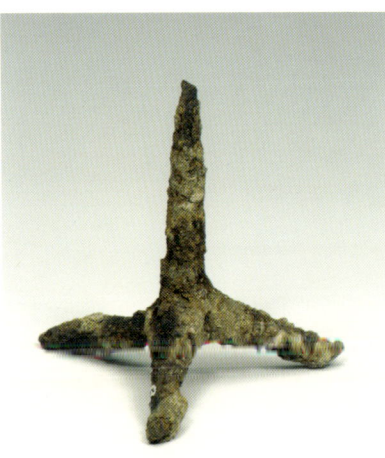

Caltrop
Han dynasty (206 BCE–220 CE)
Iron
6.5 (h) cm
Collection of the National
Museum of China (C6.218)

This corroded iron spiked
obstacle is named *jili*
after the puncture vine
(*Tribulus terrestris*), which
it resembles in shape.
Soldiers often strung
together large numbers
of these objects and placed
them on the ground across
a road or in front of a wall
to form a hazard to delay the
advance of enemy cavalry.

Spearhead with hook
Han dynasty (206 BCE–220 CE)
Bronze
37.9 (l) cm
Collection of the National
Museum of China (C5.1475)

This spearhead with hook
was originally attached to
a long pole and used as a
thrusting weapon to spear
and lacerate the enemy.
The blade is wide and flat
and has a raised central
ridge and a rounded tip.
A hook, at the connecting
point of the blade and collar
that holds the shaft, may
have been used to catch and
hold enemy soldiers or force
them to dismount.

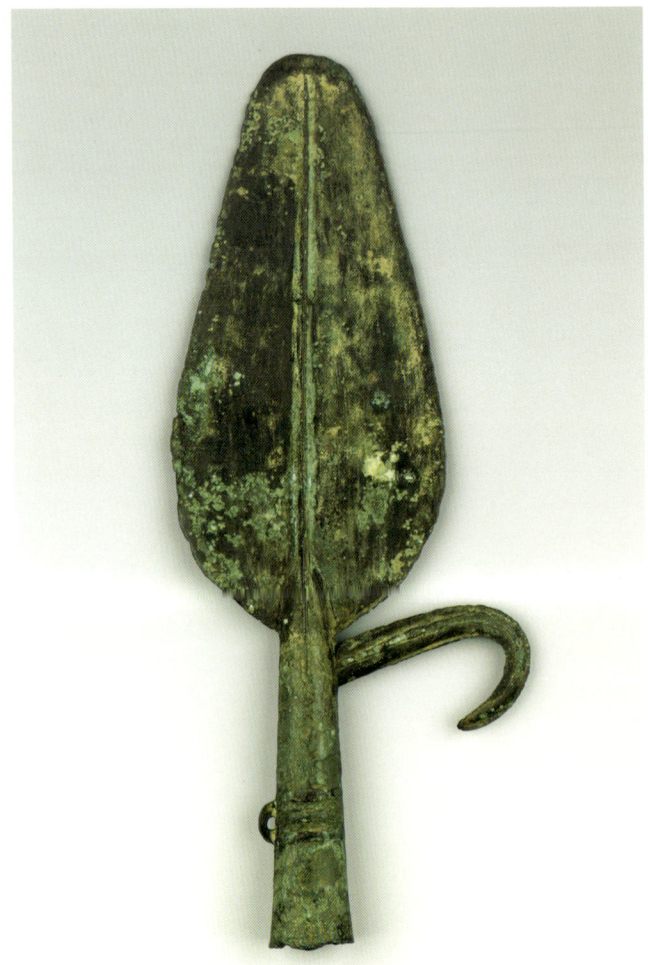

Crossbow mechanism
Western Han dynasty
(206 BCE–8 CE)
Excavated in 1978–80 from the
mausoleum site of the King of Qi,
Zibo, Shandong province
Bronze with gilding
16.6 (w) x 15 (l) cm
Collection of the National
Museum of China (K10063)

This gilded crossbow mechanism is beautifully crafted. Each of the components demonstrate the design and technical refinements that allowed standardisation of the process of manufacture. Despite having been buried for more than 2000 years, the gilding on the mechanism is well preserved.

The crossbow mechanism comprises four parts: the housing of the mechanism (*guo*), the hook (*ya*), sights (*wangshan*) and trigger (*xuandao*). The body is shaped like a rectangular box which is narrow in the front and wide at the back, with a groove on the upper surface to hold the shaft of the bolt. The hook catches are positioned on both sides of the arrow groove, and behind the left hook catch is the sights, which functioned as an aiming system. The trigger, located under the body, is rectangular in shape and bears the following inscription engraved on one side: 'Made by ☐ craftsman He'.

This object was excavated from a sacrificial pit belonging to the mausoleum site of the King of Qi in Zibo, Shandong province, dating from the Western Han dynasty. Its component parts are similar to those of earlier crossbows from the Warring States period and the Qin dynasty, but differs in the addition of the outer housing or casing (*guo*), a taller sights and a longer trigger. The introduction of the casing increased the force and effectiveness of the crossbow, and the improved sights and trigger allowed increases to the pull on the bowstring, as well as to the shooting range and accuracy of the weapon. This crossbow mechanism offers important physical evidence for research on the evolution of crossbow design and the effectiveness of weaponry.

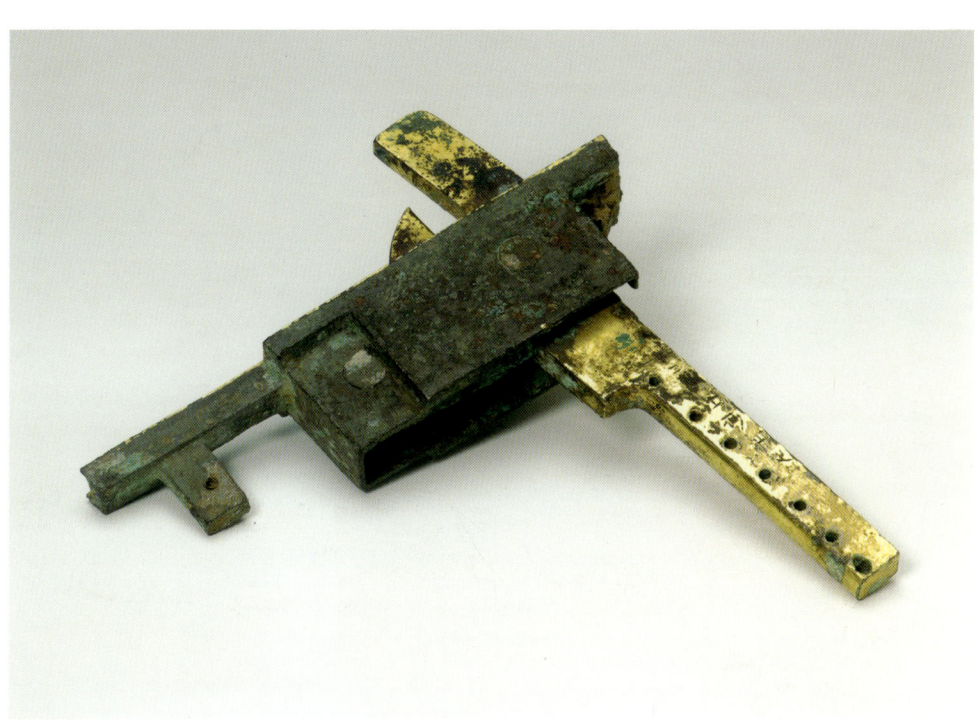

Dagger
Han dynasty (206 BCE–220 CE)
Bronze
27 (l) cm
Collection of the National
Museum of China (C5.3326)

This dagger is like a short sword and was used to kill or wound the enemy from close range. The design and construction suggest that it was made and used by northern nomadic fighters. The dagger blade is flat, with sharp edges, a rounded tip and raised central ridges on each face. The handle is decorated on one side with a pattern of connected lozenges; on the reverse side there is a slit where the metal has been folded over but not joined. The end of the handle has been shaped to form the head of a bird with a large eye and openwork beak.

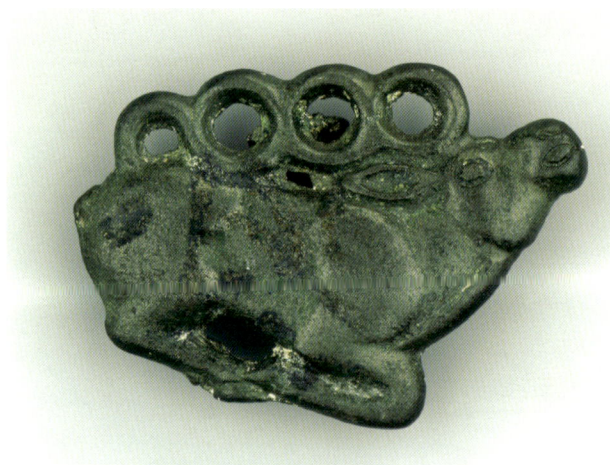

Ornament
Western Han dynasty (206 BCE-8 CE)
Unearthed at Ih Ju League, Inner Mongolia
Bronze
6 (l) cm
Collection of the National Museum of China (Mengbo 91)

This ornament takes the shape of a kneeling deer with its head raised and mouth open. The animal's antlers have been stylised and form four circles to create a pleasing design that is typical of the northern steppe or 'Ordos style'.

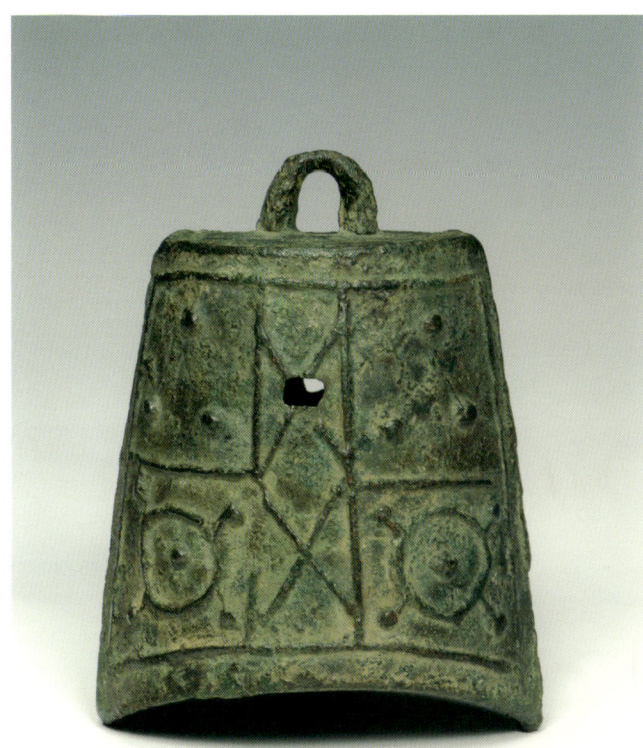

Bell
*Western Han dynasty
(206 BCE–8 CE)*
Unearthed in 1956 at Erlanhugou,
Qahar Barun Garan Hoit Banner,
Inner Mongolia
Bronze
11 (h) cm
Collection of the National
Museum of China (Mengbo 15)

When this bronze bell was
unearthed, it was discovered
with carriage ornaments.
It therefore probably formed
part of the ornamentation
of a carriage. Known as a
bell of the *yong* type, its
solid walls, ovoid shape and
loop make it a rare example.

Belt-hook
*Western Han dynasty
(206 BCE–8 CE)*
Unearthed in 1950 at Wa'ertugou,
Zhungar Banner, Ih Ju League,
Inner Mongolia
Bronze
3 (w) x 5.2 (l) cm
Collection of the National
Museum of China (Mengbo 18)

Belt-hooks like this were
attached to a leather strap
and used to secure garments
around the waist. A raised
bronze knob on the back
of the piece served to secure
it to the leather strap, which
was then fastened around
the waist with a hook
or loop attached to the
other end of the strap.

The belt-hook was
developed as a fastening
mechanism by northern
nomadic and pastoral
peoples, and reflected
the requirement that their
clothing facilitated horse
riding and herding.

Belt-hooks were made
in a wide variety of shapes
and from different
materials, most often
bronze. This belt-hook
depicts a galloping
Xiongnu horseman
and is extremely animated,
despite its small scale.
The design is clever,
and the flowing tail
of the horse doubles
as the belt-hook.

The Xiongnu were an
ancient nomadic and
pastoral people who lived
on the Eurasian steppe
for more than 2000 years.
For a time, they established
an empire that extended
to the Yinshan Mountains
in the south, Lake Baikal
in the north, the Liaohe
River in the east and
beyond the Pamirs to the
west, embracing today's
northern China, Mongolia,
southern Siberia and much
of Kazakhstan.

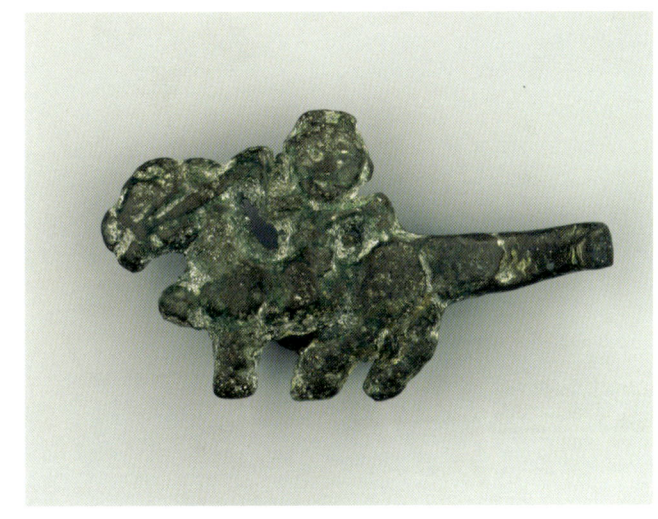

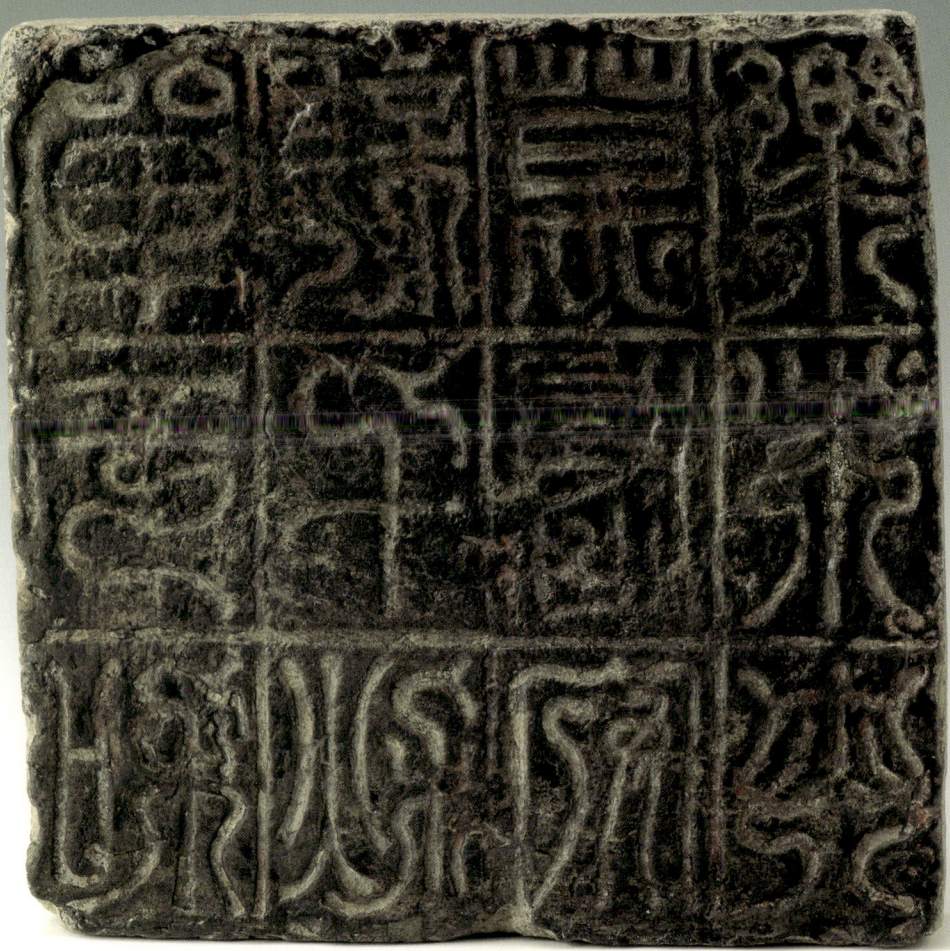

Mould
Western Han dynasty
(206 BCE–8 CE)
Unearthed at Hohhot, Inner Mongolia
Earthenware
30.2 (w) x 30.2 (l) x 5 (d) cm
Collection of the National
Museum of China (Y443)

This unusual square mould is marked up to form a twelve-section grid, with each rectangular section containing a carved Chinese character. The characters are read from top to bottom, beginning in the upper left corner, and may be translated as: 'The *shanyu* obtained peace through diplomatic marriage; may he live forever; may peace and happiness reign' (*Shanyu heqin, qianqiu wansui, anle wei yang*)

The inscription refers to the Han dynasty's diplomatic policy of alliances effected through marriages of Xiongnu *shanyu* or kings with Han Chinese women in order to achieve peace between the two ethnic groups. The inscription is written in seal script, which characterises official orthography dating from the Han dynasty.

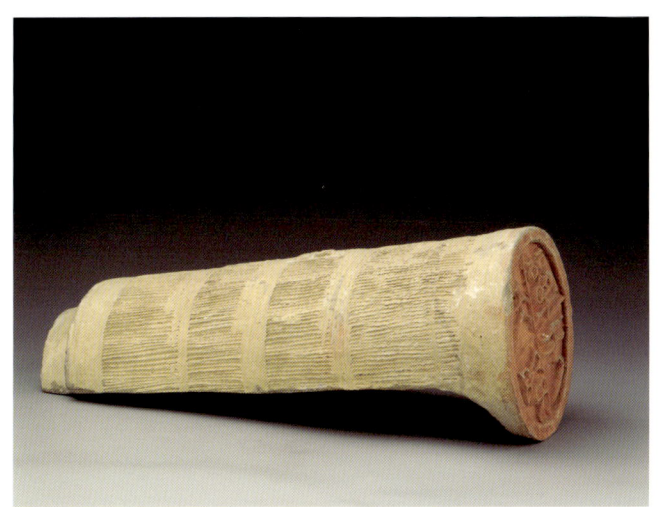

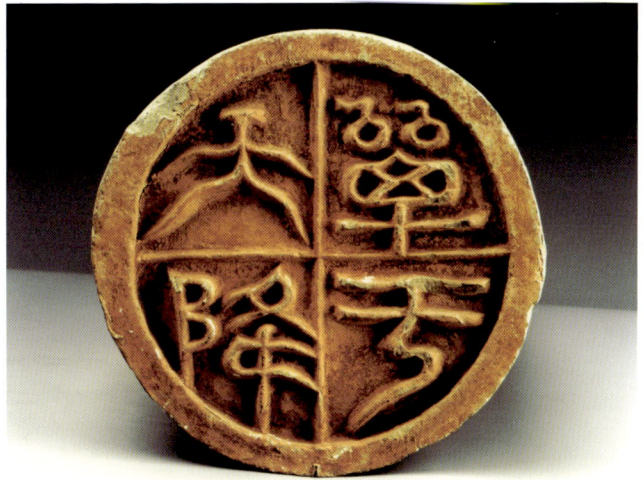

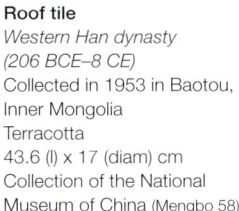

Roof tile
Western Han dynasty
(206 BCE–8 CE)
Collected in 1953 in Baotou,
Inner Mongolia
Terracotta
43.6 (l) x 17 (diam) cm
Collection of the National
Museum of China (Mengbo 58)

The end of this roof tile is decorated with four Chinese characters placed in each of four equal quadrants. The inscription reads: '*Shanyu* descends from heaven' (*Shanyu tian jiang*). *Shanyu* was the title of the king or *khan* of the Xiongnu people, and this tile attests to the power and influence of the Xiongnu at that time. The Chinese characters are written in a transitional style of calligraphy between seal script and clerical script. This tile-end is the same size and style as those used in the Central Plains region. It was possibly used in a residence built for one of the Xiongnu rulers during the Han dynasty.

*Zhaojun travels beyond
the Wall*, **handscroll**
Qing dynasty (1644–1911)
Ink and colour on paper
30 (h) x 629 (l) cm
Collection of the National
Museum of China (14.2594)

Detail opposite
Full handscroll following pages

The handscroll depicts the Chinese court beauty Wang Zhaojun and the king, or *shanyu*, of the Xiongnu, Huhanye, with their retinues on a hunting expedition beyond the Great Wall. The painting is known in Chinese as 'Zhaojun travels beyond the Wall' (*Zhaojun chusai tu*). Wang Zhaojun, also known as Wang Qiang and referred to by later generations in China as Concubine Ming, was chosen to enter the palace as a concubine during the reign of Emperor Yuandi (reigned 48–33 BCE) of the Han dynasty.

It is said that, unable to attract the attention of the emperor, she volunteered to marry the Xiongnu king, thereby effecting a diplomatic marriage on behalf of the Chinese court. She met with the approval of Huhanye and in 33 BCE assumed the 'foreign' surname of Hu'e. As part of a diplomatic effort to improve relations with the Xiongnu, Wang Zhaojun is said to have followed the Chinese emperor's orders to observe their customs after her marriage. The story of the self-sacrificing Wang Zhaojun has been told and re-told over the centuries. Many romantic poems, dramas and paintings have been created depicting various interpretations of her story.

The first known painting of Wang Zhaojun was by Yan Liben (c 600–73) of the Tang dynasty. The earliest extant painting is by Gong Suran, a female Daoist painter of the Southern Song dynasty (1127–1279). Many paintings of Wang Zhaojun were made during the Yuan, Ming and Qing dynasties.

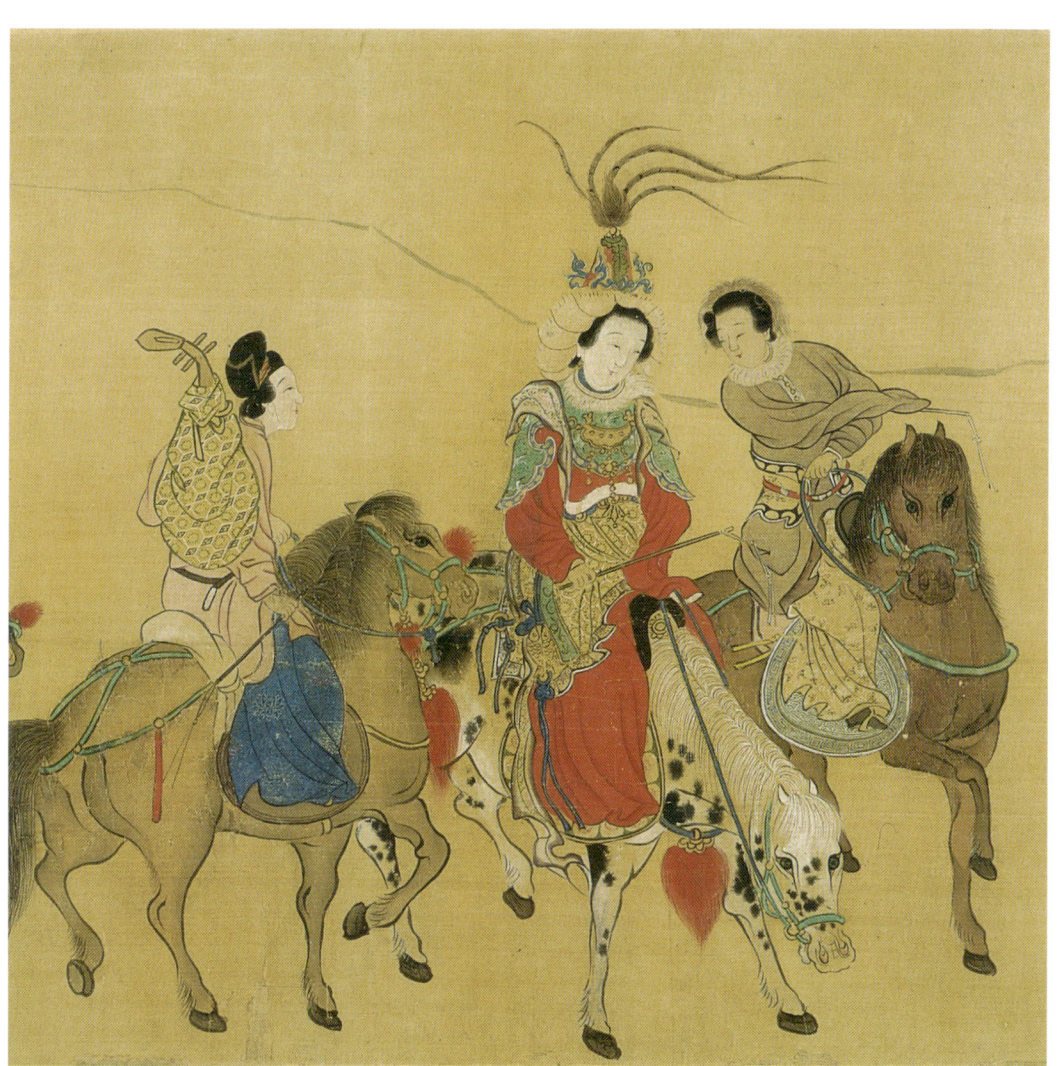

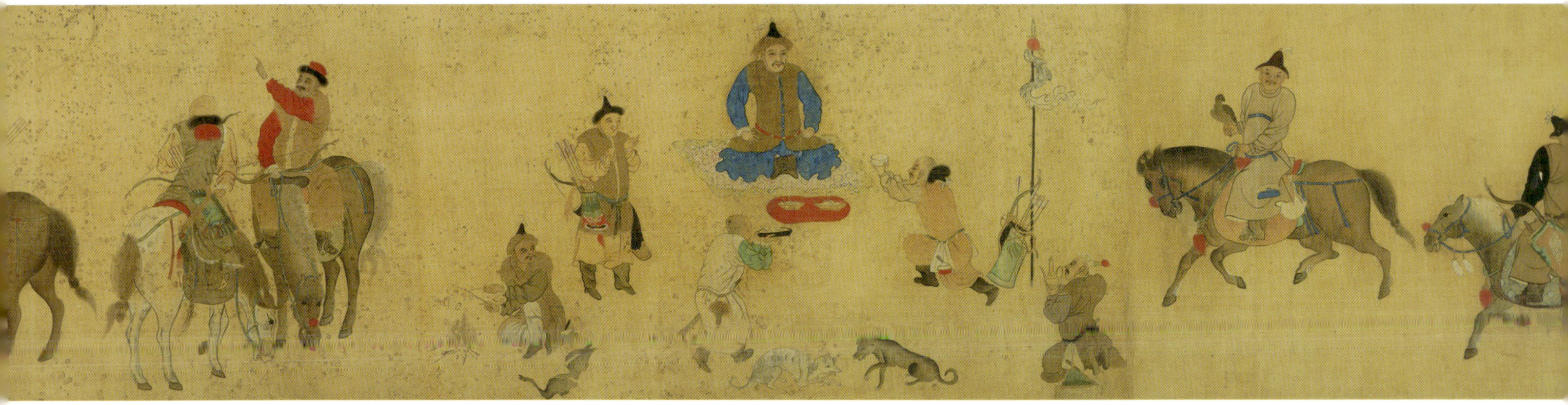

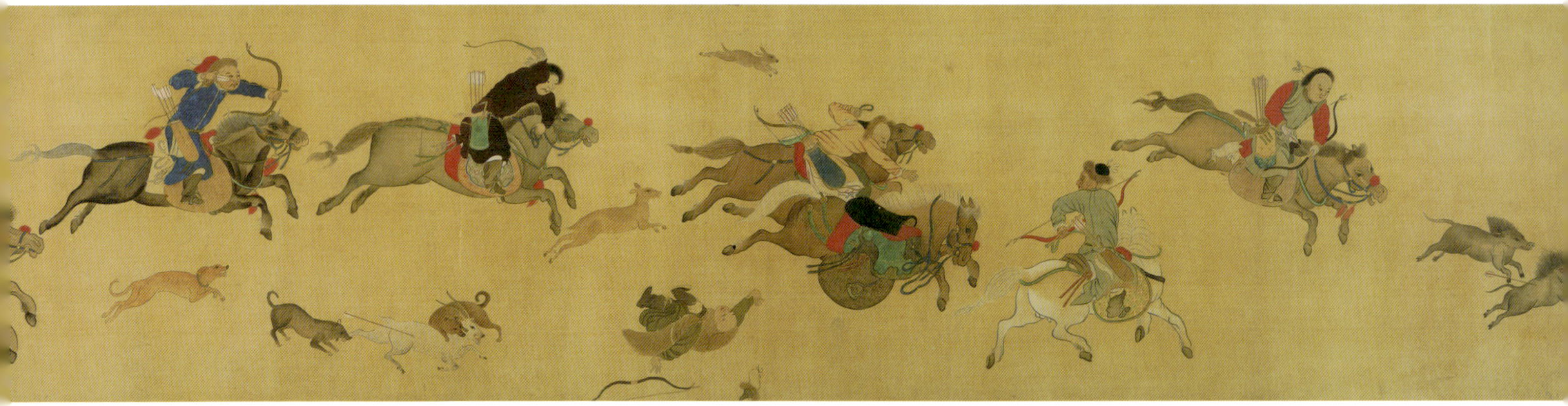

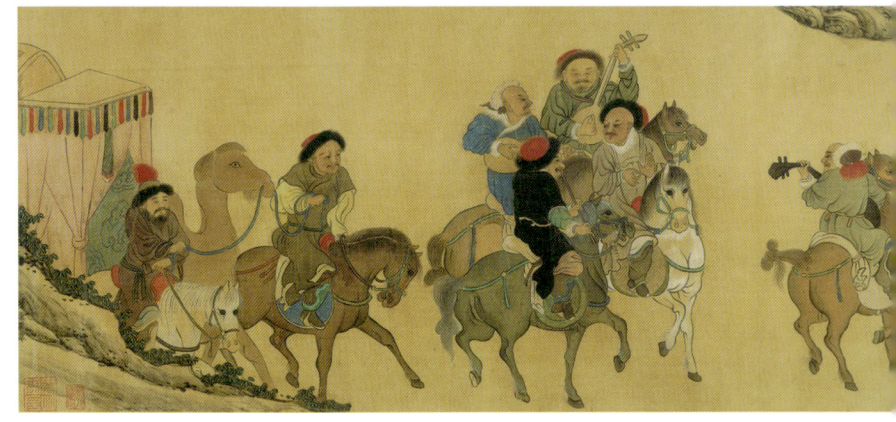

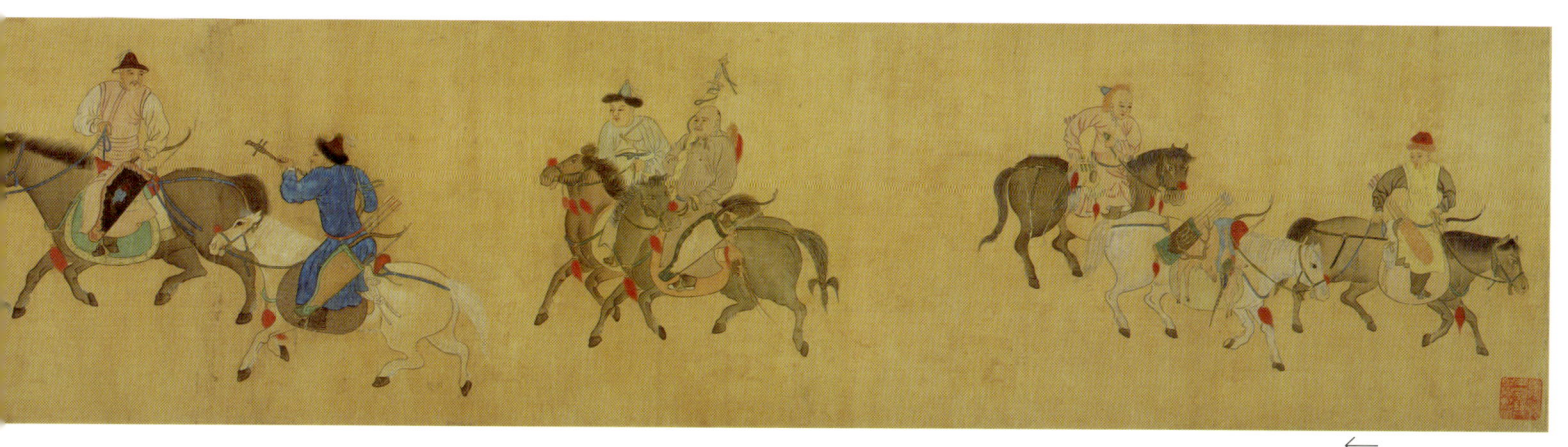

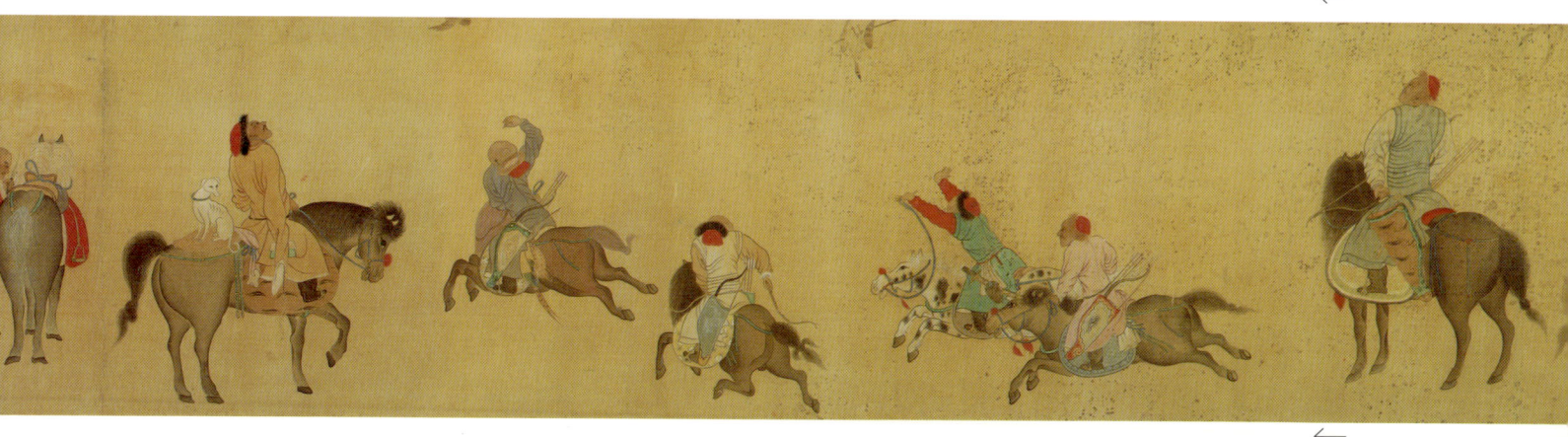

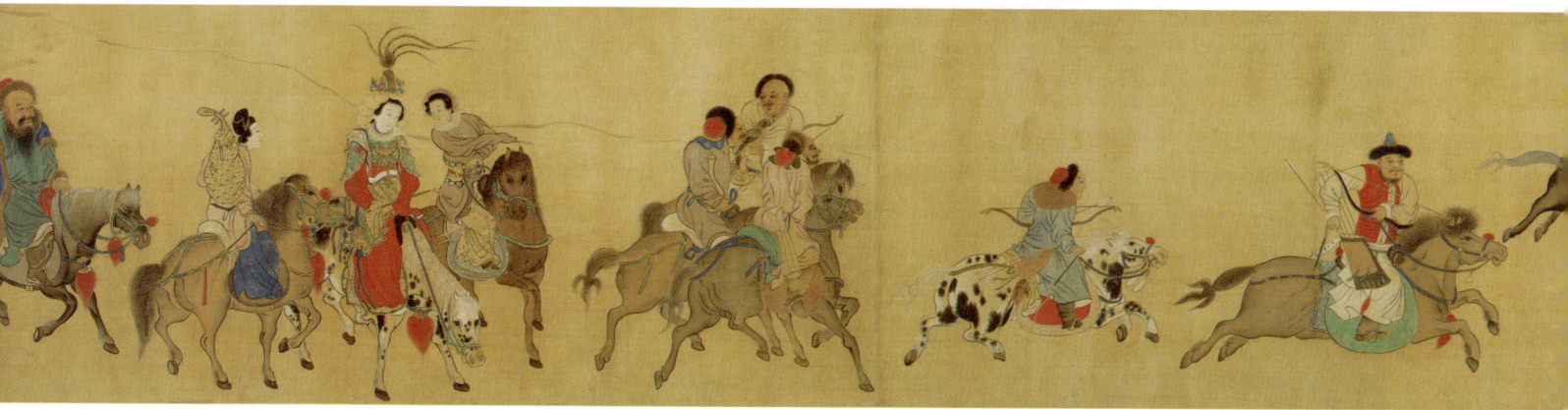

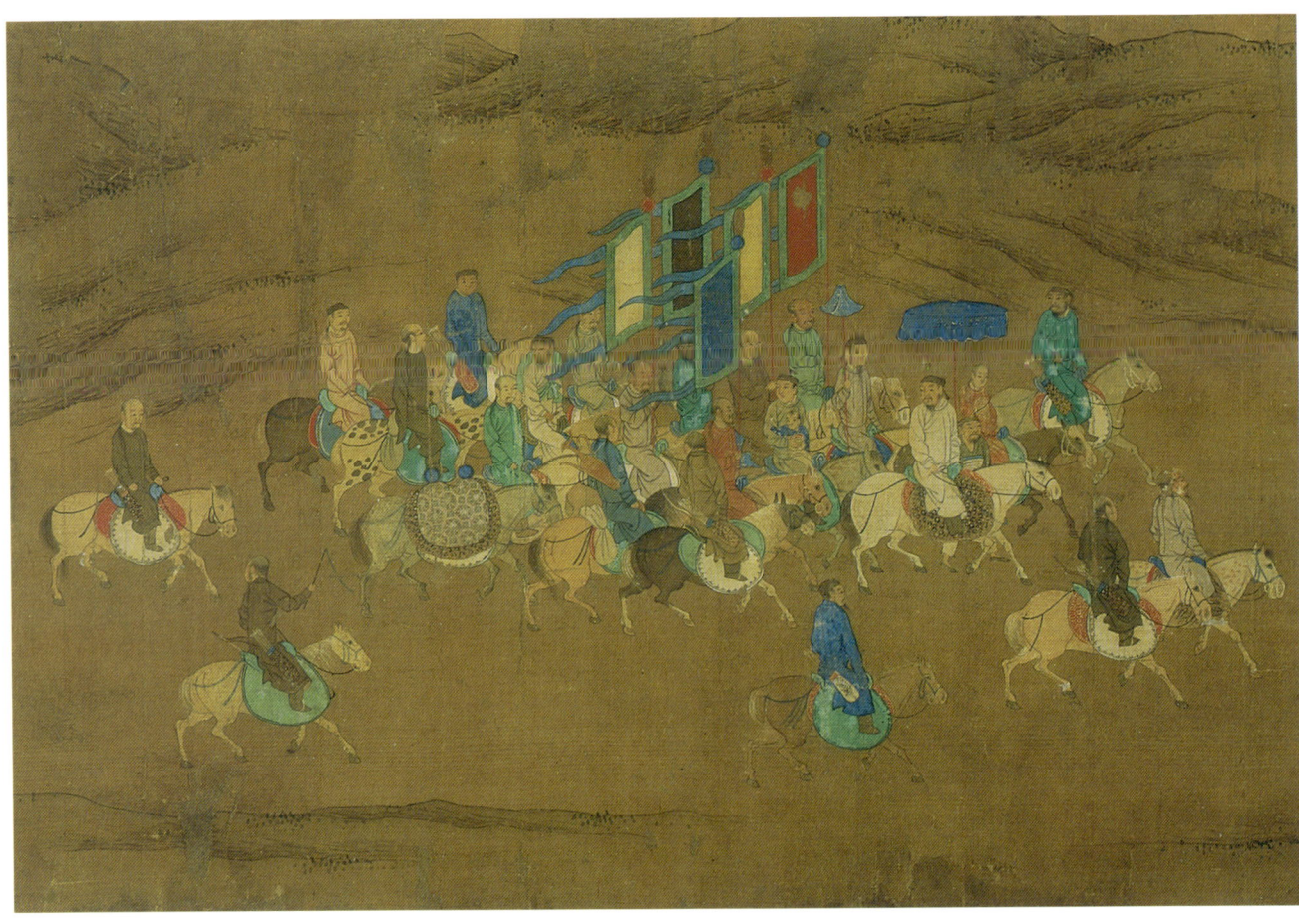

Concubine Wen's return,
handscroll
Ming dynasty (1368–1644)
Ink and colour on silk
32.2 (h) x 245 (l) cm
Collection of the National
Museum of China (14.2595)

This handscroll comprises three sections and depicts the story of Cai Yan, better known as Cai Wenji, an ethnic Han female writer, who during the Eastern Han dynasty was married to King Zuoxian of the Xiongnu. The painting known as Concubine Wen's return (*Wenji gui Han tu*) depicts her return to Chinese territory. Cai Wenji, the daughter of the talented scholar Cai Yong, was a poet to whom the musical masterpiece, 'Eighteen passages for northern music' (*Hujia shiba pai*) is ascribed. Cai Wenji lived in the southern lands of the Xiongnu for twelve years and bore the king two sons. The paintings depict the preparations for Cai Wenji's departure, capturing her reluctance to leave King Zuoxian, their children and attendants.

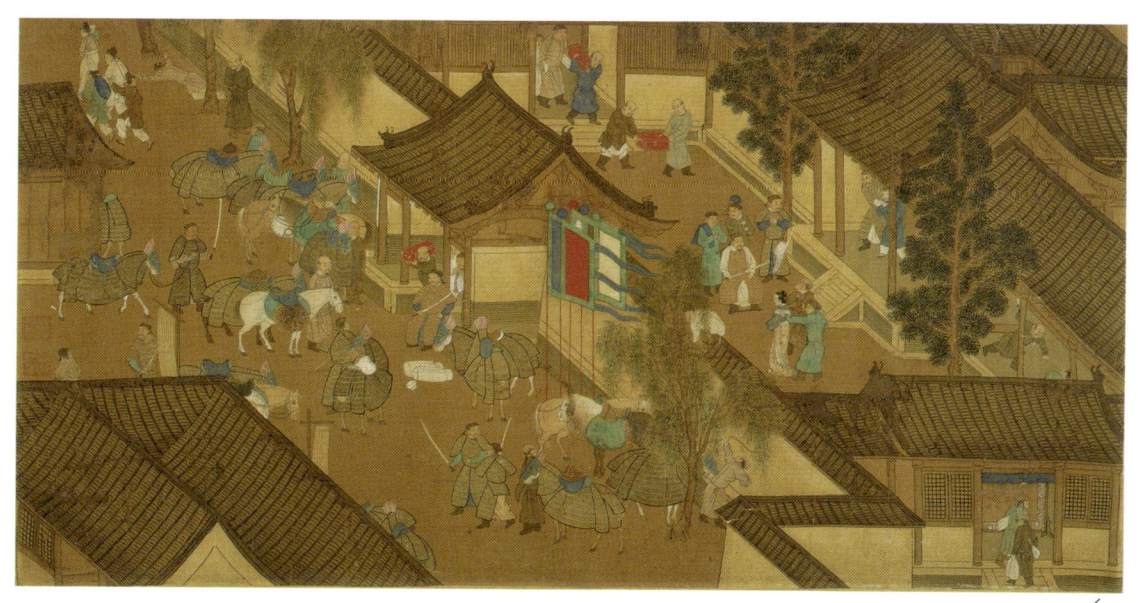

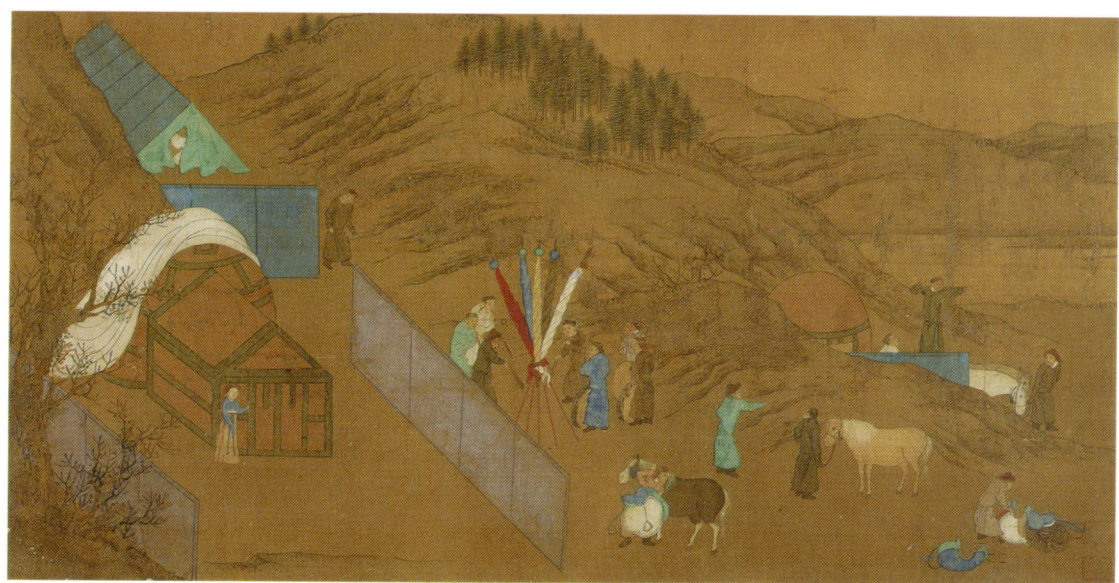

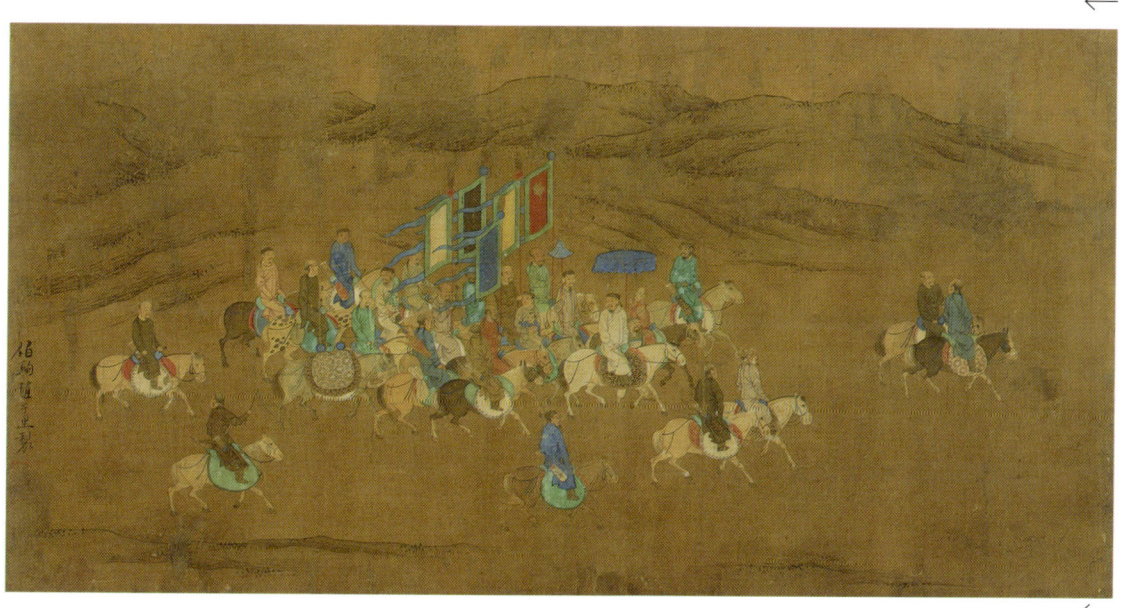

Silk fragment
Western Liang dynasty (400–21)
Unearthed in 1967 at the
Astana cemetery, Turfan,
Xinjiang autonomous region
Silk, plain weave, red ground
with resist pattern
6.6 (w) x 5.7 (l) cm
Collection of the National
Museum of China (K10296)

This silk textile fragment was excavated from the Astana cemetery outside Turfan in Xinjiang. It is a fine plain-weave silk with a pattern of white lozenges set against a deep red ground. The pattern has been created using a method of resist or tie-dyeing (known as *cuojie*, *cuohua*, *or cuoyunjie* in Chinese), one of the early forms of textile patterning.

During the reign of Emperor Han Wudi (reigned 140–87 BCE) of the Han dynasty, Zhang Qian (?–114 BCE) was sent as an envoy to the Western Region on two occasions to gather information about natural conditions, social customs, products and the methods of transportation used in the various kingdoms. Zhang Qian's missions mark the beginning of officially recorded cultural and economic exchanges between China and the lands to the west. Despite the wars and chaos associated with the final years of the Eastern Han dynasty, the Silk Road trade routes were kept open.

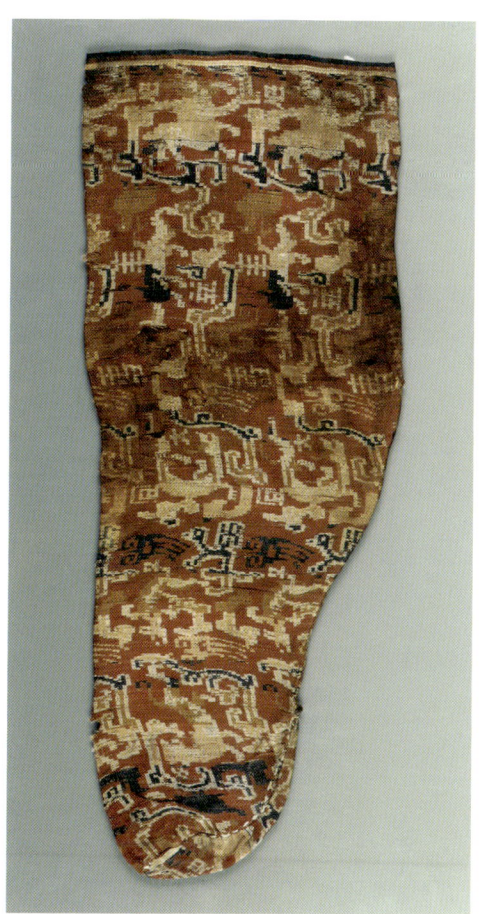
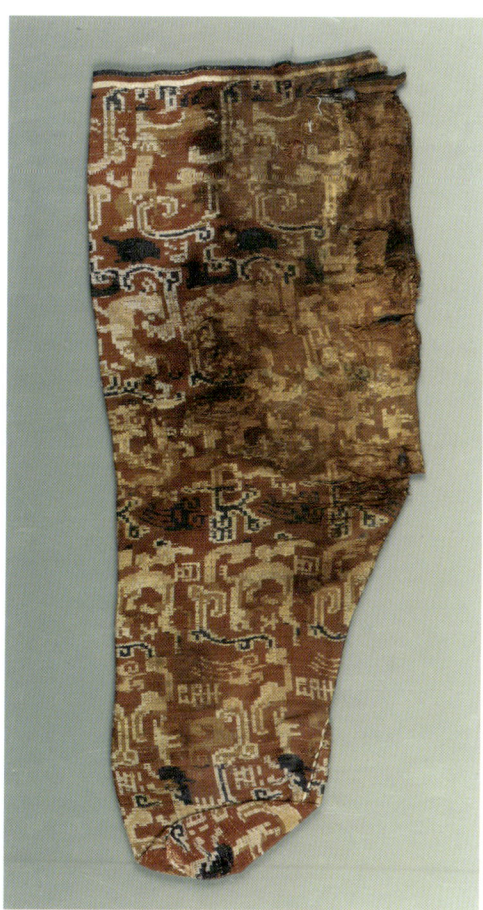

Pair of socks

Han dynasty (206 BCE–220 CE)
Excavated in 1959 at Niya,
Minfeng county, Xinjiang
autonomous region
Silk, warp-faced compound
plain weave
43.5 (h) x 17.3 (w) cm
Collection of the National
Museum of China (Y764)

This pair of silk socks was made using warp-faced compound plain weave. The design, made from silks dyed in five different colours, incorporates birds, animals and the Chinese characters meaning 'May your years be prolonged, may you be favoured with many sons and grandsons' (*Yan nian yi shou da yi zi xun*) written in clerical script.

During the Warring States period (475–221 BCE), the technique of warp-patterning improved, but the designs were rather stiff. By the Western Han dynasty (206 BCE–8 CE), designers sought to move beyond these technical limitations and express curves. Subjects became more compelling and included legendary animals and mystic landscapes. Chinese characters were sometimes incorporated in the ground weave to convey auspicious sentiments.

In the *Book of Odes* (Shi jing), the compilation of which is traditionally attributed to Confucius, woven garments using warp-faced compound plain weave (*jin*) were referred to as equal in status to coats made from rare furs because of their sophistication and beauty.

In 138 BCE, Emperor Han Wudi of the Western Han dynasty dispatched Zhang Qian as an envoy to the Western Region to open up trading routes from the capital in Chang'an (present day Xi'an) through Gansu and Xinjiang to Central Asia, Iran, India and Europe — one of the routes along which silk and other commodities were transported. In the late nineteenth century this led Baron Ferdinand von Richthofen to coin the term 'Silk Road', to describe the main conduits for economic and cultural exchange between China and the West.

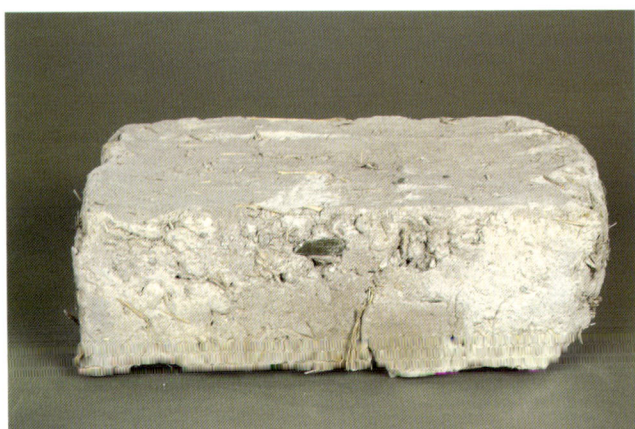

Adobe brick
Western Han dynasty
(206 BCE–8 CE)
From a beacon tower of the Han
dynasty Great Wall in the Xihu
(West Lake) area of Dunhuang,
Gansu province
Earth, grasses
17 (w) x 35 (l) x 12 (depth) cm
Collection of the Municipal
Museum of Dunhuang,
Gansu province (DB1910)

This type of adobe brick was
a major building material
for constructing beacon
platforms and towers in
some areas. It comprises
earth and gravel, mixed
with grasses or reeds. Water
was added to this mixture,
which was then shaped
in a mould and dried in
the sun. Remains of Han
dynasty beacon towers
indicate four different
methods of construction:
layers of pounded earth;
layers of earth and stones
mixed with branches
of Chinese tamarisk and
diversiform-leaved poplar,
with a layer of reeds every
20 to 30 centimetres;
alternating layers of cut
stone and reeds; and courses
of adobe brick with a thin
layer of reeds between every
four or so layers of adobe.

Frame for shooting arrows
Han dynasty, from the reign
of Han Wudi of the Western
Han to the early Eastern Han
dynasty (100 BCE–100CE)
Unearthed at the Jinguan
site of a military officer's
headquarters in Jianshui,
Ejina Banner, Inner Mongolia
Wood
41.8 (h) x 42.5 (w)
x 6.5 (central cylinder diam) cm
Collection of the Gansu Provincial
Research Institute of Archaeology
(74EPT34:02)

This timber device, called
a *muzhuanshe*, was built into
the parapet on the upper
part of defensive walls in
frontier areas during the
Han dynasty. The central
wooden cylinder with a
narrow rectangular window
could be rotated about a
vertical axis. The window
could be opened to allow
soldiers to observe and
shoot at enemies, or closed
to protect them from enemy
arrows. Many devices of this
type have been discovered
in frontier areas along the
Hexi Corridor, suggesting
that they were an important
element in the defensive
system of the Han dynasty
Great Walls.

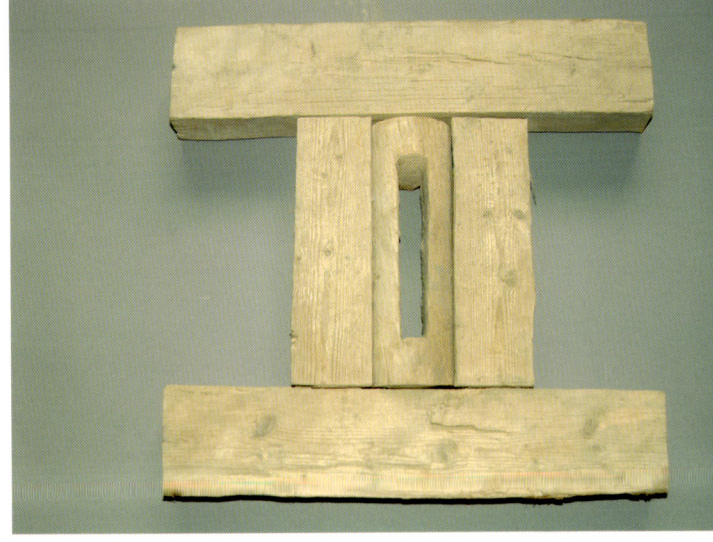

Travel permit
*Western Han dynasty
(206 BCE–25 CE)*
Unearthed in 1998 at Xiaofangpan,
Dunhuang, Gansu province in 1998
Wood
3.4 (w) x 9.2 (l) cm
Collection of the Municipal
Museum of Dunhuang,
Gansu province (DB2371)

This item permitted army personnel to access passes, roads, rivers and ferries. Made of wood, its length, size and shape were determined by the material used in its production, since there were no strict regulations governing the dimensions of permits. When personnel serving in the military wanted to travel on business or for private reasons, they were required to have a permit for identification. The receipt of such a permit or pass was called an 'issuance' (*fafu*) or 'grant' (*fengfu*) in formal documents. In addition, the round-trip time, and the times of departure and return were recorded in order to check that the permit-holder returned on schedule.

Such permits differed in type, according to the destinations, business and identities of the permit-holders. Ordinary military personnel, including their relatives, would use a common travel permit affording passage through passes, along roads or rivers and the use of fords and ferries, but military officers on government missions or those of high rank would be issued with special passes. People holding special permits would be cordially received, in terms of both catering and accommodation, and their luggage, carriages and horses would be attended to. In the military system of the Han dynasty, there were detailed rules and regulations that stipulated the procedures and authority for issuing such permits.

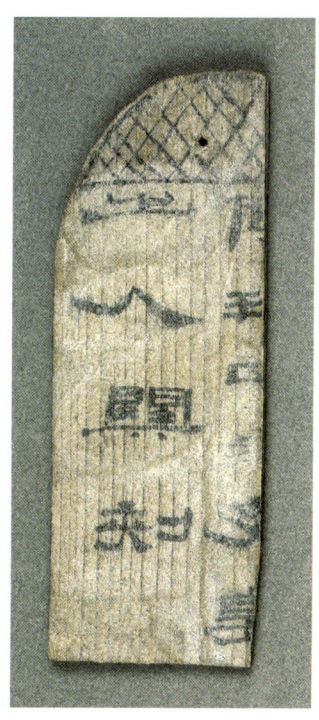

Inscribed slips
*Western Han dynasty
(206 BCE–8CE)*
Unearthed in 1998 at Xiaofangpan,
Dunhuang, Gansu province
Wood
0.9 (w) x 1. 23.2 (l) cm;
2.2 (w) x 2. 20.4 (l) cm
Collection of the Municipal
Museum of Dunhuang,
Gansu province (DB4959, DB4960)

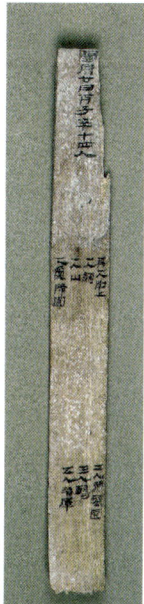
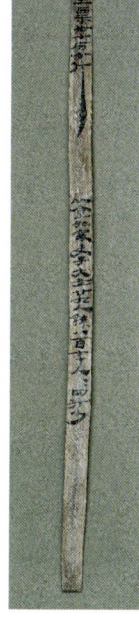

The inscriptions on these two wooden slips record events in the lives of soldiers and their families who lived in farming garrisons along the Great Wall. The inscription on one has been interpreted to mean: 'The issuing of 37 *dan* and 7 *sheng* of millet to twenty-nine sons and daughters of frontier officials. In total, 870 people were granted grain, almost 4 *sheng* per person.' The inscription on the other slip reads: 'Fourteen people died on the 20th day of the intercalary month in the *bingzi* year.'

The Han dynasty implemented a system of cultivating virgin lands along the Great Wall and troops were garrisoned to 'develop' them by farming. During the reign of Emperor Han Wudi, men aged between twenty-three and fifty-six had to serve in garrisons at the frontier for one year, to make up for the perceived shortage of personnel along the Great Wall lines in remote areas. The virgin lands cultivation system, established in the Han dynasty and perpetuated by subsequent dynasties, was a strategic measure designed to create self-supporting garrisons. The system in the Dunhuang area was described as a mixture of either cultivation and defence or farming and military training. Farmer-soldiers became an important component of the military system: soldiers doubled up as farmers who cultivated lands and paid rent. The implementation of the system dramatically strengthened the military forces available for defending the Great Walls and, at least partially, solved the problem of supplying the garrisons with grain.

Xiaofangpan, known as Yumenguan or Jade Gate Pass in the Han dynasty, was about 150 kilometres east of Lop Nur, located at the western end of the Hexi Corridor. It is said that Yumenguan acquired its name because it straddled the route along which jade from the Western Region was imported along the Silk Road trade routes to the Central Plains area. Jade Gate Pass was established in the sixth year of the Yuanding period (111 BCE) to the south of the Great Wall line. The outer city of Jade Gate Pass has vanished, but large numbers of inscribed slips have been recovered in excavations, providing valuable insights into the lives of the people who lived there in the Han dynasty.

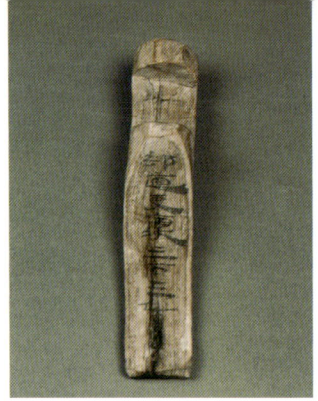
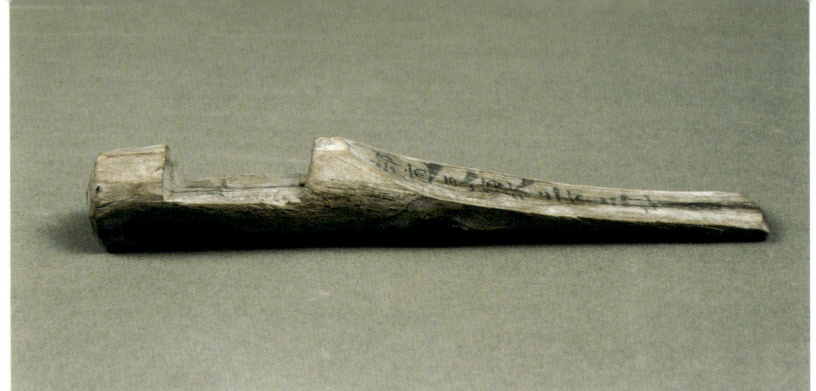

Document marker
Han dynasty (206 BCE–220 CE)
Unearthed in 1989 at a Han dynasty beacon tower at Houkeng, Dunhuang, Gansu province
Wood
2.3 (w) x 13 (l) x 11.8 (d) cm
Collection of the Municipal Museum of Dunhuang, Gansu province (DB0657)

This piece of timber, called a *jian*, was attached to a document or letter, and functioned like an envelope. The inscription indicates that the document to which it was attached was concerned with grain receipts: 'One official was distributed 3 *dan* and 2 *dou* of millet.'

In the Han dynasty, there was a large variety of documents, which could generally be divided into those issued by central and local government authorities. For the purposes of document delivery, the senders would write the destinations, types and numbers of documents on the *jian*. The organisation responsible for delivering

the documents would note down their times of receipt and despatch, as well as their points of origin and destinations. Such documents provide valuable evidence for the study of the postal and document recording systems of the Han dynasty.

Permit
Western Han dynasty (206 BCE–8 CE)
Unearthed at a Han dynasty beacon tower at Qingshuigou, Dunhuang, Gansu province
Wood
1.8–1.5 (w) x 15.1 (l) x 0.6 (d) cm
Collection of the Municipal Museum of Dunhuang, Gansu province (DB4958)

This object, known as a *bujingfu*, was a type of permit authorising soldiers and officers in beacon towers to light a beacon fire warning of an enemy attack. Beacon fires were an important military warning and communications system in ancient China. Lines of beacon platforms and towers were commonly built along frontiers, strategic passes and roads. In the Han dynasty the beacon fire system for relaying signals from tower to tower was highly developed. Tablets excavated from the Majuanwan site in

Dunhuang provide evidence of the comprehensive nature of the military defence facilities in Dunhuang in the Western Han dynasty.

The lighting, signalling and burning times of beacon fires were recorded for checking later. The system of signals between beacon towers included the use of fire with signals (*feng*), the use of marker-posts (*biao*), smoke signals (*yan*), firebrands or torches (*juhuo*) and the firing of stacks of combustible vegetation (*jixin*). The first three types of signals were used in the daytime. A torch was used for issuing warning signals at night, while the burning of firewood and other dried vegetation could be carried out both in the daytime and at night. To ensure the strict execution of signalling procedures,

a set of regulations was formulated by the frontier defenders of the Han dynasty and promulgated at the levels of the central government, prefectures and regional commanderies (*buduwei*). The *Record of beacon fire on the frontiers* (Saishang fenghuo pinyue) states: 'One stack of combustible vegetation, two beacon fires and two torches should be lit when more than one enemy crosses our border [at night]; one stack of combustible vegetation, three beacon fires, and three torches should be lit when more than 500, but less than 1000, enemies assault our tower [at night]; two stacks of combustible vegetation, three fires, and three torches [at night] should be lit when more than 1000 enemies cross our border.'

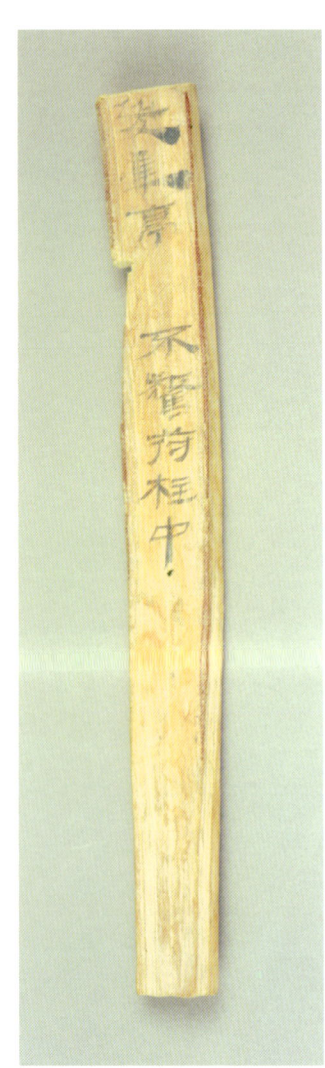

Inscribed slips

*Han dynasty, from the end
of the Zhaoxuan reign of the
Western Han to the Zhanghe
reign of the Eastern Han,
86 BCE–105 CE*
Unearthed at the Jiaquhouguan
site in the Han dynasty Juyan
protectorate, Ejina Banner,
Inner Mongolia
Wood
1.5 (w) x 39 (l) x 0.2 (d) cm
Collection of the Gansu
Provincial Research Institute of
Archaeology (EPF16:5; EPF16:16)

Emperor Han Wudi of the
Han dynasty ordered the
construction of the western
extension of the Great Wall
in the Hexi Corridor, from
Lingju (today's Yongdeng,
Gansu province) to Yanze
(Lop Nur), and dispatched
garrisons to the region.
These military forces
included officers designated
military officers below
general (*duwei*), watch
tower officers (*houguan*),
team leaders of the watch
towers (*houzhang*) and
directors of watch towers
(*suizhang*), together with
large numbers of soldiers.
The many inscribed slips
unearthed at beacon towers
and forts in Gansu vividly
record events from this
time. Beacon towers were
constructed at intervals of
approximately 2 kilometres,
and they were connected by
fortified walls in most areas.
Additionally, there were
forts, watch towers and
other defensive structures.

The *Record of beacon fire
on the frontiers* contains
specific instructions
regarding the circumstances
in which signals should be
sent; the two slips illustrated
here record some of these.
The first slip describes the
different signals to be sent
in accordance with the
different times and locations
in which enemy forces made
their appearance, as well
as detailing how other
troops at the frontier should
respond to different signals.
The slip reads: 'If the enemy
attacks the eastern side of
Houyuan beacon tower at
Sanshijing during the
daytime, a signal fire shall
be lit, as well as a timber
stack, and smoke signals
released above the watch
tower; at night, firewood
shall be lit, and a torch shall
be held on the watch tower
until next morning.'
The second slip reads:
'Information must be
transmitted quickly in
the form of an official call
to arms by infantrymen,
and by swift cavalry
if it is windy or raining,
and smoke and fire cannot
be released if the Xiongnu
have penetrated the walls.'
In the nearly two centuries
from 86 BCE to 105
CE, it is said that beacon
fires were continuously lit.

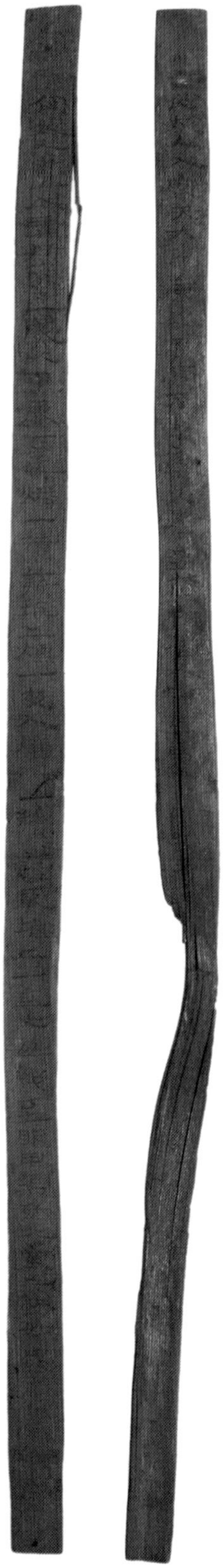

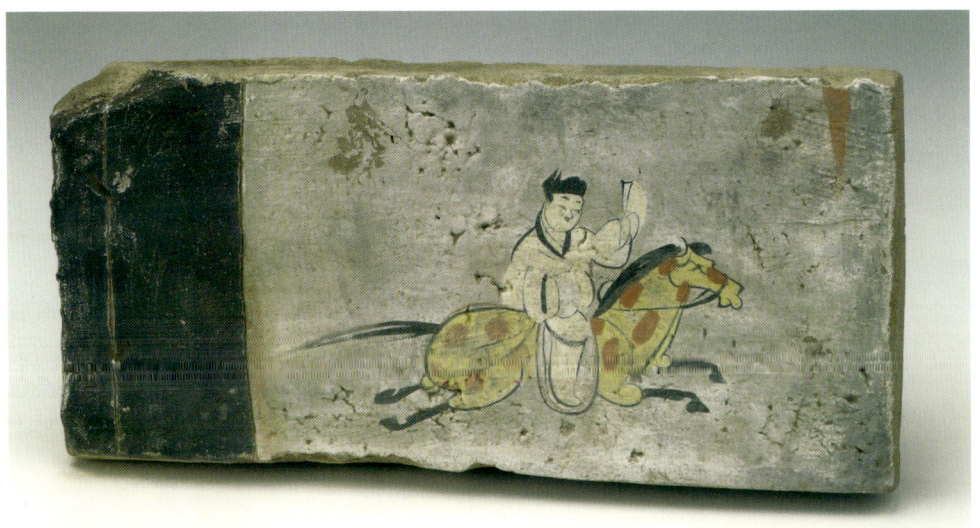

This painted tomb brick depicts a messenger on horseback, holding a document high in his left hand and the reins in his right hand, galloping to his intended destination. With sure, spare brush strokes and strong naturalistic colour, the artist has created a vivid representation of the messenger and his horse. The painting shows how important communications were relayed on horseback between post-houses along the western extension of the long walls built during the Han dynasty.

Painted tomb brick
Western Jin dynasty (265–316)
Excavated in 1973 from a tomb at Jiayuguan, Gansu province
Earthenware with pigment
17.9 (h) x 36.7 (w) x 4.6 (d) cm
Collection of the National Museum of China (K1042.41)

Historically, Jiayuguan Pass was under the jurisdiction of Jiuquan. Jiuquan is located in the mid-western section of the Hexi Corridor in Gansu province and has long been a centre of east-west transport and communication. To the south it borders the Qilian Mountains and to the north it joins the Gobi Desert. From the time when Emperor Han Wudi of the Han dynasty ordered the building of the Hexi Corridor section of the Great Wall, soldiers and civilians stationed there guarded the passes along the western walls and cultivated land in agricultural colonies run by the military. These agricultural colonies provided material support to the army, and consolidated defence. Later generations continued to follow this practice.

In 1972 and 1973, eight tombs in this area dating from the Wei and Western Jin dynasties were excavated, and six were found to contain some 600 painted tomb bricks which were used to decorate the walls of the tombs. In most instances each brick depicts a single vignette of the life of soldiers and civilians defending the borders and cultivating land in the Hexi area.

Painted tomb brick
Western Jin dynasty (265–316)
Excavated from a tomb
at Jiayuguan, Gansu province
Earthenware with pigment
18 (h) x 36.3 (w) x 4.5 (d) cm
Collection of the National
Museum of China (K1042.8)

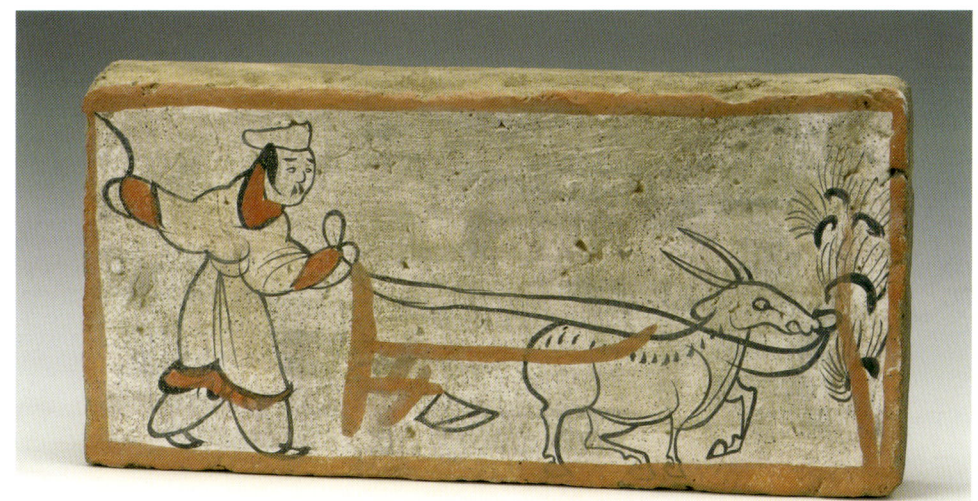

This painted tomb brick
depicts a farmer driving
an ox-drawn plough.
During the Han dynasty,
farming colonies were
established around
the main passes along
the walls built to protect
the trade routes, with farms
to provide food for the
soldiers and their families.

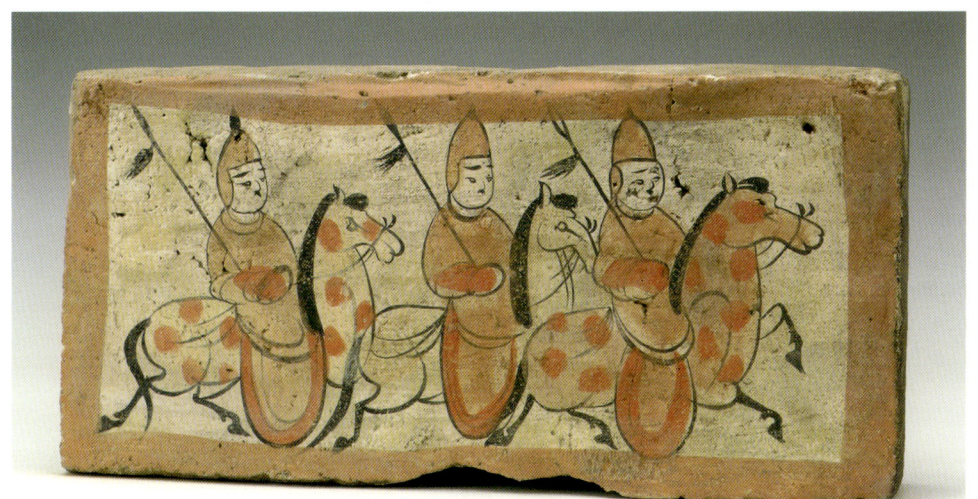

Painted tomb brick
Western Jin dynasty (265–316)
Excavated from a tomb
at Jiayuguan, Gansu province
Earthenware with pigment
17.5 (h) x 36 (w) x 4.6 (d) cm
Collection of the National
Museum of China (K1042.45)

This painted tomb brick
depicts three warriors
wearing helmets, holding
long spears and riding
on horseback.

Mounted guard
Eastern Han dynasty (25–220)
Unearthed in 1969 at Leitai,
Wuwei, Gansu province
Bronze
54 (h) x 33 (l) cm
Collection of the Gansu
Provincial Museum (22612:1, 300:4,
300:2, 22615:3)

In 1969, a large group of bronze figures and objects that formed an impressive guard of honour for a high-ranking official were excavated from the front chamber of an Eastern Han dynasty tomb at Leitai, Gansu province. The deceased was most likely a commandery governor, one of the highest ranking positions in the Han dynasty. This set of funerary objects included fourteen bronze carriages of different kinds, thirty-eight bronze horses, one bronze ox, fourteen chariots, seventeen mounted guards and twenty-eight escorts. One of the objects is this bronze horse with a saddle and a mounted guard holding a halberd. The halberd, a common weapon at this time which combined the functions of spear and dagger, was also used as a ceremonial weapon. The posture of the horse, with its open mouth and raised head and tail, presents a lifelike appearance. Also discovered in this tomb was the famous Flying Horse (*feima*) from the Eastern Han dynasty.

Wuwei was the capital of Wuwei prefecture in the Han dynasty and a garrison post along the Silk Road trade routes.

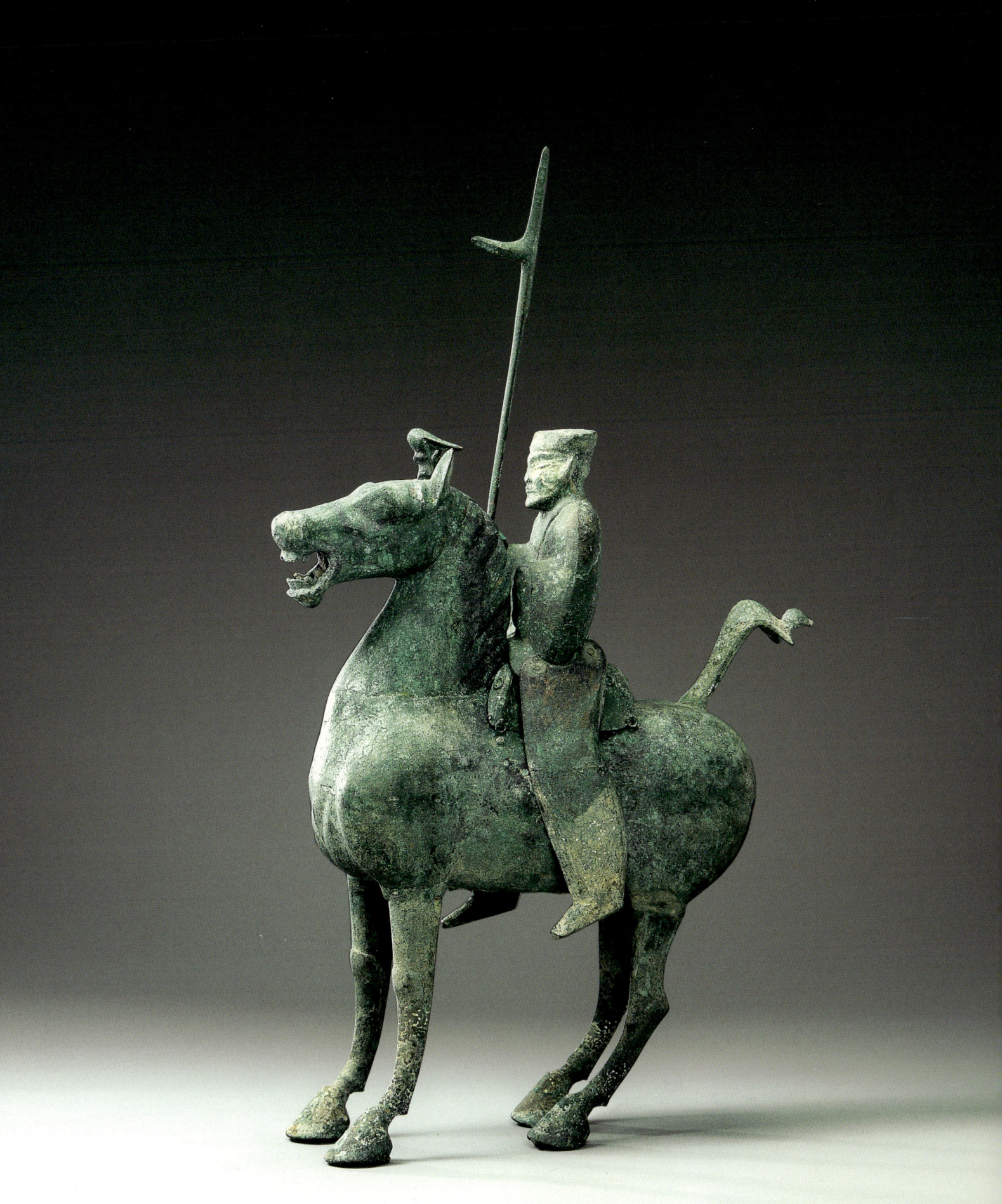

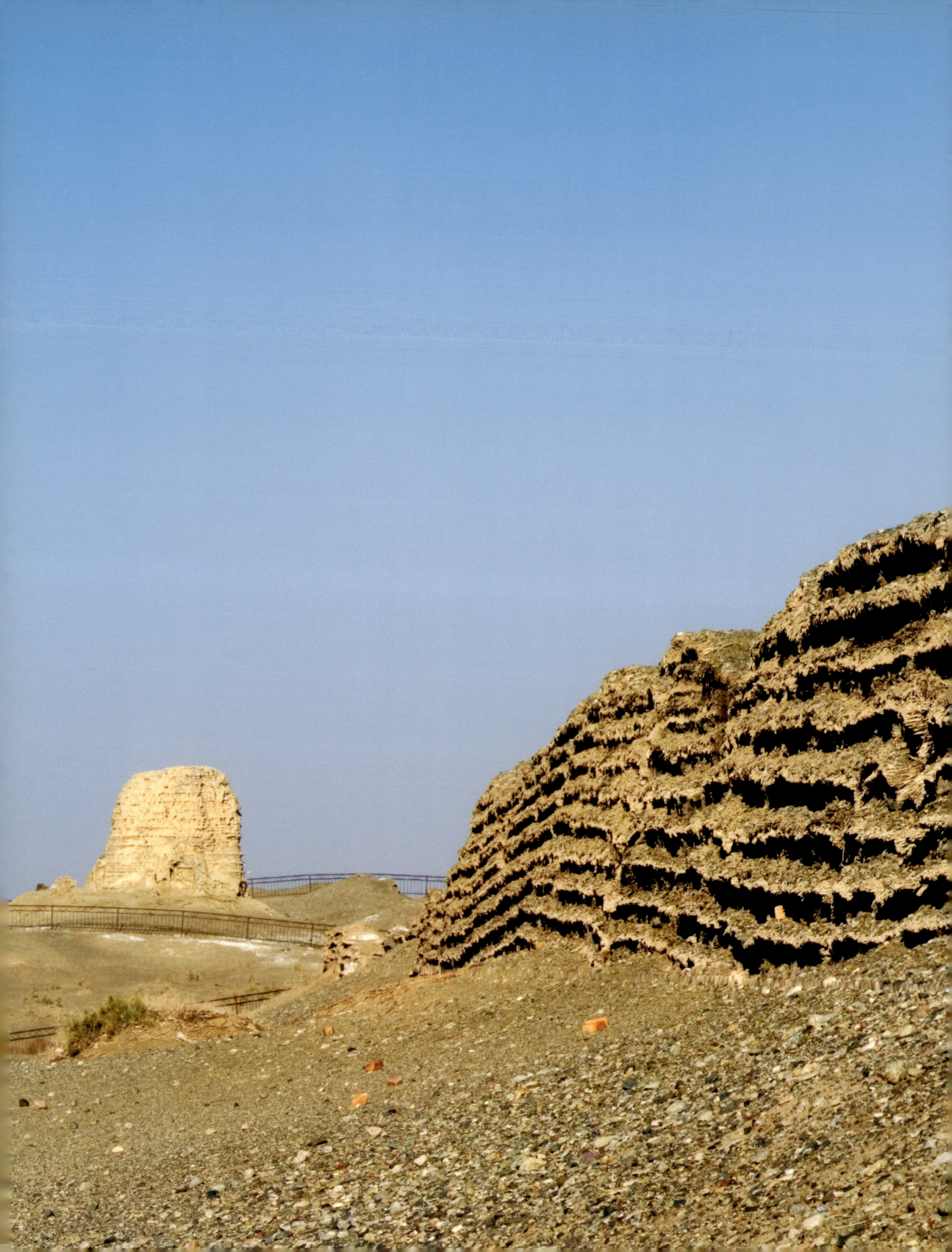

FOUNDATIONS

I watered my horse at the Long Wall caves by Chen Lin (d 217)

I watered my horse at the Long Wall Caves,
Water so cold it hurt his bones;
I went and spoke to the Long Wall boss:
'We're soldiers from Taiyuan — will you keep us here forever?'
'Public works go according to schedule –
Swing your hammer, pitch your voice in with the rest!'
A man'd be better off to die in battle
than eat his heart out building the Long Wall!
The Long Wall — how it winds and winds,
Winds and winds three thousand li;
here on the border, so many strong boys;
in the houses back home, so many widows and wives …

Excerpt from a translation by Burton Watson

Remains of the Han dynasty Great Wall and beacon tower, Majuanwan, Dunhuang, Gansu.
Photo: Jean-Francois Lanzarone

Material culture of the Walls

WANG YUEQIAN

Early historical records describe the threat posed by the nomadic peoples of the northern grasslands to the settled agriculturalists of the Central Plains of what is now called China. This changing relationship between the peoples of the Central Plains and the nomads would become a leitmotiv of Chinese dynastic history. The Great Walls were conceived during a period of 'cold weaponry' warfare between these groups. Their appearance was intimately connected with the evolution of Chinese society and politics and the interplay of its various cultures over several millennia.

Reliable records show that contact between these ethnic groups began in the Zhou era. In the early period of the Western Zhou (c 1100–771 BCE), a capital was established first in Feng and later in Hao, both in the vicinity of present-day Xi'an in Shaanxi province. Powerful ethnic groups lived to the north of these capitals. They threatened the security of the Zhou, which was forced to adopt defensive measures. These included building a series of beacon platforms and towers along the border regions for relaying signals and information on enemy movements. The beacons played a similar defensive role as the Great Walls that were built later. An historic incident which highlights the significance of beacons to state security is the example of King You (reigned 782–771 BCE), who played a hoax on his own feudatory lords by activating the fire beacons, thereby losing the trust of his people, so that when the minority Quanrong people launched an attack he could not summon desperately needed support. This sparked a series of cataclysmic events which led to the final collapse of the Western Zhou, the move of the capital to the east by King Ping and the establishment of the Eastern Zhou dynasty (771–256 BCE). During this time, the struggle for territory between the peoples of the Central Plain and the surrounding ethnic groups continued. During the Spring and Autumn (770–476 BCE) and following Warring

States (475–221 BCE) periods, the kingdoms of Qin, Zhao and Yan all constructed long walls along their northern frontiers, with the object of resisting invasion by the Xiongnu and other nomadic peoples. The walls of this time were built separately and did not form a continuous barrier.

By the third century BCE, Qin Shihuang (reigned 221-210 BCE) created a unified empire, establishing a centralised authoritarian state with himself as the first emperor of all China. He ordered that the walls of the Qin, Zhao and Yan kingdoms be joined together, and the construction of the first true Great Walls of China began.

Few remains of the Qin Great Walls survive. Almost all subsequent dynasties, however, built and repaired Great Walls. What is interesting is that this work was not only carried out by the Qin and Ming dynasties founded by the majority Han ethnic group, but also by the Northern Qi, Northern Zhou, Northern Wei and Jin dynasties that were established by northern nomadic and semi-nomadic peoples who had entered the Central Plains region. During the time of the Ming dynasty (1368–1644), the construction of Great Walls continued, prompted primarily by the need to resist incursions by various Mongol groups, designated the Tata and Wala by the Ming. From the Hongwu to the Wanli reign periods

(1368–1620 inclusive), the imperial court undertook more than twenty large-scale wall-building programs and built a 'border wall' running from Jiayuguan Pass in Gansu province in the west all the way to Hushan in Liaodong in the east, a distance of more than 6000 kilometres. This activity is reflected in the art works and other cultural production of that period.

One might well ask why so many historical events took place around the artificial divide of these Great Walls. The north of China was much like a stage on which, from ancient times onwards, there was a changing cast of players, including the Xiongnu, Tujue, Khitan, Jurchen and Mongols. In the Central Plains area, especially after the advent of the bronze age, productive forces advanced rapidly, attaining an unprecedented level of technical sophistication. The people of the plains produced a wide variety of high-quality bronze objects, including ritual vessels, musical instruments, weapons, carriage and horse fittings, as well as tools. For example, the tally of Qi, Lord of E, of the Warring States period, a bronze object featuring seal script characters inlaid in gold, is a token of exemption from taxation issued by the King of Chu, and documents exemption for wheeled vehicles (see p 67). It is an object of great beauty, and one that also provides valuable information on regional culture and on the advanced state of land transportation in the Central Plains.

Such objects and the culture that produced them proved attractive to outsiders who would enter the Central Plains, peaceably or under force of arms, to acquire them. Large groups of farmers and artisans were abducted. Many others fled south to escape the depredations, leading to extensive economic collapse. In response, and to exert their authority, rulers of the Central Plains ordered the construction of walls.

Qin Great Walls

Although the Great Walls were built to serve defensive purposes, they never totally divided the peoples who lived on either side of them.

The Great Walls did, however, greatly influence the development of weaponry and fighting power. Most probably from the Western Zhou period onwards, bronze-making skills advanced to the stage when a single mould could be used several times, accelerating production. The development of commerce in the Spring and Autumn period required large quantities of metal currency, spurring bronze technologies to even more dramatic advances, and mining, smelting and casting attained new levels of achievement. More intense warfare prompted the various states to develop and refine weaponry for their armies: they produced bronze dagger-axes (*ge*), spears (*mao*), swords (*jian*), halberds (*ji*) and arrowheads (*zu*) (see pp 70, 71, 73) dramatically strengthening the fighting power of their armies. Protective bronze armour and helmets came into

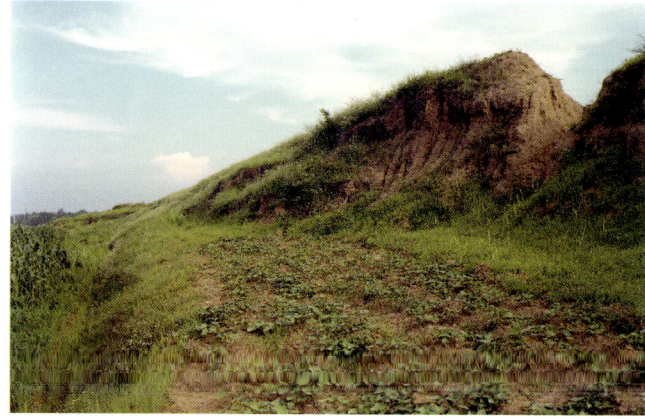

Remains of the wall built by the State of Yan during the Warring States period, in Suicheng, Hebei.
Photo: Cheng Dalin

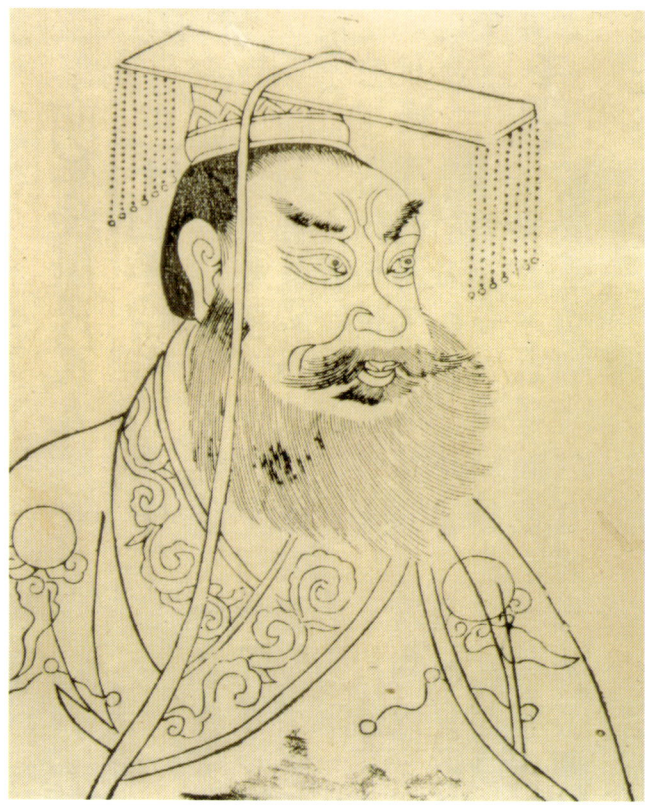

Portrait of Emperor Qin Shihuang (259–210 BCE), from the Ming dynasty woodblock-printed edition of *Collected images of heaven, earth and man* (Sancai tuhui) by Wang Qi and Wang Shouyi.
Reproduced courtesy National Museum of China

general use, critically increasing military efficiency as well (see p 70). Although a small quantity of iron objects was produced (see p 72), iron was rarely used in the weaponry of the period.

At the same time, the northern nomadic and semi-nomadic peoples harnessed metalworking techniques for the manufacture of weapons. Battle scenes decorate some of the bronze items from this period, giving us a visual perspective on the warfare of the time (see p 69).

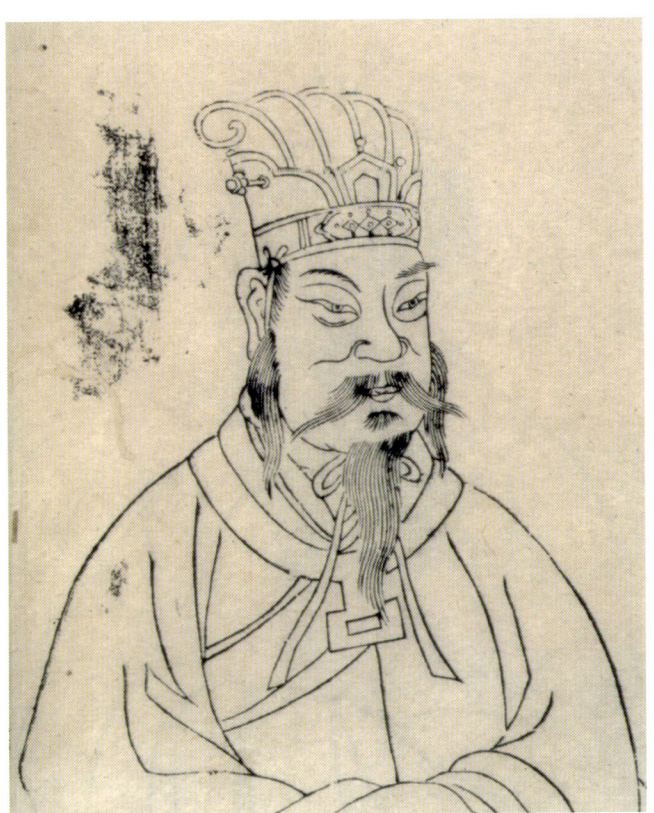

Portrait of Emperor Han Wudi (156–87 BCE), from the Ming dynasty woodblock-printed edition of *Collected images of heaven, earth and man* (Sancai tuhui).
Reproduced courtesy the National Museum of China

In districts of modern-day western Liaoning and eastern Inner Mongolia, archaeologists have unearthed helmets, armour and short bronze swords with curved blades which may once have belonged to the Donghu people. The decorative animal motifs make them distinctive (see pp 74–75) and reflect the finesse of the northern craftsmen working in bronze.

After Qin Shihuang unified China, he standardised weights, measures, written scripts and currency in order to consolidate his centralised autocracy, an act that had a stabilising effect on society as a whole (see p 76). He also launched a major military offensive against the Xiongnu people and began linking the scattered defensive walls of the Qin, Zhao and Yan states to form a continuous long wall — or 'great wall' — to protect the security of the Qin dynasty (221–206 BCE). In addition, he relocated hundreds of thousands of households to what is today the Ordos region of Inner Mongolia to farm the virgin lands there and prevent the Xiongnu from encroaching southwards. The Qin emperor extended the Zhou walls in this region to protect these new settlements. Thus, the walls also acted as an agent of expansion into new territory. The Qin continued to use the military tally system through which the emperor personally wielded control over the military (see p 77). We have noted that

the use of iron weapons was not yet common and most of the Qin's offensive weaponry, such as swords, arrowheads and crossbow mechanisms, were still made of bronze (see pp 80–81). Only a small number of weapons were made of iron. From the pottery figurines made at that time we can see that the development of armour and helmets had already been greatly improved and their use seems to have been widespread.

The crossbow had made its appearance by the Spring and Autumn period at the latest. It was widely used in the Warring States period, and the Qin dynasty continued to deploy it. According to archaeological and written evidence, there were at least two types of crossbow. The *bizhangnu* was fired off the arm and the *juezhangnu* from a kneeling position. The latter had greater firing power. The shape of the mechanism of the Qin crossbow was basically similar to that of the Warring States prototype: the arbalester, or archer, placed the arrow on the stock in order to fire it from a crossbow without a deep bore. The bronze firing mechanism had four main components: the hook (*ya*), sights (*wangshan*), a locking ratchet casing (*niu*) and a trigger (*xuandao*). The sights enabled the arbalester to fix the target; the ratchet worked together with the trigger to either lock the bow or fire, and the hook controlled the bowstring. The stock of the crossbow was made of wood with a wooden bow attached to it at the front. Strips of leather strengthened the outside of the frame. The arbalester aligned the hook in the sights, locked the weapon using the ratchet and trigger, placed an arrow on the stock (*nubi*) and drew the bowstring to the hook. He lined up the target, pulled back the trigger, releasing the ratchet mechanism and the string, firing the arrow at its target. The design of the Qin crossbow was simple, very scientific and practical, with an accuracy exceeding that of a simple bow and arrow. It came to play a major role in warfare.

So did the introduction of cavalry forces with mounted archers. This was another innovation from the Warring States period embraced by the Qin. It was developed by King Wuling of Zhao (reigned 326–299 BCE), who recognised that the traditional fighting methods of the Central Plains were less effective than those of the northern nomadic peoples. He reorganised his army into a cavalry force trained in light cavalry charges and long-range archery. By rapidly raising the military efficiency of his army, he consolidated his rule.

King Wuling also adopted the dress of the nomadic warriors. Battle dress consisted of close-fitting, narrow-sleeved jackets, which were fastened at the waist with a leather belt and belt-hook and were worn with trousers and long leather boots. Many scholars consider that the belt-hook originated among the northern nomadic and pastoral peoples, and was then popularised and refined by the Han, although it is still the subject of debate. Archaeological discoveries demonstrate that during the

Spring and Autumn period the belt-hook was being used to hold leather belts in place in the Central Plains region (see p 72). Later, in the Warring States, belt-hooks became a fashion in personal adornment, as their workmanship grew more sophisticated and their shapes and ornamentation more complex. Apart from securing a belt around the waist, they were used to suspend daggers, swords, paring knives, mirrors and seals.

Defending the Han empire

The Han dynasty (206 BCE–220 CE) perpetuated and strengthened many aspects of the Qin system, including the construction of walls. Han efforts to build Great Walls must be understood in the context of the social environment of the time, particularly the relationship between the Han and the peoples to the north. Because the rulers of the Central Plains were accustomed to conducting trade and other exchanges along the land routes to the west, during the Qin a stable communication route developed along the Hexi Corridor running east to west through modern-day Gansu which became an important part of the Silk Road. But after the third century BCE, the northern Xiongnu peoples had grown quite powerful. Taking advantage of the opportunity provided by the dynastic transition from Qin to Han, they rode south and occupied the Hexi Corridor. This meant that they controlled all the states of China's Western Region, cutting the roads, and therewith the trade routes, linking the Han dynasty to the lands to the west. Because the early Han rulers were unable to resist the Xiongnu they were forced to develop a system of diplomatic intermarriage that entailed betrothing Han princesses to the Xiongnu rulers. But the Xiongnu remained belligerent and launched incursions into the areas south of the Great Walls, continuing to pose a serious threat to Han political authority.

During the time of Emperor Han Wudi (140–87 BCE), the power of the dynasty was strengthened, providing the conditions that allowed the Han to strike back at the Xiongnu. On successive occasions, Emperor Wudi despatched the military commanders Wei Qing and Huo Qubing to lead large armies against the Xiongnu. These armies drove the Xiongnu outside the Great Walls and eventually recovered control of the regions of Ordos and Hexi. Emperor Wudi also sent Zhang Qian (?–114 BCE) on a diplomatic mission to the Western Region and laid the foundation for the establishment of the Silk Road trade routes. During the reign of Emperor Xuandi (147–67 CE), the Han dynasty established protectorates in the Western Region, which provided effective control of the area. The borders of the Western Han were extended north beyond the Yinshan Mountains and west as far as Central Asia. To consolidate Han rule over the Western Region and to provide security for the trade routes, the emperor extended the Great Walls along the Silk Road as far as Lop Nur in modern-day Xinjiang province. The Western Han constructed fortifications, in the north

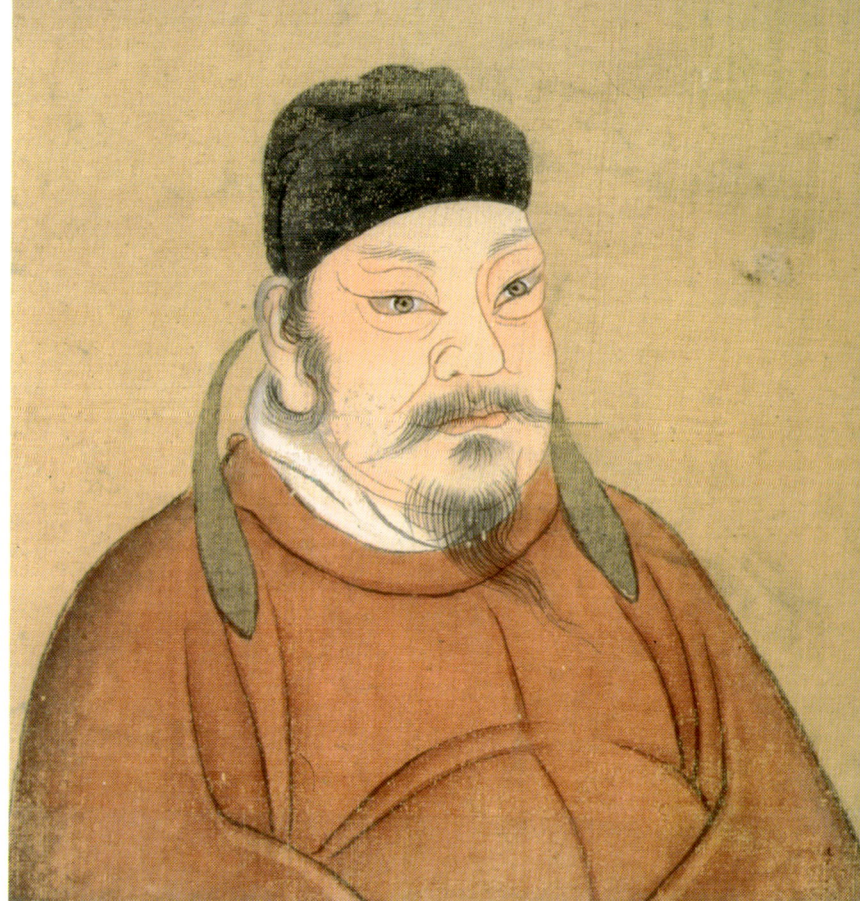

Portrait of General Huo Qubing (140–117 BCE) by an unknown artist of the Qing dynasty. Album leaf, ink and colour on silk. Collection of the National Museum of China

at Juyan, and despatched well-armed troops to defend them. It also built many sections of the Great Walls and related structures, such as beacon platforms and towers, walled forts and watch posts.

At the beginning of the twentieth century, expeditions discovered more than a thousand inscribed wooden slips, manuscripts and large quantities of relics dating from the Han dynasty at these sites. These chronicle various aspects of Han society, such as ethnic groupings, cultures, types of economic production and customs, and they reveal the influence of the Han Great Walls on the development of east-west communications, trade and cultural interchange. As the Han dynasty grew strong and flourished, the Xiongnu went into decline and finally split into smaller groups, and their rulers took the initiative to repair relations with the Han dynasty. During the reign of Emperor Yuandi (48–33 BCE), Wang Zhaojun, the daughter of a palace lady named Liang, was married to the Xiongnu king. As a result of this marriage, the two nations enjoyed a harmonious relationship for more than forty years. Because the diplomatic marriage was backed on this occasion by a powerful polity, the relationship was qualitatively different from earlier examples of diplomatic marriage when the Han dynasty was weak. Its effect can be seen in the later relationship between the Han and the Xiongnu, as demonstrated by the popularity, during the closing years of the Eastern Han dynasty, of the story of Cai Wenji, who lived, albeit unwillingly, among the

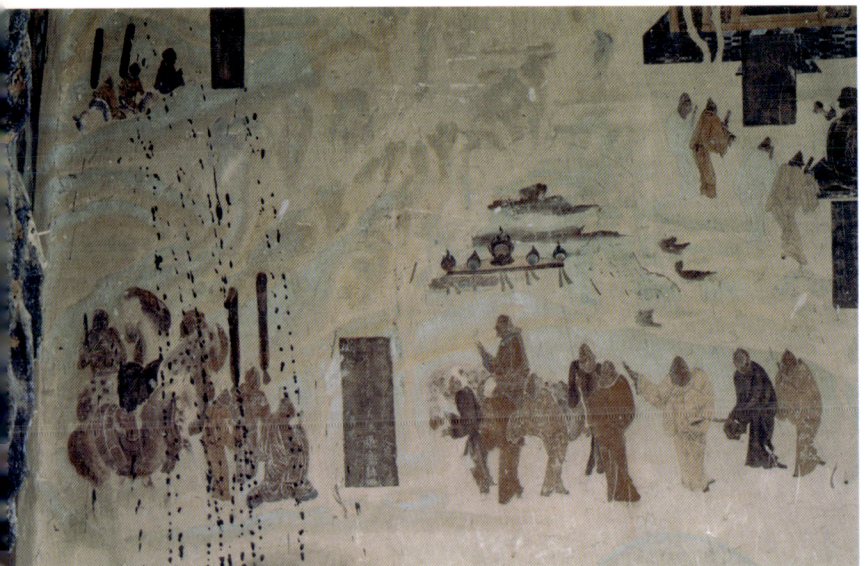

Detail of a Tang dynasty (618–907) mural painting in cave 323 at the Mogao Caves, Dunhuang, Gansu, depicting the diplomatic journey of Zhang Qian to the Western Region.
Reproduced courtesy the National Museum of China

Xiongnu, but introduced elements of Xiongnu musical culture to the Central Plains (see handscroll pp 98–99, and Bulag pp 216, 219).

During the Han dynasty, then, relationships between the Central Plains people and the northern nomadic and semi-nomadic peoples, especially the Xiongnu, alternated between periods of peace and warfare. When the forces controlling the Central Plains were strong, they kept the Xiongnu in check and a period of peace would prevail. When they were weak and ineffectual, the Xiongnu would breach the walls and threaten the Han state. The Great Walls separated ethnic groups physically and they effected a geographic division which lessened conflict and tension.

When Zhang Qian was despatched to the Western Region by Han Wudi, he was charged with forging alliances with countries to the west in order to surround the Xiongnu. This aim was never realised but the mission established trading links in the west, creating the conditions that led to the opening up of the Silk Road. The extension by the Han dynasty of the Great Walls along the Silk Road was crucial in guaranteeing these major trading routes remained open.

Chinese silk, lacquer goods, bamboo items and paper were transported to the west along these roads under the protection of the Great Walls, contributing to the development of cultural life. Buddhism, Manichaeism and, much later, Islam, as well as new forms of culture and art, such as music and dance, were introduced into the Central Plains. Fruits and vegetables, such as the grape, walnut, pomegranate, cucumber, garlic and carrot, also entered China along the Silk Road routes. At the same time, the Han cultural influence spread to the

Xiongnu, who eventually adopted the clothing, language and handicrafts of the Han court, as can be seen from artefacts of the period (see p 93). Many objects found in Xiongnu aristocratic tombs have a strong Central Plains character. These include bronze weapons, horse bridle fittings and ornamental items decorated with realistically depicted animals, all of which display a high standard of technical artistry (see pp 90–91). Culturally and economically, the Han dynasty also benefited from relations with its neighbour. They imported large numbers of horses raised and trained by the Xiongnu, leading to the development of horse breeding in the plains. Han Chinese also learned advanced riding skills and the ways of equestrian warfare from the Xiongnu, dramatically improving the fighting capabilities of their armies (see p 91).

The most important weapon, however, remained the crossbow (see p 89). The Han greatly refined the crossbow technology of the Warring States and Qin dynasty. Although the operational principles of the mechanism were basically the same, the weapon's accuracy was increased and its offensive capability strengthened. A track with a casing was carved into the wooden stock, stabilising the firing procedure and preventing the weapon from injuring the soldier's arm — a common problem with early crossbows. Secondly, the sighting fitting was raised and calibrated, allowing the weapon to be more accurately aimed at targets at different distances.

Great Wall culture after the Han

In the time up to and including the Han dynasty, the Great Walls represented a clear line of demarcation between the world inside its boundaries and that outside. However, this symbolic significance changed over time: for most of the dynastic period after the Han, the Great Wall region was politically divided, in a state of civil war, or parts of it were included in a unified state.

After the Han dynasty fell, China descended into a long period of turmoil. The dynasties of the Central Plains region were constantly changing and northern peoples invaded in large numbers, establishing their own kingdoms inside the Great Walls. Chinese historians describe this period as 'the turmoil brought to China by the five Hu [or barbarian] peoples' (wu Hu luan hua). Stability only returned with the Sui–Tang period beginning in the late sixth century. During this tumultuous time, the Great Walls effectively lost their defensive function and their ability to vouchsafe the economic or cultural development and prosperity of the Central Plains. There were ceaseless population shifts, times of peace interspersed with periods of slaughter and bouts of wall-building: those living outside the walls in one period would, in the next, find themselves living within a new great wall. Large numbers of material objects illustrating these processes remain in the vast region along the walls, as do foreign objects in many different styles that demonstrate the high degree of contact and trading with lands to the west that was occurring during this period. Many gold and silver coins and other objects from Persia and elsewhere are among the discovered foreign artefacts (see p 145).

The Tang dynasty (618–907) was a period of great cultural openness, of the ready absorption of foreign cultural influences. During this period the Great Walls did not play any apparent role in preventing inter-ethnic migration for the Tang controlled lands on both sides of the walls. Tang dynasty works of art depicting 'barbarians' are common (see pp 142–144).

In the post-Tang period, a succession of northern peoples founded the Liao, Western Xia, Jin, Yuan and Qing dynasties, some of which claimed dominance over territory south of the Great Walls. The origins of these polities differed and some were more short-lived than others, but all of them achieved a synthesis with the original culture of the Central Plains. The dramatic process of their acculturation is reflected in their currency, scripts, handicrafts and decorative arts (see pp 149, 152–55, 162–63).

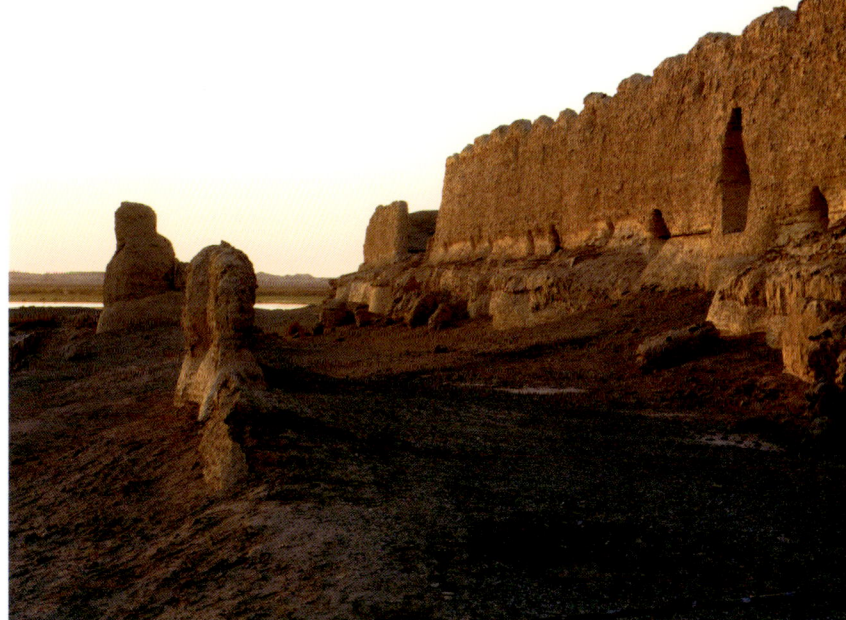

Remains of a Han dynasty military grain warehouse at Hecangcheng (Dafangpan), along the defence line of the Jade Gate Pass, Dunhuang, Gansu.
Photo: Jean-Francois Lanzarone

Of all the polities that followed the Han, the Mongol-Yuan dynasty (1271–1368) was the most influential. Its founder, Chinggis (Genghis) Khan, not only united the Mongol tribes, but he attacked and eliminated, in turn, the Western Xia, Jin and Southern Song dynasties, and his armies subjugated Central Asia. His successors carried on his mission of conquest and dramatically expanded the Yuan empire until it straddled Eurasia. It was in response to the demonstrated might of the Mongols that the next dynastic rulers of China, the Ming, embarked on an unprecedented project of wall-building, for which they paid an enormous human cost. The scope of the Ming dynasty's program of building Great Walls exceeded that of all previous eras.

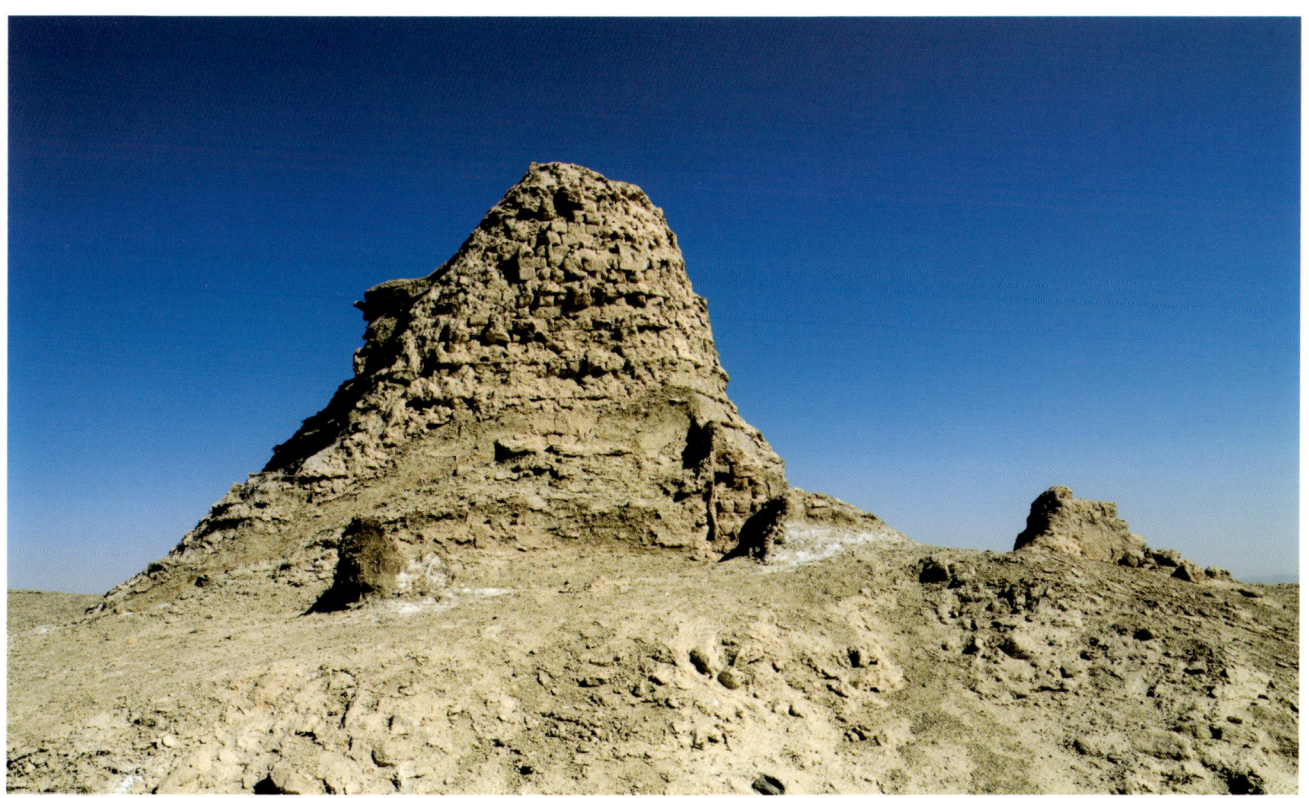

Remains of a Han dynasty beacon tower in Dunhuang, Gansu.
Photo: Jean-Francois Lanzarone

Woodblock print reproduced from the *Biography of Taizu* (Taizu shilu), recording the seige of Ningyuan by the Manchu Prince Nurhachi in 1626 and the use of Manchu assault ladders and 'sky-vibrating' bombs.

As a result of the invention of gunpowder after the Tang dynasty, methods of warfare changed. Gunpowder, cannon and other forms of artillery presented new challenges to the defensive capability of the Great Walls (see pp 200–01). The walls had posed significant obstacles for cavalry armed with knives, spears and crossbows, but did not provide an impregnable defence against more modern weapons. The Ming dynasty's strengthening of the Great Walls was effective to some degree, but wall-building was no longer proving socially beneficial. Its many negative effects included the national closed-door policy of the mid and late Ming periods.

The Great Walls played a positive defensive role at particular times, when they served to preserve social peace and stability, guaranteeing the security of people's lives and property, and strengthening the rule of dynastic houses. However, the historical record shows that whenever a dynasty became corrupt and fell into decline, the Great Walls invariably failed to prevent incursions and did little to prevent dynastic collapse: the military effectiveness of the walls depended on human factors. Ultimately, the Great Walls benefited those living near them, bringing together people of different ethnicities, polities and cultures in large-scale interchange and acculturation.

TRANSLATED BY BRUCE GORDON DOAR

Delimited boundaries and Great Wall studies

BRUCE GORDON DOAR

The interdisciplinary field of research within China known as 'Great Wall studies' (*changchengxue*) was established in the late 1980s. Despite its formulation as a discipline, however, Chinese scholarship on the Great Walls can still be subsumed under a number of categories — such as general history, historical geography, ancient mythology, military history, ethnology and archaeology — which acquired their contemporary forms in the 1920s.

Great Wall studies, as promoted in China, cannot be separated from the Great Wall Society (GWS) although, according to the entry on the subject in *The Great Wall encyclopaedia*,[1] the impetus for the establishment of Great Wall studies was provided by a conference on Great Wall conservation and research held in 1977 in Hohhot under the auspices of the State Cultural Relics Enterprises Management Bureau, at which the call for the establishment of such a field was made by a number of speakers. The GWS, described as 'a mass [or non-official] intellectual organisation', was not founded until a decade later, and then as the formal response to a proposal for the establishment of just such a group at a 1979 gathering organised by the State Cultural Relics Bureau. Further impetus for the establishment of the society came in 1984, when Deng Xiaoping issued his 'Great Wall declaration' — 'love our China; repair our Great Walls' (*ai wo Zhonghua, xiu wo changcheng*) — initiating nationwide patriotic 'activities' on this theme. The society was formally set up at the Great Hall of the People in Beijing on 25 June 1987.

The constitution adopted at the time the society was established stated its aim as being 'to study, conserve, restore and publicise the Great Walls, and to proclaim the glorious spirit of the Chinese people'.[2] The study of the Great Walls was defined as 'conducting research on the position, function and value of the Great Walls in the historical development of the Chinese people.'[3] The definition and scope of Great Wall studies given in *The Great Wall encyclopaedia* encompasses these same stated aims and areas, including conservation and tourism.[4]

A number of scholars concerned with historical, heritage and conservation issues — including Cheng Dalin, Dong Yaohui, Hou Renzhi, Luo Zhewen, Shan Shiyuan, Shi Nianhai and Zheng Xiaoxie — were involved with the GWS from around the time of its inception. Their sense of social engagement and their practical academic bent ensured that the society became engaged with heritage and conservation issues, promoting research on aspects of the history of the Great Walls. When Great Wall studies was first broached as an intellectual field, however, it was not given any rigorous definition; indeed, it simply incorporated all academic and popular studies of the Great Walls.

In 1994, the GWS published *The Great Wall encyclopaedia*, a reference work that represents the thinking on what constituted Great Wall culture (*changcheng wenhua*) and studies at the time. *The encyclopaedia* remains the first port of call for any scholar wanting an overview of the existing scholarship, even though there is an over-enthusiasm for tourism evident in its editorial priorities. Conservation and cultural heritage issues, which have become much more prominent today, receive only cursory treatment.

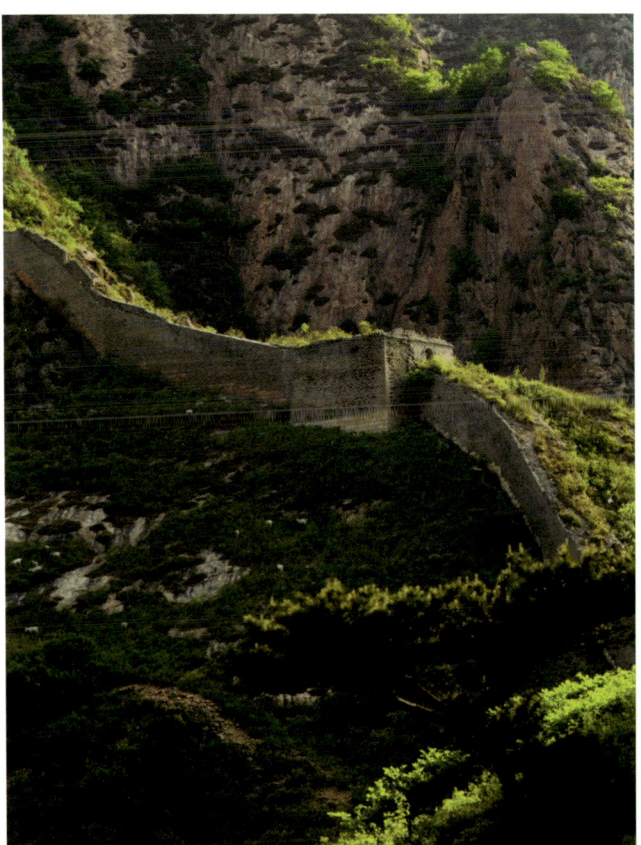

The Ming dynasty Great Wall near Jiumenkou, Funing, Hebei.
Photo: Jean-Francois Lanzarone

As an academic field, Great Wall studies acquired final definition at an international conference on Great Wall studies, held in Beijing from 23 to 25 September 1994.[5] In his opening address, the historical geographer Hou Renzhi asked: 'What is the Great Wall?' And he commented, 'There are many answers to this question, but all are incomplete.' From the perspective of military engineering systems, he said, 'The Great Wall is an object of fixed warfare, and in terms of a unified war strategy, it is both a man-made structure which intensifies and enhances a determined battlefield, and a massive, solid defensive system which has taken shape over an immense distance, fixing locations and uniting them, and thereby establishing a hierarchical formation.'[6]

Attempts to define 'the Great Walls', or for that matter Great Wall studies, are invariably coloured by the discipline of the particular scholar essaying them. The 1994 conference was the forum where the grab-all categories of Great Wall studies and culture proffered in the early days of the GWS were finally subjected to intellectual scrutiny. Dong Yaohui stated, 'A concept that we must first clarify is changchengxue [Great Wall studies]. To date, there has been a great hue and cry about this "field", and most people are under the impression that all research on the Great Walls counts as Great Wall studies. This relatively crude view has seriously impeded the development of just such studies.'[7]

In one of his articles, Dong Yaohui cited the following definition: 'Great Wall studies is a branch of knowledge derived from comprehensive research, and a discipline that engages in synthesizing research on the Great Walls. It is an epistemological science concerned with the Great Walls, and its task is to bring together the various aspects and levels of understanding of the Great Walls into a synthetic whole.'[8]

However inadvertently, Dong Yaohui's insistent paper was perhaps the kiss of death for Great Wall studies as a discreet social science category. As a macro-field, or all-inclusive category, it might continue to serve academia and the GWS as a rubric of convenience or social organisational tool, like Dunhuang studies or any other area study, but it is doubtful that the intellectual synthesis that Dong Yaohui sought to conjure up will ever eventuate, no matter how desirable an interdisciplinary approach might be. Since the 1994 conference, Dong Yaohui has gone on to publish many articles on the walls, none of which fulfils the criteria that he articulated.

Defining Great Wall studies

The more comprehensive the study of the Great Wall systems has become, the more difficult it is to separate it from the entirety of the Chinese history of architecture, warfare, foreign relations, politics and diplomacy. The walls shed light on many subjects: for example, 'the study of their ruins' has been characterised as 'a kind of archaeology of foreign policy'.[9]

Proceeding from Hou Renzhi's definition of the Great Walls as a system of military engineering structures, the wall complexes of the various dynasties can, for example, be viewed as a set of architectural structures when seen at close quarters. Or they can be regarded as a system of defences with an infrastructural support network, which ultimately defined and altered the entire economy, geography and culture of a vast region, called in contemporary Chinese the Great Walls belt (changchengdai) or Great Walls zone (changcheng quyu); this region lies between an inner agricultural region inhabited by Han Chinese and an outer herding and hunting area that was the preserve of nomadic peoples. The farming colonies established to aid in Great Wall construction programs also served to introduce agriculture to areas where it had not been previously practised. The unearthing by archaeologists, in Gansu, the Ordos region of Inner Mongolia and the Liaoyang district of Liaoning province, of Qin-Han iron ploughshares, coins, weights and measures has provided material evidence of the spread of agriculture and of the economic mechanism for exchange in that period. At every turn evidence of the interdependence of farmland and steppe is reinforced by archaeological finds.

In stressing the environment as the determining factor in the construction of the walls, rather than defining a region by virtue of the existence of constructed walls,

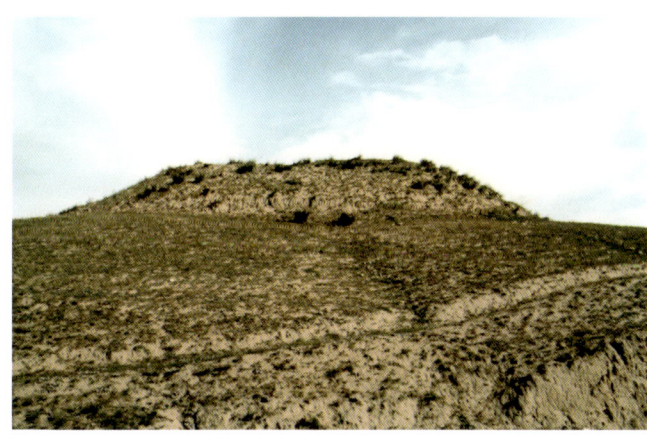

Remains of walls built by the State of Qi during the Warring States period, at Changqing, Shandong.
Photo: Luo Zhewen

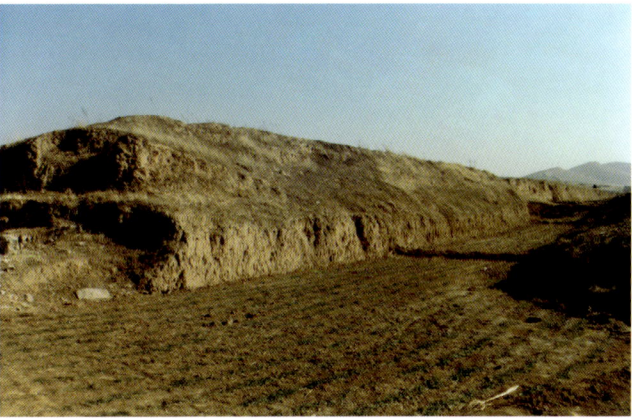

Remains of walls built by the State of Zhao during the Warring States period, at Baotou, Inner Mongolia.
Photo: Luo Zhewen

some scholars have questioned the pure 'military' nature of some of the complexes. Baiyin Chagan, an archaeologist from Inner Mongolia, for example, has examined the great walls of the Yan, Zhao and Qin states of the Warring States period (475–221 BCE) and concludes that different walls served different functions, even though it was traditionally believed that these walls were designed to resist and halt the Xiongnu people moving south. He has argued that in the state of Yan the walls along its southern border served as a defence against the Qi and Zhao states, but the northern wall served as a border delimiting nomadic and agricultural economies and peoples.[10] Guo Guanghong, a historian from Shandong province, has questioned whether defence was the motive in the construction of the Qi walls, which run from Changqing county near the present-day Shandong capital of Jinan to the coast at Qingdao. Built between 685 and 555 BCE, these walls, he argues, were designed to secure the salt monopoly of the Qi rulers and to prevent salt smuggling.[11]

If, in the first instance, the Great Walls are defined as a set of military structures, scholars disagree regarding the extent of the military system in which the walls were supposedly the central element: for example, does the system of Great Walls include the defensive towns and farming colonies (*tuntian*) founded in their vicinity? Scholars also ask whether all the walled structures were exclusively, or primarily, defensive? Definitions that stress the defensive nature of the various Great Wall complexes sometimes overlook the 'offensive' military nature of the walls as imposed structures that constitute a presence akin to the bases of occupiers. The Great Walls could also form part of a pre-emptive, or aggressive, military strategy, as was practised by Emperor Han Wudi (reigned 140–87 BCE) or the early rulers of the Ming dynasty (1368–1644). Moreover, the beacon towers were message-relaying facilities, which could also convey information for offensive military purposes.

The Manchus, for example, emulated this offensive aspect of Great Wall warfare with startling success. Although the Manchu administrative policy of great unity (*da yitong*) was developed after the Qing dynasty (1644–1911) had been firmly established in the Central Plains region and has been described as an innovative ethnic construct in Chinese history,[12] this new peaceful concord rested on military achievement. According to old Manchu texts, some dating back to the sixteenth century, the Manchus copied the defensive Ming beacon-fire system of the Liaodong region. Zhao Zhiqiang has documented the hierarchical structure of fire beacon forts — called in Manchu *bang, pan, tu, derhi, poo* and *holdon* — that they constructed and developed. The Manchus also emulated the Ming use of cannon as a signalling technique, as well as using drums and bells, turning them into an effective element in an offensive, rather than defensive, military strategy in mobile, highly organised warfare.[13]

The history debates

From the 1990s onwards, many of the debates in historiography initiated by Gu Jiegang (1893–1980) from the mid 1920s onwards continue to remain relevant, as a new generation of 'sceptics' (*yigupai*), of whom Wu Rui is representative, pits itself against those historians, exemplified by Li Xueqin, director of the Institute of History of the Chinese Academy of Social Sciences, who describe themselves as 'explicators of the past' (*shigupai*).[14] Most of the terms of reference would be familiar to historians of the 1920s, the debate being a continuation of perennial disagreements regarding the authority of ancient texts, exemplified by the evidential (*kaozheng*) school of scholarship of the Qian-Jia period of the mid eighteenth to early nineteenth centuries. Modern historians are also indebted to China's fine traditions of historical geography, specifically those related to the Great Walls that emerged from the mid Ming period onwards.[15] Today's debates can be distinguished by the greater significance of the role archaeology can, and does, play in historical studies.

Studies of the Great Walls have also been influenced by new historiographical models, as indeed have all aspects of Chinese history. The historian Gu Jiegang was prompted to conduct archaeological fieldwork and, in 1938, was responsible for discovering remains of the Qin wall at Lintao in Gansu province. Yet ancient historical sources are often still regarded as the ultimate guides and arbiters for archaeologists and historians alike: for example, in discussions of wall-building by the Warring States, historians often include the walls of the Zhongshan state, together with those of Chu, Qi, Wei, Zhao and Yan, even though no remains of Zhongshan walls have yet been discovered.[16]

Similarly, the discussion by historians of the pre-Qin period is frequently influenced by models that conform to archaeological cultures. Although traditionally Qin has been regarded as one of seven major 'warring states', the archaeological identification of many other small states of the period has lent weight to the depiction of Qin as a unique cultural region, conforming to the new view of Eastern Zhou history from an archaeological perspective. Li Xueqin, for example, has identified seven archaeologically defined cultural regions for the later period of the Eastern Zhou — the Qin, Central Plains, northern (Beifang), Shandong (Qi-Lu), Chu, southern (Wu-Yue) and south-western (Ba-Shu-Dian) — and this model has been adopted by Hu Minghuan in his discussions of the Qin Great Walls.[17]

The archaeological view

In recently published historical writing, few scholars ignore the new findings of archaeology, taking their cue from such early twentieth century innovators in historiography as Wang Guowei (1877–1927) and Guo Moruo (1892–1978), although purely textual studies do continue to appear. The contribution of Chinese archaeology to the development of Chinese historical research in the twentieth century highlights its affinities with history rather than with anthropology, as is usual in the Euro-American tradition. Chinese archaeology (kaoguxue) reveals a respect for texts, although archaeology shorn of the fieldwork experience of excavating is usually classified as 'artefactology' (wenwuxue).[18] Apart from surveys, most archaeological excavations conducted in China are salvage operations dictated by the destructive aspects of either plunder or construction. As far as the Great Walls are concerned, most archaeological fieldwork has only been conducted since the 1950s. Between 1955 and 1959, for example, teams assigned to excavate promising sites uncovered by reservoir construction in the Yellow River valley surveyed and conducted trial excavations of sections of the western great walls of the state of Wei in Huayin and Dali counties in Shaanxi.[19]

Chinese archaeologists sometimes link the construction of great or long walls with the general practice of building walls (cheng) around towns and cities (both also simply termed cheng); both types of wall are taken to serve as an indicator of a degree of settled social development, generally termed 'civilisation' (wenming).[20] Walls in themselves serve to demarcate not only space but time, and they have a qualitative role to play for different branches of history. Architectural boundaries and the delineation of space within the development of cultures in China led to the formation of polities different from the city-states of ancient Greek history and historiography, and the materials used in the construction of the various great walls also serve to delineate separate cultural building traditions that developed in different parts of China.

Generally speaking, in the pre-Ming period, the north-east of China and the mountainous eastern areas of Inner Mongolia had a tradition of stone masonry and stone fortified settlements going back to the Hongshan, post-Hongshan (Danangou) and Xiajiadian Upper and Lower archaeological cultures, which date from 4000 to 1500 BCE; the Yellow River valley and the Central Plains

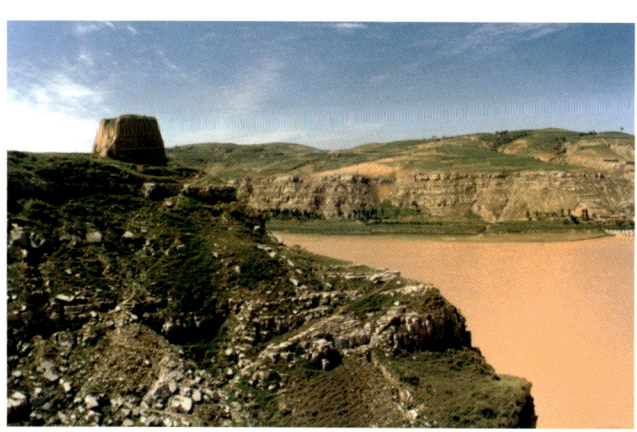

Remains of a beacon tower and earthen wall along the bank of the Yellow River at Pianguan, Shanxi.

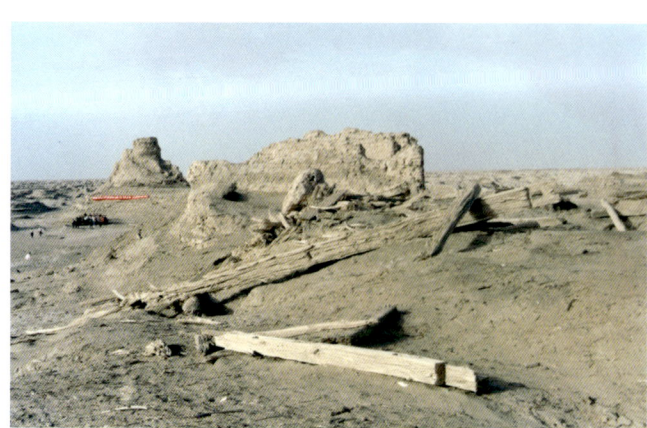

Remains of the ancient city of Loulan on the Silk Road, Lop Nur, Xinjiang.
Photos: Luo Zhewen

area had a tamped-earth building tradition also from the neolithic era onwards; and the north-western areas of China had disparate traditions of building in adobe and timber. The Great Walls in different parts of China reflect these diverse cultural traditions.

A periodisation schema

Although prehistoric archaeology has developed its own cultural categories and periodisation schemes, using scientific methods and typological classification, Great Wall construction falls mostly within the literate period of Chinese history, and archaeologists employ conventional historical dynastic references, although the discussion of regional cultures for the pre-Qin period can be at variance with traditional historical terminology. Many periodisation schemes covering the development of Great Wall construction are equally serviceable for either an archaeological or a textual approach to Great Wall history, but that of Li Wenlong is more strictly 'archaeological' in its approach.[21]

Li argues that the history of the Great Walls can be divided into four stages or forms (*xing*): a 'primitive [or original] stage' (*yuanshi xing*), in which the construction of walls serves as a signifier of Chinese civilisation, as suggested by Su Bingqi in his *A new investigation of the origins of Chinese civilisation*;[22] an 'initial stage' (*chuji xing*) that encompasses the Spring and Autumn (722–476 BCE) and Warring States periods, in which walls were constructed but rivers were also used to form boundaries; a 'basic stage' (*jiben xing*) from the Qin-Han to the Sui-Tang period, between 221 BCE and 907 CE, which Li characterises as 'the period when the feudal system in China was established and developed to a flourishing stage';[23] and, finally, a 'stage of completion' (*wanbei xing*), which 'can be divided into two intimately connected periods, the Jin Dynasty [1115–1234] and Ming Dynasty'.[24]

Li's schema seems flawed by the inclusion in the 'basic stage' of the Tang dynasty (618–907), which most scholars agree was not a period of wall construction. Cheng Cunjie has argued quite conclusively that the Tang did not construct walls to defend itself against northern nomadic peoples, choosing instead to build fortified border towns and cities, especially in the period up to the reign of Emperor Xuanzong (712–56) and, furthermore, these were located along the lines of communication between the nomads and the south.[25] This highlights the irony whereby the walls remain a 'presence' throughout Chinese history, even if only as an option for foreign policy or military action of the central government, whether or not wall construction was taking place.

Li Wenlong's 'stage of completion' omits the Yuan (1271–1368) and Qing dynasties, although any military history of China must acknowledge the Mongols' ability to besiege walls and the Manchus' success in emulating the beacon-fire system of the Great Walls to their own

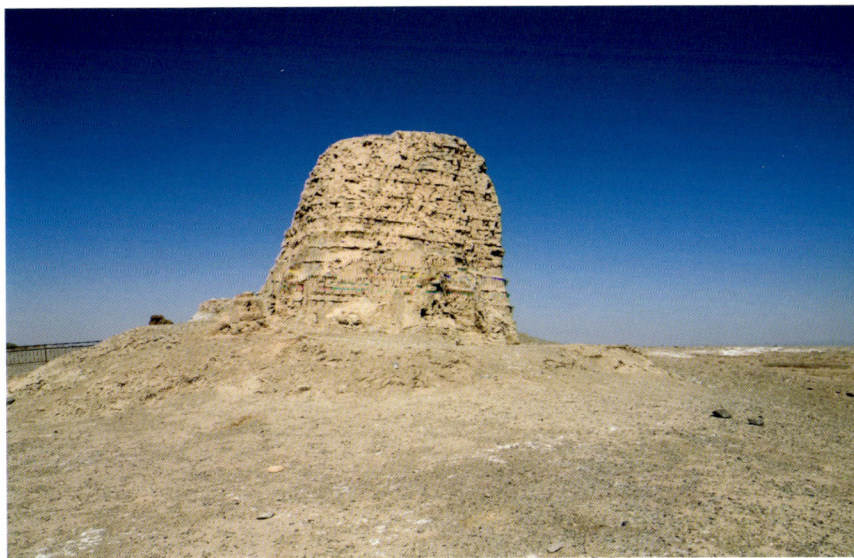

Remains of a Han dynasty beacon tower at Majuanwan, Dunhuang, Gansu.
Photo: Jean-Francois Lanzarone

military advantage. The Manchus rose to prominence in north-eastern China, where there were various ancient traditions of constructing fortifications from stone, of which the Gaogouli-Koguryo architectural traditions are typical.[26]

Surveying the pre-Qin walls

Over recent years, there has been a steady increase in the level of knowledge related to general wall construction in the various states during the Spring and Autumn and Warring States periods. Archaeological work in Shandong, for example, has uncovered many remains of the state of Qi and of its capital Linzi near the modern city of Zibo. Linzi's walls have been unearthed and some archaeologists have conjectured that Guan Zhong (Guanzi), the strategist and advisor to Duke Huan of Qi, may have been the designer of the walls of the capital and those throughout the state.[27]

During Li Wenlong's 'initial stage', many states and small states constructed great walls, and archaeologists continue to map and survey their remains. The work proceeds slowly, with often surprising results. Archaeologists setting out to survey the pre-Qin Great Wall complexes may rely only on ancient textual evidence. Toponymic knowledge and ancient historians and geographers often prove to be surprisingly reliable guides: for example, ancient texts record that the northern wall of Yan, constructed after the state conquered territory of the Donghu around 300 BCE, ran for approximately 1000 kilometres from Zaoyang (near present-day Dushikou, Hebei) in the west to Xiangping (present-day Liaoyang in Liaoning) in the east. This wall passed through Fuxin and Zhangwu counties in Liaoning and from the 1960s onwards archaeologists searched for its remains without success. In 1980, the archaeologist Sun Jie found remains of the wall in Fuxin and subsequently traced its course through that county for 95 kilometres. Then, in 1986–87, Sun traced its route for 160 kilometres through Zhangwu county to the east and discovered that a second outer wall connected with the original wall at Bajiazi.[28]

The Qin Great Walls of the Warring States period have, not surprisingly, attracted the greatest interest among archaeologists and historians, and there are many ongoing disputes about the identification of sections mentioned in Sima Qian's *Records of the historian* (Shi ji), notably about the walls around ancient Gaoque,[29] and the interpretation of the terms *qianluo* and *sai* walls. References to Great Walls are scattered thinly throughout Sima Qian's work, by virtue of its organisation into separate chronicles of states, tables, biographies and thematic essays. Often one reference offers information contradicting that in another, and there is disagreement about the interpretation of terminology.

Ou Yan and Ye Wansong challenged the interpretation of the references to *qianluo* throughout *Records of the historian* and conceded that the word could refer to some form of wall or constructed barrier. But they argue that it is irrelevant whether the *qianluo* was a wall running along the bank of the Luo River or a scooped-out section of the bank rendering it precipitous, as Shi Nianhai first argued: they point out that the passages scattered through Sima Qian's text show that some areas along the western bank of the Luo River, such as Linjin and Luoyin, were still part of the territory of Wei in the sixth year of the reign of Qin Marquis Jian (409 BCE), and that therefore the walls of the Qin state could not have been constructed in the domain of hostile Wei.[30] *Records of the historian* has rarely been regarded as such an infallible source of historical information, but Ou Yan and Ye's interpretation is at variance with the conclusion of some textually reliant Ming and Qing dynasty scholars, who argue that the Shangjun *sai* was built as a defence against the Xiongnu, rather than the State of Wei.[31]

The Qin-Han construction period

Although the Qin dynasty Great Walls can be seen as the culmination of wall-construction programs of the Warring States period, most scholars bracket the Qin-Han Great Walls as a single entity. During the four centuries covered by the Western and Eastern Han dynasties (206 BCE–220 CE), wall-building in the north was only undertaken during some periods. Most construction work was focused in the Hexi Corridor in Gansu and further west. Aurel Stein was the first archaeologist to document the remains of Han and Jin dynasty walls in the north-west.[32] Survey work of remains of Han dynasty walls (called *changcheng, fengsui,* and *chengzhang*) from Gansu to the Ejina River Valley in Inner Mongolia was conducted in the course of the North-western Scientific Expedition in 1927.[33] In 1942, the North-western Historical and Geographical Survey Team conducted an expedition

that documented remains of Han dynasty walls in Gansu at the Jade Gate and Yangguan passes, as well as areas to the east.

Since 1949, cultural relics and archaeological teams in Inner Mongolia and Gansu have been active in further surveying and documenting the Han Great Walls. In Gansu a survey in the Hexi Corridor, which began in 1979, has continued during separate seasons to the present day. An interim report on the findings to date, accompanied by detailed maps of the documentation, by Wu Rengxiang was published in 2000.[34] Archaeological work in Gansu and Inner Mongolia has also resulted in the discovery of a large number of Han inscribed wooden slips at Juyan, Jiayuguan and other sites, and these have enabled historians to correlate field work with the extensive archives available, and build up an increasingly sophisticated picture of the political geography of the north-west in the Han dynasty.[35] The correlation of sites and documents has also enabled scholars to understand the terminology for walls developed in the Han dynasty in the north-west, where architectural traditions of building with adobe and daub were brought within the Great Wall inventory. An excellent and clear exposition of this new understanding of the particularities of such structures as *sai, zhang, wu, sui* and *guan* is included in Wu's report, where he modestly states that 'after many decades of work we now have some preliminary understanding of these.'[36]

Inner Mongolia has also been the focus of extensive archaeological survey work, which falls into three roughly defined sections: eastern, western and central sections, both above and running diagonally through the Ordos region.[37] The results of these surveys can be appreciated in the mapping of the Han Great Walls that appears in the recently published atlas of Inner Mongolian cultural relics.[38]

After General Huo Qubing drove the Xiongnu from Han dynasty territory about 121 BCE and the Hexi Corridor was opened up, a line of ramparts was constructed to protect the trade routes between the Central Plains and the far west that were part of what is called the Silk Road, of which the Hexi Corridor formed a vital stretch. Li Bingcheng, a historical geographer, was involved in the archaeological mapping of the Hexi Corridor's Great Walls from Yongdeng county north of the Yellow River in Gansu and west of Dunhuang.[39] Here the Han walls run roughly parallel to, but several kilometres to the north of, the Great Wall of the Ming dynasty, and some sections are still in good condition. In the eastern section of the Hexi Corridor are the remains of two separate Ming walls, testifying to a change in borders during that dynastic period. Li Bingcheng, who set out to determine whether there were similar adjustments and constructions during the Han dynasty, and whether extra protective walls were constructed at that time, published a report on a section of Han wall, from Xuci county to the ruins of the ancient city of Aowei, which run between 3 and 12 kilometres north of one stretch of a Ming dynasty wall in a heavily desertified area.[40]

For historians and archaeologists, many of the problems in studying the Han Great Walls arise from the attempt to correlate texts and finds, highlighting one of the aspects of Chinese archaeology that sometimes sets it apart from other archaeological traditions. Some scholars, such as the Dunhuang specialist Li Zhengyu,[41] insist that, given the large number of cities, fortifications and communication posts that historical records suggest once dotted the landscape of north-western China, the identification of ancient sites by historical geographers is one prerequisite for future archaeological work, and that the multiplicity of cultures in the Dunhuang area around ancient Guazhou and Shazhou has compounded the problems of focusing on the toponymy and geography of this pivotal region at the end of the Hexi Corridor. Much hinges on how the remains of the network of defensive posts and their administrative function are interpreted.

The Jin and Ming walls
Li Wenlong's 'stage of completion' is also problematic because wall-building in the Jin and Ming dynasties was quite different from that in the Han dynasty and earlier. Indeed, in the early and late Ming periods it was also quite different in nature from that of the Jin. However, Li has argued that construction of the Jin dynasty walls, designed to foil the Mongol cavalry, as well as the many forts providing bases and support, represented technical advances that were perpetuated by the Ming.[42]

A textual study of the Jin trench (jiehao) system, known in vernacular Chinese as 'Genghis Khan's border walls', was undertaken by Wang Guowei in the 1920s. But it was only between 1958 and 1981 that limited surveys of Jin walls were conducted by the archaeological institutes of Heilongjiang, Inner Mongolia and Jilin.[43] In recent years scholars have also discussed the Jin walls in Hebei.[44]

The Ming Great Walls have also been examined by archaeologists, although prior to 1949 most historical research on the Ming walls was textual and only a few passes and watchtowers had been studied. In 1952, after Guo Moruo proposed that the main sites of the Great Wall be restored, the Cultural Relics Bureau dispatched personnel to Badaling and Shanhaiguan and Jiayuguan passes to survey, design and undertake restoration work. In 1956, a ground survey of the Great Walls was conducted with a view to determining which sections and passes be proclaimed 'key sites' (zhongdian) as protected units at either the national or provincial level. In 1981, the bureau set up four small teams to conduct a survey of the entire length of the Ming Great Walls. As a result of several surveys, the overall idea of the distribution, direction, structures and state of preservation

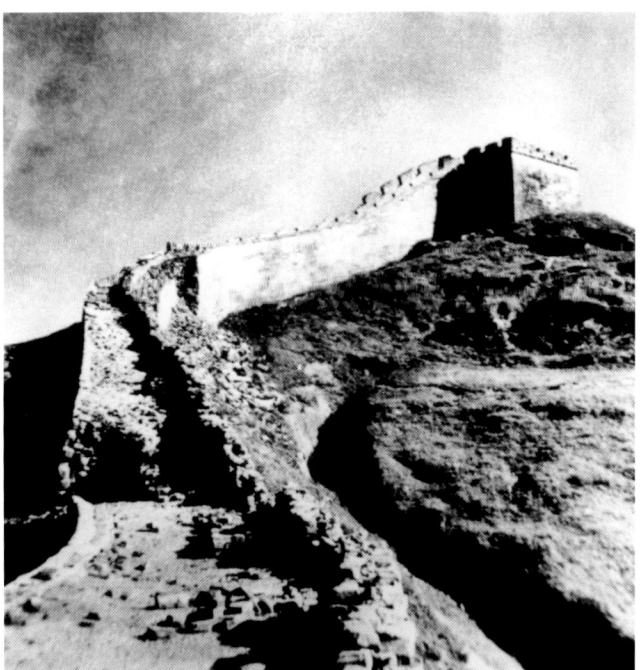

The Ming dynasty Great Wall at Badaling, Changping, Hebei, as it appeared in 1948 prior to restoration.
Photo: Luo Zhewen

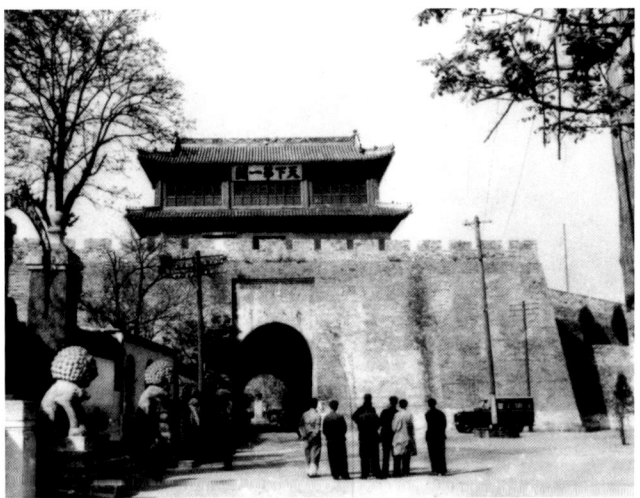

The Ming dynasty pass at Shanhaiguan, Hebei, as it appeared in 1953 prior to restoration.
Photo: Luo Zhewen

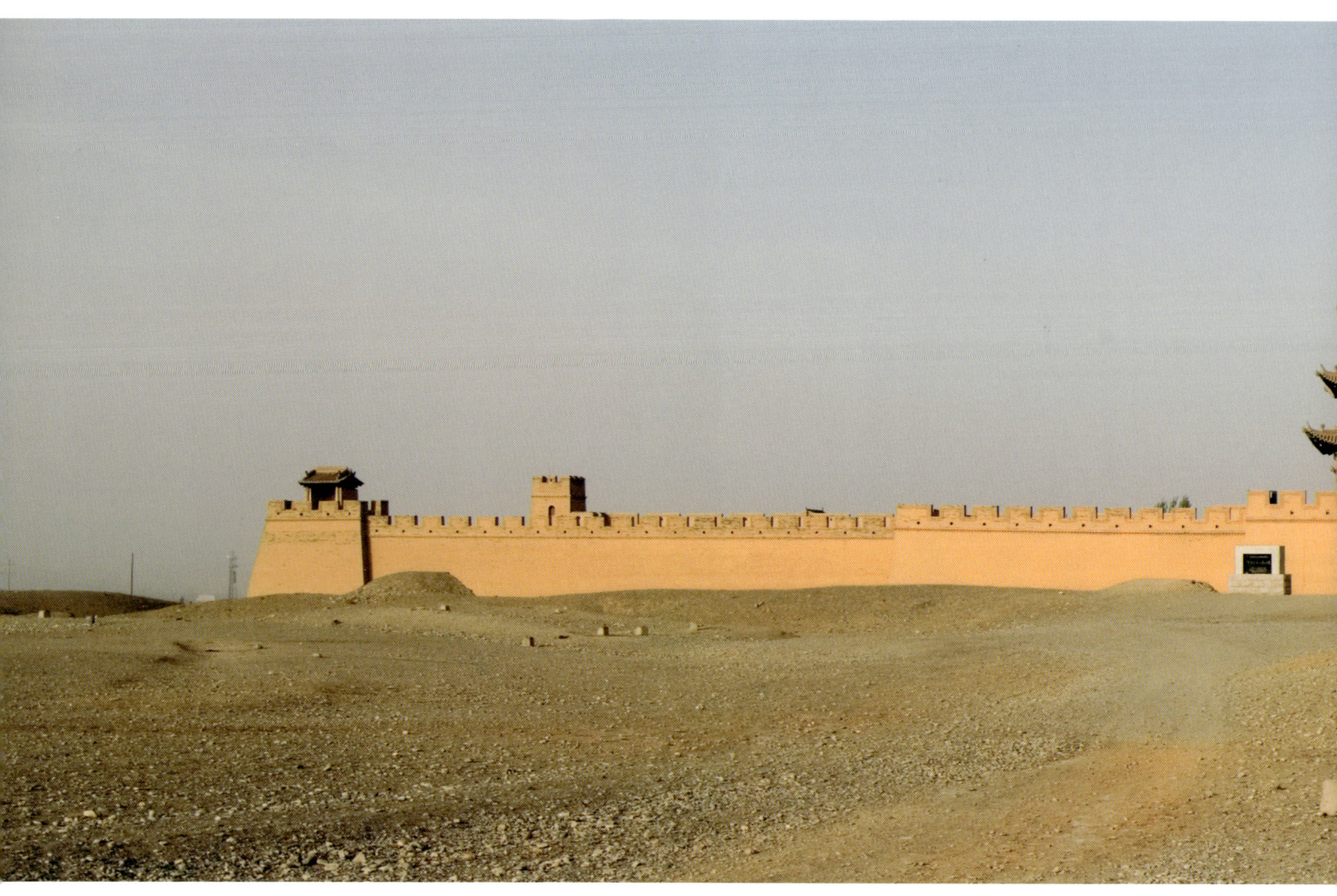

was ascertained. In 1981, the Jinshanling section in Luanping county, Hebei, and the Mutianyu section in Huairou, Beijing, were surveyed, restored and opened to the public.[45] Excavation work has been conducted in recent years at the Hushan site, regarded as the eastern end of the Ming Great Walls.[46]

In 1985, archaeologists working in Qianxi county, Hebei, near the Ming wall, unearthed the remains of an intact kiln capable of firing 500 bricks at a time. On seven of the 403 recovered bricks were incised or relief characters reading 'Zuosan' (Left three), believed to be the serial number of the kiln. Two kinds of bricks used in sections of the Great Walls in the region are identical to these unearthed bricks, which measure 41 by 20 by 10 centimetres. According to Luo Zhewen, the construction of each metre of the Great Walls would have required the entire output of twenty-two full firings of a kiln of this size, so that if the entire length of the Ming Great Walls were covered with bricks, the natural fuel this would have required would have exacerbated the ecological damage the brick walls undoubtedly caused.[47]

Conclusion

The attempt to create a social science called Great Wall studies has failed, but under the auspices of the Great Wall Society the effort to do so has provided many scholars working within a wide range of disciplines with a forum for presenting the results of their research. Many of these disciplines are branches of history. Yet it is also clear that any comprehensive history of the Great Walls must be interdisciplinary. Despite the need felt by some historians to reinforce archaeological findings with textual proof and the persistence of near canonical faith in the veracity of ancient writings such as *Records of the historian*, scholars of the Great Walls now rarely ignore the findings of archaeology. Indeed, it is the slow, steady and incremental documentation through archaeology of many thousands of sites and artefacts that will eventually result in a better understanding of the walls. Some of this archaeological detail has been provided over the last fifty years, but it will be some time before any comprehensive moving map of the Great Walls is completed.[48]

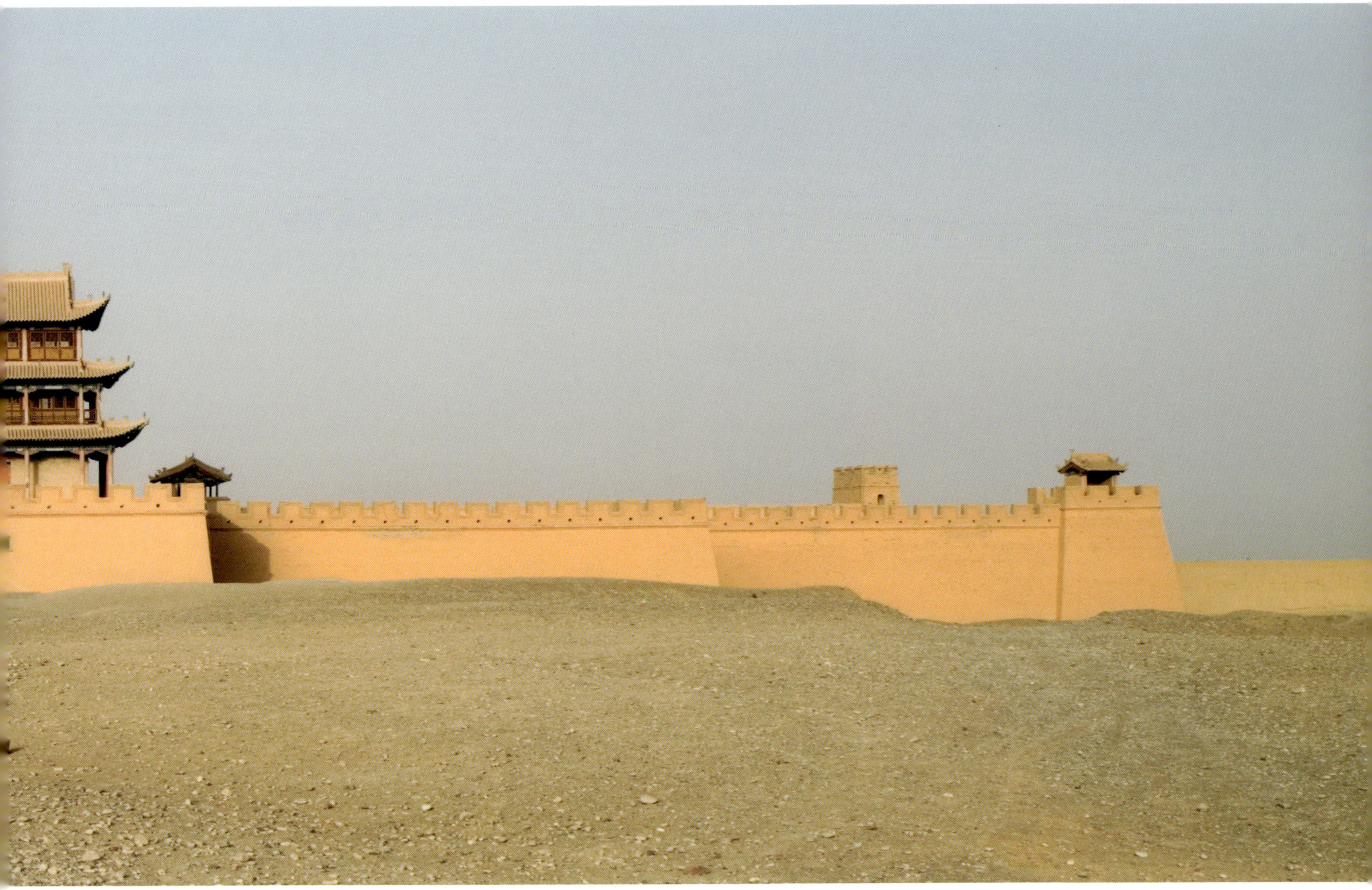

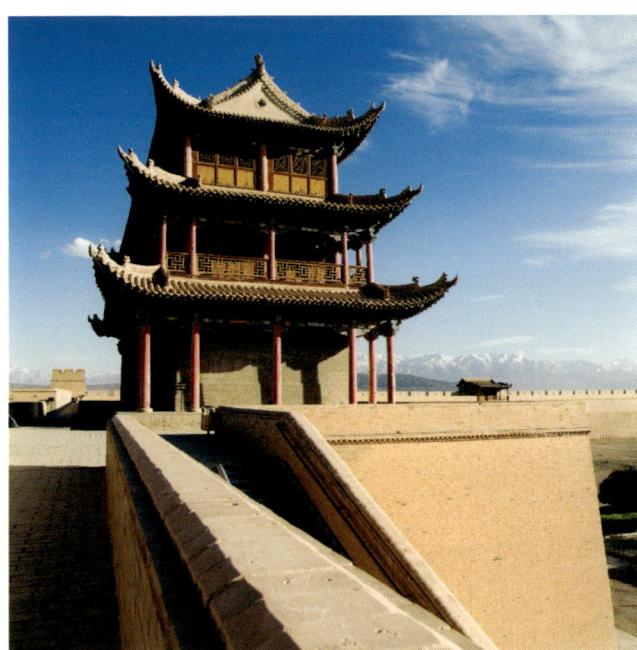

Above and top: The restored Ming dynasty pass at Jiayuguan, Gansu.
Photos: Jean-Francois Lanzarone

Steaming through the Wall

INTERVIEW WITH YANG ZHENTAO BY SANG YE

The Great Wall at Qinglongqiao Bridge, north-west Beijing, was first constructed in the Northern Wei dynasty (4th century CE), and rebuilt in the Ming, over 1000 years later. In the early twentieth century, at the end of China's imperial history, a breach was made in the wall for the construction of a railway. This engineering feat was overseen by Zhan Tianyou, also known by his English name Tien-yu Chan, a graduate of Yale University.

Zhan died in 1919 and a bronze statue of him was erected next to the Great Wall to commemorate his engineering achievements. In 1966, at the time of the Cultural Revolution, the Red Guards from the Railway Academy toppled the statue of this 'bourgeois intellectual', and splattered it with red paint. The statue was eventually cleaned and restored, and it stands next to the Great Wall today.

Yang Zhentao, forty-five years old, is the deputy stationmaster of the Qinglongqiao Bridge train station, Beijing branch of China Railways.

This is a fourth-grade station. According to China Railways, this means we are the lowest priority station for passenger and goods transportation. But this fourth-class stop of ours is pretty special since we were the first station designed, built and managed by Chinese. And this line was the first to penetrate the Great Wall and connect the interior to the world 'beyond the pass'. This was once a very important station, but that's all in the past. What remains is mostly symbolic. But symbols mean something too, and I must say that I do feel a sense of pride working here.

Last year, 2005, marked the centenary of our railroad. In the words of Zhan Tianyou from 100 years ago, 'China was just coming to the realisation that we needed our own railroads.' The first central rail bureau was established and Zhan was made the chief engineer. Under his direction, construction on the Beijing-Zhangjiakou line began in

September 1905 and the line was inaugurated four years later. The first stage was only 201 kilometres long, and the most difficult terrain was right here at Qinglongqiao Bridge: although it's only 16 kilometres from Nankou to Badaling, the difference in altitude is over 800 metres. Even today's electrically powered trains couldn't make that grade, let alone the steam engines back then.

Zhan Tianyou laid tracks in a zigzag formation to deal with the problem of getting the trains up and down the hills. He used two engines, one to haul the train from the front up the first stage of the incline halfway up the hill, and another at the back to push the train up the rest of the zigzag track. When the train reached the apex of the V grade, it would stop and the two engines would change roles: the one at the front would now push, while the one that was at the back would pull, thus getting the train over the next incline. After much consideration, Zhan Tianyou decided to put the exchange station here in the valley at Qinglongqiao Bridge. So this station became the pivotal point for the whole system. Because of the herringbone or V-design, the length of the tunnel through Badaling could be reduced by half. This saved a lot of time and money too. Even after the line went into operation in 1909, construction continued, and seven years later the line was extended from Zhangjiakou to Datong in Shanxi province. Another five years after that the line from Datong to Baotou in Inner Mongolia was completed.

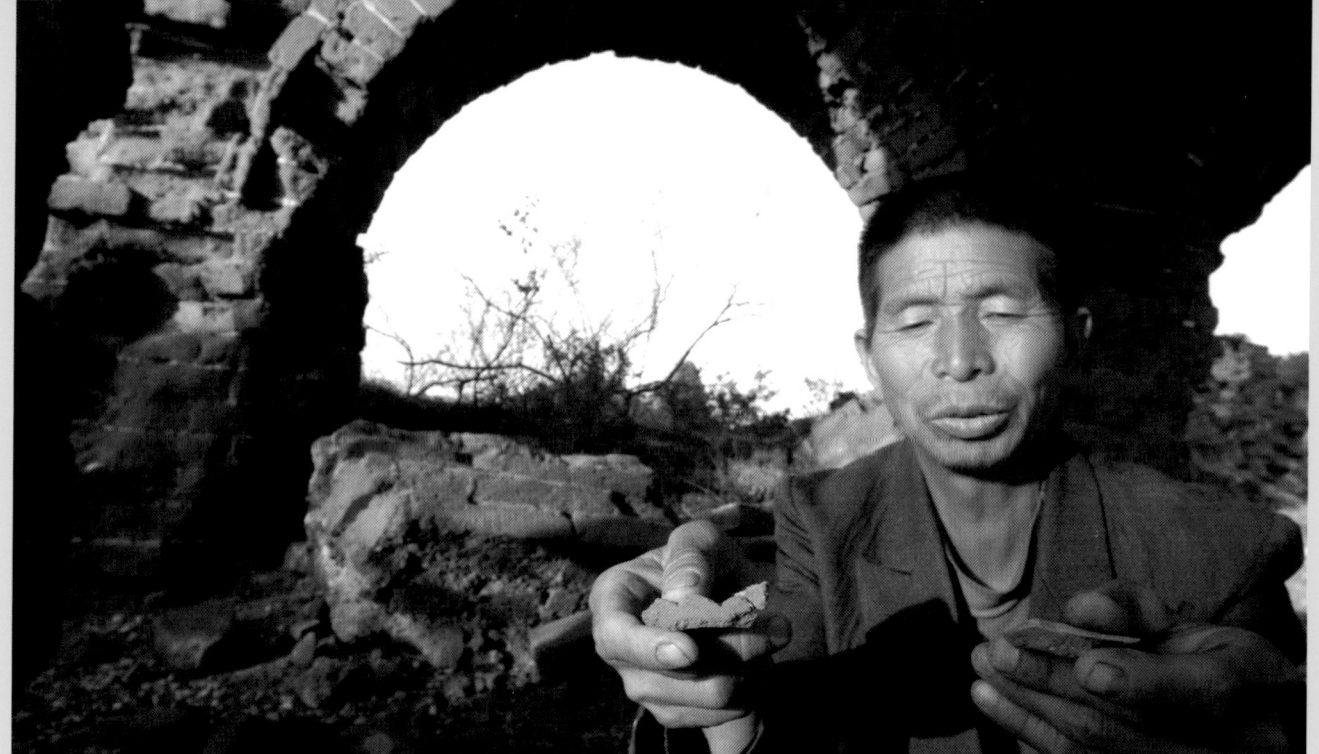

Old Sun, holding a piece of brick from the Great Wall, explains, 'This is something my ancestors left me.' His soldier-ancestors migrated from south China to guard the Wall. He sees himself as having a responsibility to continue the family tradition of protecting the Wall.

He walks 50 kilometres a day along the Wall, to protect it from abuse by tourists. This is not a paid job. He hopes his son will become a doctor.
Photo: Y W Jiang; location: Funing county, Hebei

Zhan Tianyou's headquarters were here at Qinglongqiao Bridge station. He lived here with his family for two years, and they billeted with another family by the name of Ji. The house is still here. Following Zhan's death, the Chinese Society of Engineers along with rail workers on this line erected a bronze statue of him here at the station. In 1982, his wife's grave was moved here too; originally it was near the Summer Palace, but no one was looking after it there and the area had been rezoned for residential development.

Although we're not far from the major tourist attraction of the Badaling Great Wall, few people come here to see Zhan Tianyou. We're not on the tourist map, and few visitors to the Great Wall have any idea of the special significance of this railway line.

We are the caretakers of Zhan's statue and his grave. For all of us who work here at the Qinglongqiao Bridge this is both a duty and an honour. I believe that there's not enough effort made to educate people about Zhan Tianyou. He deserves to be properly commemorated. He recognised the dangers of China being closed to the outside world and locked in upon itself. He understood the need to learn from the progressive thinking and technology of the rest of the world. He also put his beliefs into action. By day he'd survey the mountains on his little donkey, while at night he designed his railroad by the light of a small kerosene lamp until he finally was able to break through the Great Wall of China and build our first railroad.

For years people have claimed that the V-line was invented by Zhan Tianyou. In fact, it wasn't his invention at all. American mines had been using this design for ages. Zhan doesn't need false praise. His greatness doesn't lie in what he invented, it lies in the fact that he led the Chinese out into the world.

After they opened the line from Fengtai in south-west Beijing to Shacheng in Hebei province in 1950, ours was no longer the main rail artery. Naturally, our little station didn't matter any more either. Staff numbers dropped from the original fifty-four people to fourteen. There are still many empty buildings around here. Apart from upgrades to the control panel, the rest of the station is pretty much the same as it was. The buildings are just as Zhan Tianyou left them, though they did get a paint job in 1994. Five trains pass through here every day, and then there's the weekly Trans-Siberian that takes passengers from Beijing via Ulaan Baatar in Mongolia to Moscow.

I started working for the railroad in 1980, after graduating high school; that's a quarter of a century now. I make 1500 yuan [$A250] a month. It's a low wage. The tour guides and trinket hawkers working up at Badaling just over the hill make much more. Even the young girls sent by the Forestry Bureau to keep an eye on the trees get 2500 [$A415]. But I'm happy working here, because it's truly special.

It's a full 100 years from the time when they laid down that first track for the Beijing-Zhangjiakou line to the building of the Qinghai-Tibet rail link. Qinglongqiao Bridge enjoyed its heyday. Though we'll never be that important again, this is the starting point for China's first railroad. Thousands of trains have passed this way.

TRANSLATED BY GEREMIE R BARMÉ

Northern dynasties to Yuan dynasty

Headdress ornament
Northern dynasties (386-581)
Unearthed in 1981 at Darhan
Mumingan Banner, Ulanqab
League, Inner Mongolia
Gold, precious and semi-precious
stones
19.4 (h) cm
Collection of the National
Museum of China (Y2047)

Ox-head and deer-antler shaped ornaments such as this were known as *buyao* and were used on headdresses worn by the Xianbei people in the Northern dynasties period. The Xianbei were a nomadic people, many of whom lived on the steppes of Mongolia where they engaged in hunting deer, boars, hares and other grassland animals as well as herding oxen, sheep, horses and camels. The peach-shaped leaves attached to the ends of the antler-like forms shake with the movement of the wearer. The base of the ornament was cast, and decorated with applied gold ornamentation and inlaid with precious and semi-precious stones.

According to historical records, such headdress ornaments date back to the Han dynasty and during the Wei-Jin and Northern and Southern dynasties periods they became popular among ethnic groups of northern China. At that time, to wear a headdress ornament such as this was a symbol of status.

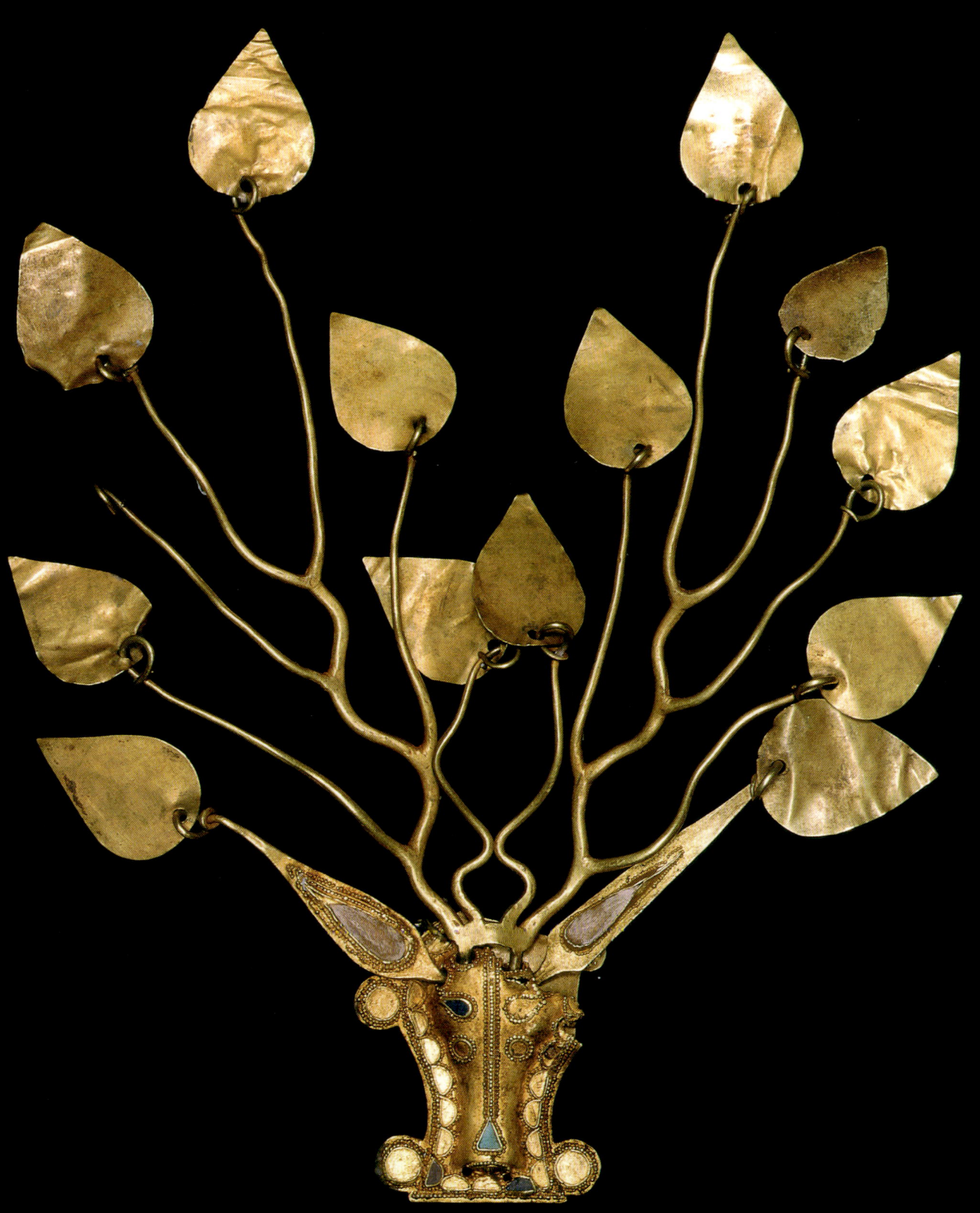

Horse equipage
Sixteen States period (304–439)
Unearthed at Ji'an, Jilin province
Gilt bronze
Saddle bridge: 25.4 (h) x 50.5 (w) cm
Collection of the National
Museum of China (K9814)

This set of gilt bronze objects comprises parts of a horse's harness (*maju*) that dates from the Sixteen States period and was unearthed at Ji'an in Jilin province. It is made up of saddle-bridge ends, stirrups, strap buckles, a gag bit and several small harness ornaments. During the Han dynasty, the Xiongnu people were already using saddles and in the following Western Jin dynasty the Xianbei people began to use the saddle stirrup. By the Sixteen States period the harness had been greatly improved, with the use of the saddle-bridge, buckled girth strap, stirrups and bit, making horse riding a much more comfortable experience and providing riders with greater stability and control of their mounts. As a result, cavalrymen began to use heavier armour, and carry larger and stronger bows and other weapons.

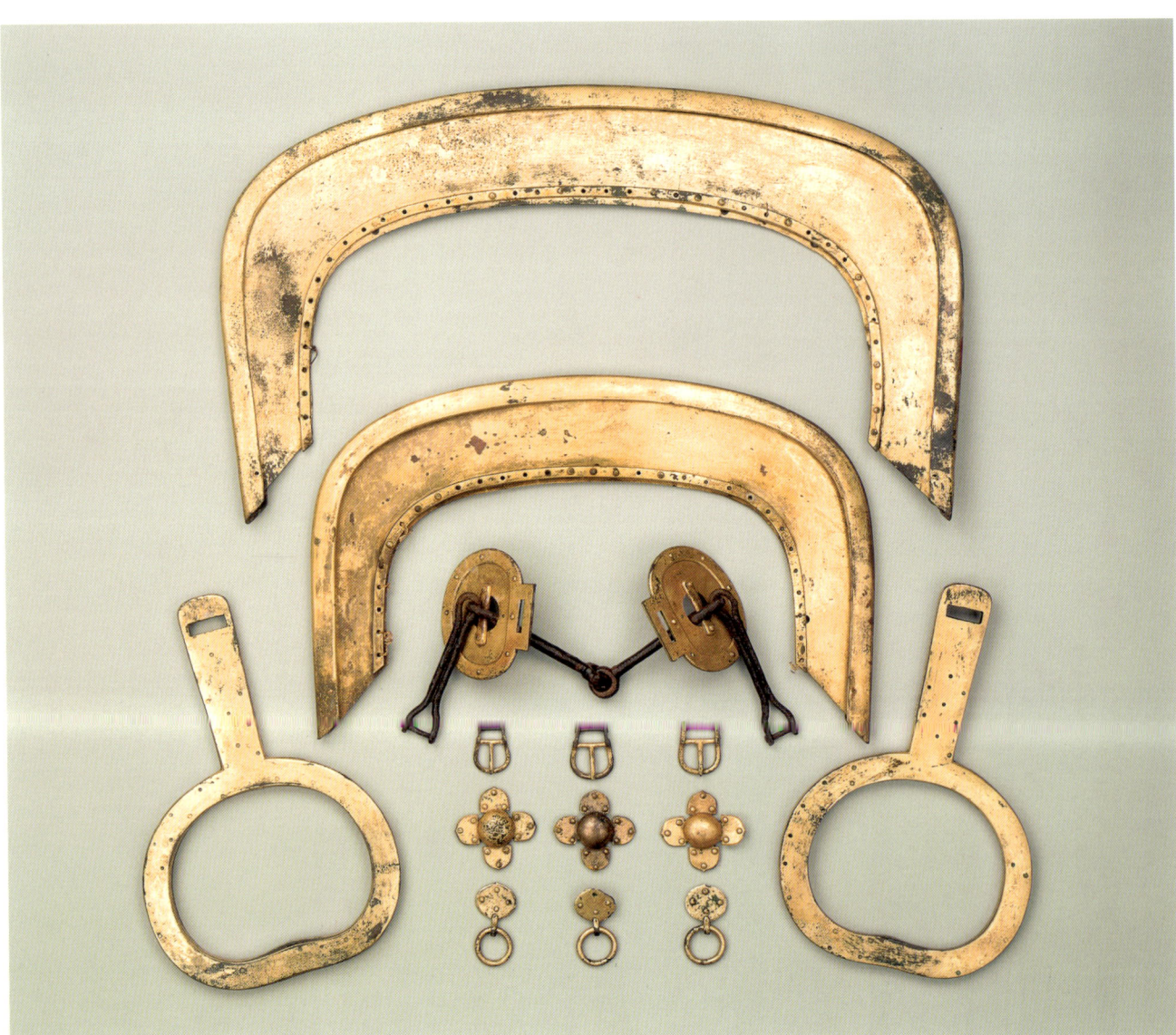

Object to exorcise evil spirits
Northern Wei dynasty (386–534)
Unearthed at Tumd Banner,
Inner Mongolia
Gilt bronze
3.6 (h) x 3.3 (l) cm
Collection of the National
Museum of China (Mengbo 105)

This small gilt bronze creature was used to exorcise evil and is known as a *bixie*. Its divine purpose is suggested by the large head with curling horns and the wing-like patterns on its body. It is seated on all fours with its mouth open, as if to scare off evil spirits. The object was made during the Northern Wei dynasty, established by the Tabgach (known in Chinese as Tuoba) group of the Xianbei people. The central, and original, sphere of influence of the Northern Wei was northern Shanxi and the central area of present-day Inner Mongolia.

A *bixie* is a winged animal that originated in Western Asia, and images can be found as far afield as the Byzantine empire, the eastern Mediterranean and the Eurasian grasslands. *Bixie* take different forms, such as lions, tigers, horses or camels, and according to historical documents they share features with the mythical *qilin*, *fuba* and *tianlu*. This *bixie* shares the characteristics of horses and camels, and follows representations dating from the Western Han period.

The *bixie* was introduced into China and was adapted and integrated with local cultures during the Western and Eastern Han, Wei and Jin periods. Many *bixie* of this kind have been discovered in archeological excavations, and are now to be found in public and private collections.

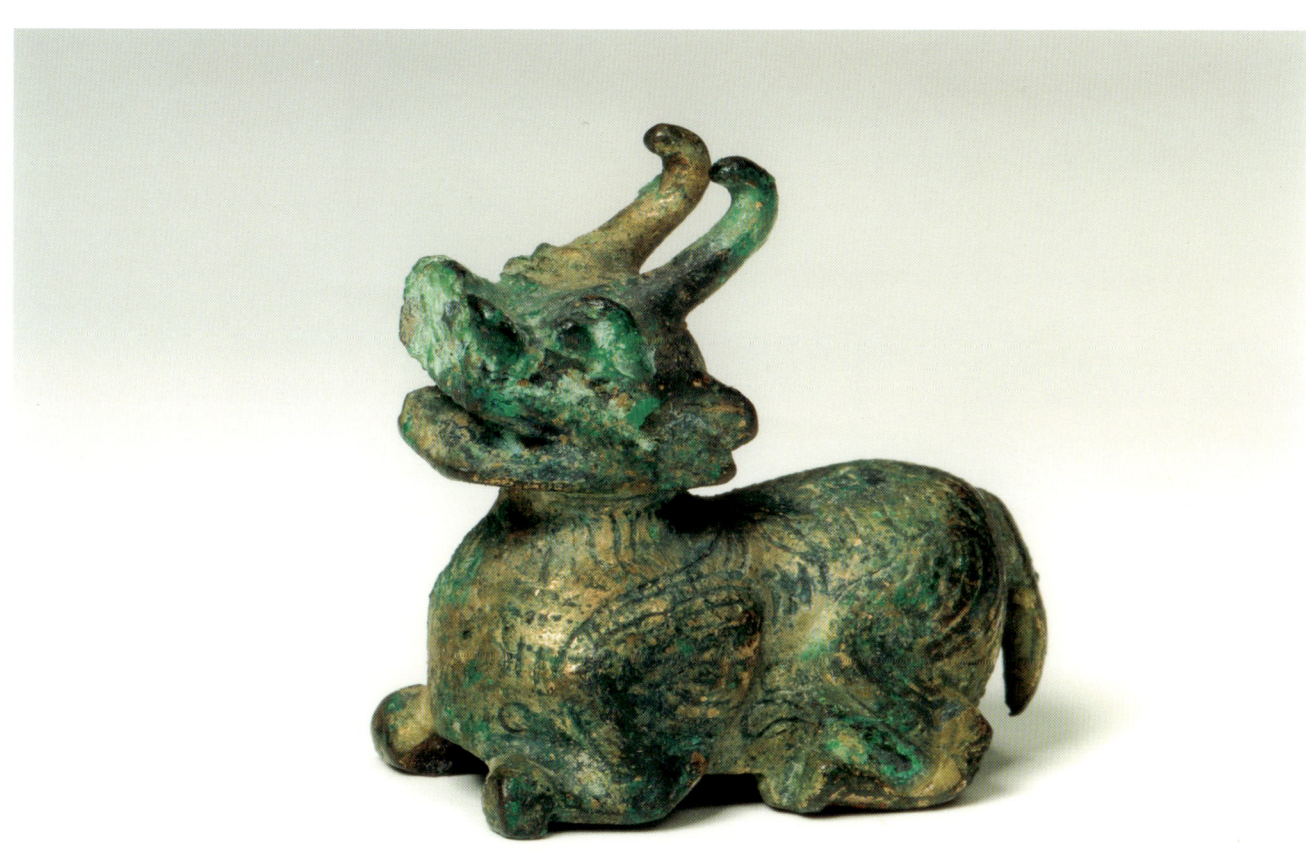

Female musician
Northern Qi dynasty (550–577)
Unearthed in 1973 at Shouyang,
Shanxi province
Earthenware with pigment
28.2 (h) cm
Collection of the National
Museum of China (K9900)

This standing female figure is depicted holding a lute-like instrument, known as a *pipa*. The *pipa* originated in Central Asia. The celebrated Han dynasty beauty Wang Zhaojun is often depicted playing or carrying a *pipa*, a symbol of her marriage to the Xiongnu king and her life of exile north of the Great Wall. The representation of the *pipa* with this funerary figure indicates the extent of cross-cultural exchanges that existed before and during the Northern Qi period.

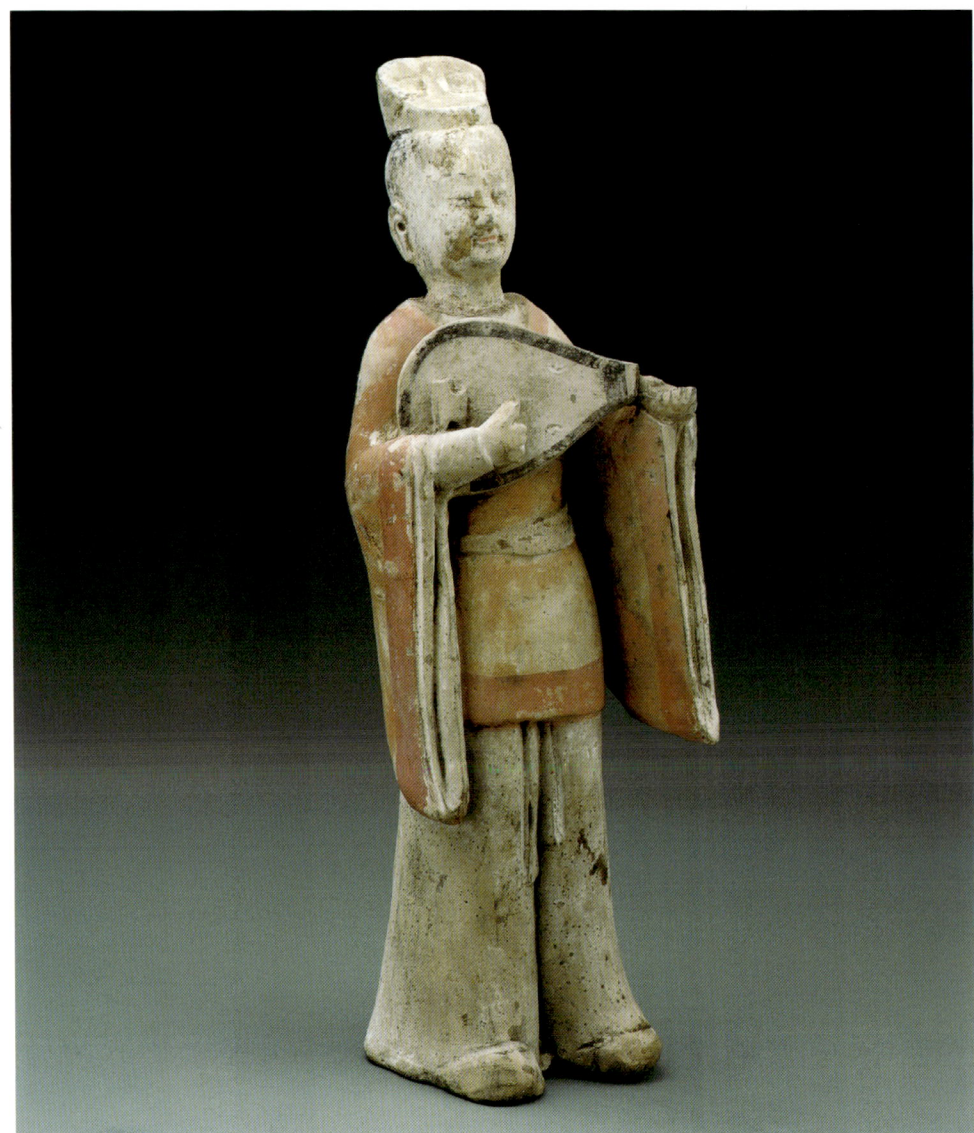

Flask
Northern Qi dynasty (550–577)
Excavated in 1971 from the
tomb of Fan Cui (dated 575),
Anyang, Henan province
Glazed earthenware
20.5 (h) cm
Collection of the National
Museum of China (K9931)

The shape of this yellow-glazed flask is influenced by the pilgrim's flask, which originated in West Asia. It has a flattened form and two eyelets to allow it to be lashed on to a saddle. The flask is moulded and on each side has the same pattern of a centrally placed dancer and four musicians, described in Chinese texts as depictions of *Hu* people. *Hu* is a generic term for people of non-Han origin who inhabited what is now northern and western China. Here they are depicted with large deep-set eyes, high-bridged noses, thick beards, narrow-sleeved costumes and long boots. The central figure dances on a lotus flower, which represents a small round carpet used for the whirling dance that was a popular form of entertainment in the sixth and seventh centuries. The two musicians in the front play the lute (*pipa*) and cymbals and those in the background play the flute and clappers.

The flask was found in 1971, during the Cultural Revolution, when peasants alerted authorities to antiquities they had uncovered while building an irrigation system in Anyang in the Central Plains region. The site was found to contain a tomb that belonged to Fan Cui, a high official at the Northern Qi court at Ye, who had died in 575. The tomb contained more than seventy burial objects, including ceramic vessels and figurines and a number of flasks similar to this one. The flasks provide an insight into life at the Northern Qi court and the significant presence of Central Asian people at the court.

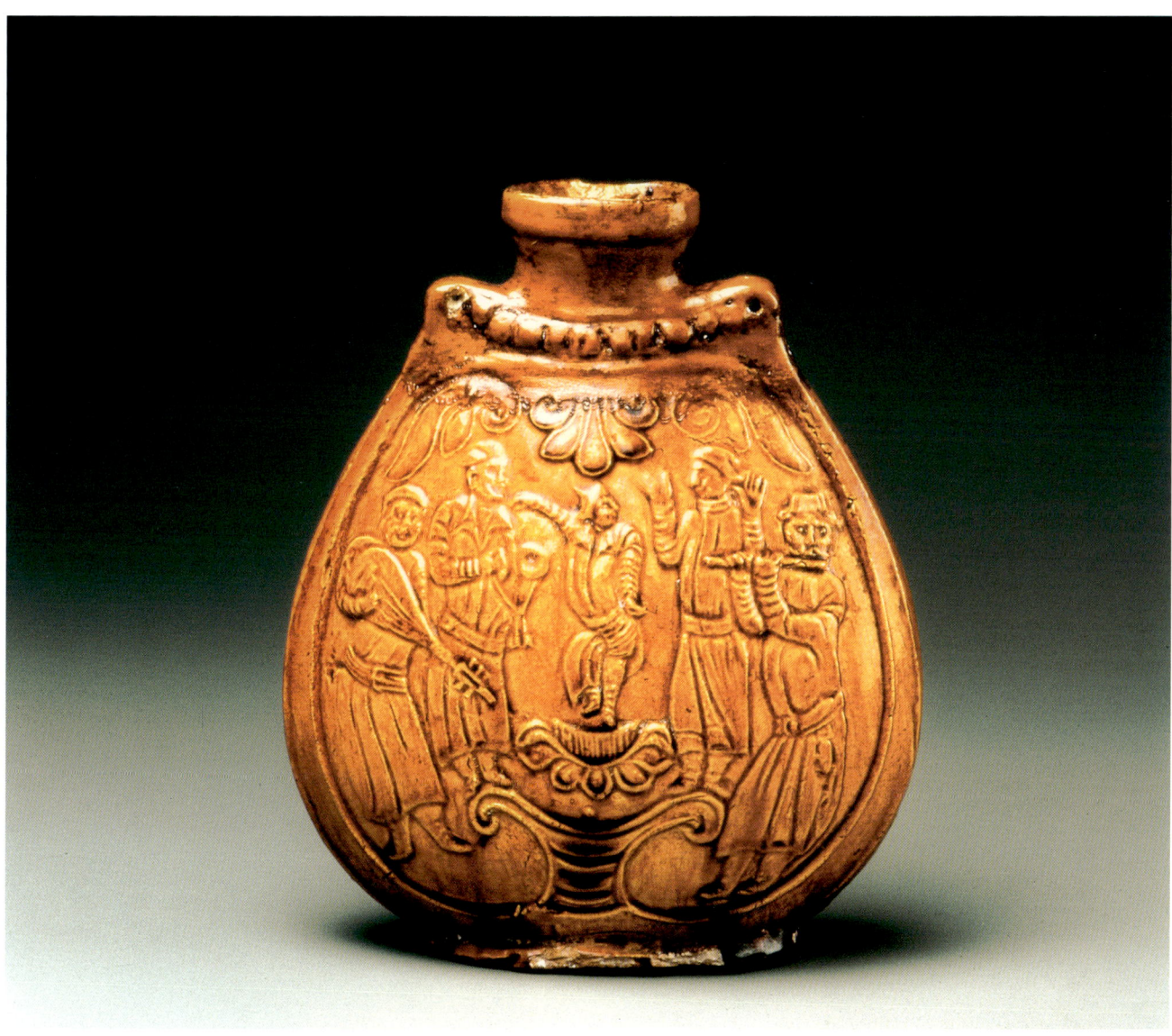

Figure
Northern Qi dynasty (550–577)
Excavated in 1955 from the
tomb of Zhang Susu (dated 559),
Taiyuan, Shanxi province
Earthenware with pigment
24 (h) cm
Collection of the National
Museum of China (Jinbo 379)

This painted earthenware figure wears dress that is characteristic of the Xianbei people: notably, a distinctive hat, an inner garment that comes to the knees, an outer garment that is fastened at the waist with the right shoulder exposed, and wide-legged trousers that are tied under the knee. The figure appears to have once held something, possibly a wooden weapon, which has since perished. His face has been sensitively modelled with lively eyes and a distinguished-looking moustache painted with ink.

This figure was excavated from the tomb of Zhang Susu, a member of a northern nomadic clan living in the Northern Qi. It is one of a number of funerary objects, including farmyard animals and objects intended for use in the afterlife.

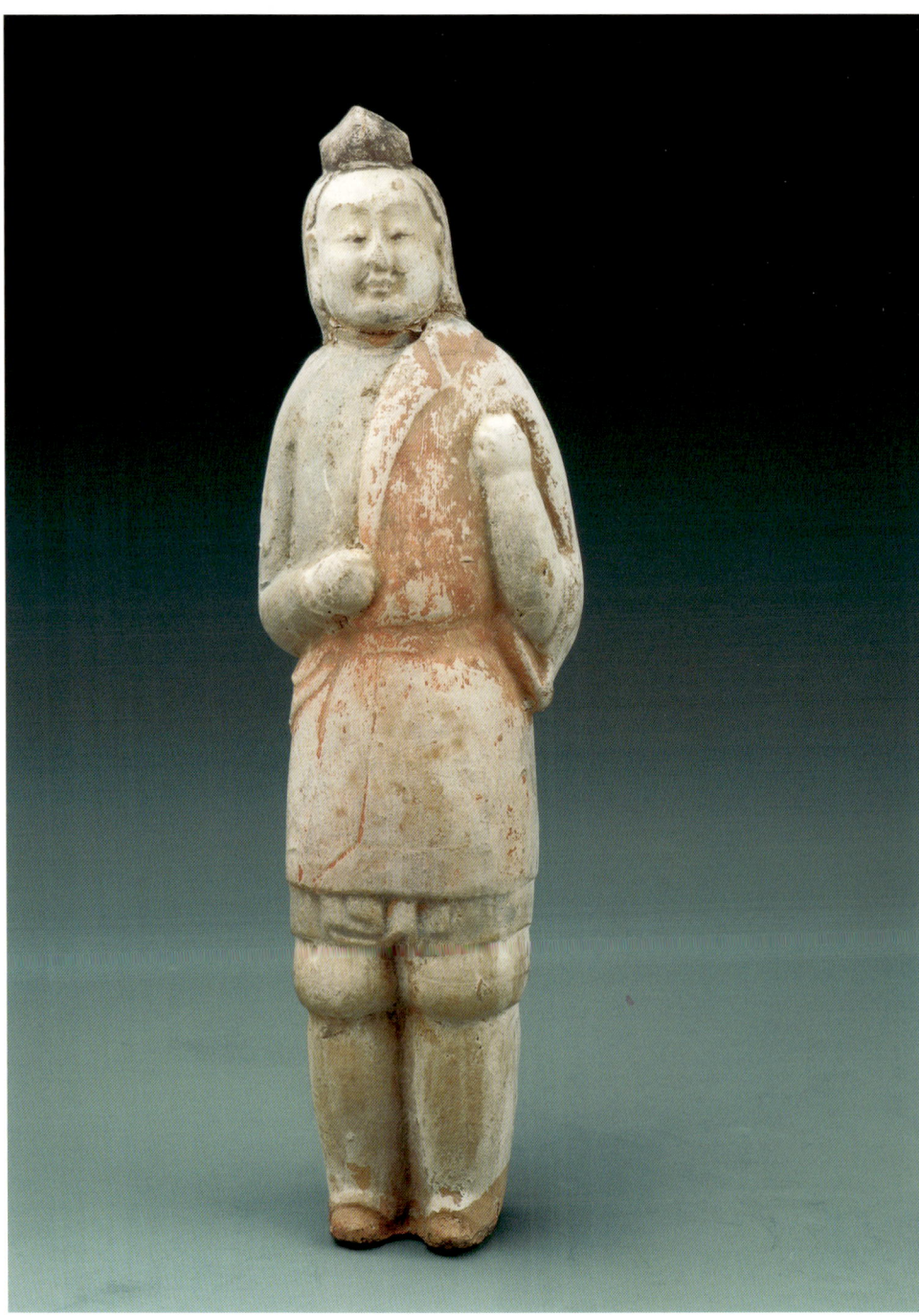

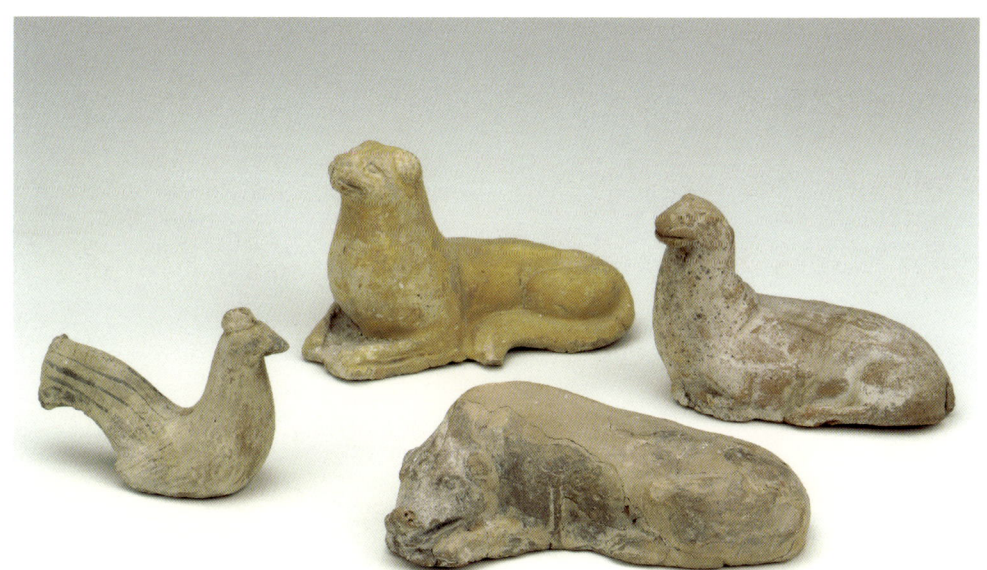

Hen, dog, pig and sheep
Northern Qi dynasty (550–577)
Excavated in 1955 from the
tomb of Zhang Susu (dated 559),
Taiyuan, Shanxi province
Earthenware with pigment
Chicken: 14 (h) x 11 (l) cm; dog: 8 (h)
x 15 (l) cm; pig: 7.5 (h) x 16.5 (l) cm;
sheep: 6 (h) x 12.5 (l) cm
Collection of the National
Museum of China (Jinbo 340,
Jinbo 329, Jinbo 341, Jinbo 326)

Zhang Susu was from
a northern nomadic family
and lived during the
Northern Qi dynasty.
His tomb was found in
Taiyuan in present-day
Shanxi province (then
known as Jinzhou), which
was an economically
developed region to the
south of the Great Wall.
As in other parts of China
at that time, agriculture
was the main mode of
production for the majority
of the population.

The many objects that
were found buried with
Zhang Susu represented
the necessities that
he needed in the afterlife,
including farmyard animals
such as a dog, pig, sheep
and hen. The quantity
of objects found in Zhang's
tomb suggests he was not
an ordinary farmer, but
rather a relatively wealthy
one, or at least one who
yearned for a better life.

**Stove, grinding
stone, well and toilet**
Northern Qi dynasty (550–577)
Excavated in 1955 from the
tomb of Zhang Susu (dated 559),
Taiyuan, Shanxi province
Earthenware with pigment
Stove: 12.5 (h) x 11.5 (w) cm; grinding
stone: 5.5 (h) x 7.2 (base diam) cm;
well: 5 (h) x 8.5 (diam) cm; toilet:
7 (h) x 9 (w) x 10 (d) cm
Collection of the National
Museum of China (Jinbo 336,
Jinbo 337, Jinbo 338, Jinbo 386)

Along with models of the
farmyard animals found
in the tomb of Zhang Susu
there was also a group
of models of domestic
equipment and facilities
of the kind that would
be expected in a functioning
well-to-do rural household
at the time. These consist
of a stove, a grinding stone,
water well and toilet, which
collectively demonstrate
the lifestyle or aspirations
of the man with whom
they were buried.

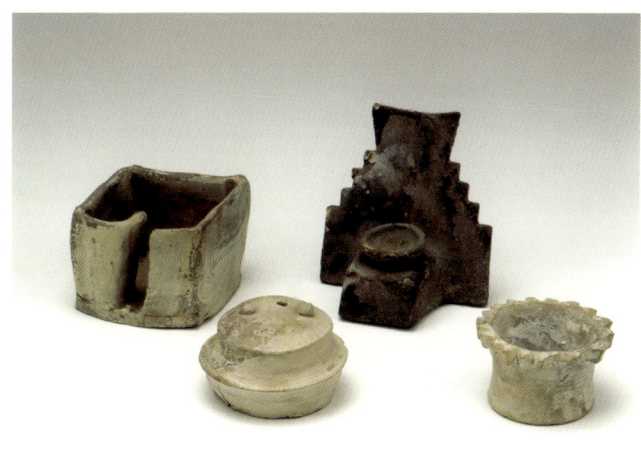

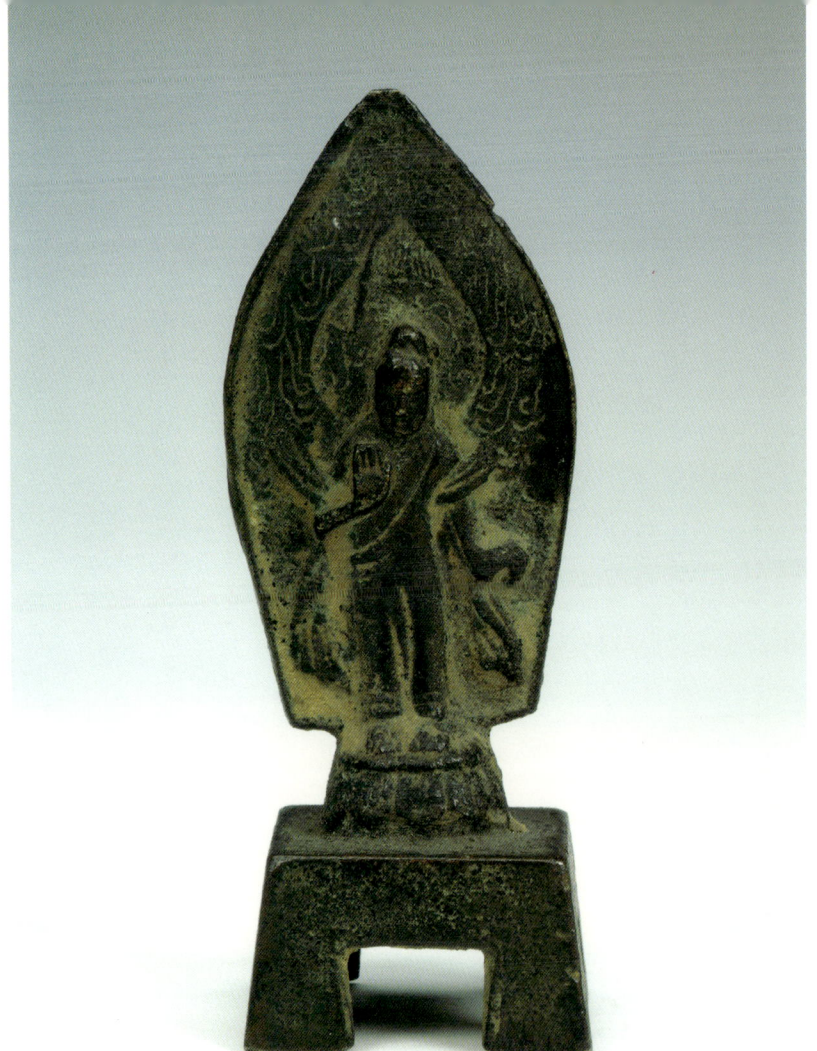

Amitabha Buddha
Northern Qi dynasty (550–577), dated 551
Bronze
12.1 (h) cm
Collection of the National Museum of China (C5.2235; donated by Mr Huo Mingzhi, 1949)

In the Han dynasty, one way Buddhism was transmitted to China from India was via the Hexi Corridor in Gansu province, an important section of the Silk Road. But it was not until the Southern and Northern dynasties and the Tang dynasty, a time when traditional Chinese culture was greatly influenced by cultures from beyond the Great Wall, that Buddhism came to exert a significant influence within China.

This statue of Amitabha, Buddha of the Western Paradise, dates from the time of the Northern Qi, which was one of the Northern dynasties. It has a peach-shaped aureole incised with upsweeping rays of light. The raised right hand is open and held before the chest in the *mudra* (hand gesture) expressing fearlessness (*abhayamudra*); the left arm hangs beside the body with the hand in a gesture of benevolence (*varamudra*). The left shoulder is draped and the figure stands barefoot on a lotus base, which is supported by a four-legged pedestal inscribed: 'This Buddha was made by the Buddhist acolyte Yang Rong on the 2nd day of the 9th month in the 2nd year of the Tianbao reign [551]'.

This figure has many features that are typically associated with buddha figures: for example, a high bun and the wearing of a *kasaya* leaving the right shoulder bare rather than collar pendants. It is worth noting that bodhisattvas and not figures of buddha are usually represented with silk draped over one shoulder. Although this example embodies characteristics that are associated with both buddha and bodhisattva figures, the inscription makes it clear that the statue is a buddha.

Shrine
Tang dynasty (618–907)
Stone
41(h) x 31 (w) x 10.5 (d) cm
Collection of the National
Museum of China (C10.264)

The figures that form this Buddhist shrine are carved in high relief. The upper register comprises a central buddha deity figure, flanked by attendants, bodhisattvas and guardian figures. The lower register depicts kneeling donors. The buddha figure holds an alms bowl in the left hand and a staff or *khakkhara* in the right, and wears a cassock with the right shoulder exposed. Two attendants standing on either side press the palms of their hands together in an attitude of reverence. A bodhisattva and guardian figure stand on the outer side of each disciple. The bodhisattva to the left of the buddha holds an object up in the right hand and carries an amphora (*kundika*) in the left. The bodhisattva on the right holds both palms together in front of the chest. All stand on lotus pedestals.

According to Buddhist iconography, a figure holding a staff and alms bowl is usually the Bhaisaijya Buddha, or the Medicine Buddha, but in this case the retinue features characteristics associated with Sakyamuni Buddha. The two attendants standing on either side of the buddha figure, one old and the other young, are the two foremost disciples of Sakyamuni: Mahakasypa and Ananda. The figure on the left holding the amphora appears to be the bodhisattva Avalokitesvara; therefore it follows that the figure standing to the right would be the bodhisattva Mahasthamaprapta.

On the basis of the figures flanking the buddha figure, it is most likely that the central deity is Sakyamuni Buddha. The distinctive attributes given to Sakyamuni reflect the influence of Central Asian cultural traditions on Buddhism, which was introduced into ethnic Han regions via the Silk Road trade routes. The statue, with its eclectic iconography highlights the popularity of Bhaisaijya in the Tang dynasty and the popularity of worshipping this buddha, who offered the hope of preventing illness and curing disease.

The worship of Bhaisaijya Buddha originated from the worship of the Medicine King in Central Asia, beyond the Great Wall. The Zoroastrian scripture, the *Avesta*, indicates an association in Iranian culture between the worship of light and that of the Medicine King, a tradition acculturated within Buddhism. Statues of Bhaisaijya Buddha were common in areas of Han ethnic settlement during the Tang dynasty.

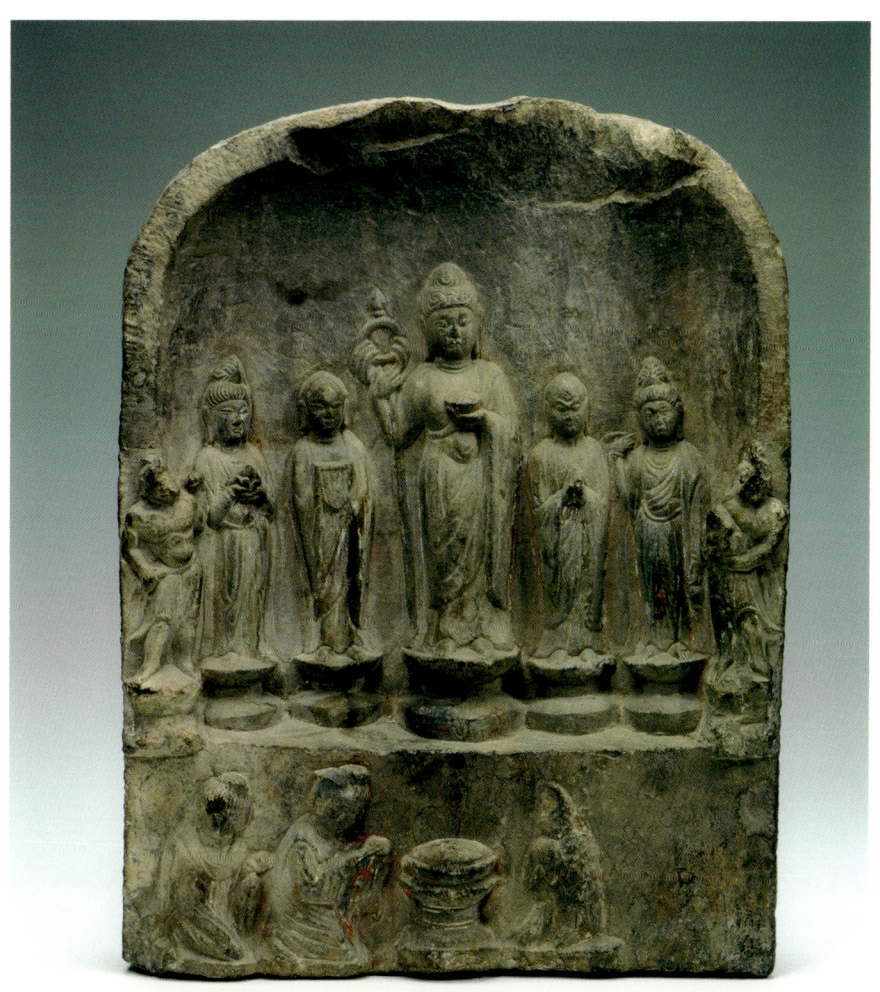

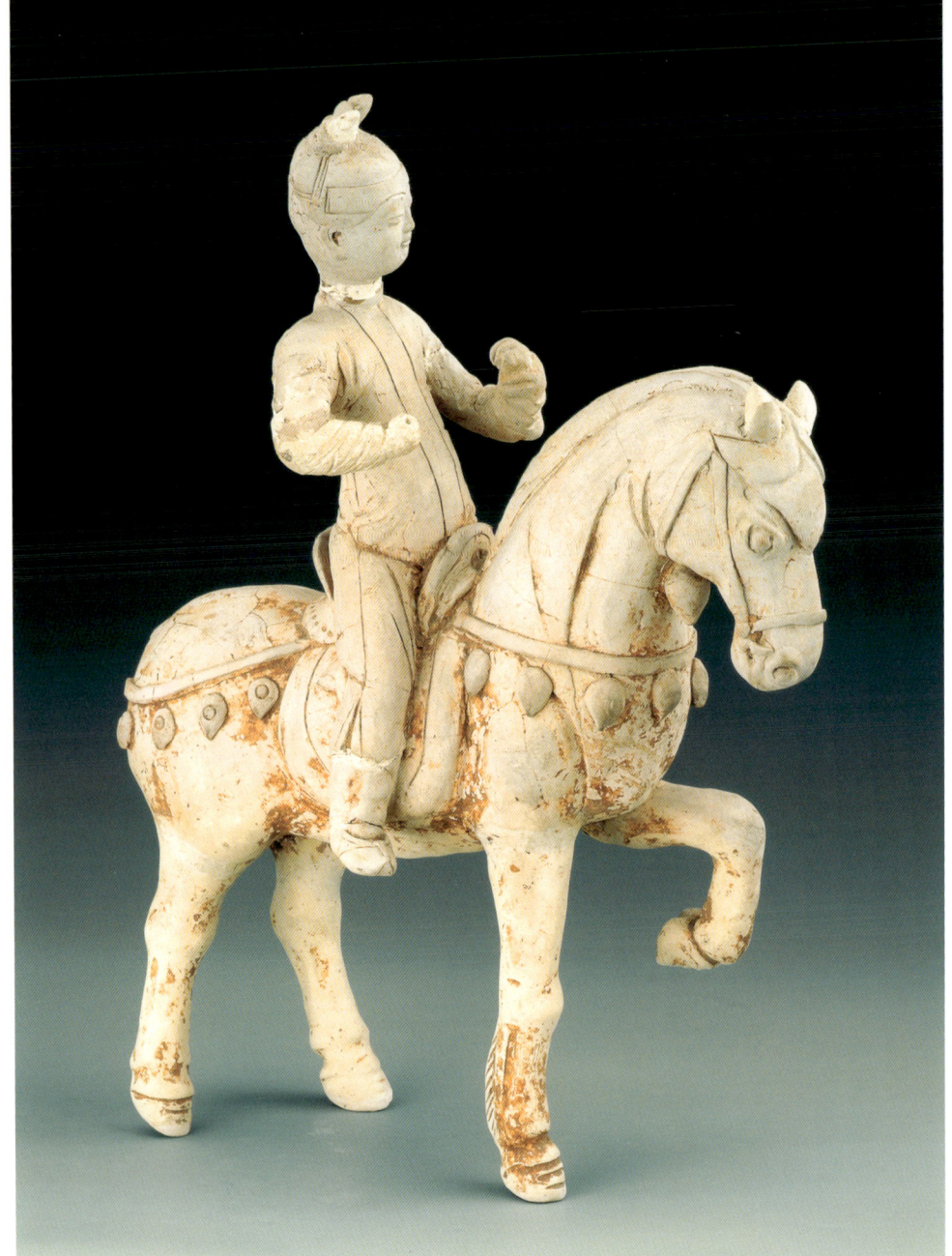

Female equestrian figure
Sui dynasty (581–618)
Unearthed in 1956 at Guizishan,
Wuhan, Hubei province
Earthenware
37.5 (h) cm
Collection of the National
Museum of China (Ebo 132)

This rider wears a garment with tight-fitting sleeves, trousers and boots, all of which are characteristic of northern nomadic dress. She sits on the saddle in a spirited attitude and holds what would have been the reins in both hands. The horse raises its front leg as if preparing to gallop, which imbues the sculpture with a great sense of movement. During the Sui and Tang dynasties many northern cultures, in which it was common for women to ride horses, came to exert a considerable influence on society.

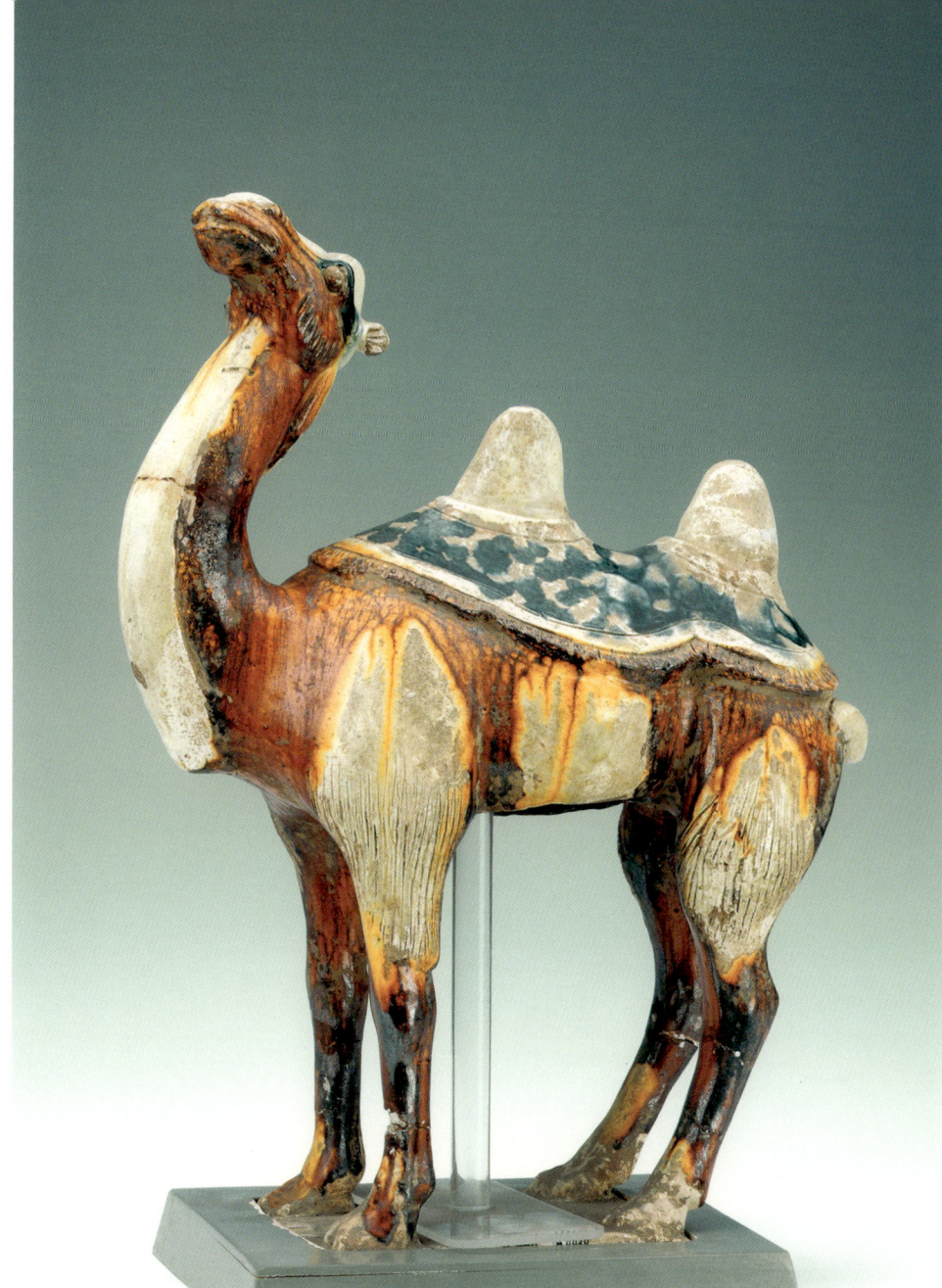

Camel
Tang dynasty (618–907)
Unearthed at Guanlin Fittings
Factory, Luoyang, Henan province
Glazed earthenware
39.5 (h) x 29 (l) cm
Collection of the National
Museum of China (K9939)

Camels were the major mode of transport along the ancient Silk Road trade routes and thus made an extraordinary contribution to commercial and cultural exchange between China and the West. Many tricolour glazed camels have been found buried in the tombs of the wealthy in the Central Plains area dating from the Tang dynasty, when trade between Central Asia and the West flourished.

This camel rears its head and has wide open eyes. The slant of the two humps and the short curly tail that clings to the left flank create a realistic and animated depiction. The camel's body is covered with a yellow-brown glaze and on its back is a 'felt rug' created by alternating spots of blue and white glaze.

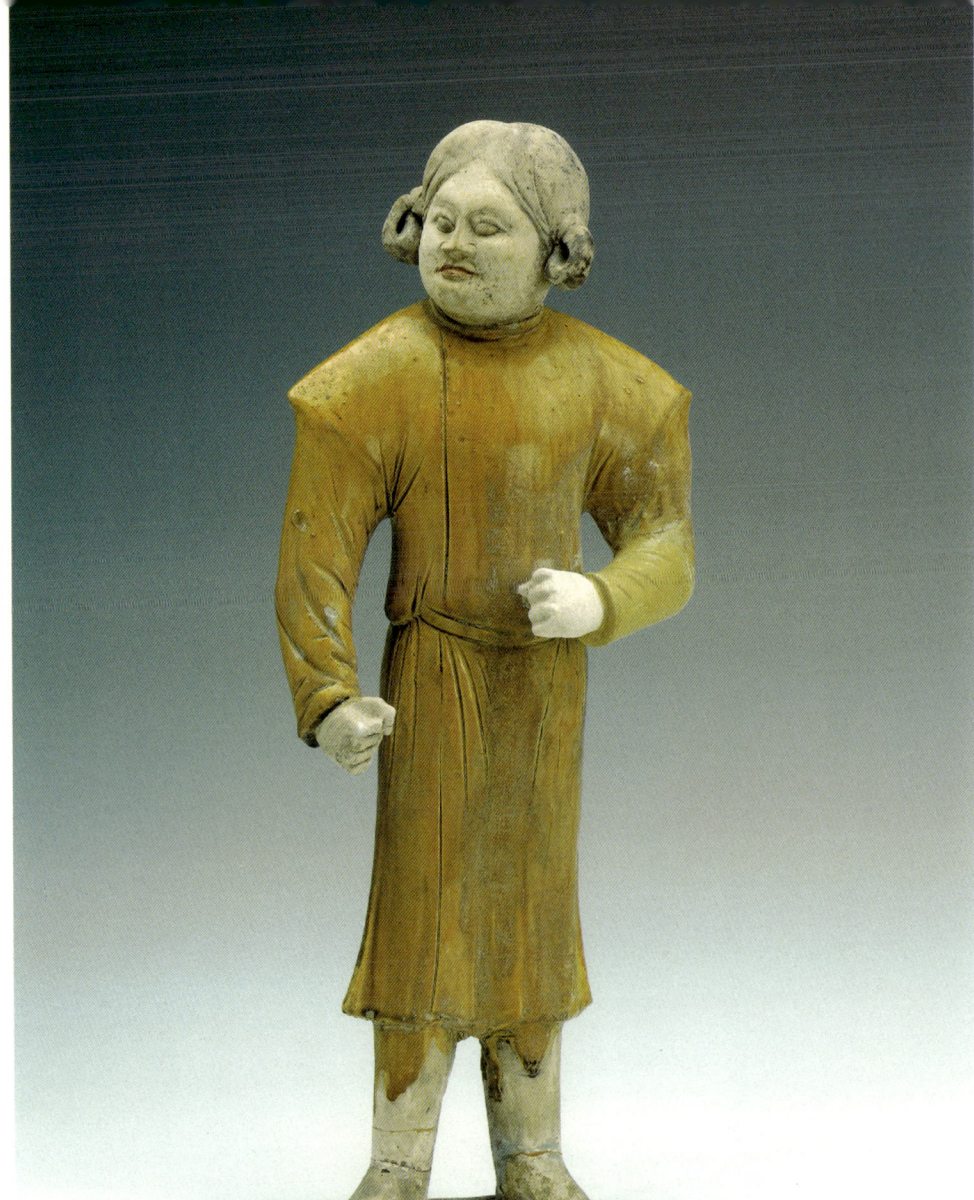

Figure
Tang dynasty (618–907)
Excavated in 1957 from the tomb
of Xianyu Tinghui (dated 723), in Xi'an,
Shaanxi province
Glazed earthenware with pigment
41 (h) cm
Collection of the National
Museum of China (K6846)

This figure has a distinctive hairstyle and pronounced facial features: notably, thick eyebrows, large eyes and a wide nose, which suggest it is a depiction of a person from West Asia.

He wears a round-collared Han Chinese outer garment belted at the waist and a pair of long boots. The arms are active and the fists clenched which, together with the turning posture, suggest that the figure may originally have been leading a horse by the reins.

This figure was excavated from the tomb of Xianyu Tinghui (660–723), located north-west of Nanhe village in the western suburbs of Xi'an. Xianyu Tinghui was the scion of a family of military officials from Yuyang in Hebei province. He achieved high rank during the reign of Xuanzong (reigned 712–56), and when he died, the emperor ordered the imperial workshops to make funerary objects for his tomb.

Figure

Tang dynasty (618–907)
Excavated in 1957 from the tomb
of Xianyu Tinghui (dated 723), in Xi'an,
Shaanxi province
Glazed earthenware with pigment
41 (h) cm
Collection of the National
Museum of China (K6847)

The physical appearance of this figure, with deep-set eyes, a high-bridged nose and thick beard, suggest it is a depiction of a person from Central or West Asia. The facial features have been highlighted with pigments to further animate his expression.

The hands clenched into fists are held up in front of the chest which, together with the twisting pose of the body and slightly bent head, suggest that he may originally have been leading a camel.

As with the preceding figure, unearthed from the same tomb, the clothing is typical of Han Chinese people and therefore reflects the cultural exchange and integration between China and West Asia during the Tang dynasty.

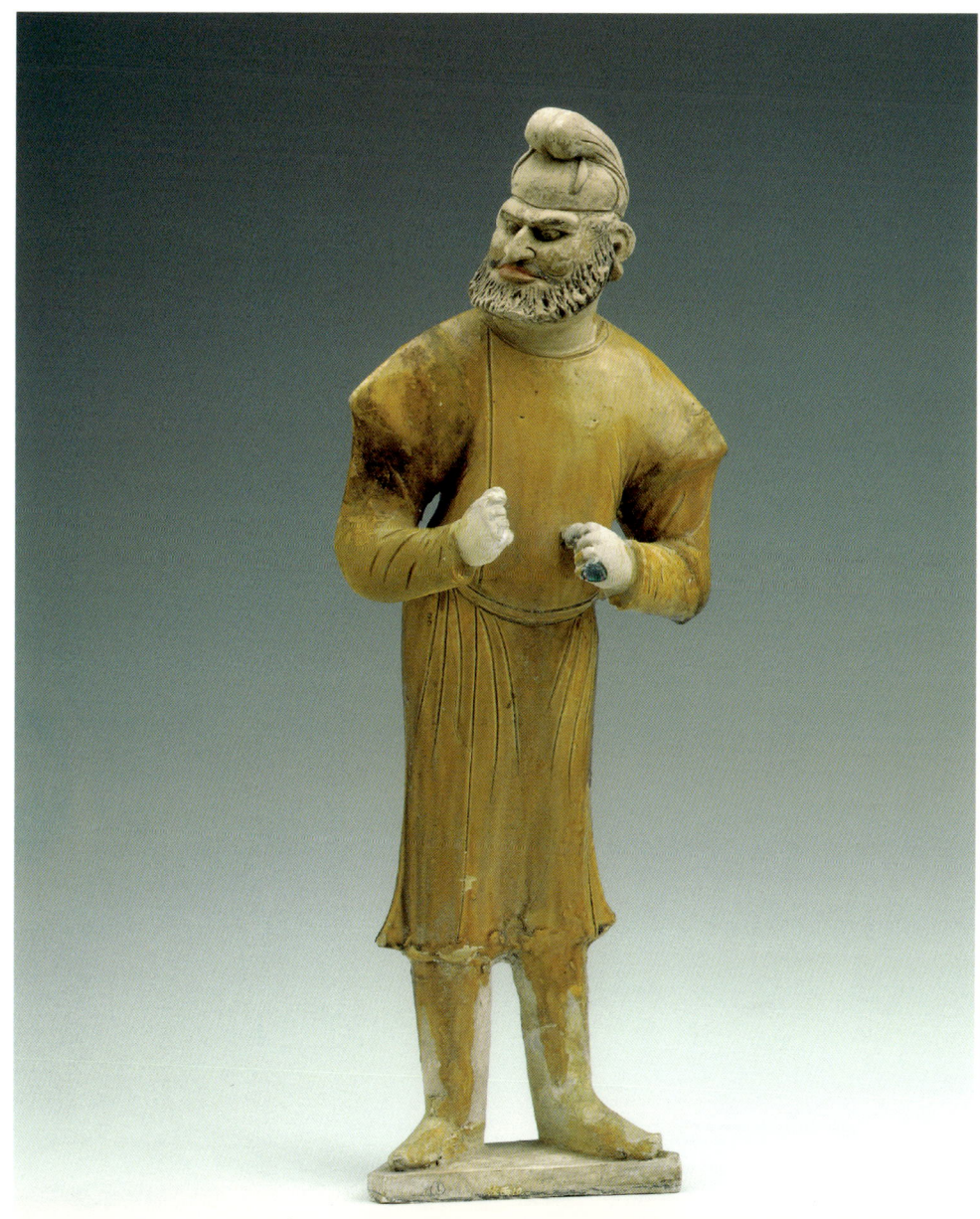

Figure
Tang dynasty (618–907)
Said to have been excavated
in Xi'an, Shaanxi province
Earthenware with pigment
28 (h) cm
Collection of the National
Museum of China (C3.984)

In the Tang dynasty, indigenous people with curly hair from South and Southeast Asia and from Africa were known as Kunlun people. At this time, enslaved Kunlun people commonly presented acrobatic performances for Chinese aristocrats and bureaucrats. They were known as 'Kunlun slaves' and are frequently mentioned in the literature of that period. This barefoot figure has tight curls and wears a garment with a round neckline and close-fitting sleeves, a sash which falls from his shoulder to his waist, and tight-fitting pants. One arm is raised, which suggests that he was originally holding an implement.

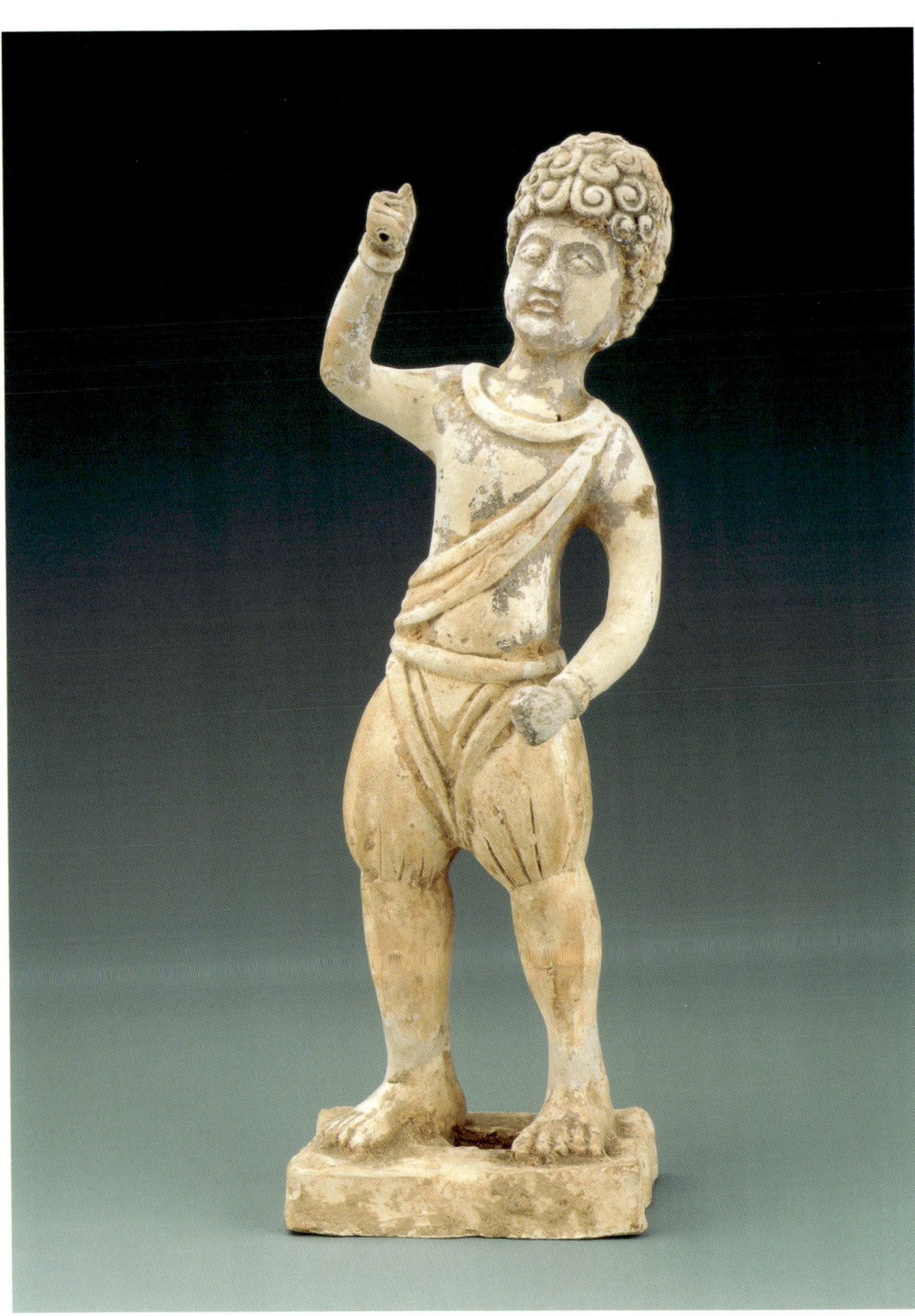

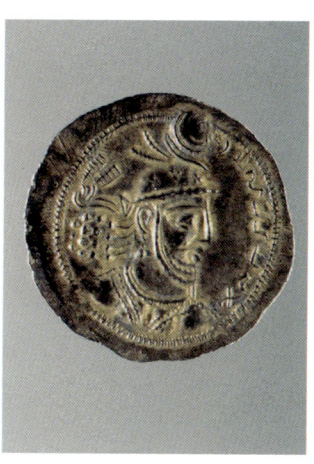
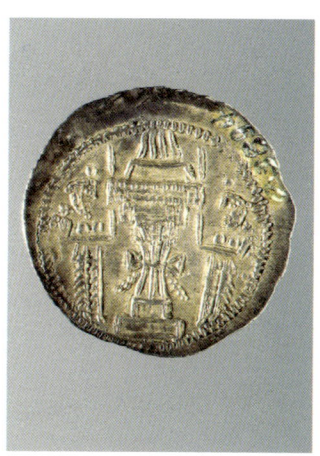

Silver coin of Ardashir II
Late fourth century CE
Unearthed at the ancient city of Gaochang, Turfan, Xinjiang autonomous region
Silver
3.1 (diam) cm
Collection of the National Museum of China (Xinbo 28.2/2)

This coin features the portrait of the Sassanian Persian ruler Ardashir II (reigned 379–83) on the obverse in the typical style of Persian coins of this time. The hemispherical crown the king is wearing is surmounted by a spherical motif decorated with two flying ribbons. The king has a high-bridged nose, deep-set eyes, thick beard, wavy hair and ears decorated with pearls. The well-preserved inscription reads: 'Servant of Ahura Mazda, Sacred Ardashir, King of all Kings.' On the reverse is a fire-altar and flames flanked by figures wearing coronal headdresses and ribboned costumes with raised swords.

The large numbers of Persian silver coins found in China serve as material evidence of friendly relations between the two empires and of frequent commercial exchanges via the Silk Road. Historical records also demonstrate that the Sassanian empire had very close political contacts with China: during the period from 455 to 521, Persia sent more than ten diplomatic missions to China.

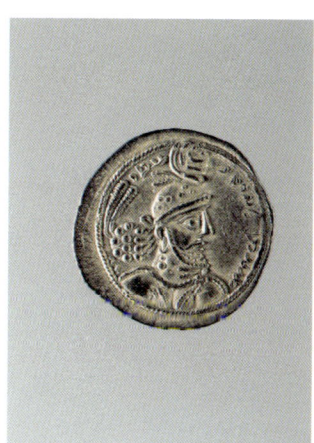
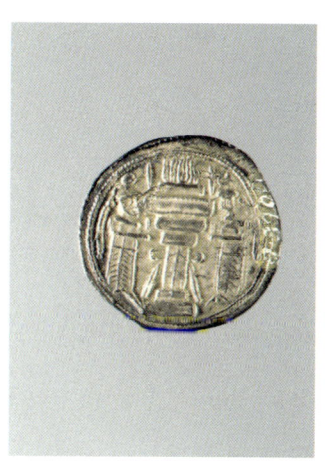

Persian Silver Coin of Shabuhr II
c 326–79
Unearthed at the ancient city of Gaochang, Turfan, Xinjiang autonomous region
Silver
2.8 (diam) cm
Collection of the National Museum of China (Xinbo 28.1/2)

At the centre of the obverse is a portrait of Shabuhr II, The inscriptions identify the portrait as 'Sacred King Shabuhr'. The reverse side is the same as that on the coin of Ardashir II.

Gaochang, where these two coins were found, is an ancient city site in Turfan, Xinjiang, and was located on the Silk Road trade route connecting East and West.

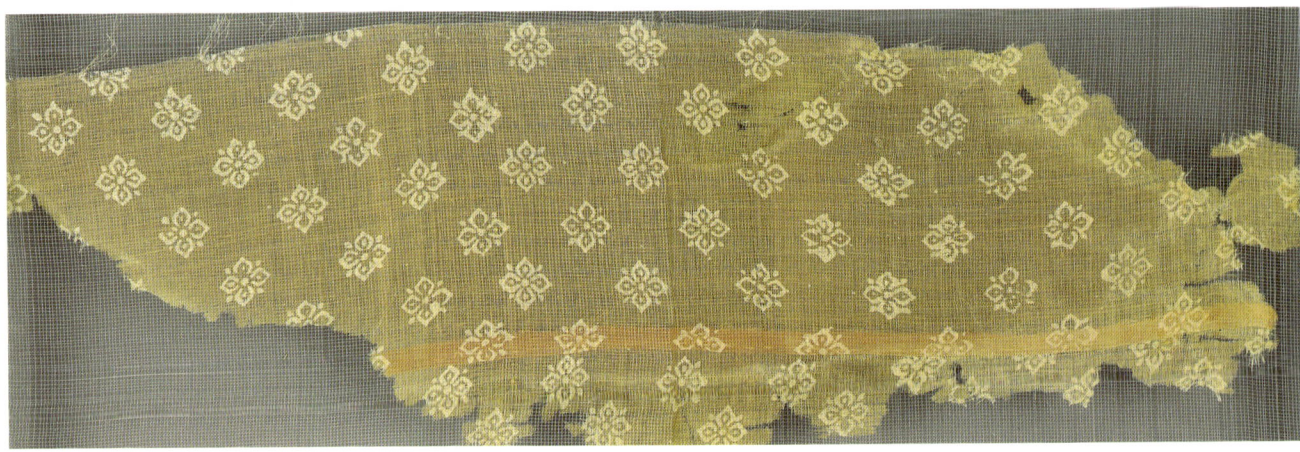

Textile fragment
Tang dynasty (618–907)
Unearthed in 1968 at the
Astana cemetery, Turfan,
Xinjiang autonomous region
Silk gauze
17.5 (w) x 5.1 (l) cm
Collection of the National
Museum of China (K10295)

The pattern on this textile, which looks like a persimmon calyx, was drawn using an ash (*huixie*), rather than wax-resist stencilling process.

The persimmon calyx was a popular decorative motif used on damask silk in the Tang dynasty. The renowned Tang poet Bo Juyi refers to such a textile in one of his poems: 'The beauty with red sleeves weaves damask persimmons; So at the inn, when buying wine, you should try some made with pears.'

Chinese textiles patterned using wax-resist stencilling first appeared during the Eastern Han dynasty and gradually became popular during the Wei and Tang dynasties. Due to the small-scale production of wax in the Central Plains area, ash rather than wax was used during the Tang dynasty. Later, during the Ming and Qing periods, ash was widely used to produce the stencil-patterned blue and white cotton cloth that is popular today.

This textile fragment is one of many that have been unearthed from the Astana cemetery in Turfan in the Xinjiang region.

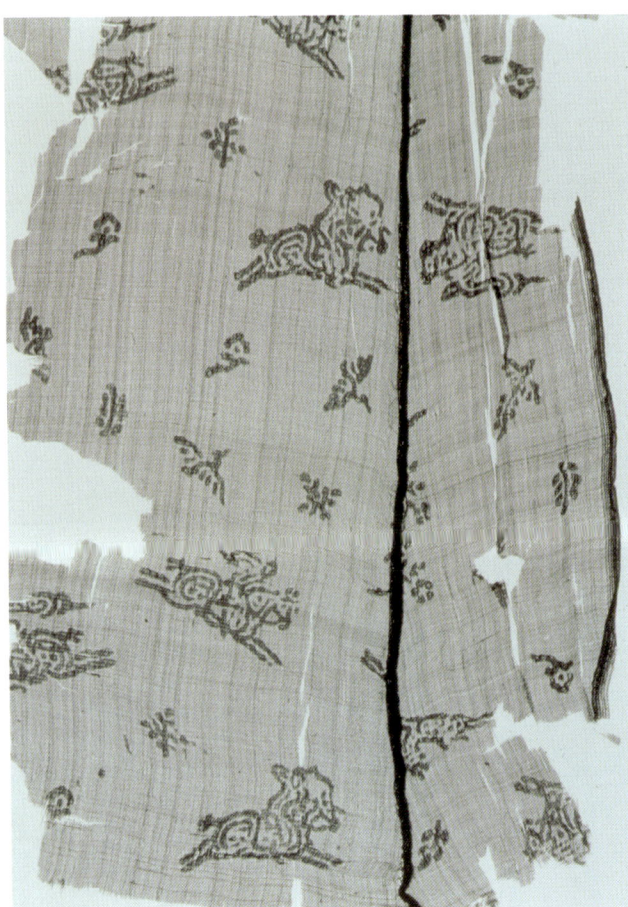

Textile fragment
Tang dynasty (618–907)
Unearthed at Turfan, Xinjiang
autonomous region
Silk gauze
18 (w) x 35 (l) cm
Collection of the National
Museum of China (Jie 1043)

This pale green silk gauze fragment is patterned with a stencilled hunting scene. It was found in a tomb dating to the mid Tang dynasty. The design depicts soldiers riding horses at high speed, while shooting bows and arrows and unleashing weighted rope projectiles, and causing birds to take flight. The patterns comprise simple lines and dots and are highly animated: this fragment is a particularly fine example of the plain-weave silk textiles from the Tang dynasty.

Textile fragment
Tang dynasty (618–907)
Unearthed in 1968 in Turfan,
Xinjiang autonomous region
Silk, weft-faced
compound plain-weave
7.5 (w) x 26 (l) cm
Collection of the National
Museum of China (Jie 1037)

The weaving technique used in this silk textile is unusual and involves fine and even brown warp threads and thicker weft threads. The pattern is composed of seven interlocking hexagons, stripes and the Chinese character for 'auspicious'. It is likely that the textile was produced in a city with a large Chinese population such as Gaochang, or present-day Turfan in Xinjiang.

A larger textile length with a similar pattern was excavated from Tomb 169 (dated 588) in the Astana cemetery, Turfan, in 1972–73 and is in the collection of the Xinjiang Uyghur Autonomous Region Museum. It is thought that these textiles are examples of the *jin* silk with white ground (*bai di jin*) recorded in ancient Turfan texts. Weft-faced compound weave textiles were produced in Xinjiang, which was an important centre on one of the Silk Road trading routes during the Han and Tang dynasties.

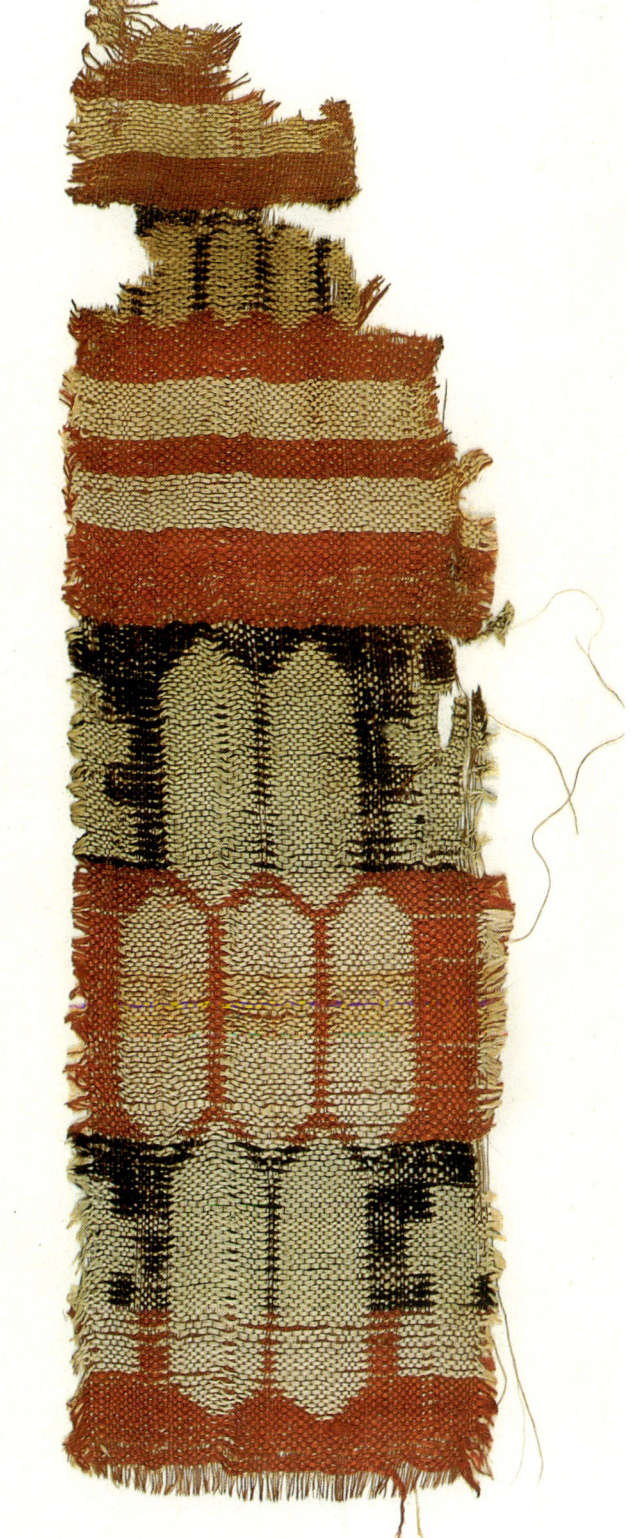

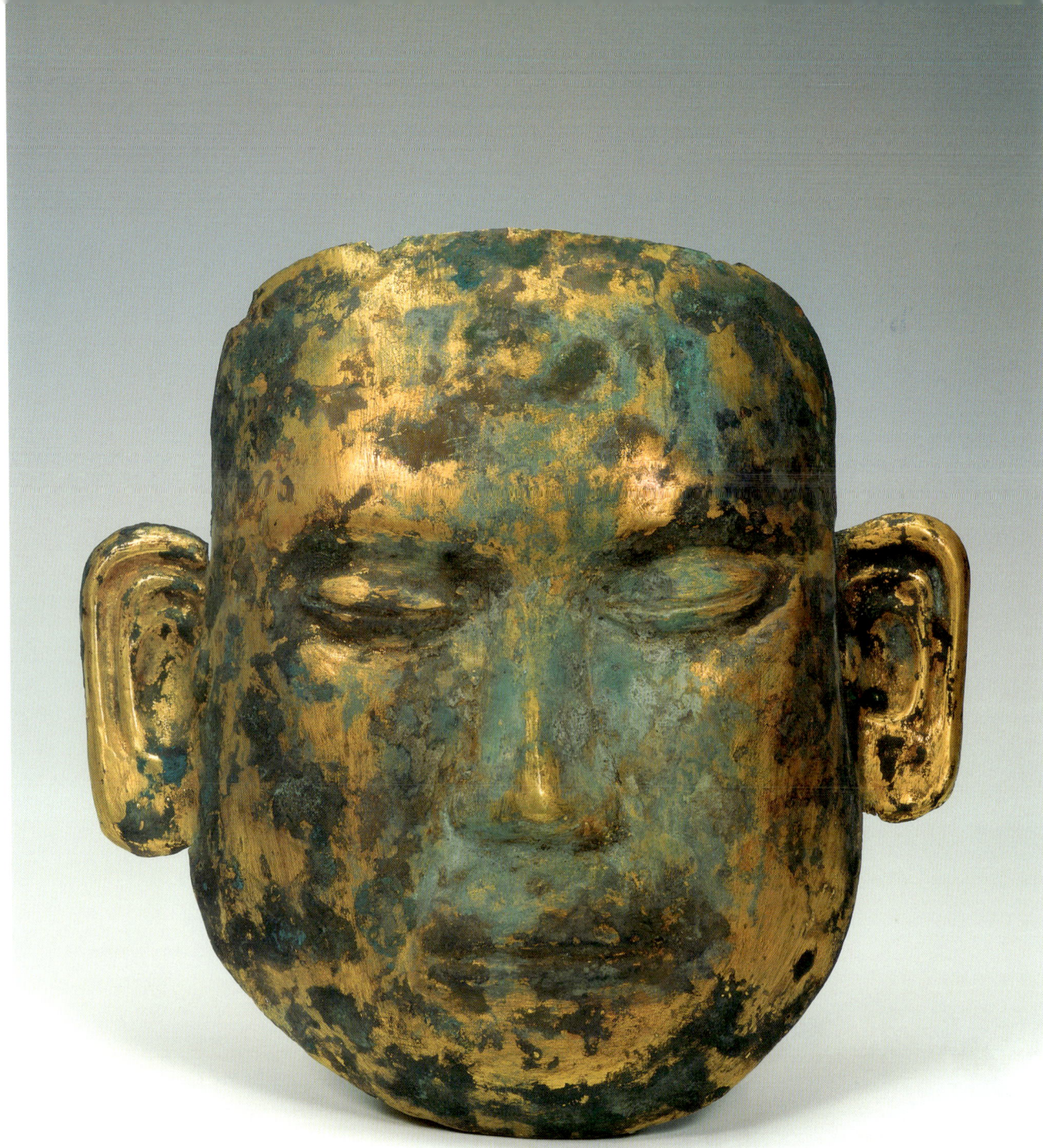

Death mask
Liao dynasty (916–1125)
Gilt bronze
23 (h) x 23.2 (w) cm
Collection of the National
Museum of China (C5.3713)

During the Liao dynasty, the Khitan (Qidan) nobility observed the custom of covering the face of the dead with a mask made of precious metal and encasing the body in a shroud made from silver wire. Like European death masks, these objects were modelled on the face of the deceased and were made from bronze, gilt bronze or gold, the type of metal conveying the status of the dead person. This example was made by hammering thin sheets of bronze on to a mould of the deceased's face and then gilding the finished object.

In China, such 'death masks' were unique to the Khitan people. They enhanced the preservation of the deceased, and were regarded as a way of paying respect to the deceased, by preserving the living visage.

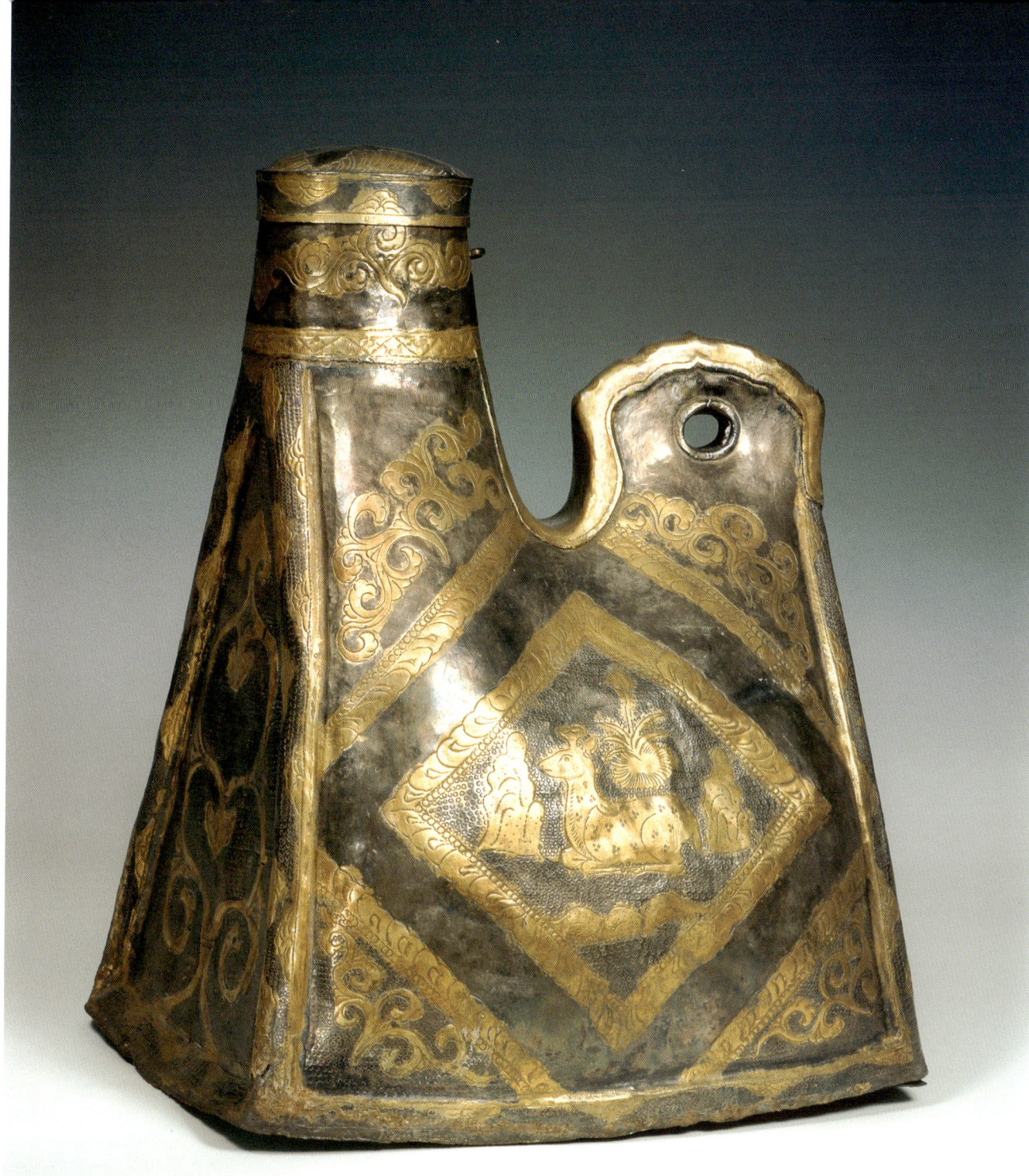

Pilgrim flask
Liao dynasty (916–1125)
Gilt silver
Unearthed in 1979 from a hoard
in Chifeng, Inner Mongolia
26.5 (h) x 5.5 (mouth diam)
x 16.6 (base w) x 21.2 (base l) cm
Collection of the National
Museum of China (Y2053)

The shape of the flask is inspired by leather containers for carrying water made by the Khitan, who founded the Liao dynasty. Raising from a rectangular flat base, the flask has a tall cylindrical spout and cover and a bracket-shaped handle pierced to allow a cord to be passed through it so that the flask could be secured to a saddle. It is ornamented with a Tang-inspired design of flowers, and on each side there is a rhombus framing a kneeling deer in a landscape setting with rocks, hillocks and vegetation. The flask, of a form used by nomadic peoples, is also influenced by Han Chinese metalworking techniques and reflects the high degree of Han Chinese influence in Liao dynasty decorative arts objects.

Pilgrim flask
Liao dynasty (916–1125)
Stoneware
25 (h) x 9 (base w) cm
Collection of the National
Museum of China (C4.2594)

This white-glazed pilgrim flask, known as *madeng hu*, was used to carry wine or water. Originally made from leather, it was an everyday article used by the Khitan people while hunting, grazing and warring. After the Khitan rose to power in northern China in the tenth century, they occupied major kiln sites in Dingzhou and Cizhou, and Chinese artisans were brought north of the Great Wall to create a ceramic industry. Ceramic flasks began to take the place of leather vessels, and in many cases the ceramic forms retained a nomadic style. This flask imitates a sewn leather vessel, with prominent edges and stitched seams that emulate the original nomadic form. The flask has a tall cylindrical spout to prevent the liquid inside from spilling and two bracket handles that have been pierced to allow the vessel to be tied to a saddle. Two small three-dimensional monkeys — one of the horary animals of the Chinese zodiac — ornament the bracket handles. The arms and legs of the monkeys grip the brackets, giving the impression that they too are riding on horse back.

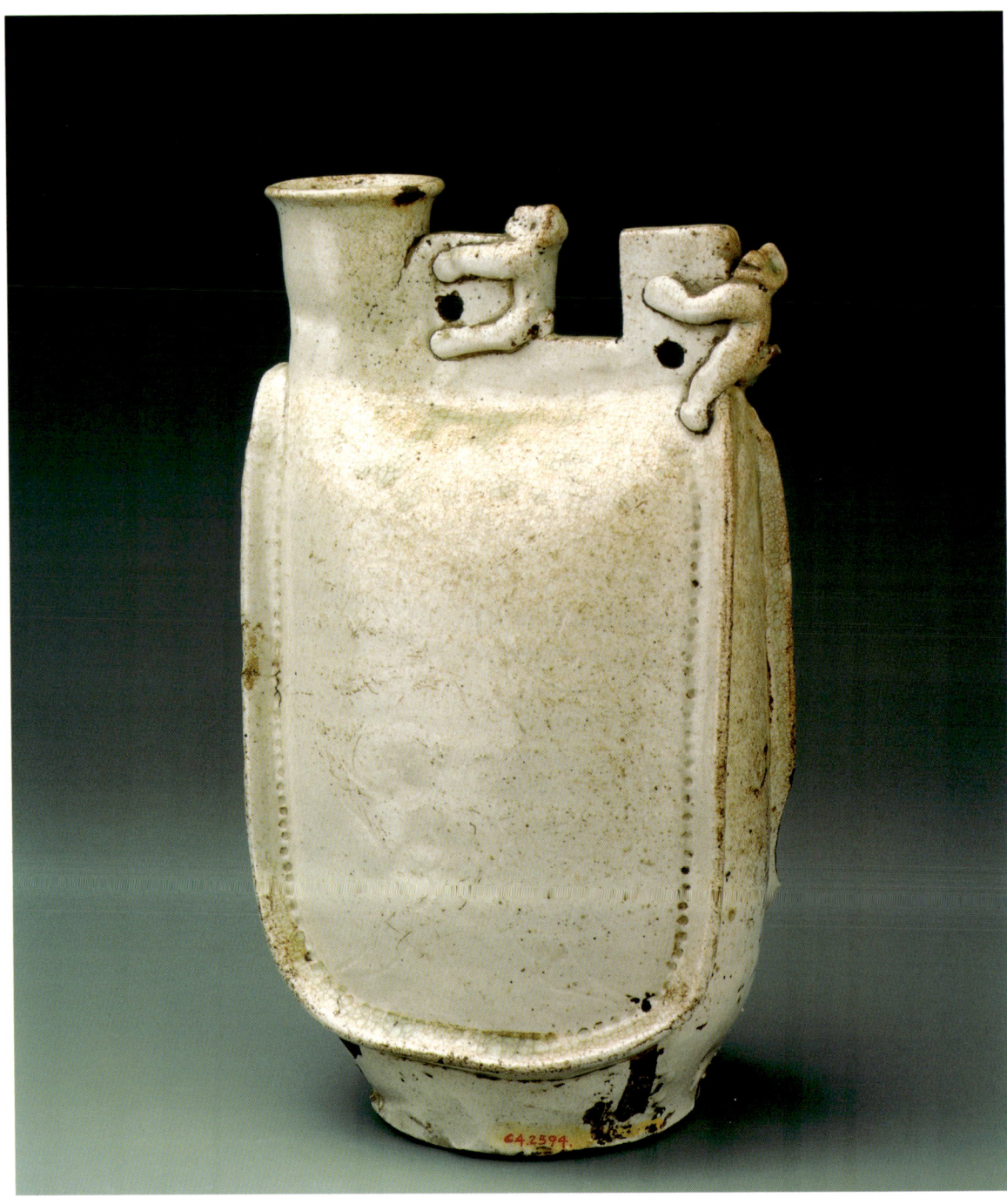

Vase
Liao dynasty (916–1125)
Stoneware
34.5 (h) x 9.5 (mouth diam)
x 7.5 (base diam) cm
Collection of the National
Museum of China (C4.3822)

This long-necked ceramic vase is typical of Liao dynasty ware and the form and decoration relate closely to the nomadic lifestyle of the Khitan. Tall vases like this were popular: they did not take up much space in a Khitan yurt and could be readily attached to a saddle.

The vase has an ovoid body, a cylindrical neck and a large flaring mouth. The petal-shaped mouth is also practical for it serves as a funnel to prevent liquid from spilling. The vase, covered with a white slip and transparent glaze, is decorated with an

incised design of wild flowers which has been highlighted with yellow glaze. The motif depicted is a fully grown plant complete with roots, which suggest a tree of life or perhaps a herbal plant used and valued by the Khitan.

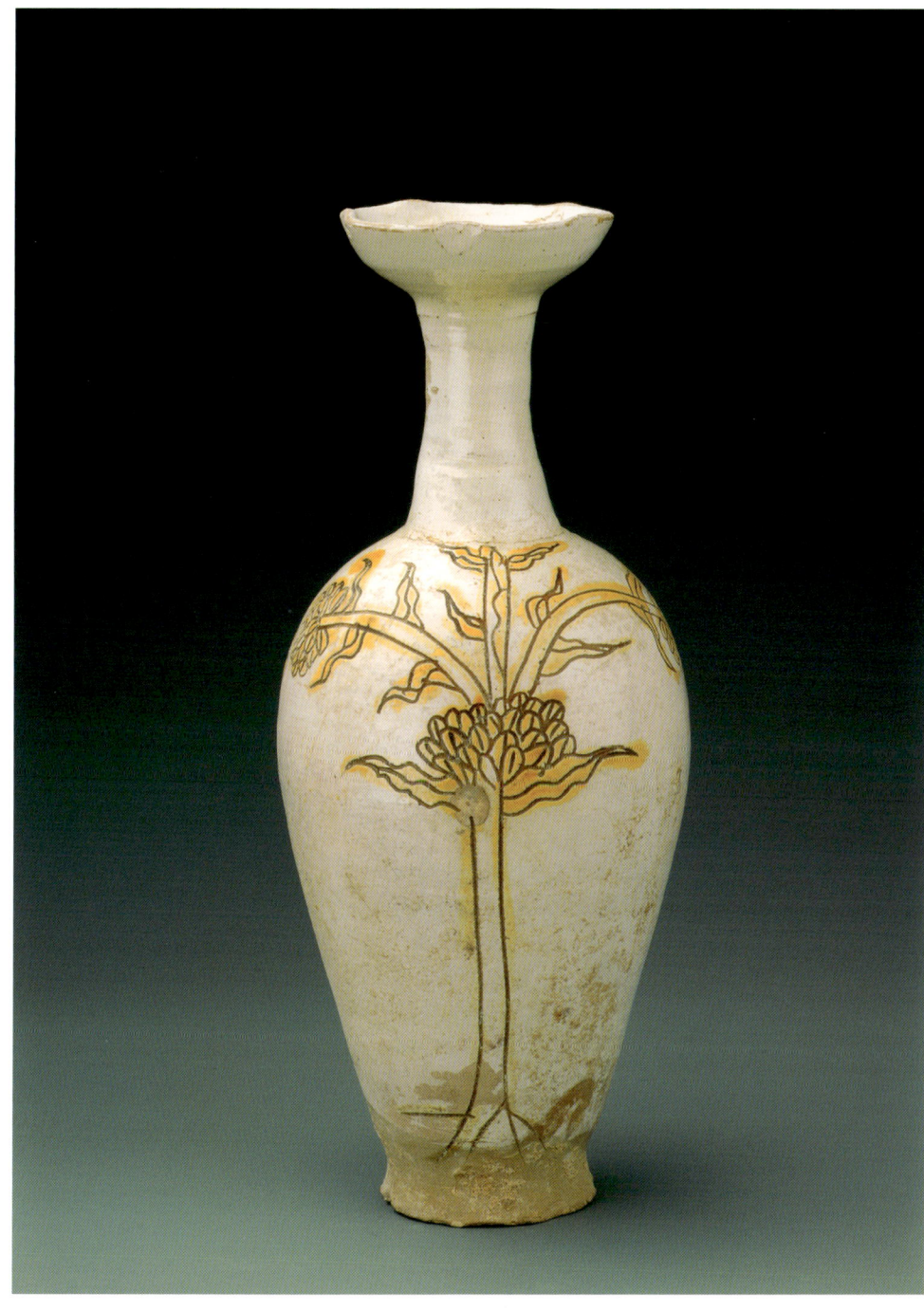

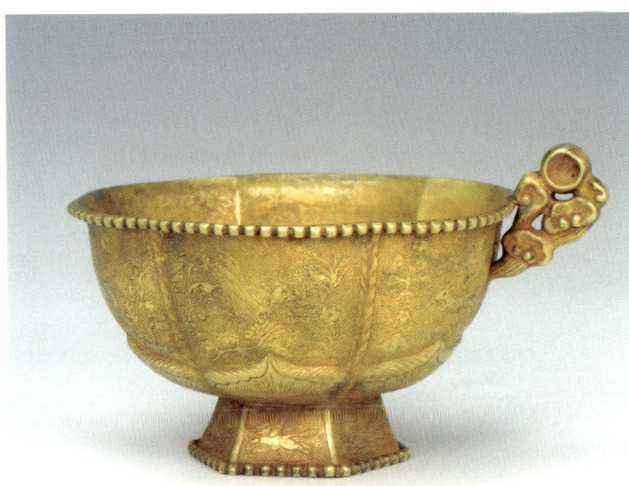

This fine gold cup was most likely used for wine or on ceremonial occasions by a Khitan aristocrat. The art and technology of the Central Plains region, as well as Iranian and Sogdian metalwork traditions, exerted an influence on the technique and design of Liao dynasty goldware and can be clearly seen in this vessel. The cup is shaped like a lotus flower with a row of smaller petals at the base, and suggests the strong influence of Buddhism. The rim and foot are decorated with a beaded edge that can also be seen in Tang dynasty and Central Asian metalwork. The external body of the cup is decorated with a finely worked all-over design of flowers, birds and animals, and the inside with a dragon chasing a *cintamani* pearl, surrounded by lotus petals. Incising is a traditional technique used in the decoration of gold objects. By using different metalworking tools, different effects could be created. This technique is still widely used in China today.

This cup is similar in style and decoration to Tang dynasty gold vessels excavated in Hejiacun in the southern suburbs of Xi'an, Shaanxi province, in 1970. The site was the former residence of a cousin of the Emperor Xuanzong, Prince Pin (Li Shouli), who died in 741. The hoard included 216 gold vessels, many of which displayed Persian, Sogdian and other Western influences as well as many Chinese and foreign coins.

Cup
Liao dynasty (916–1125)
Gold
6 (h) x 9 (mouth diam)
x 4 (foot diam) cm, 155.5 g
Collection of the National
Museum of China (C7.565)

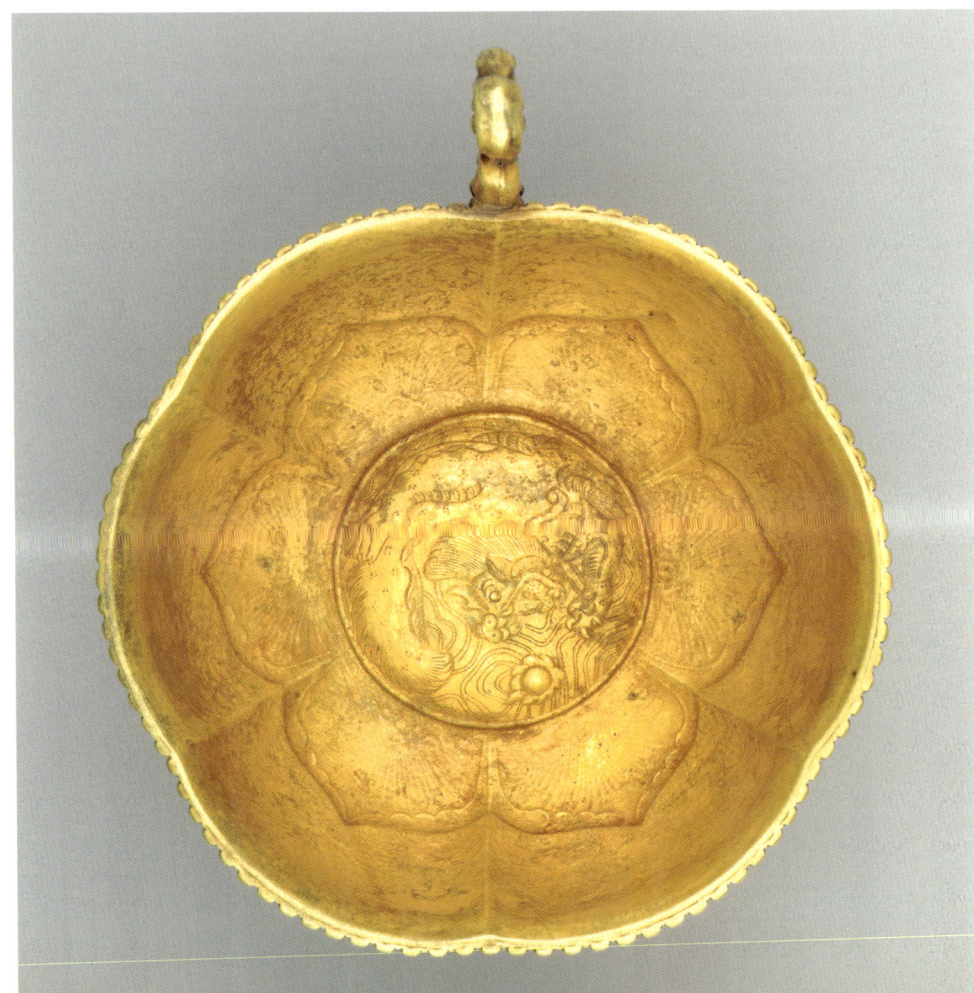

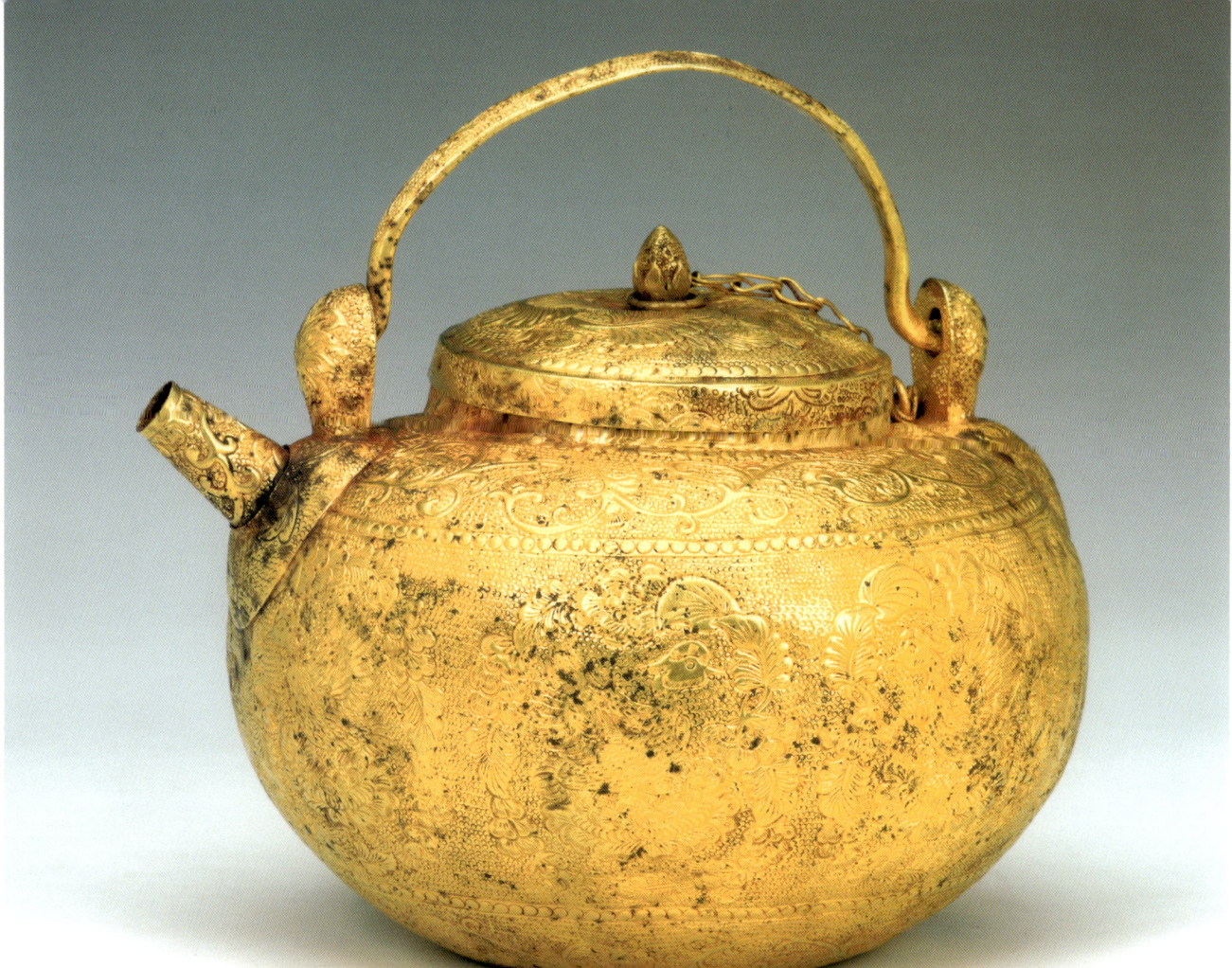

Serving pot
Liao dynasty (916–1125)
Gold
8.5 (h) cm
Collection of the National
Museum of China (C7.550)

This gold pot was used for serving wine or water. It is decorated with an all-over incised design of scrolling floral forms around the shoulder and base, and eight roundels containing nesting mandarin ducks around the centre of the body. The pot has a solid arc-shaped handle, which is attached to the body of the pot with two supports decorated with a floral design. The round lid is also decorated with a flower and leaf pattern.

The bud-shaped knob on the lid is connected to the body of the jug with a gold chain. The pot was made using a traditional Chinese technique of hammering and folding sheet gold.

Coin

Liao dynasty (916–1125)
Copper
2.42 (diam) cm, 2.7 g
Collection of the National Museum
of China (H8.122/Y1595; donated
in 1957 by Mr Luo Bozhao)

This coin bears an inscription in Khitan 'small script'. The graph at the top signifies 'longevity', the graph opposite it 'eternal' or 'long', on the right 'good fortune' and that on the left 'virtue'. The inscription is auspicious and was intended to confer long life, good fortune and virtue.

The Khitan, an ancient ethnic group living north of the Great Wall, established the Liao dynasty in 916. They first appear in Chinese records in the fourth century. Over the centuries they had extensive contact with Han Chinese and their state exhibited aspects of both Chinese and Khitan cultures. The Liao dynasty was conquered in 1125 by the Jurchen (Nüzhen), who established the Jin dynasty.

The Liao dynasty wrote their language in two scripts: the large script and small script. The large script resembles Chinese, but the characters cannot be understood by Chinese readers.

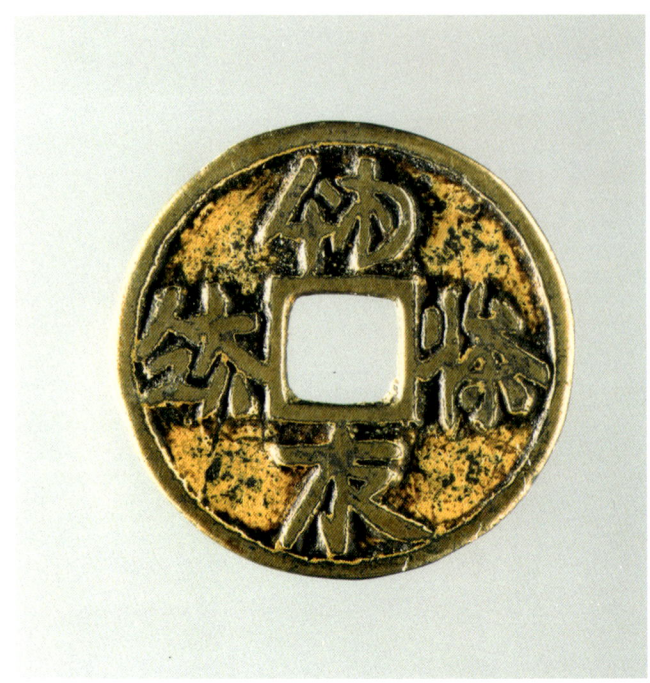

Belt ornaments
Liao dynasty (916–1125)
Gold
4.2–4.3 (w) x 6.8–8 (l) cm
Collection of the National
Museum of China (C7.558)

This set of twelve gold belt plaques would originally have been attached to either a leather or heavy silk belt, as worn by a member of the Khitan nobility. The plaques have been ornamented with a relief design of phoenix in flight, and feature fine gold filigree. This technique of ornamentation is rarely seen in Liao dynasty work, making this set of belt plaques of particular interest.

The rectangular plaques are known as *kua* in Chinese, and the two with rounded edges, where the belt was fastened, are called *chawei*. Both types have apertures on their undersides to allow them to be attached to a belt.

After the Khitan people established the Liao dynasty, attire became rigorously codified as a means of defining social hierarchy in the Han Chinese ritual style. The different materials used for the manufacture of belt plaques demonstrated a person's social status. Belt plaques made from jade and gold were worn by people of the highest rank and status; those of lower social gradations wore plaques of silver or bronze.

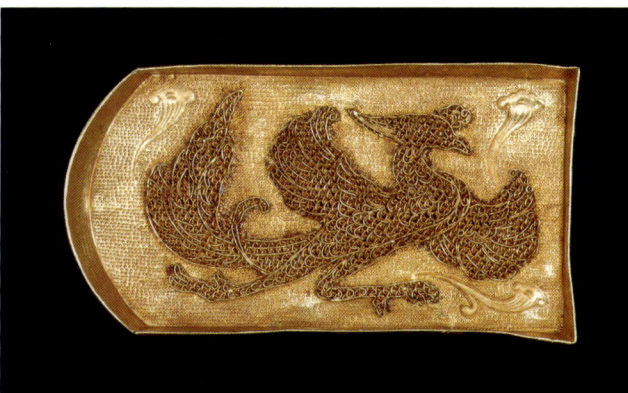

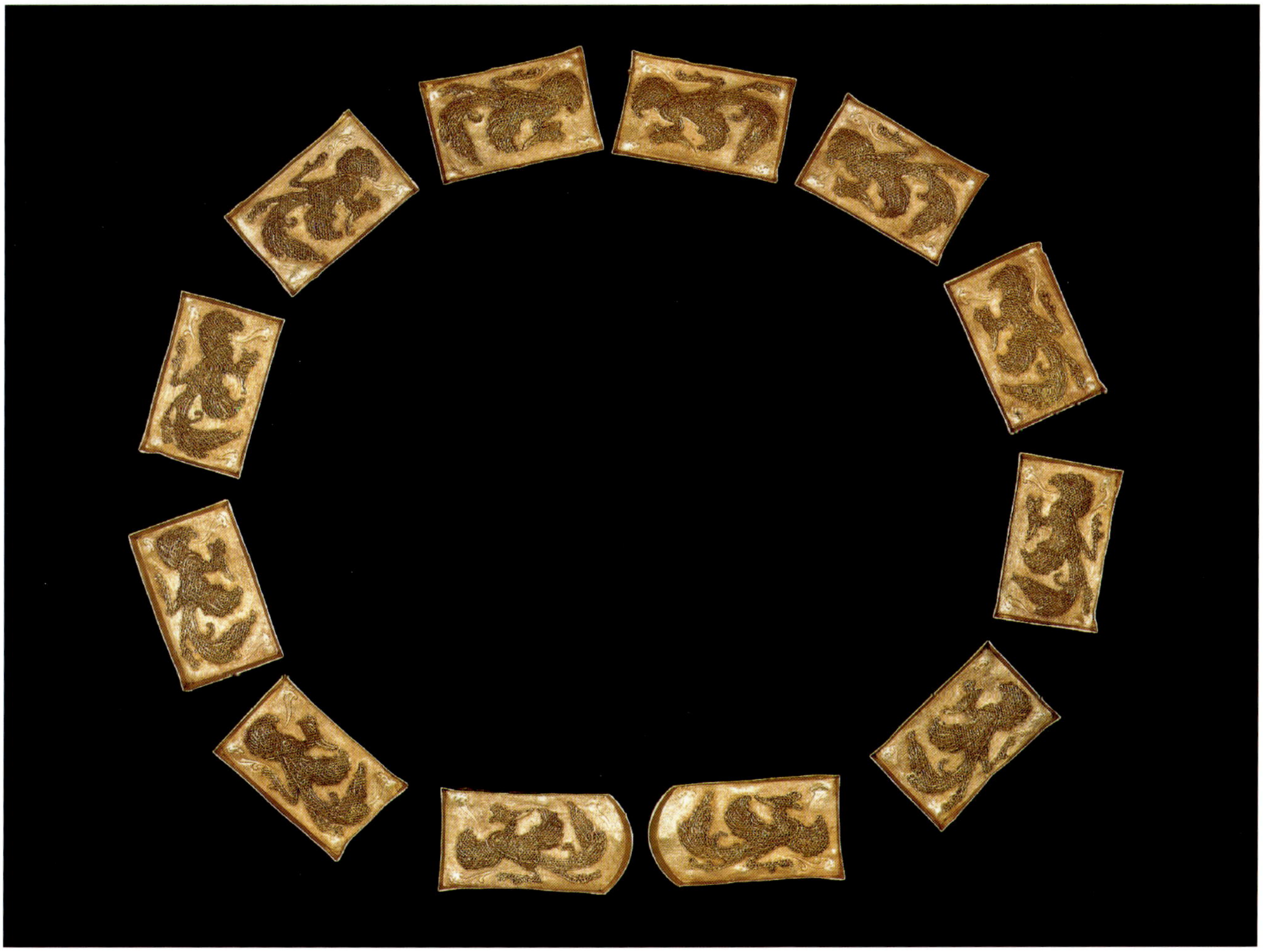

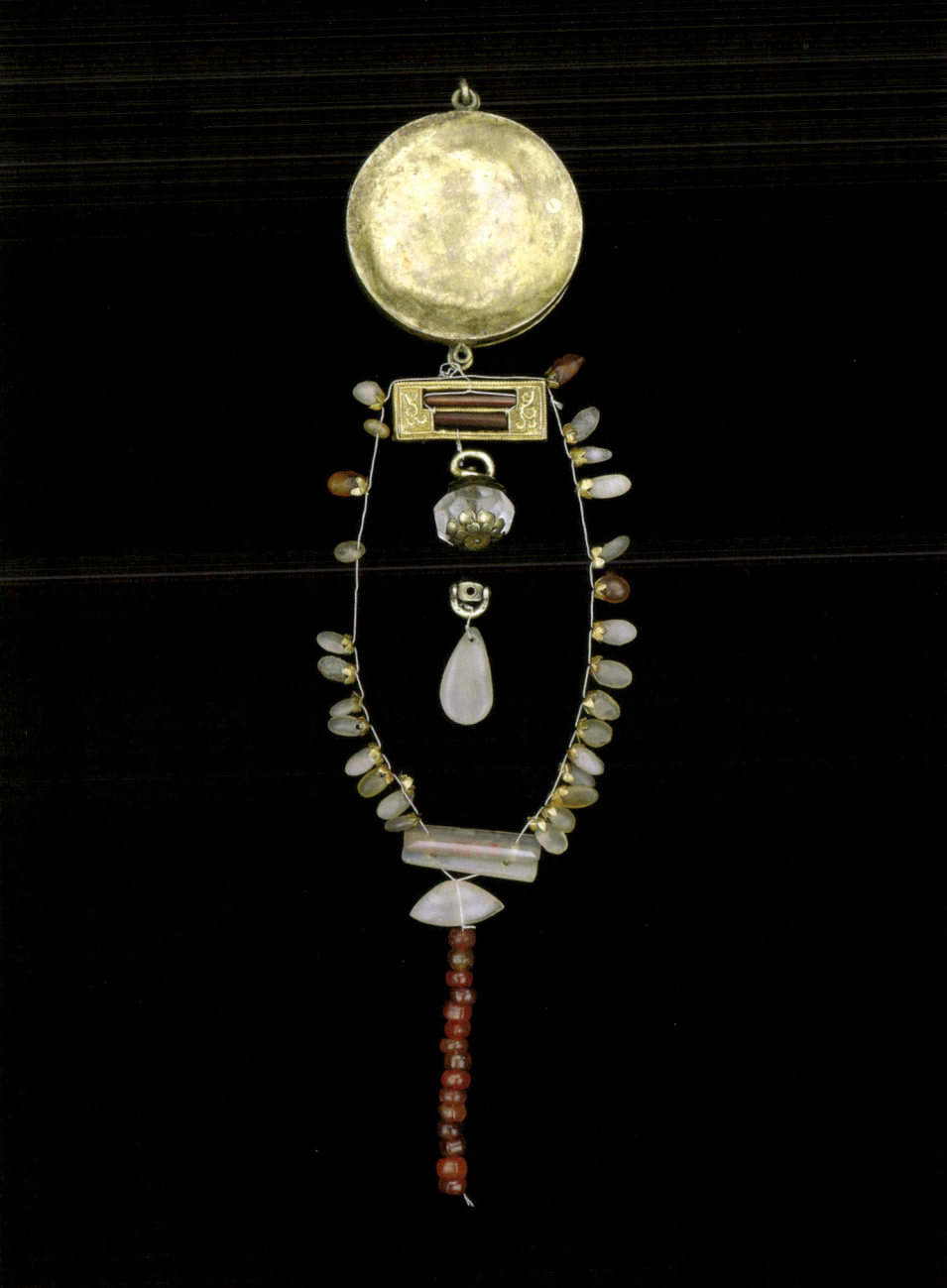

Pendant accessory
Jin dynasty (1115–1234)
Unearthed from a Jin dynasty
tomb in Zhongxing, Suibin county,
Heilongjiang province
Gold, silver, agate, crystal, jade
37.7 (l) cm
Collection of the National
Museum of China (K9856)

This pendant dress accessory would have been worn by a Jurchen noblewoman and dates from the mid to late Jin dynasty. It was worn suspended from a belt, and was both practical and decorative. The accessory comprises a round gilt silver casket, which closes with a snap clasp, and a rectangular gold pendant engraved with a pattern of interlocking floral sprays and inset with red agate. A faceted crystal, ornamented top and bottom with a flower made from a cut sheet of silver, is suspended from the pendant, together with a piece of jade in the shape of a teardrop. Hanging from and surrounding the rectangular gold pendant is a string of small agate jewel pieces, each of which is fastened to the string with a leaf-shaped gold cap, and at the lower end are two additional shaped pieces of jade and a string of red agate beads.

Mirror
Jin dynasty (1115–1234)
Unearthed in 1976 at Acheng county, Heilongjiang province
Bronze
2.5 (w) x 43 (diam) cm, 4300 g
Collection of the National Museum of China (Y2010)

This bronze mirror is the largest extant mirror dating from the Jin dynasty, founded by the Jurchen people of northern and north-eastern China. In 1115, the Jurchen army was successful in its southern campaigns and defeated both the Liao and the Northern Song to occupy a large area and proclaim the Jin dynasty. During this period many Jurchen people moved to the Central Plains where the ethnic Han Chinese were predominant. The form and design of the mirror is distinctively Han and suggests acculturation of the Jurchen during the Jin dynasty.

The reflective surface of this mirror is plain polished bronze. Its decorative back has a raised knob at its centre with a hole through which a silk cord would have been threaded to allow for handling: the size and weight of the mirror suggest that it would have been placed on a stand. Two carp appear to swim playfully around the knob in a confined circular space, their fins spread and tails curved, creating waves with the speed of their movement. The scales on the low-relief bodies of the fish are precise and help to accentuate the impression of realism and three-dimensionality. The waves appear as concentric lines, which form swirls and add to the visual interest of the imagery. The outer border of the mirror is decorated with a pattern of aquatic plants. The two carp could be the blending of the Makara (Pisces) motif from Buddhism. To ethnic Han Chinese, the carp conveys a hope for prosperity.

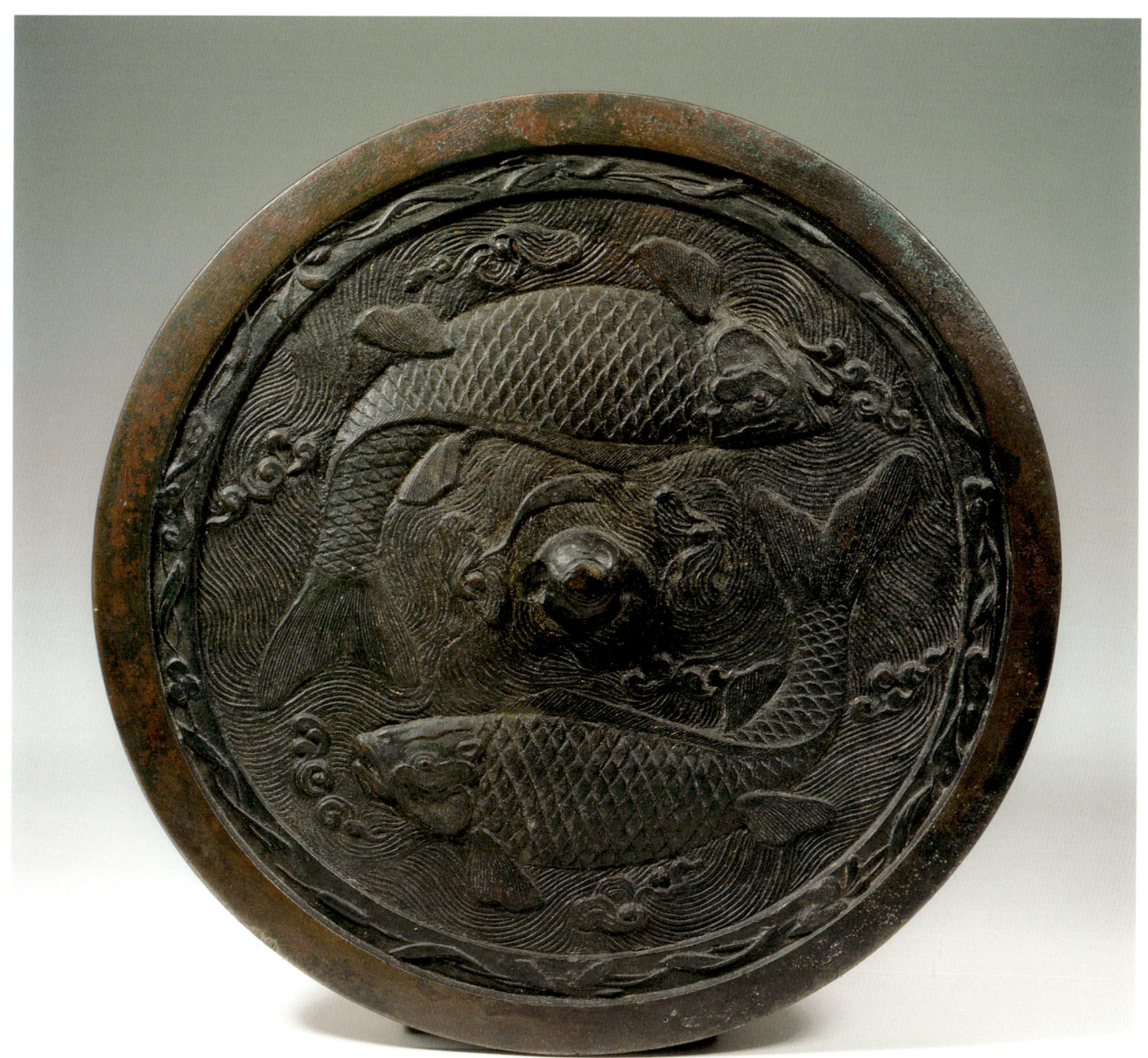

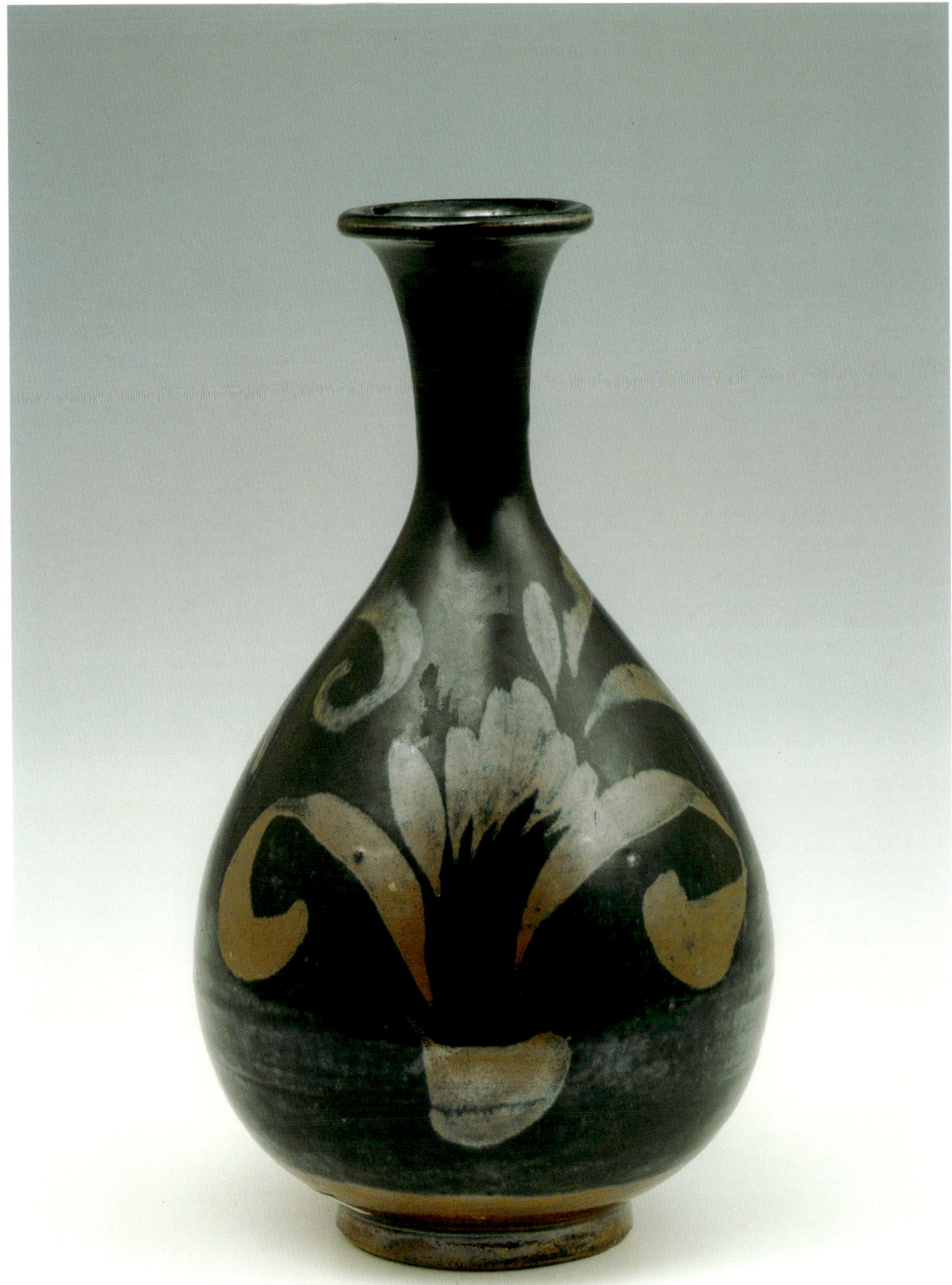

Vase
Jin dynasty (1115–1234)
Stoneware, Cizhou ware
Guantai, Hebei province
31.5 (h) x 7.5 (mouth diam)
x 9 (foot diam) cm
Collection of the National
Museum of China (C4.3704)

Black-glazed wares were the most common ceramic type for everyday use in northern China, because the clay used for its manufacture was not of the highest quality and it was more easily fired than white porcelaneous clay.

To add aesthetic diversity to black-glazed wares, craftsmen decorated the vessels with ferrous pigments, creating freehand abstract patterns and impromptu designs — as on this vase, which creates an inkwash effect.

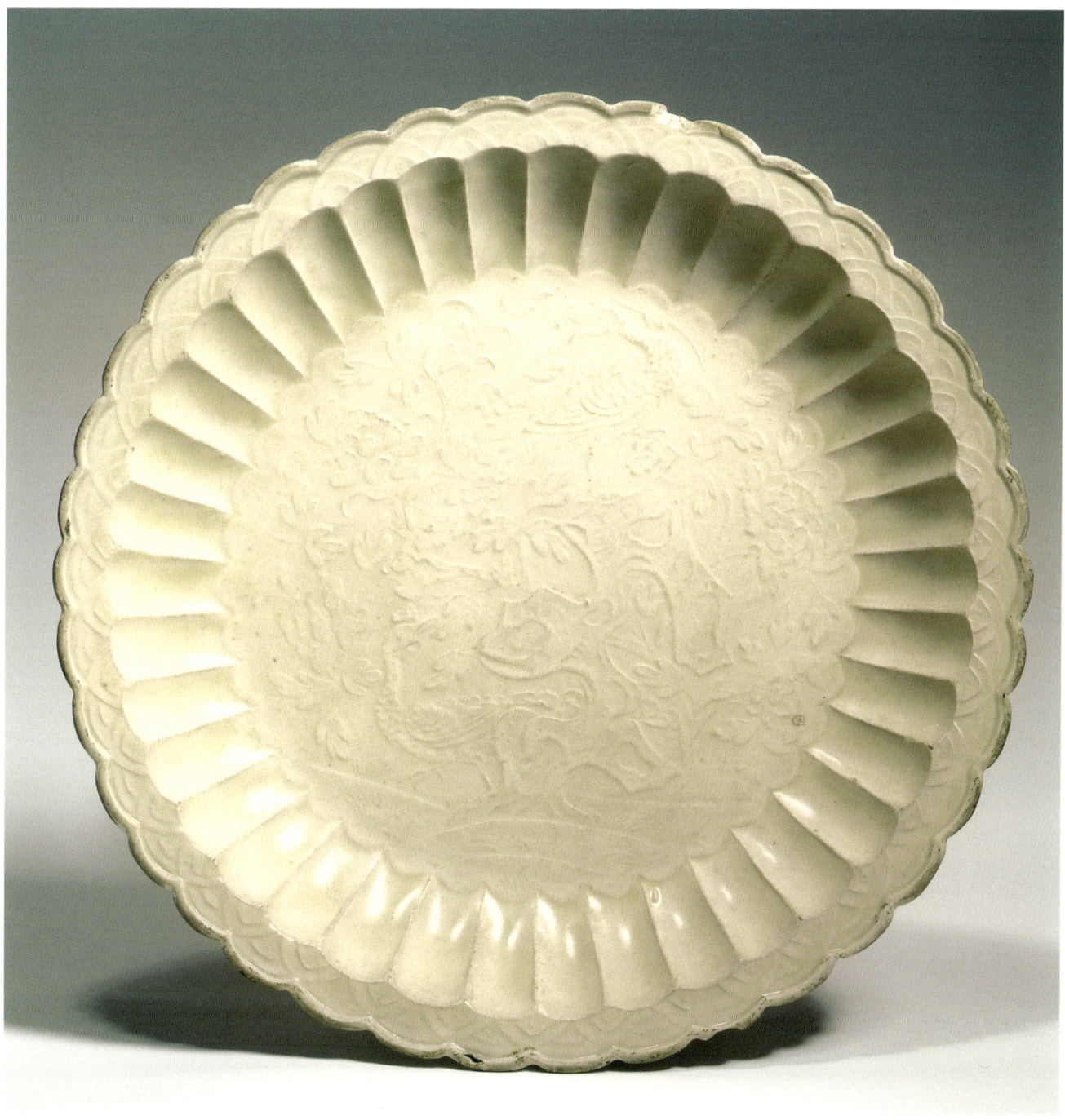

Dish
Jin dynasty (1115–1234)
White porcelaneous ware, Ding ware
22.7 (mouth diam) x 3 (d) cm
Collection of the National
Museum of China (C4.3062)

The fine moulded design on this plate features peacocks and peony flowers. Images of peacocks and peonies appear frequently on Tang dynasty porcelain and represent fortune, happiness and prosperity.

The process of imprinting the pattern on to this plate involved the use of a carved mould, which was pressed into the half-dry body before glazing and subsequent firing in the kiln. The imprinting technique is a simple and highly efficient way to standardise patterns and is suited to mass production. It was used in China from the third century onwards.

In the Jin dynasty, the Ding kiln of northern China was renowned throughout the country for its white glazed wares and exerted a great influence on ceramic manufacture in surrounding areas.

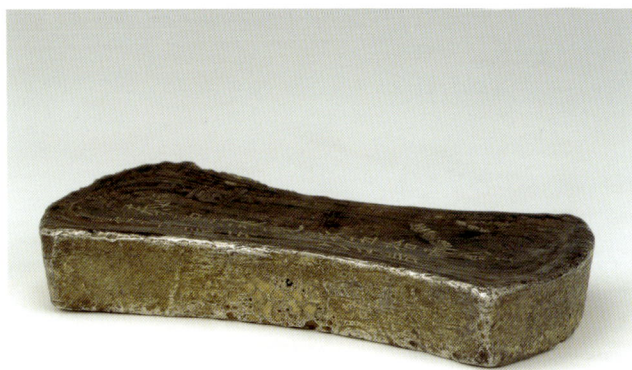

Ingot
Jin dynasty (1115–1234)
dated 1206
Unearthed at Lintong,
Shaanxi province
Silver
8.7 (w) x 14.5 (l) cm
Collection of the National
Museum of China (K7946)

During the Jin dynasty, silver became widely used for both commercial transactions and the payment of taxes on which the government was dependent for funding civic projects. This ingot was specifically created to pay a government levy. Its inscription reveals that it weighed 50 *liang*, which was the tax in the autumn of the 6th year of the Taihe reign of Jin emperor Zhangzong (1206), and was weighed by an official whose name was Xu Yan. During the Jin dynasty 1 *liang* of silver was equivalent to 39.94 grams.

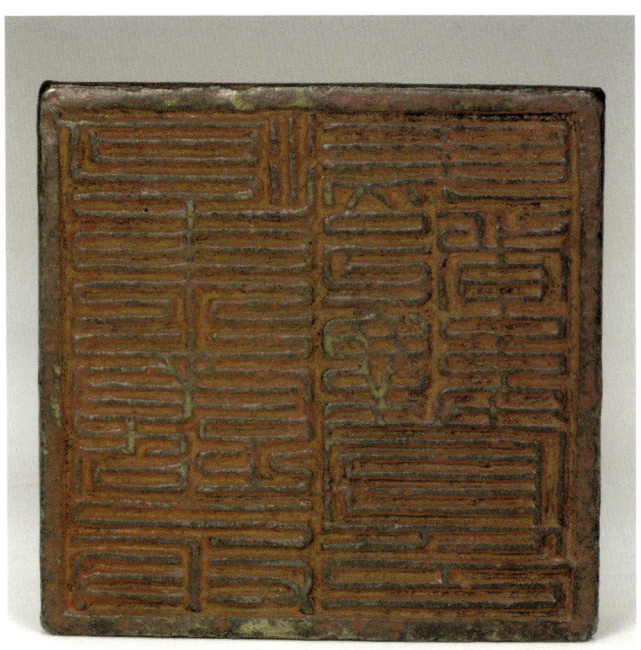

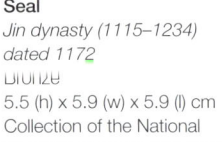

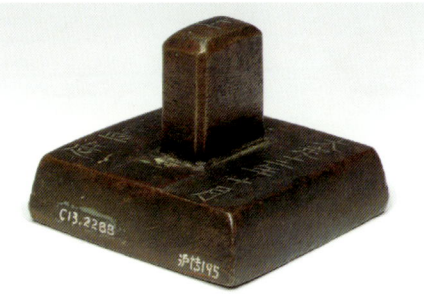

Seal
Jin dynasty (1115–1234)
dated 1172
Bronze
5.5 (h) x 5.9 (w) x 5.9 (l) cm
Collection of the National
Museum of China (C13.2288)

The raised inscription in seal script on this seal reads 'Seal of marshal of troops and horses in Hedongnan circuit' (*Hedongnan lu bingma-duzongguan*). The circuit (*lu*) was the highest local administrative unit in the Jin dynasty and the jurisdiction of the Hedongnan circuit covered the northern area of present-day Shanxi province. The 'marshal of troops and horses' was the highest ranking officer in charge of the military forces within a circuit, making this seal that of the commander in charge of the forces in the northern Shanxi area in the Jin dynasty. On the back of the seal are Chinese characters reading '10th month in the 12th year of the Dading period' and 'Made by the Shaofujian', which indicates that the seal was cast in 1172 by the government body responsible for imperial production.

Coin
Western Xia dynasty
Tianqing period (1194–1205)
Copper
2.4 (diam) cm, 3.2 g
Collection of the National
Museum of China (H8.173;
donated in 1957 by Mr. Luo Bozhao)

The characters inscribed on the ingot read from the top, clockwise: 'Tian' 'Qing', 'Yuan' and 'Bao'. Tianqing was a reign title of Zhao Chunyou, Emperor Huanzong of the Western Xia dynasty. *Yuanbao* was the name given to silver ingots used as money in ancient China.

The Western Xia dynasty was established by the Tangut (Dangxiang), an ancient ethnic group once living in areas adjacent to the Great Wall. The dynasty was officially established in 1038 and, under the influence of Han culture, developed civilian and military systems, introduced ritual music and cast coins. The Western Xia was conquered in 1227 by the Mongols, who established the Yuan dynasty.

The Western Xia had its own language with characters based on the Chinese regular script, but with more strokes. Numismatically, the Western Xia was significant for being the first non-Han group in Chinese history to cast coins with inscriptions in their own language. The Western Xia coins bore reign titles in both Western Xia and Han characters.

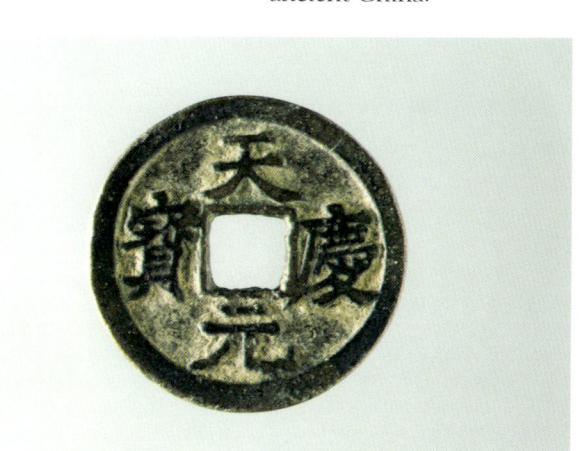

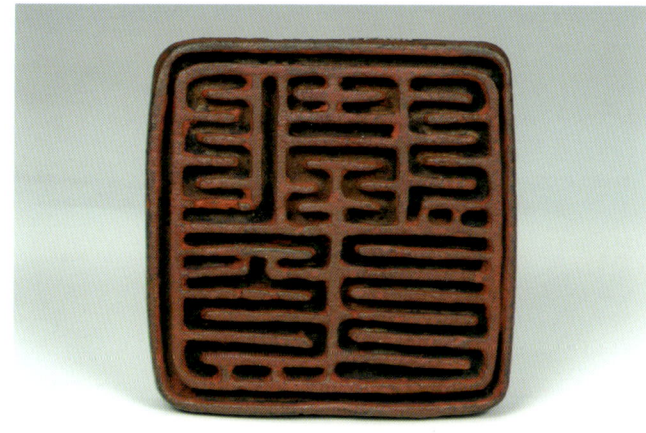

Seal
Western Xia dynasty (1038–1227)
Unearthed at Tongxin,
Ningxia Hui autonomous region
Bronze
1.9 (knob h) x 5.3 (w) x 5.5 (l) cm
Collection of the National
Museum of China (K9863)

Seals were used in ancient China to authorise official and civil exchanges of documents and letters. This is an example of a four-character Western Xia seal and is one of the dynasty's official seals. It is cast with Western Xia seal characters meaning 'chieftain's seal'. On the reverse is an inscription in Western Xia script,

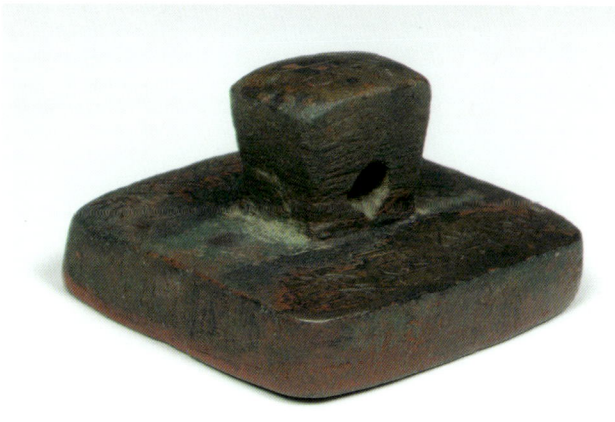

the characters of which were based on Chinese regular script. Engraved on the right and left sides of the back of the seal are the date and the name of its owner. The square knob in the middle is carved with one character meaning 'up' to ensure the seal was used with the correct orientation.

Official seals of Western Xia were made of gold, silver and bronze, but most surviving examples are of bronze. They were used by chiefs in their capacity as military or civilian officials.

Vase
Western Xia dynasty (1038–1227)
Stoneware, Lingwu ware
34.8 (h) x 9 (mouth diam)
x 10.1 (bottom diam) cm
Collection of the National
Museum of China (C4.3586)

This vase, fired at the Lingwu kiln in the Western Xia capital, has a typical thick glossy brown glaze. The surface of the body has an incised and cut away design of peony flowers and waves and the plain style reflects the aesthetic of the Tangut people. The knife-cut marks of the incised pattern can be clearly seen and there has been no attempt at meticulous trimming. For firing there is an unglazed area around the shoulder, which allowed vessels to be efficiently stacked in the kiln without adhering. Brown-glazed stonewares like this were used by Western Xia nobility.

Founded in 1038, the Western Xia dynasty was located in north-western China and ruled until 1227, during which time there were ten ruling emperors. At various times, the Western Xia was in rivalry or in alliance with the Northern Song, the Liao and the Southern Song dynasties. In 1227, the Western Xia was conquered by Chinggis (Genghis) Khan's armies.

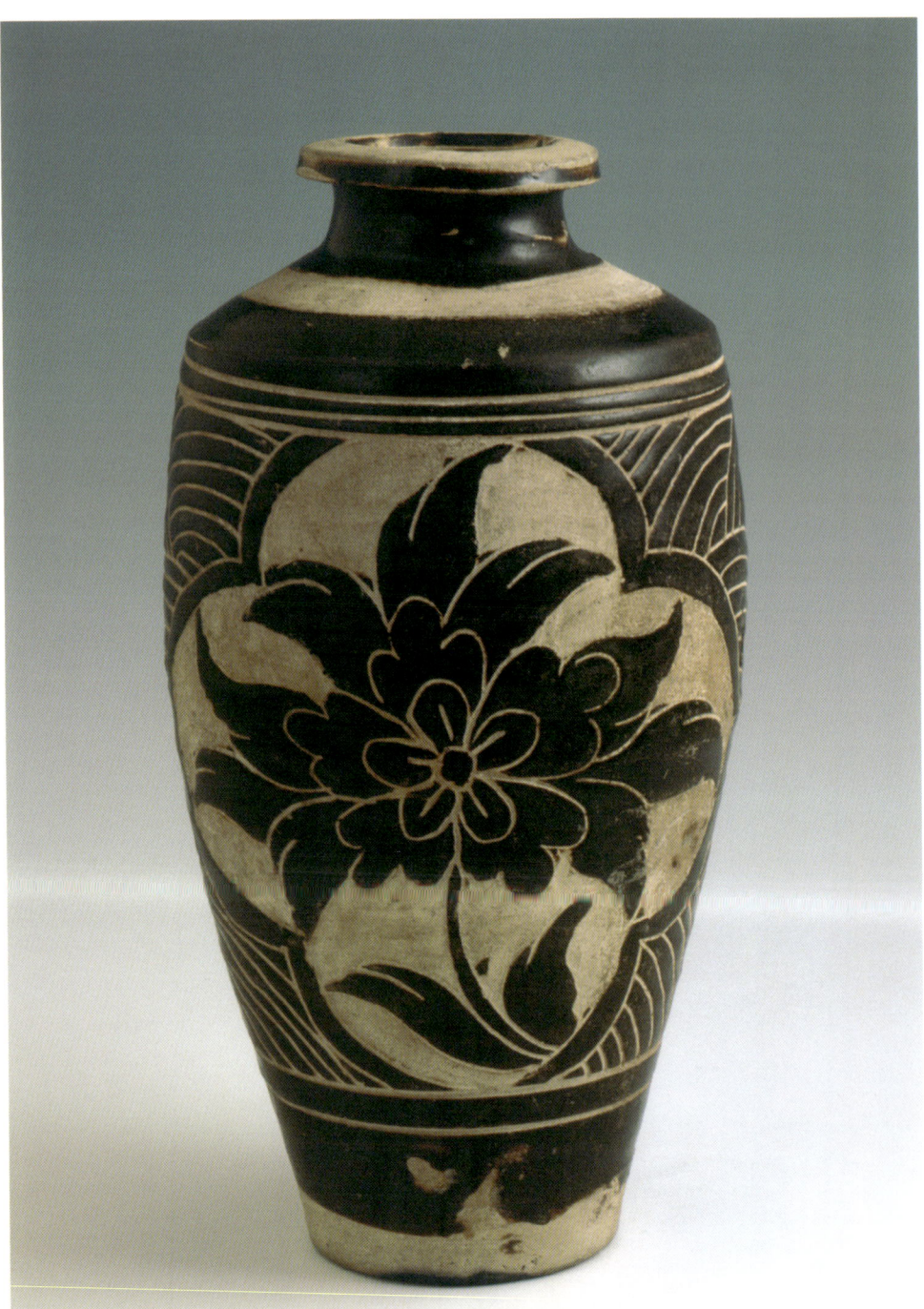

Flask
Western Xia dynasty (1038–1227)
Collected from Haiyuan county,
Yinchuan, Ningxia Hui
autonomous region
Stoneware, Lingwu ware
33.3 (h) x 31.5 (w)
x 9 (mouth diam) cm
Collection of the National
Museum of China (C4.3598)

This rounded flask has a slightly flattened profile with small loop handles. It is decorated with a pattern of peonies created when the brown glaze was cut away when half dry, exposing the natural colour of the clay. Peony patterns can often be seen on Western Xia ceramics as a symbol of prosperity and happiness expressed through the grace and elegance of that flower. The flask is a practical form designed to be either tied to a saddle or laid flat on the ground.

The imitation stitching around the edge of the flask reflects the fact that the shape of the vessel owes its origins to examples made from leather.

Combining beauty and practicality, this flask is a typical article of everyday use of the Tangut people. The Lingwu kiln, located in Lingwu, Ningxia Hui autonomous region, was a ceramic kiln inside the territory of the Western Xia. There are few surviving examples of Western Xia porcelain, and intact flattened flasks are very rare.

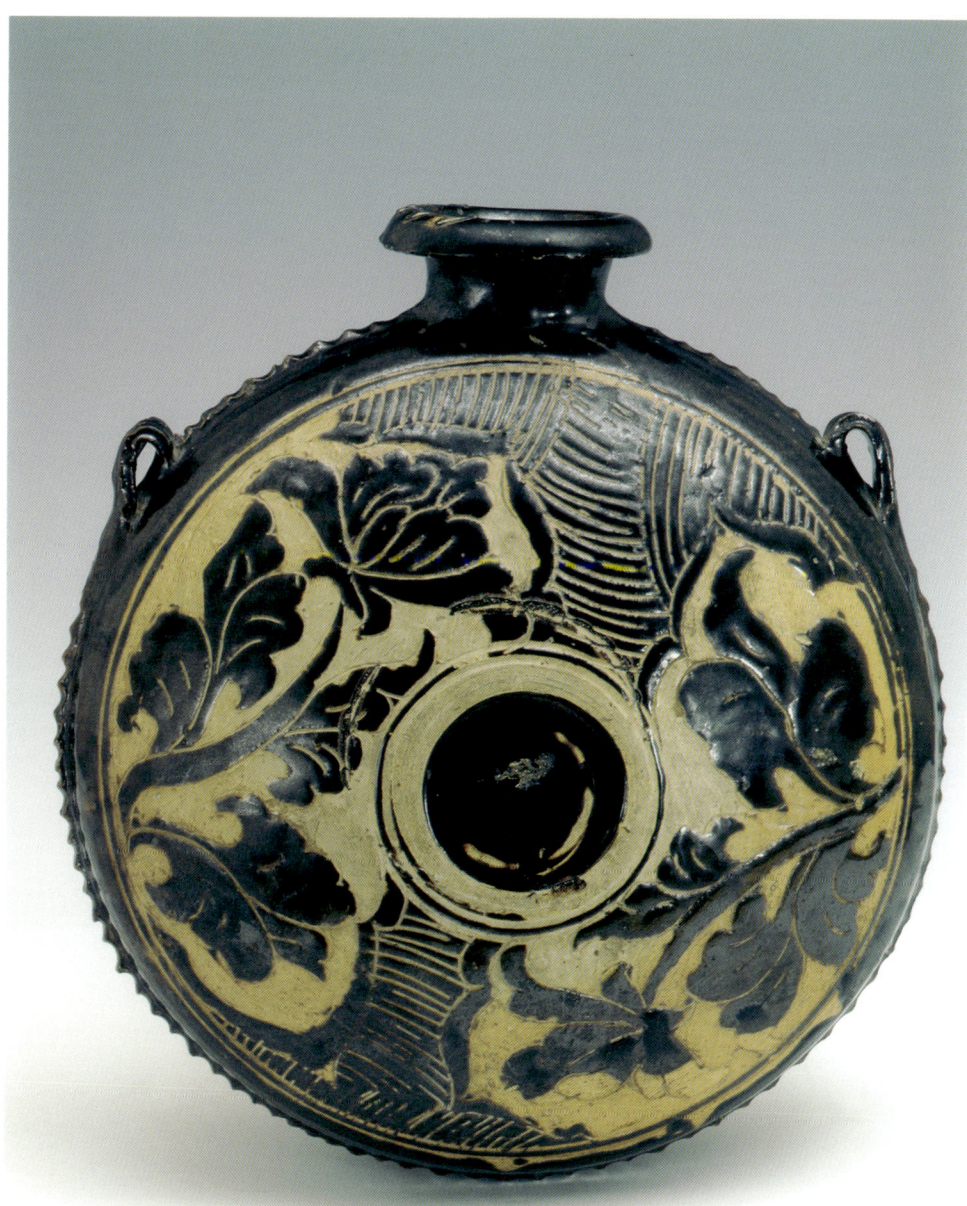

The front surface of this silver plaque is incised with three lines of gilt characters — 'Urgent heaven-bestowed imperial edict of Chinggis Khan' — and the reverse is engraved with two Khitan characters which mean 'walking horse'. In 1206, Chinggis (Genghis) Khan established a great empire of peoples living on the Mongolian plateau. To facilitate the transmission of decrees, the delivery of goods

and materials, and communications, Chinggis Khan ordered the construction of a network of post-houses based on a postal system previously used by the Khitan in the north-east of China.

This silver permit was issued by the government as an authorisation for the bearer to use post-houses and horses. The post-houses had to offer transport, catering and accommodation to the person holding the plaque.

The descendents of Chinggis Khan further developed this system. After the Yuan dynasty was established by the Mongols, networks of post roads centred at Dadu (today's Beijing) were established. These radiated in every direction, leading to all parts of the vast Eurasian empire ruled by the Mongols. In the late period of Emperor Shizu's reign, the number of post-houses exceeded 1500.

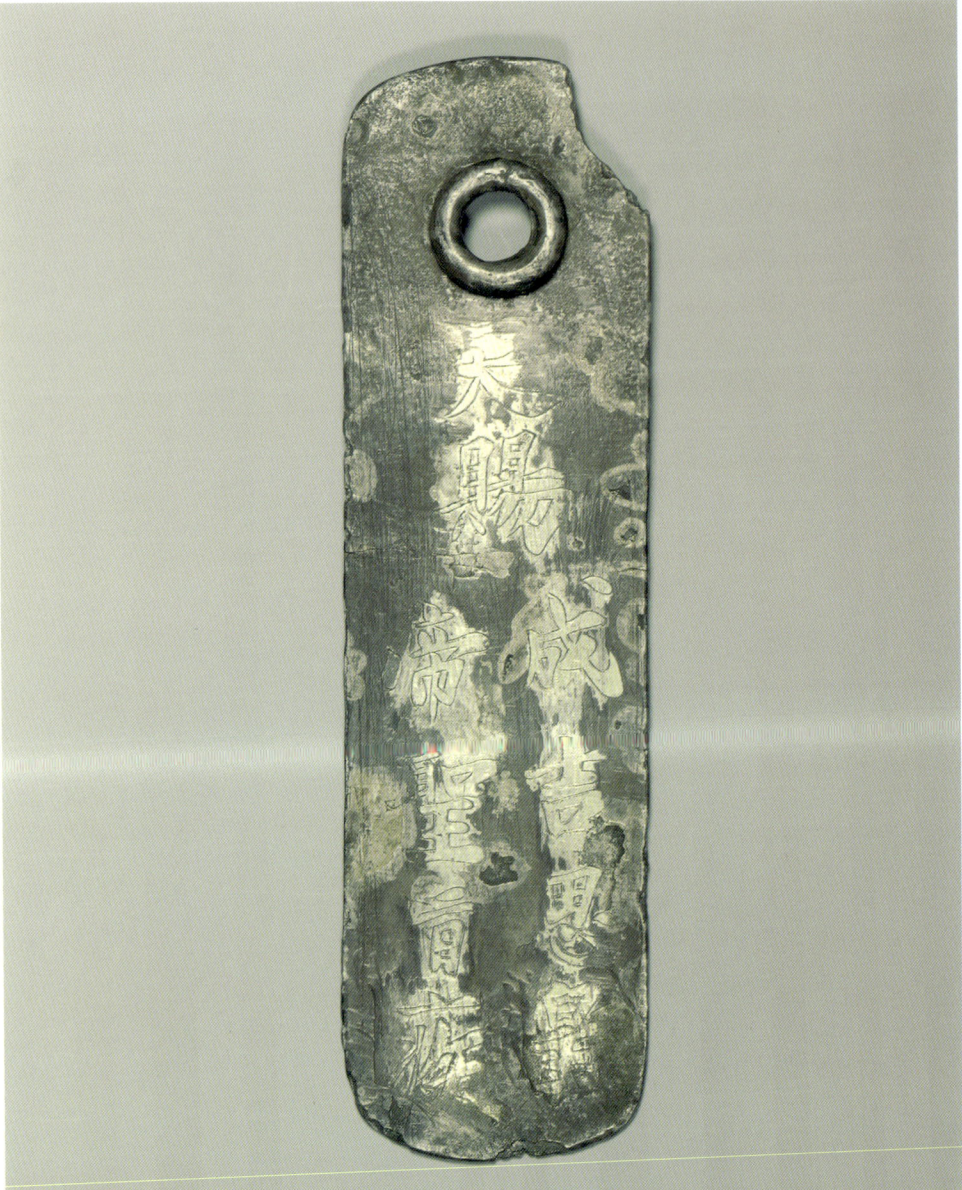

Permit
Reign of Chinggis Khan (1206–27)
Silver
6 (w) x 21.5 (l) x 0.3 (d) cm
Collection of the National
Museum of China (C7.538)

Portrait of Chinggis Khan
Ming dynasty (1368–1644)
Ink and colour on silk
48 (w) x 75.5 (l) cm
Collection of the National
Museum of China (Y1084)

Chinggis Khan, whose original name was Temuchin, was born into the Kiyat-Borjigid nomad tribe in the north-east of present day Inner Mongolia. In the early years of the thirteenth century, he was elected as the chief of the tribe and united Mongolia after years of war. At the Kurultai meeting of tribal leaders in 1206, Temuchin was elected as the leader of all Mongol tribes and proclaimed 'Chinggis Khan'. He established a Mongol empire with new military, political and legislative systems, and extended his territory through military invasions. His armies conquered much of the Jin empire in northern China, and started campaigns in Central Asia. In 1227, he died in his military camp when his army was about to invade the Western Xia empire in north-western China. After his grandson Kublai Khan founded the Yuan dynasty, he was honoured with the posthumous title of Yuan Taizu.

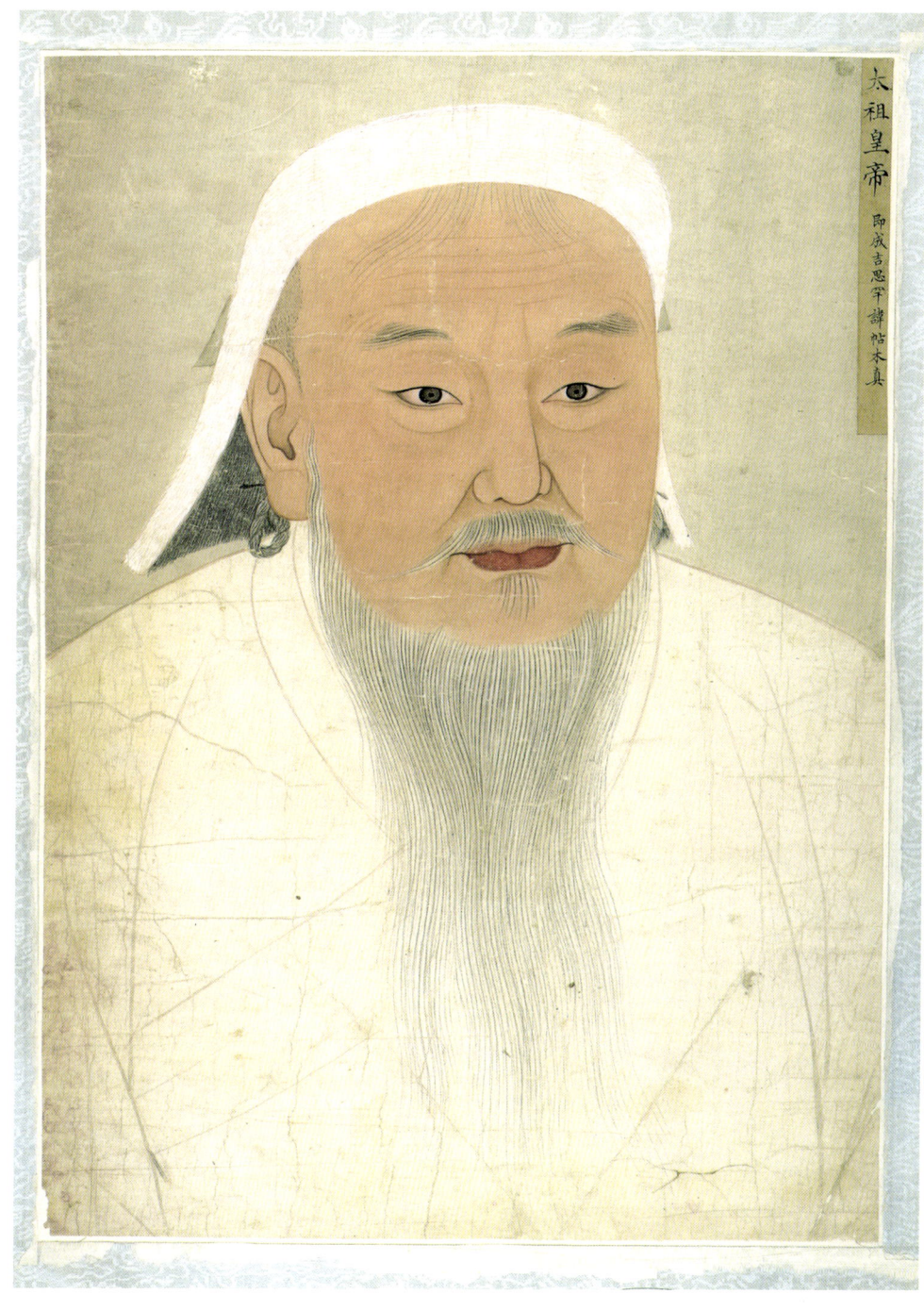

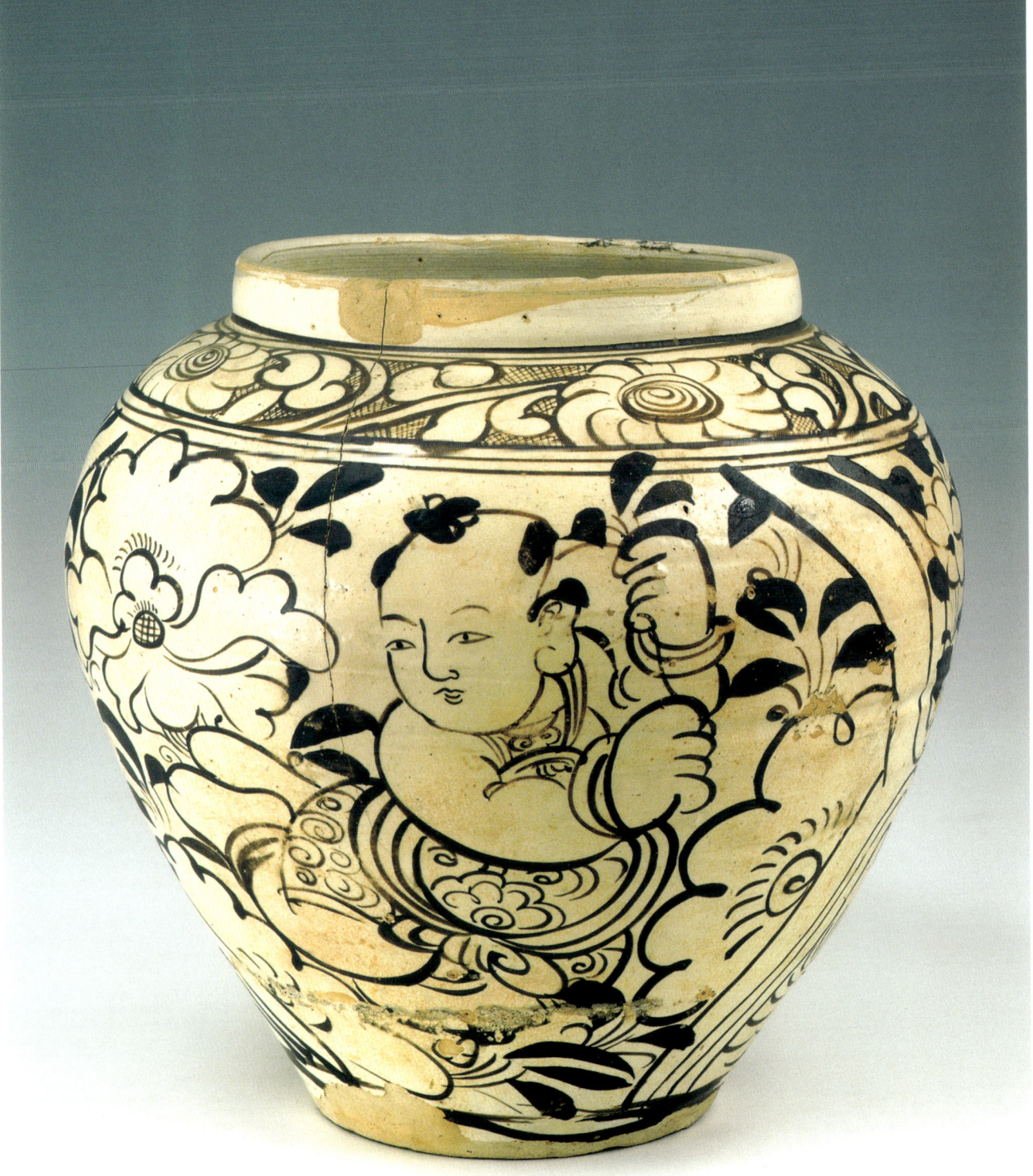

Jar
Yuan dynasty (1271–1368)
Salvaged in 1994 near a sunken Yuan dynasty ship in the Sandaogang sea area in Suizhong, Liaoning province
Stoneware, Cizhou ware
30 (h) x 18.5 (mouth diam) x 31 (belly diam) x 12 (bottom diam) cm
Collection of the National Museum of China

During the Yuan dynasty, ceramics painted in brown on a white ground were popular in northern China. The most famous wares were from the Cizhou kilns in Cixian county (present-day Hebei province), which in time expanded to other centres in Henan, Shanxi and Shandong provinces.

Cizhou ware was predominantly for domestic use and included vessels such as jars, plates, bowls, vases, basins and kettles, as well as pillows and small-sized toys. The designs feature motifs including children at play, as on this example, as well as birds, animals, landscapes, figures and flowers.

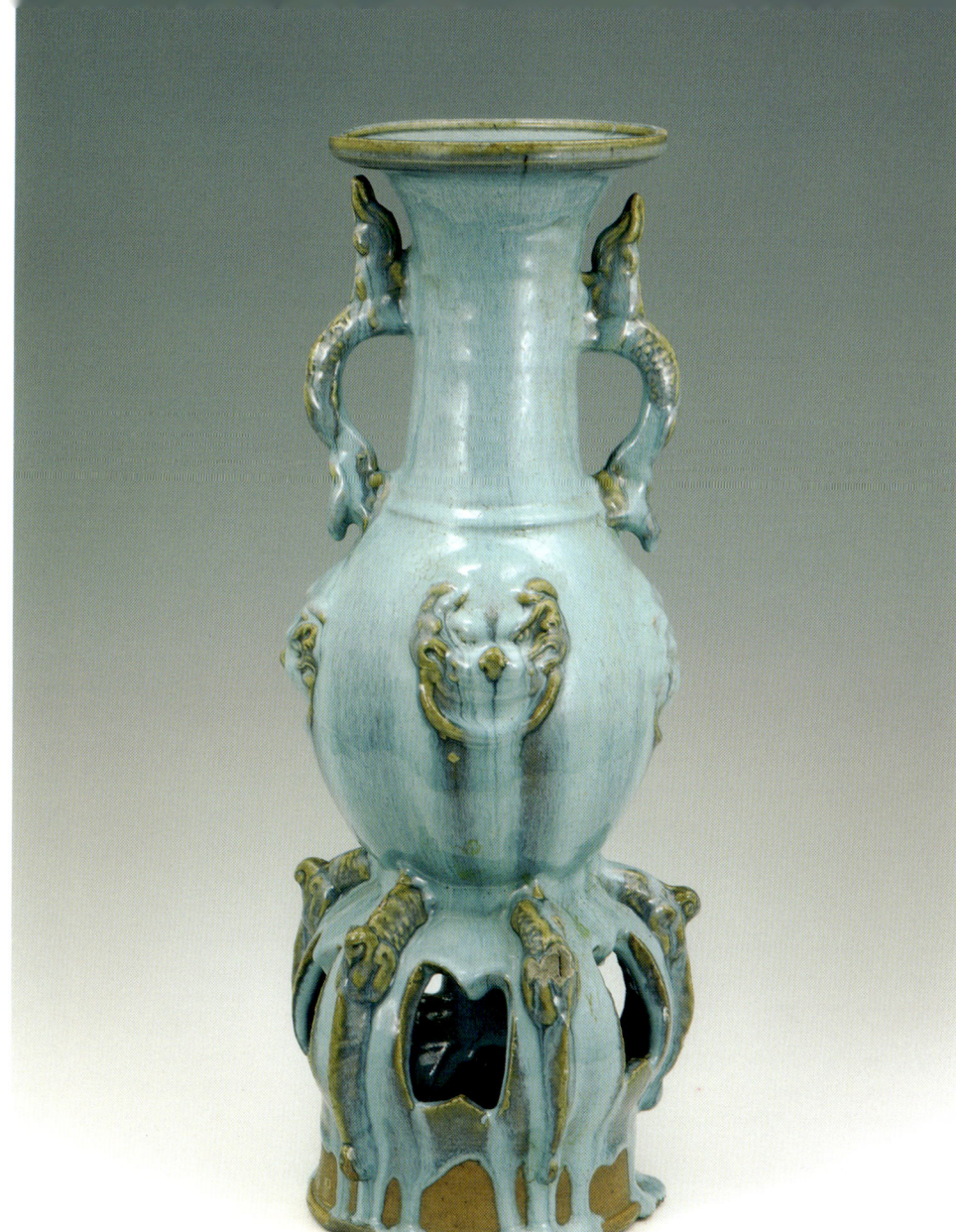

Vase on openwork stand
Yuan dynasty (1271–1368)
Unearthed in 1970 from the ruins
of Baita village, Fengzhou city,
I lohhot, Inner Mongolia
Stoneware Jun ware
58.5 (h) x 17 (mouth diam)
x 18 (foot diam) cm
Collection of the National
Museum of China (Jie 1147)

This large and imposing
porcelain Jun ware ritual
vase is one of a pair found
in a hoard in Hohhot in
Inner Mongolia in 1970.

The Jun kilns were founded
in the early Northern
Song dynasty and flourished
during the late years of
the dynasty.

The distinctive sky-blue
glaze of Jun ware has long
been prized by connoisseurs.
During the Yuan dynasty
Jun kilns also operated
in Henan, Hebei and
Shanxi provinces, making
the ware more accessible
and popular in northern
China. It is thought that
this large vase was produced
in Guantai, Hebei province.

Many Jun ware objects
have been excavated in
the hinterland of Inner
Mongolia. Most of them
are sacrificial and ritual
objects that date from
the Yuan dynasty and are
blue, the colour preferred
by the Mongol rulers.

The majority of the Jun
wares produced during
the Yuan dynasty were
objects used by people
in everyday life such as
cups, plates, bowls and jars,
which makes this large vase
unusual and rare. The most
common colours were sky-
blue or moon-white and
the glaze was usually thick
and opalescent. The vase's
all-over glaze is thick but
uneven and has gathered
at the bottom of the vessel
during the firing in
a phenomenon popularly
known as 'flowing glaze'.

Coin (front and back)
*Yuan dynasty, Zhiyuan period
(1335–40)*
Copper
4.1 (diam) cm, 21.7 g
Collection of the National
Museum of China (H8.888 / Y1628)

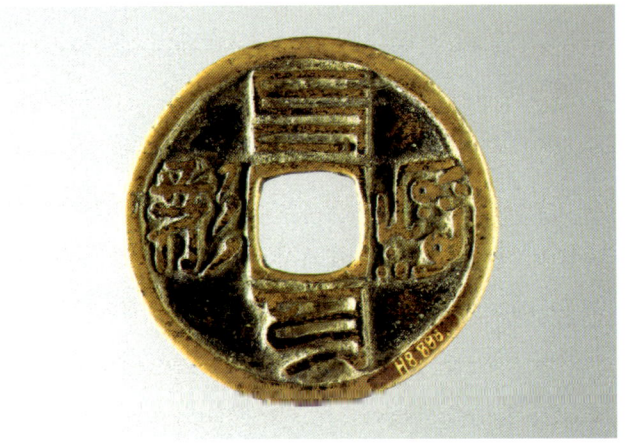

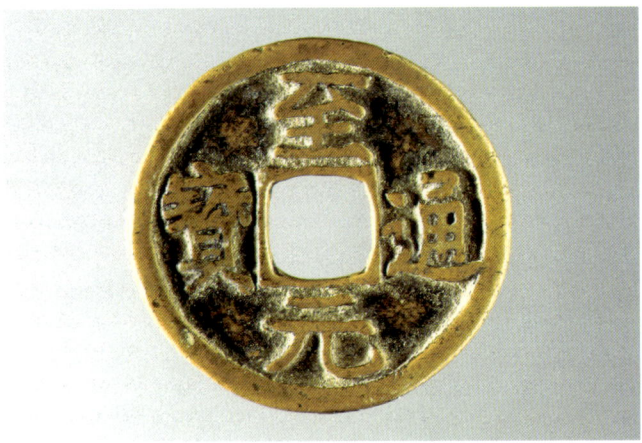

This coin was cast during the Zhiyuan period (1335–40) of the reign of Emperor Huizong in the Mongol-Yuan dynasty. One side is inscribed with characters in regular Han Chinese script: *Zhiyuan tongbao*. The other side has inscriptions in three different northern languages: the characters above and below *zhi zhi* are 'Phags-pa characters, the character on the right, *tong*, is an old Uyghur or Chagatai character, and the character on the left, *bao*, is a Western Xia character. The existence of a coin with inscriptions in four different scripts suggests that these scripts were in widespread use across the country at that time. It should be noted, however, that this coin was most probably made for commemorative purposes rather than as currency.

In addition to coins with inscriptions in 'Phags-pa and Han Chinese characters, the Yuan dynasty also cast coins bearing inscriptions in other northern languages.

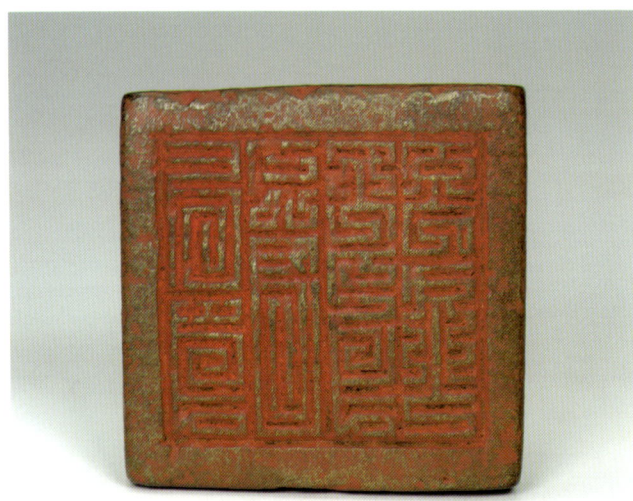

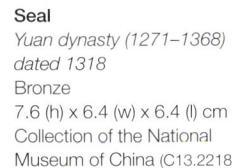

Seal
*Yuan dynasty (1271–1368)
dated 1318*
Bronze
7.6 (h) x 6.4 (w) x 6.4 (l) cm
Collection of the National
Museum of China (C13.2218)

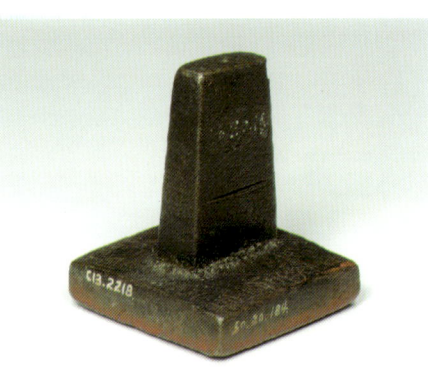

This bronze seal features Mongolian characters. On one side of the back of the seal are Chinese characters which may be translated as 'Seal of a Mongol military officer *baihu*', and on the other side: 'Made by the Board of Rites, Imperial Secretariat in March of the 5th year of the Yanyou period' (1318). A Mongol military *baihu* was a military officer of the Yuan dynasty, which indicates this was an official seal.

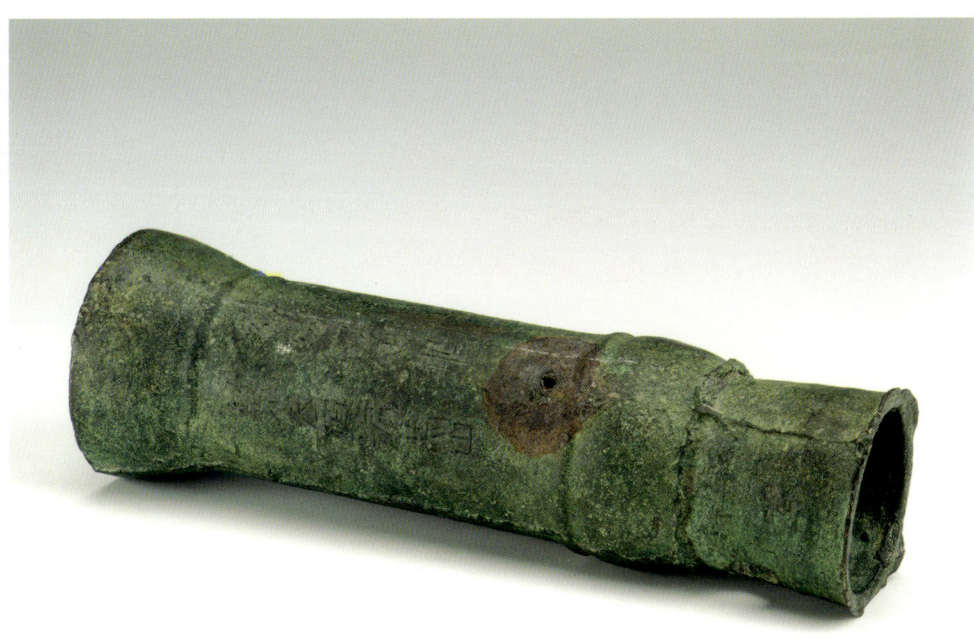

Cannon
Yuan dynasty (1271–1368)
dated 1332
Unearthed in 1935 at Yunjusi Temple,
Fangshan, Beijing
Bronze
35 (l) x10.5 (front aperture diam)
x 7.5 (rear aperture diam) cm, 6.94 kg
Collection of the National
Museum of China (Y195)

This is the earliest documented Chinese cannon. It has an inscription which reads: 'No 300 of the expeditionary army on the border of the Sui [commandery] on the 14th [day of the second month] of the 3rd year of the Zhishun reign [1332].'

From the eleventh to the thirteenth century, rapid developments in many military technologies occurred in China. One example is the widespread use of firearms in battle, which had a great influence on Chinese history. The Mongol army acquired the expertise to make early timber ballistic weapons from artisans captured during its campaigns, and they further developed this expertise to make metal firearms. Among these was a large-calibre predecessor of the cannon, which could launch stones.

The inscription on the body of this object indicates that the cannon is number 300 of a batch, from which we gain an insight into the scale of production at that time. This bronze cannon of the Yuan dynasty comprises three parts: bore, gopher hole and tail. The cannon muzzle is bowl-shaped and is much bigger than the cannon bore. In practice, the cannon would be installed upon a wooden bracket secured by iron bolts. The shooting angle could be adjusted by inserting a wedge under the cannon body, and the shooting distance by adjusting the quantity of gunpowder. Not only the gopher hole but also the cannon bore was filled with powder. The shells, round stones placed in the muzzle, were pushed out by expanded air produced after the gunpowder burned. During the Yuan dynasty developments in gunpowder compounding techniques meant that the burning rate was accelerated, which produced more explosive force and made cannons and blunderbusses more powerful and destructive.

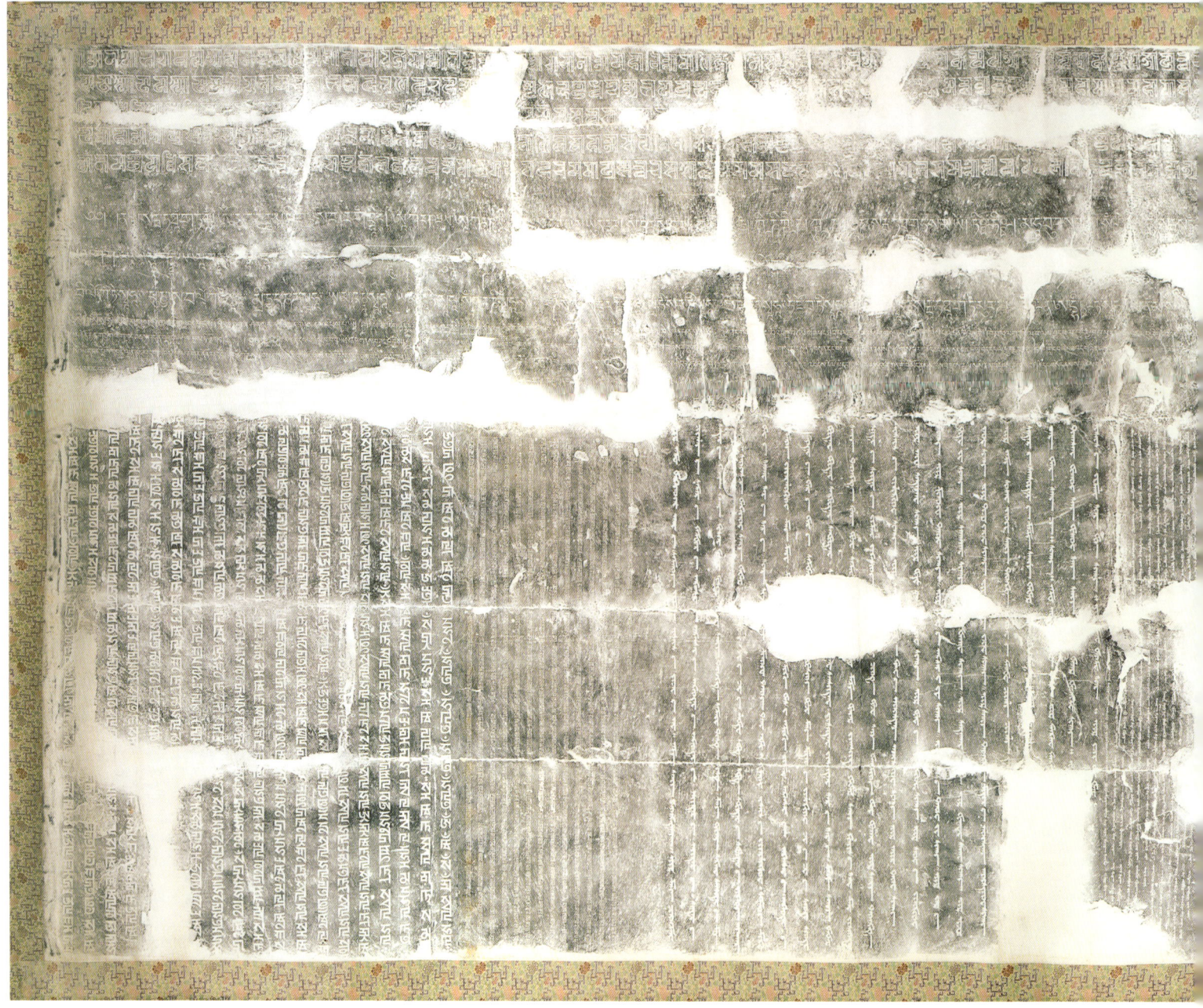

Rubbing

From the Cloud Terrace (Yuntai),
Yuan dynasty (1271–1368)
dated 1345
Ink on paper
246 (w) x 627 (l) cm
Collection of the National
Museum of China (Chen 5)

Juyongguan, an important pass in the Ming dynasty Great Wall, is located north-west of Beijing. At the pass there is a structure called the Cloud Terrace (*Yuntai*) built in the 5th year (1345) of the Zhizheng period during the reign of Emperor Huidi of the Yuan dynasty. The terrace is 9.5 metres high, 26.84 metres long from east to west, and 17.57 metres deep from south to north. On top of the terrace there were three small stupas, which no longer exist. There is a 5-metre-high passage through the structure from south to north.

The stone walls inside the Cloud Terrace are inscribed with mantras from the *Dharani Sutra* and an inscription recording its construction. The horizontal lines above are in Sanskrit and Tibetan, and the vertical lines are, from left to right, in Mongol, Old Uyghur, Tangut and Chinese. The Chinese characters at the end of the inscription read: 'Written by Monk Decheng from Baoji Temple in Chengdu of Western Shu on an auspicious day in the 9th month of the 5th year of the Zhizheng period [1345]'. The inscriptions are in languages that relate to peoples living in the northern and north-western regions.

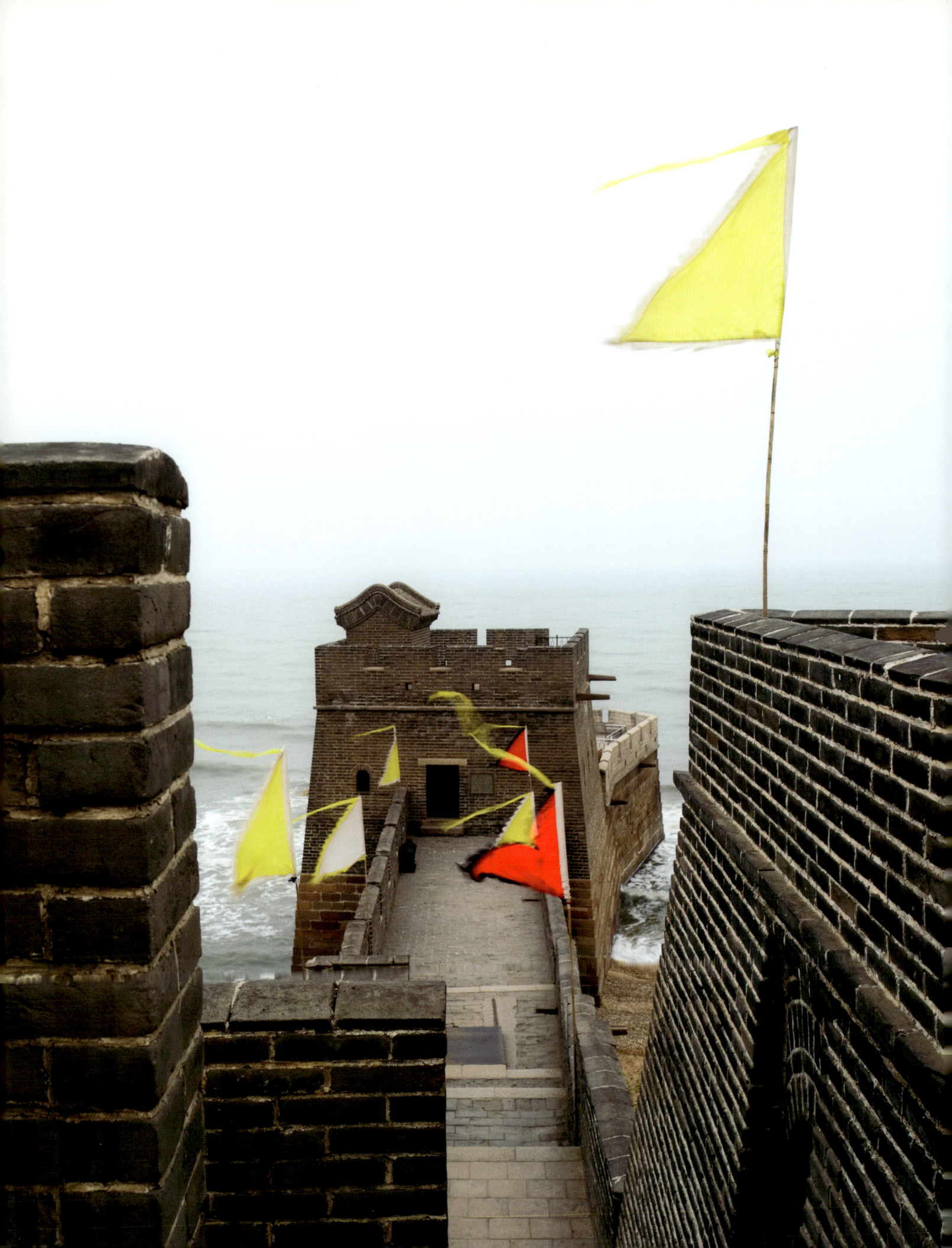

FORCES

At fifteen I joined the army, a ballad from the Han dynasty (206 BCE–8 CE)

At fifteen I joined the army,
At eighty I first came home.
On the road I met a villager,
'At my home what kin are there?'
'Look over there — that's your home!'
Pine, cypress, burial mounds piled, piled high,
Hares going in through dog-holes,
Pheasants flying in through rafter tops;
The inner garden grown wild with corn,
Over the well wild mallow growing.
I pound grain to serve for a meal,
I pick mallow to serve for broth.
Once broth and meal are cooked
I'm at a loss to know whom to feed.
I leave by the gates, look east.
Tears fall and soak my clothes.

Translated by Anne Birrell

Old Dragon's Head, Shanhaiguan Pass, Hebei.
Photo: Jean-Francois Lanzarone

The Wall at work

YANG WENHE

In the spring of 1982, the National Museum of Chinese History made an extraordinary acquisition in the form of more than 670 individual folded pages bound in a folio. Years of exposure to damp had caused the binding to come apart and reduced some of the pages to little more than dust. The inscribed labels attached to many of the illustrations had also come loose. Yet this ragged folio was nothing less than *Plans of the Jizhou commandery of the Ming Great Walls* (Ming changcheng Jizhen tu).

It was impossible to ascertain the original number of pages. What remained were the plans of some of the passes and the areas they controlled within the twelve circuits of the Jizhou commandery north of Beijing: the Huangtuling, Damaoshan and Yiyuan passes of the Shimenzhai circuit; the Jieling and Qingshan passes of the Taitouying circuit; the Lengguan Pass of the Yanheying circuit; the Jijiazhuang and Heigu passes of the Caojiazhai circuit; Chaohechuan of the Gubeikou circuit, and the Baima and Dashuiyu passes of the Shitangling circuit. In all, there were plans of eleven passes under the jurisdiction of different circuits. There were also a number of pages of tables indicating the number of troops deployed, both local and from other commands.

The plans had belonged to Kang Junxiang, whose family had lived in Machang village in Jize county, Hebei province, for generations. We travelled there to meet with him. Kang traced his lineage back to Kang Yingqian, a *tanhua* graduate who had won the third highest place in the imperial examinations of the Ming dynasty (1368–1644), and whose academic achievements had been extolled in a stele, letters of encomium and recorded in a clan genealogy. Kang Junxiang was the Ming scholar's fourteenth-generation descendant. During the Cultural Revolution, when Red Guards scoured the country for traces of old culture to destroy, Kang Junxiang's mother hid the plans inside a basket made from willow fronds.

Although the Red Guards found and confiscated the encomiums and several other ancient texts, the plans escaped detection.

A passage in the eighteenth-century Qianlong-period *Gazetteer of Jize county* (Jize xianzhi) devoted to 'Personages' relates the following about Kang Yingqian:

Kang Yingqian's personal name was Yizhi; he styled himself Niandong. In the jiachen *year of the Wanli reign period [of the Ming dynasty, 1604] he successfully attained the Advanced Scholar degree in the metropolitan examinations. His first official appointment was as magistrate of Chenzhou. Later, he rose ... to become magistrate of Jinjingkou [present-day Zhenjiang]. He allocated more then 100,000 taels from the prefectural treasury for coastal defences, and although his subordinates suggested that this was improper, he sternly rejected their advice. He was then promoted to the position of assistant administrator of Shandong Province and placed in charge of military ordnance and troops for the Liaodong maritime circuit defence. ... After Liaoyang fell [in 1621], he was left without troops to man the defences, and so was ordered to return to the [imperial] Court ... There, he pre-empted criticism by confessing to error. When the military commissioner Xiong Tingbi memorialised that he had rendered great services in transportation and bandit suppression, the emperor felt kindly towards him, and did not pursue the issue of his impeachment … after spending several years working towards redressing the injustice done to him, he returned to his hometown. There he composed* Writings from Zhan Studio [Zhanzhai yigao] *and his mother, Lady Chen, was presented with an honorary title.*

According to Liu Xiaozu's *Gazetteer of the four commanderies and three passes* (Sizhen sanguan zhi), Liaodong was part of one of the four commanderies — Ji, Liao, Chang and Bao — located north of the capital; it was known as Jizhen, or the Jizhou commandery. In the later years of the Wanli reign period (1573–1619), the military governor Xiong Tingbi initiated the construction of the Liao permanent garrison and built towers, creating a unified defensive system from the four commanderies. Kang Yingqian's important position in the Jizhou commandery at Liaodong gave him access to the military plans. When the Manchu leader Nurhaci attacked Liaoyang in 1621, Kang Yingqian took the plans home so that they would not fall into enemy hands. They remained in the Kang family, together with the encomiums and other texts, for well over three centuries.

The plans are drawn on heavy paper waterproofed for painting. The Great Walls, mountain ridges, gullies, streams and slopes are depicted in ink and colourwash. Stamps of watchtowers and lookout platforms, encampments, forts, beacon towers and relay beacons indicate their positions within the overall structure of the Great Walls.

The painting shows the influence of the mid- to late-Ming imperial atelier style. To portray rugged mountains and slopes, the artist employs the 'axe-blade stroke' of landscape painting. The Great Walls resemble a long dragon which snakes along the contours of the precipitous Yanshan Mountains for 500 kilometres, and winds its way between the lines of the peaks that form the Chongshan Range. Where each watchtower rises above the line of ramparts, a triangular pennant hangs from its north-eastern corner, indicating martial preparedness.

In the illustrations, 'tiger skin' (*hupi*) stones and grouting face the outer surface of the ramparts, which are topped with battlements. The walls are shown facing west. The uniform depiction of all the watchtowers, beacon towers, encampments and forts does not do justice to the architectural variety of the Ming Great Walls. But the maps were not created for artistry or verisimilitude, but to provide logistical information.

The lines of demarcation between military circuits (*lu*) bear white, brown, red and blue labels. On the labels are written the names of the defending armies, their troop quotas and their budgets (expressed in silver taels), the

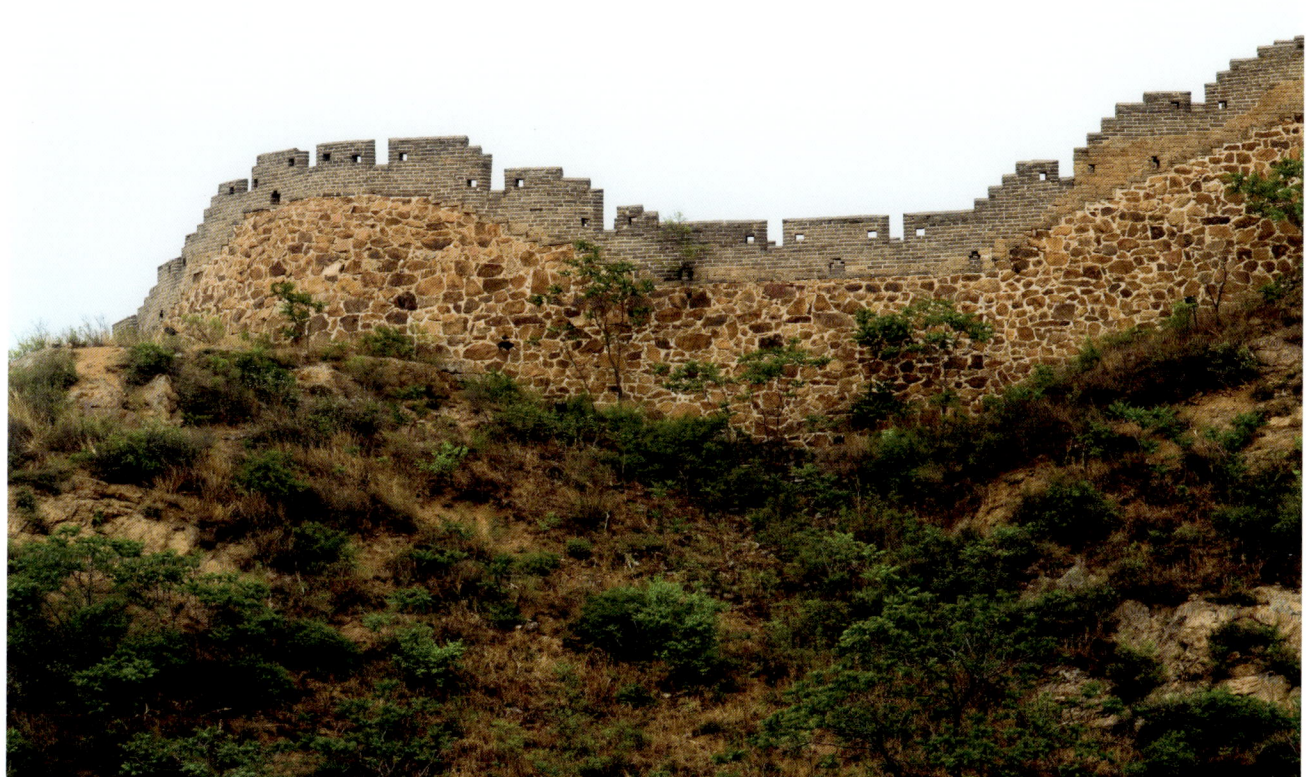

The Ming dynasty Great Wall at Jinshanling, Luanping, Hebei, built with 'tiger skin walls' (*hupi qiang*).
Photo: Jean-Francois Lanzarone

names of the demarcation lines themselves, and the distances — in both *li* and paces — between each strategic pass, watchtower and beacon tower. The watchtowers and beacon towers are marked with their construction dates. There is also detail on the areas covered by various kinds of military scouts, as well as other data not available in other historical documents.

Reading the plans

The plans played a role in the design and construction of the Great Walls, as well as functioning as defence plans for the Jizhou commandery. Construction of the ramparts in that commandery began early in the Ming dynasty, but the watchtowers on those ramparts date from 1569, the third year of the Longqing reign. In the section on 'Edicts and memorials' of his *Gazetteer of the four commanderies and three passes*, Liu Xiaozu writes: 'It was originally proposed that three thousand watchtowers be built in total in the Jizhou and Changping sections of the walls, and that these be ordered into high and low priority tasks. Top priority was given to 1500 of these structures.' Five years later, in 1574, Supreme Commander Yang Zhao presented a memorial to the throne which stated, 'I have heard that the construction of watchtowers in the Jizhou commandery over successive years has exhausted the strength of the armies, but now I can report that this building work has been completed.' This passage signals that 1500 watchtowers had been built.

The work on the Great Walls was supervised by men with the title of 'Patrolling Pacification Inspecting Censor'. Wei Huan, in the 'Jizhou commandery' section of his *A study of the nine commanderies of the empire* (Huangming jiubian kao), quoted a memorial of 1539, written by Inspecting Censor Dai Jin, in which he describes his duties:

> Upon encountering a section of the wall at the passes which is either [too] low or narrow, inspecting censors order local military officers to rebuild, urgently, the deficient section in conformity with regulations. The walls require constant upkeep, as does military ordnance; there are a number of cases of damage clearly requiring repair. Other long-term defensive strategies should also be implemented, and a full-day meeting called every year for the grand defenders and commandants of the commanderies to present illustrated plans for all proposals they make to the government. As before, a system whereby inspectors, commissioned by the central government, conduct successive inspections. If several months intervene between inspections, and if in an exigency there are no available inspectors, then the grand defenders and commandants of the commanderies … should be empowered to issue the relevant effective orders.

The explanations on the labels attached to the Jizhou commandery plans conform completely with the regulations implemented in the Jiajing period (1522–66). We know that the maps were used both for building plans and inspections. But from their general content

and certain details not included on the labels, as well as from changes made to some of them, we also know that they were not the original reference plans used by inspectors, but copies employed by military commanders.

The plans locate south at the top, east on the left and west on the right. In this they differ from other post-Song dynasty maps as well as another Ming dynasty map, *The nine commanderies* (Jiubian tu). The reason for this was that most military commanders, when at headquarters, sat at desks facing south; such an orientation made the plans easy to read. Significantly, this also ensured that strategists were able to view the Great Walls as though from the outside, as their enemies did. In fascicle 225 of *Ming documents on statecraft* (Ming jingshi wenbian), Weng Dongyao, quoting a rescript by Weng Wanda to *Explanation of the plan presented of the external walls of Shanxi's Xuan[fu] and Da[tong] commanderies* (Jin Xuan Da Shanxi waibianqiang changtu shuo) wrote: 'The depiction of the external ramparts is more detailed than that of the internal ramparts, and all the passes are shown so that their outer areas are more distinct.' The external walls are also depicted in finer detail on these plans, which is logical given their greater defensive significance.

As the plans themselves lack dates, names and signatures, we must refer to internal evidence to date them. Blue stamps affixed to the plan indicate those watchtowers and beacon platforms that had already been constructed; those still in the planning stages are indicated with red stamps. Apart from a few landmark structures missing labels, all were built between 1569 and 1584. Of these, the seventeen watchtowers built between 1582 and 1584 bear distinctive labels. Using red, blue or yellow paper, these labels indicate the year and the name of the army that constructed the watchtower. In addition, above the name of each circuit, a broad label repeats the information regarding the year of construction, as well as the number of troops involved, their salaries calculated in silver, and their rations of grain, beans and medicines. Five of the seventeen watchtowers constructed in 1582 bear blue labels, as do four built in 1583 and one built by the spring defence shift of troops. The remaining three watchtowers, like the eight built in 1584, have red labels over-stamped with blue watchtower stamps. This enables us to conclude that the maps were created in 1583.

Building and arming the watchtowers

The Great Walls run westward through the Jizhou commandery from Shanhaiguan Pass in the east to where the Changping commandery begins, a distance of more than 600 kilometres, its ramparts undulating across the mountainous terrain. The walls include fortified passes and 1500 watchtowers, as well as encampments and forts for housing battalions on the inner side of the ramparts, and beacon towers and signal relay stations for transmitting military intelligence. On the outer side, ramps, measuring between 2 *zhang*, 5 *chi* or 3 *zhang* [8 and 10 metres] in height, were constructed to form a forward

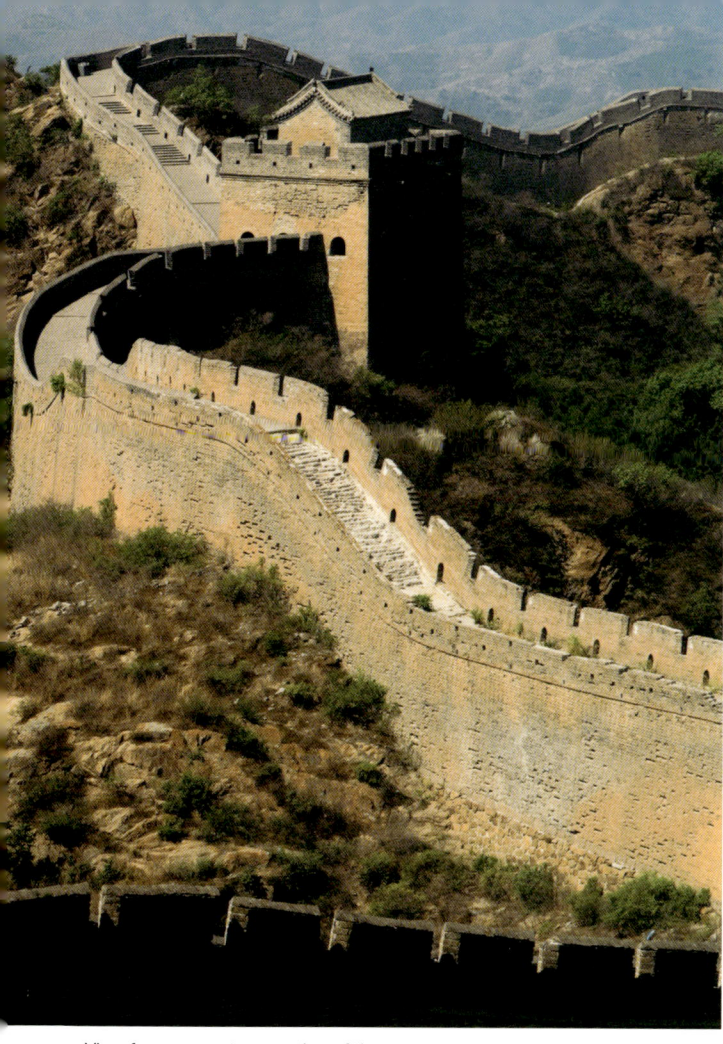

View from an eastern section of the
Great Wall at Jinshanling, Luanping, Hebei.
Photo: Jean-Francois Lanzarone

line of defensive structures which, together with the walls, constituted a comprehensive system of defences.

Regarding the building of the watchtowers, General Qi Jiguang wrote in his *Notes on military training* (Lianbing shiji zhaji):

In earlier years, when low or narrow sections of the boundary walls collapsed, small stone platforms were erected to fill the gaps and to provide some cover. However, when soldiers encountered summer downpours or winter storms, these left them with no shelter. If gunpowder was required at a particular place, it could not be transported, nor could it be kept under cover on the ramparts. If fighting was heavy and a place was surrounded by cavalry, the defending soldiers found it hard to fight back, and if the ramparts were breached the soldiers had to take flight leaving the enemy troops unopposed to pour through and depredate. Now that watchtowers have been constructed, men and horses can be deployed easily throughout the defensive network. Conflict points are blocked by structures between 3 and 4 zhang [10 and 13.3 metres] in height and between 12 and 17–18 zhang [40 and 57–60 metres] in circumference, and cavalry can ride up onto the ramparts because the base of these structures is level with the walls. The middle layers are hollow; there are embrasures set into the walls of these structures, and the defenders on the inside can discharge their weapons through the gaps between the merlons of the battlements.

The watchtowers shown on the plans resemble the military structures described in the above passage. The section on 'Edicts and memorials' (Zhishu) of Liu Xiaozu's *Gazetteer of the four commanderies and three passes* contains Liu Yingjie's ten-point summary of the advantages provided by watchtowers:

1. *The troops regard the watchtower as their home-base; inside, they are provided with firewood, water, hay and grain, and it protects them from the elements;*

2. *There they can store a plentiful, seemingly unlimited, supply of firepower;*

3. *The arrows of the enemy cannot reach them nor can structures be used to scale the ramparts, while our cannon fire and arrows can cover a greater distance;*

4. *By relying on the watchtowers, the troops lose their fear and are emboldened, making it possible also to deploy younger troops;*

5. *Their proximity to watchtowers strengthens the defensive capability of the ramps and trench walls;*

6. *Because watchtowers are constructed with regard for topography, they allow an economy of effort in handling all situations to the present day;*

7. *If cunning bandits do succeed in scaling our defences, and take us by surprise, they might capture a watchtower, but they will still be surrounded on all sides, and unable to attack from the walls, which will make them wary of attempting a deep penetrative foray;*

8. *Defending troops can hold out for a long time while awaiting reinforcements;*

9. *If bandits plan an entry they must also plan their exit; coming in, they will meet resistance, and, leaving, they will also need to be on the offensive; and finally,*

10. *Even if bandits attacking a watchtower succeed in breaching a wall, their cavalry will still be unable to charge straight through and the troops on the watchtowers can fight on fearlessly.*

In 'Accounts of walls' (Cheng zhi) found in *Treatise on military preparedness* (Wubei zhi), it states that: 'While weapons such as spears cannot be used to fight attackers positioned below the walls, those below are unable to reach those above with arrows or projectiles. Thus, thanks to the watchtowers, we can devote our energies to repelling the enemy.' These two passages succinctly summarise the important role the watchtowers played in defensive warfare.

The collection of the National Museum of China contains bricks from the Jinshanling section of the Great Wall in Hebei's Luanping county. The bricks, made from local materials, bear the inscriptions 'Made by the Valiant Battalion in the sixth year of Wanli [1578]' and 'Made by the Border Cavalry Battalion in the sixth year of Wanli'.

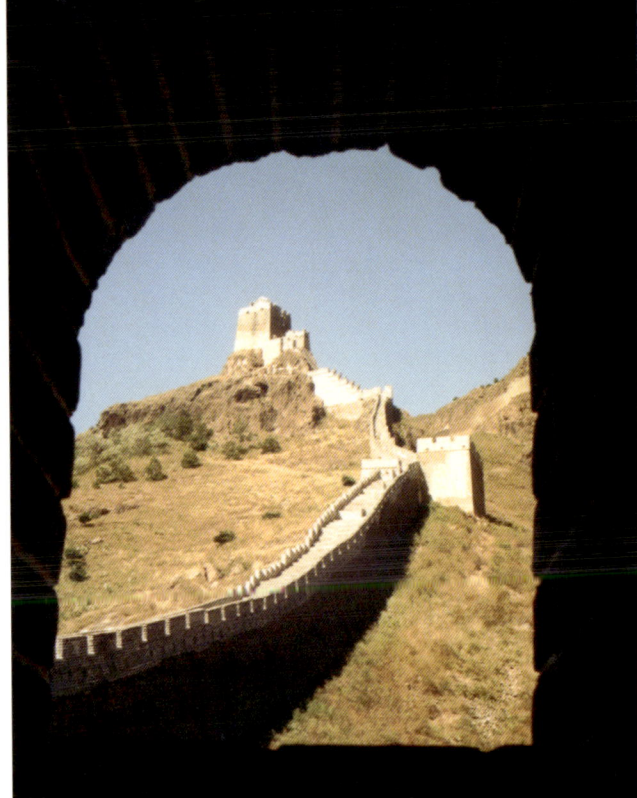

Ming dynasty Great Wall and watchtowers
at Jiaoshan Mountain, near Shanhaiguan Pass, Hebei.
Photo: Luo Zhewen

Soldiers employed various ingenious methods to construct walls and watchtowers over difficult terrain, including steep ridged mountains. The 'Edicts and memorials' section of Liu Xiaozu's *Gazetteer of the four commanderies and three passes* cites Tan Lun's 'Memorial announcing the conclusion of the autumn building roster' (Fang qiushi jun tai gongwan shu):

> The watchtower alone measures 12, 14–15 or 15–16 zhang [40, 47–50 or 50–53 metres] in height. Its base rests on a square stone foundation and in its upper section, bricks face the walls to a depth of 4 chi, 5 cun [1.5 metres]. West of Huanghua the autumn building teams faced the walls to a thickness of nine chi [3 metres]. The cost of this work was originally projected at 50 official silver liang, but additional bureaucratic costs raised this figure to 80, 90 and even 100 liang to include wages, and yet if this work had been carried out by civilians it could not have been done for 500–600 to 1–2000 jin.

Qi Jiguang's 'Memorial requesting the construction of watchtowers' (Qing jian kongxin ditai shu), fascicle 348 in *Ming documents on statecraft*, states: 'The foundation must be 30 zhang [100 metres] in width [and the watchtower] should rise to ten zhang at its highest point. Construction will require 240–250 men. Each year 70 watchtowers can be completed, making for a great improvement.' The labels on the plans indicate that between 1582 and 1584, seventeen watchtowers were built, and the notes on the related expenditure in silver *liang* reveal that, on average, each watchtower cost around 200 silver *taels*, and required the labour of 400 men.[1] As each tower took approximately four months to complete, they represent 48 000 working days.

Peng Xinwei's *History of Chinese currency* (Zhongguo huobi shi) states that in the Wanli reign period 'one *dan* [50 kilograms] of rice cost six *qian*, three *fen* and eight *li*'. From this, we can calculate that 200 *liang* of silver could purchase 313 *dan* of rice, and if 1 *dan* is 100 *jin* [50 kilograms] then that is equivalent to 31 300 *jin*, then a daily ration of rice per worker (based on 48 000 days) was 0.65 *jin* [325 grams]. If one watchtower were completed every two months, then each worker would only have received slightly more than 1 *jin* [500 grams] of rice in wages. These figures are only estimates, but they reveal that the soldiers building the watchtowers were fed little more than a bowl of watery rice soup daily. On these meagre rations they built one of the world's greatest engineering wonders.

Cannon emplacements were constructed at the outside bases of the watchtowers. Indicated on the plans by blue stamps, the low cannon emplacements abut the watchtowers on one side, surrounding a level area on which the cannons stood and using an external wall of the watchtower as their fourth wall. At the base of the front wall were two apertures, and each side wall also contained an aperture. Assuming that a watchtower measured 3 *zhang* [10 metres] across, the width of each aperture was 2 *shichi* [60 centimetres]. Above the cannon embrasures, in the centre of each of the three outer walls, was a row of eight small holes, most likely for the use of firearms (rifles and muskets). Between one and five cannon emplacements were positioned either on one or both sides of the watchtowers at thirteen strategic passes: Changbangu, Nazigu, Damaoshanguan, Dongjiakouguan, Chengzigu, Shuimensi, Pingdinggu, Yipianshi, Huangtuling, Wumingkou, Jielingkouguan, Luohandong and Heiguguan.

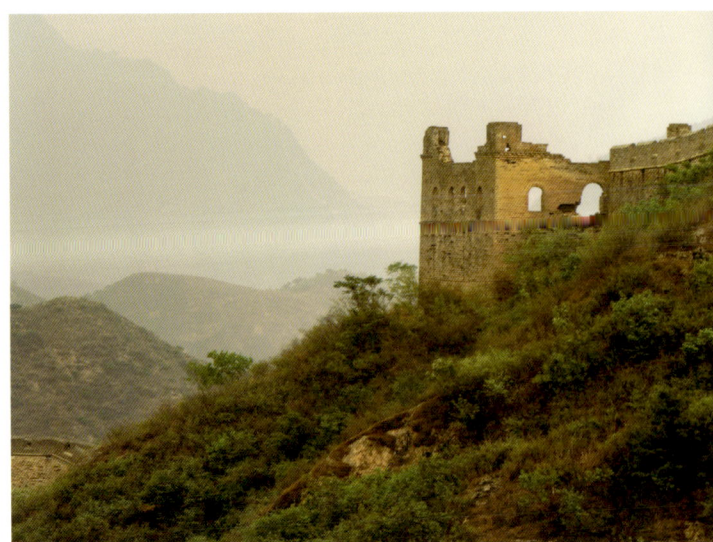

Looking east towards a ruined watchtower on the
Ming dynasty Great Wall at Jinshanling, Luanping, Hebei.
Photo: Jean-Francois Lanzarone

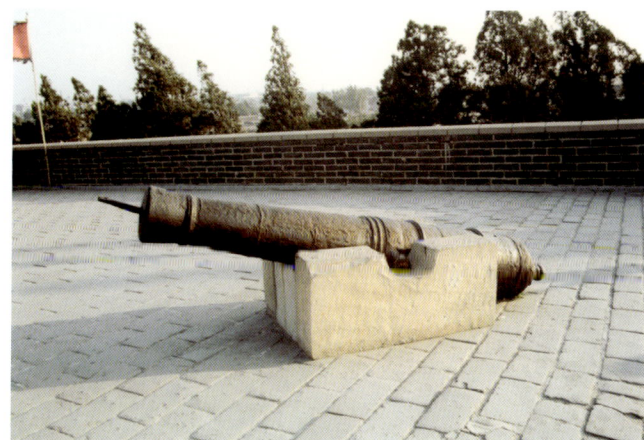

Ming dynasty cannon on the Great Wall at Shanhaiguan Pass, Hebei.
Photo: Luo Zhewen

The label underneath the symbol for the cannon fort below the Number One Watchtower at Huangtuling reads: 'The sixty cannon emplacements below were all built in the ninth year of Wanli [1581] by the military supervisor of this circuit.' This demonstrates that cannons were used in the Wanli period as part of the forward line of defence of the Great Walls. In 'Explanation of watchtowers' in his *Notes on military training*, Qi Jiguang wrote that each watchtower was fitted with eight 'Portuguese cannon' (*folangji*), seventy-two large muskets with 2160 rounds of ammunition, eight light muskets with 480 rounds of ammunition, and 200 kilograms of gunpowder. At that time cannon emplacements had still not been constructed and the installed 'Portuguese cannon' were not heavy-duty artillery.

A fairly large number of ballistic armaments have survived from Ming times. An iron barrel from a 'Portuguese cannon' in the collection of the National Museum of China is 151 centimetres long and weighs more than 50 kilograms. Two watchtower muskets — one made in 1414, the twelfth year of the Yongle reign, and the other in 1444, the ninth year of the Zhengtong reign — were unearthed from the slope at the foot of the Great Walls in Chongli county, Hebei.

To date, however, no heavy cannon manufactured prior to the Tianqi reign (1621–27) has been found. The 'Military' section of the *History of the Ming dynasty* (*Ming shi*), states that in 1529, the eighth year of the Jiajing reign, Wang Hong cast a bronze 'Portuguese cannon' with a rounded barrel and long neck nicknamed 'the generalissimo' (*dajiangjun*), which was issued to all border commands. It measured 1.65 or 2 metres in length and weighed 500 kilograms; a smaller version weighed only 75 kilograms. There were apertures in the barrel and it could fire five shots. When primed with gunpowder, 'it could fire a cannon ball for a distance of more than 100 *zhang* [333 metres].' If this record is accurate, then the heavier cannon could have first been used on the Great Walls;

however, the cannon emplacements on the Jizhou commandery plan date back only to 1581 and there is no textual documentation as to the type of cannon employed on them. The cannon emplacements shown on the maps thus pose fresh questions for historians of Chinese firepower.

Troop rosters and relay beacons

Troops defending the Great Walls were divided into 'host' troops and 'guest' troops. The host troops were local troops of a particular circuit; the guest troops came from the military commands of Yansui, Datong, Shandong, Liaodong, Zhen or Bao. The host and guest troops were further divided into the spring and the autumn rosters. Each defence season (or tour of duty) lasted for four months. The spring defence began in the second month of the lunar calendar and concluded in the fifth month, while the autumn defence began in the seventh month and ended in the tenth month. The guest troops arrived in shifts. In the 'Jizhou commandery strategies' (Jizhen jinglüe) section of Liu Xiaozu's *Gazetteer of the four commanderies and three passes*, we read:

> There were, in total, sixty host and guest troops stationed at a watchtower. Thirty were assigned to the defence of the tower and from among them, a tower leader was appointed. Thirty were assigned to the defence of the battlements, and these were further divided into six groups of five, with a leader appointed from among each group of five.

In 'Explanation of watchtowers' in his *Notes on military training*, cited above, Qi Jiguang wrote:

> At every watchtower there is a co-ordinator who is in charge of the deployment against attacks, and below him are two Masters of the Watchtower, one of whom is an assistant, and they are in charge of all weaponry inside the watchtower. For every five watchtowers there is one Master of One Hundred and for every ten watchtowers there is a Master of a Thousand, and they manage every detail in the integrated system.

The Jizhou commandery plans indicate that each circuit had an assistant regional commander and at each pass there was a supervising officer, while the Master of a Thousand and the coordinator managed key posts and boundaries in each area. The names of those 'in charge of one hundred' were recorded on the plans. Each watchtower was assigned a serial number and a name. Within each circuit the numbering of the watchtowers began from number one, and ran from east to west. The strategic rating of the pass determined the number of soldiers assigned to it: in the Huangtuling and Damaoshan pass areas, there were thirty troops posted at each watchtower; in the Yiyuankou Pass area there were forty at each watchtower; in the Shitang circuit, each watchtower had only twenty-eight men; and between thirty and thirty-seven guarded the rest. The largest number of troops were assigned to the Chaohechuan area,

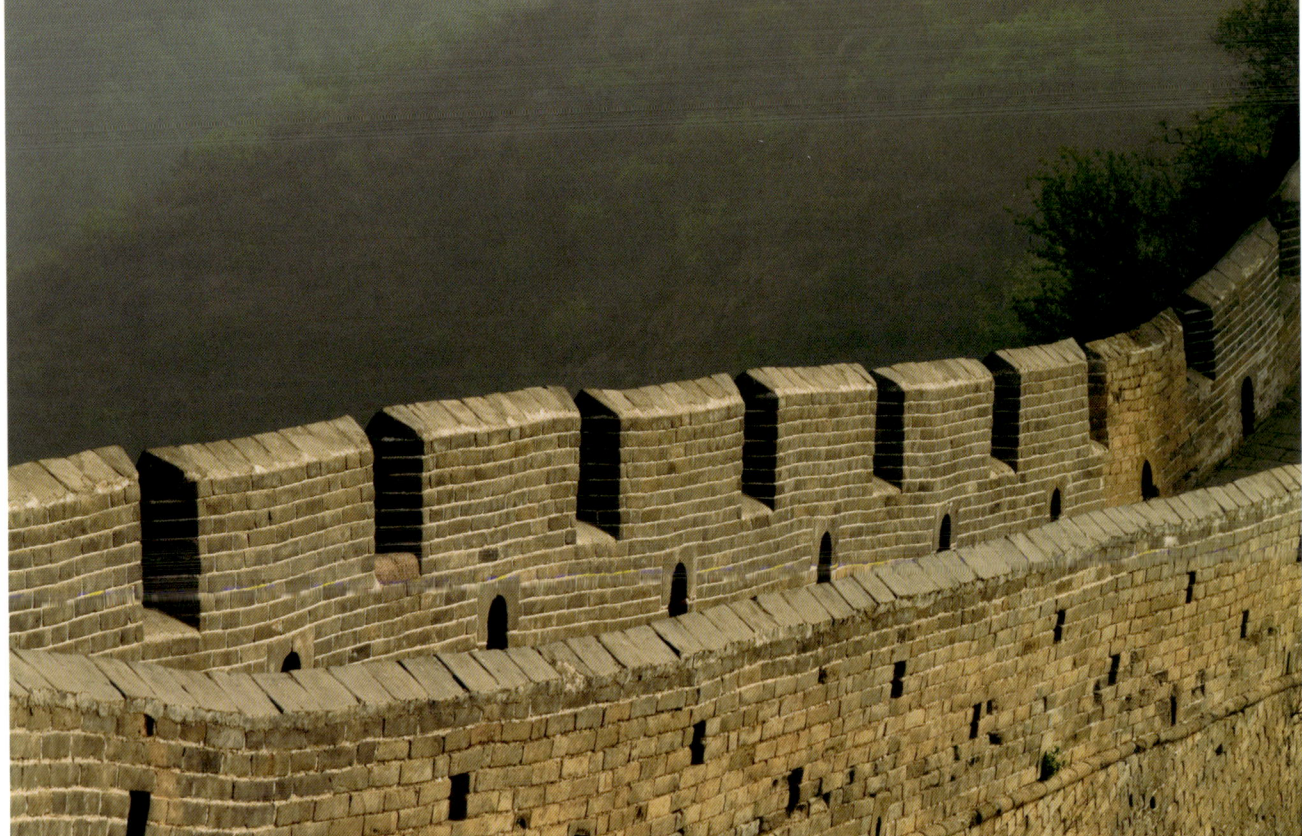

Detail of the Ming dynasty Great Wall
at Jinshanling, Luanping, Hebei.
Photo: Jean-Francois Lanzarone

where there were from fifty to sixty per watchtower, and
the names of all of them were noted.

Areas where there were no watchtowers or walls were
called 'voids'. Depending on the strategic pressure on
the area, each void was assigned between ten and fifty
soldiers. Five were assigned to each signal relay station.
The intervals between all watchtowers, fire-beacon
platforms and relay stations were indicated in measures
of either *zhang* and *chi*, or *li* and *bu* (steps).

In every circuit within a military command the men were
systematically ranked from the supervising officer down.
This reflected Qi Jiguang's military strategy: an integrated
system of managing and deploying troops in groups of six
and five.

On the plan the scouts are described as those 'staying out
at night'. There were distinctions between scouts working
in the day or at night and contingency scouts. Some of
each were assigned to every circuit. Scouts were chosen
with great care. They had to be familiar with the enemy,
speak their language and wear their clothing, as well as
be able to distinguish every landmark in the enemy's
territory. Two short-range and two long-range scouts were
selected to survey the terrain and reconnoitre strategic
landmarks. They were sent out into the field in rotation.
The long-range scouts, who operated in an area up to 300
or 350 kilometres or beyond, used locals to guide them
into enemy territory. The short-range scouts operated in
an area from between five kilometres to 50 or 100
kilometres from the pass. The scouts ferreted out

information about the enemy and formed networks of
contacts, then reported directly back to the pass, battalion
and military command. 'An examination of Liu
Daichuan's frontier proposals' (Liu Daichuan bianyi kao),
fascicle 403 in M*ing documents on statecraft*, states:

> *All three armies posted scouts and spies into the area …
> The troops stationed at the beacon towers would light fires.
> The night scouts would receive their information from the
> long-range scouts. The long-range scouts, short-range scouts
> and reporters stayed out at night gathering intelligence
> on enemy troops from beyond the passes; those gathering
> top-secret information were received the following morning
> back at camp after their return, where they imparted
> information on numbers of formations, the advances
> and retreats of enemy forces, and details of areas where
> they were encamped or roaming. Thus the armies could
> pre-empt enemy movements before battles broke out.*

The scouts served as eyes and ears for the officers
in charge of troops defending the Great Walls, who
could then relay the intelligence and prepare defences,
including the strategic deployment of military forces.

Other labels on the plans are attached to the boundary
passes of each circuit. They indicate where enemy troops
were likely to attack. Passes were given a security rating,
which determined the number of troops assigned to
guard them, and created a priority system for assigning
government troops. For example, at Jielingkou Pass
there is a note:

If the enemy troops at Daning proceed to Tuhutong via Hanluowusu, Wudalin, Luchang, Hongcaogou or Ulan Qihe, or at Qingcheng they rush eastwards via Eliqi to avoid coming out at Ulan Qihe and go on to [Tu]hutong, then they must move eastwards into the area of the Jielingkou Pass, Luohandongpu and Jianganlingkou Pass. Zhongsangpu and Xingxinggupu are on strategic roads beyond the walls and they will not be able to resist a major movement of troops.

Such definitive assessments were made on the basis of geographical knowledge and an understanding of the routes of entry. These factors determined military priorities. Such details reflect deep penetrative reconnaissance and keen intelligence.

Beacon signal relay stations were set up in roofed structures marked by five beacon poles, between each of which was a lookout. Each beacon tower was assigned a serial number; in each circuit these ran from number one all the way to the boundary of the circuit.

Most beacon towers were built on the outer side of the Great Walls and the relay stations were built on the inside. The 'Jizhou commandery strategies' section of Liu Xiaozu's *Gazetteer* records:

Cannons guard the beacon towers and the lookout posts oversee the walls. When a cannon is fired the signal is relayed on to the next beacon, and the next, until the signal is sent to every circuit, camp and fort under the military command. By day the lookouts relay information using flags and pennants, and by night they send signals by fire. The military command is divided into five circuits [or 'roads'] in both the east and west. The eastern circuit has a white flag which is seven chi [2.3 metres] square and the western circuit has a white pennant two chi [0.66 metres] wide and one zhang, two chi [4 metres] in length. At each lookout relay there are four poles, each one zhang, eight chi [4.65 metres] in height. When a military situation occurs in the daytime, the eastern circuit will raise their flag and the western circuit will respond with the white pennant. At night fires relay the signal. Whenever a lookout hears cannon fire it will relay the information to either side … If three shots are fired and then the flags or pennants are raised or the torches lit, the next beacon will respond and so the message will be spread through the ten circuits. If bandits are at a distance of more than one hundred li [50 kilometres] then one signal will be sent, if they are at a distance of 30 li [15 kilometres] then two signals are sent, and if they are approaching the walls then three signals are sent. When it is foggy or misty, the flags and fires are replaced by cannon, and unless there are three cannon shots then the appropriate number of signals is relayed.

Liu Xiaozu's *Gazetteer* and Qi Jiguang's *Notes on military training* make no mention of the more traditional use of smoke from wolf dung (*langyan*).[2] Therefore it is evident that in the Jizhou commandery there had been innovation in the ways in which relay messages were being transmitted.

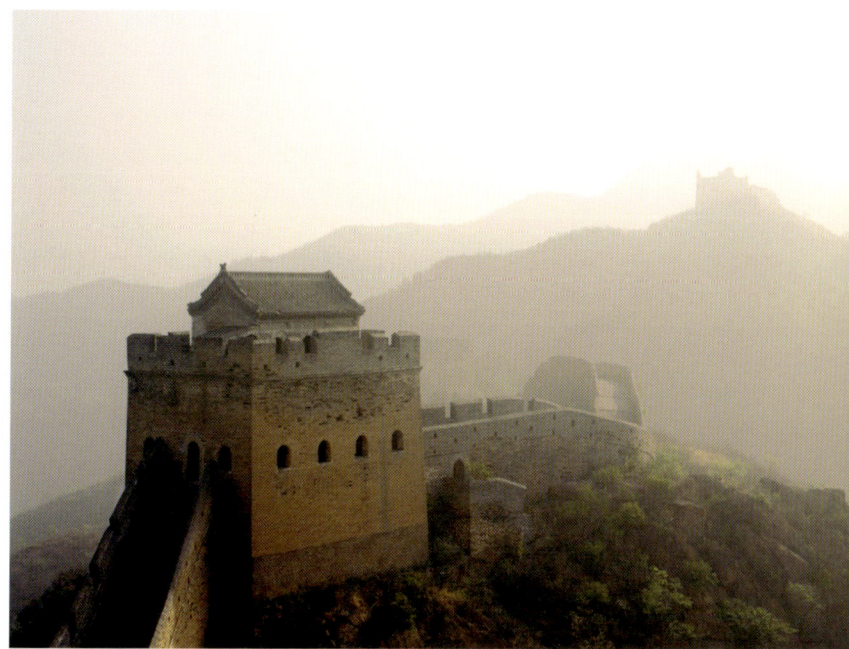

Ming dynasty Great Wall and beacon towers at Jiumenkou, at the border of Liaoning and Hebei.
Photo: Jean-Francois Lanzarone

The Great Walls of the Jizhou commandery extend through difficult terrain and precipitous mountains. It is here that the most solid section of the walls was constructed. Historians have written about this engineering feat in detail, but these plans are the only known pictorial documentation. The *Plans of the Jizhou commandery of the Ming Great Walls* not only supply new data for the study of engineering, defence, military topography and ethnic relations, but they also provide valuable clues for the conservation and restoration of the Great Walls.

TRANSLATED BY BRUCE GORDON DOAR

Manning the Wall: Qi Jiguang

LIU RUZHONG

The establishment of the Ming dynasty in 1368 forced the Mongol rulers who had reigned during the preceding Yuan dynasty (1279–1368) to retreat to the northern frontier. But the Mongols continued to harass the Ming, conducting frequent raids across the border. Securing the northern frontier was thus of paramount importance and General Qi Jiguang played a prominent role in this mission during the late Ming dynasty.

Qi Jiguang (1528–87) hailed from Penglai county in Dengzhou prefecture, Shandong province. An ancestor of Qi's had participated in the uprising against the Mongols led by Zhu Yuanzhang (1328–98), the man who founded the Ming dynasty and became its first emperor. The ancestor had been rewarded for his meritorious actions with the title of Assistant Commander of the Dengzhou Guard, a title which was inherited by his descendents. At the age of sixteen, Qi Jiguang succeeded to this position, and was diligent in securing coastal defences, auditing the cash and grain expenditure of the guard post, and punishing lawlessness and local tyrants. Later, in recognition of services rendered in the defence of the frontier, he was awarded the title of Junior Guardian of the Heir Apparent.

An example of his work in establishing law and order can be found in his 'Memorial of Qi, the communications officer of the Commander of the Dengzhou Guard to the Governor General of Shandong on the matter of local gambling', a document preserved in the Liaoning provincial archives. In this memorial from 1552, Qi highlights the problem of local gangsters in Shandong who were responsible for a wave of gambling and vice. He ordered a crackdown, urged the citizenry to adopt upright moral conduct, and called for improvements in local law and order as well as coastal defences.

In 1554, Qi Jiguang served as adjutant commander in charge of defending the Jiangsu-Zhejiang region in the south of China, including Ningbo, Shaoxing and Taizhou, from Wo pirates — marauders consisting of Japanese, Ryukyu islanders and some Chinese elements. Thirteen years later, in 1567, the emperor assigned Qi, then the area commander for Fujian, to lead a pacification campaign against the Wo pirates.

In light of his efficacy, in 1568 the court transferred him to the Jizhou commandery (known as Jizhen), in Hebei province immediately north of the capital, with a special commission to reinforce the Great Wall and strengthen frontier defences against the Mongols.

For decades the Mongols had continued to threaten Ming rule. The third Ming emperor, Yongle (reigned 1403–24), had personally led several expeditions against the Mongols and died on campaign. Under Yingzong, the sixth Ming ruler who became emperor in 1436,[1] the fortunes of the court waned in part due to the unchecked rise of eunuch influence, widespread corruption and economic stagnation. Meanwhile the Oirat Mongols were becoming more powerful. Dividing their forces into four circuits, they launched a full-scale attack on the Ming. In 1450, Yingzong personally led his army into the field against them. He was completely routed, falling into a trap laid by the enemy at Tumupu, and was taken prisoner.

The war inflicted severe damage on the Great Wall, and many fortresses were destroyed. The Mongol ruler Anda (Altan Khan) led a force to capture the Ordos region of

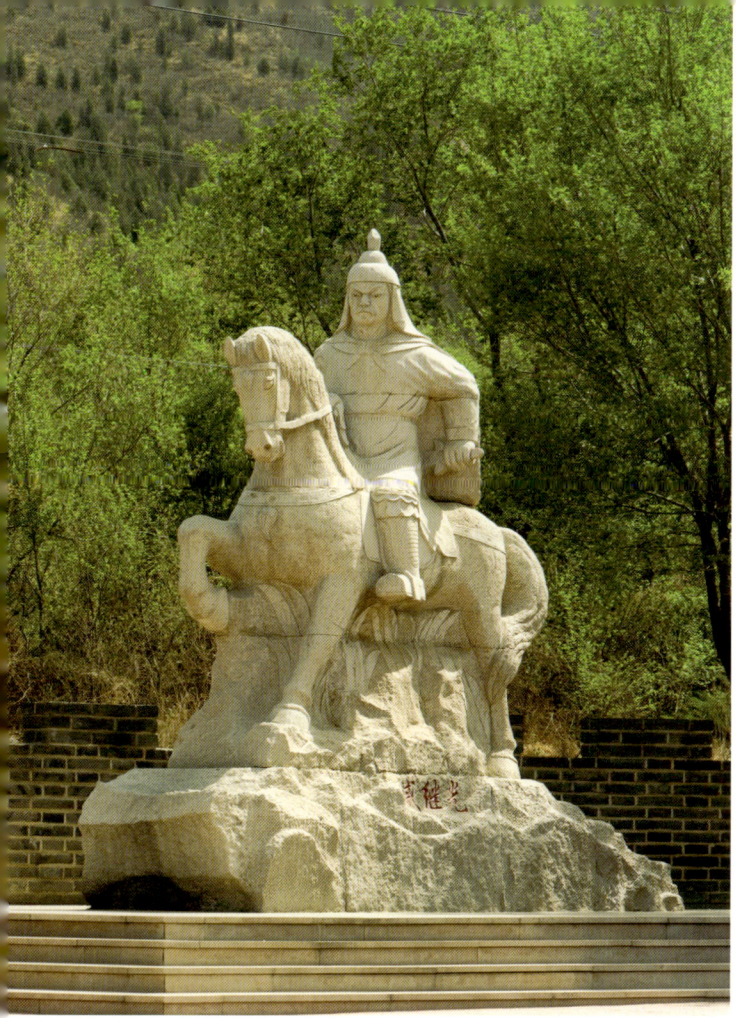

Statue of Qi Jiguang near the Great Wall at Badaling, Yanqing, Hebei.
Photo: Jean-Francois Lanzarone

the upper Yellow River for use as grazing lands. The Ming painting *Encampment of Anda* depicts this expansion of Mongol forces.[2] In 1550, in what is known as the Gengxu Incident, Anda's troops laid siege to Beijing and eventually looted the Ming capital. The Great Wall had failed to protect the dynasty and as a result, the Ming rulers set upon the task of repairing and extending their defences.

Thereafter, the Ming established regional military commands along the entire length of the Great Wall. As noted earlier, these were known as the 'nine commanderies' or 'nine garrisons'. Each commandery was led by a regional commander. A painting in the collection of the National Museum of China entitled *The nine comanderies* (see pp 198–99) depicts the garrisons from east to west: Liaodong, Jizhou [Jizhen], Xuanfu, Datong, Piantou [Shanxi], Yuzhou [Yansui], Ningxia, Guyuan and Gansu.

In 1568, Qi Jiguang was put in charge of the Jizhou commandery in Hebei province, immediately north of the capital. With a rank equivalent to regional commander, he reported directly to the military governor. He was commissioned to reinforce the Great Wall and strengthen frontier defences against the Mongols.

He located his headquarters at Santunying in Shizigou, where 300 military households of the Loyal Central Guard had been posted. According to the *Record of the reconstruction of the walls of Santunying carried out by Qi*

Jiguang, Qi extended the new wall at Santunying 'around the old south wall, for a total length of 517 *zhang* [1.72 kilometres], with a height of two *zhang* five *chi* [8.3 metres] and with a parapet of an additional five *chi* [1.65 metres] in height. At the base it was over four *zhang* [13.3 metres] and had three gates.'[3]

Qi's command was responsible for the area from Shanhaiguan in the east to Sihaiye (now in Yanqing county, Beijing) to the west. It encompassed over 1290 kilometres of walls. This made Jizhou the most important of the nine Ming commanderies, and the linchpin in the defensive network around the imperial capital.

The Great Wall within the Jizhou commandery can be divided into three sections. The eastern section, from Shanhaiguan to Shitanglu, was overseen by a district commander with three assistants, eleven divisional adjutants and six mobile field commanders. The Changping section, stretching from Mutianyu in the east to Zijingguan in the west, had one district commander, three adjutants and two mobile field generals, as well as two commanding officers and ten garrison defence leaders. The Baoding section, stretching from Zijingguan westwards to Zhiguguan, had one area commander, four assistants and six mobile field generals.

After Qi Jiguang took up his appointment, he carried out a thorough inspection of the Great Wall defences in Jizhou, paying particular attention to all vulnerable points. He noted: 'one flawed section is enough to render worthless a hundred which are sound. …[W]alls built in the spring are in ruins before the year is out. Money thus spent … gives scant return.'[4] Qi decided to carry out major reconstruction of sections of the Great Wall within his command, reinforcing the walls with brick, building more than 3000 watchtowers and restoring beacon towers.

The reconstruction of the Jizhou walls was largely carried out by soldiers. Numbers of construction battalions, each of 250 men, made bricks with locally procured materials and built some seventy watchtowers per year.

Two bricks in the collection of the National Museum of China record the details of the military units, under Qi Jiguang's command, that made them (see p 192). One is inscribed 'Made by the Valiant Battalion in the sixth year of Wanli' [1578]; the other records 'Made by the Border Cavalry Battalion in the sixth year of Wanli.' At the fortress of the Simatai Pass a brick is marked 'Made by the Left Battalion of Shandong in the fifth year of Wanli [1577]'.

An inscription on a stele from a section of the Great Wall east of Shifosi village in Yanqing county, Beijing, records that this section of the wall, measuring just under 250 metres, was constructed by the Right Cavalry Battalion under Qi Jiguang's command in the tenth year of Wanli [1582], and cites the names of the team leaders responsible for the work.

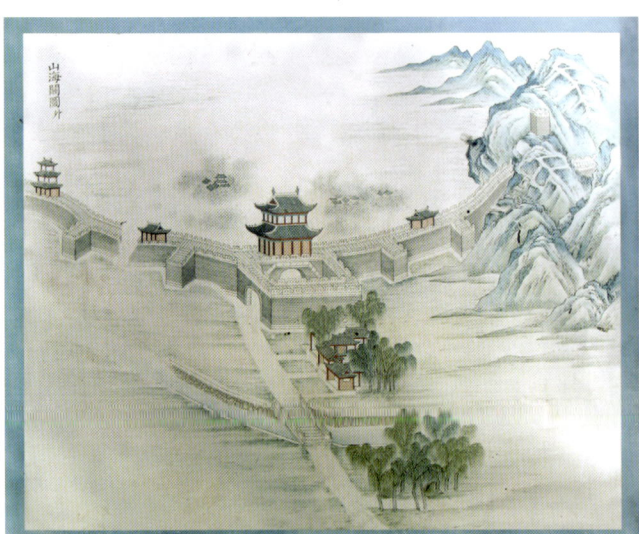

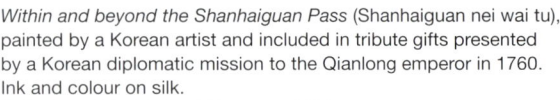

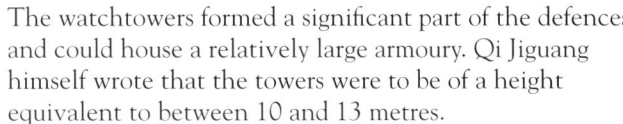

Within and beyond the Shanhaiguan Pass (Shanhaiguan nei wai tu), painted by a Korean artist and included in tribute gifts presented by a Korean diplomatic mission to the Qianlong emperor in 1760. Ink and colour on silk.
Collection of the National Museum of China.

The watchtowers formed a significant part of the defences, and could house a relatively large armoury. Qi Jiguang himself wrote that the towers were to be of a height equivalent to between 10 and 13 metres.

> *They are placed at a distance of several dozen or a hundred paces apart in vulnerable sections of the wall. Adjacent towers are designed to provide mutual support, facilitated by the construction of a cavalry wall. The watchtowers are constructed as follows: the outer foundation is in a line with the outer wall, extending up to a distance of one* zhang *and five or six* chi *[5 metres].* The enclosure of the building is left bare, with merlons on all four sides and a crenellated tower above, from which defending soldiers were able to fire cannon at the enemy.[5]

Qi Jiguang here provides a clear description of the method of construction and function of the watchtowers. They were to be built, 'in a form appropriate to the terrain, with towers closer together where the wall crosses level ground, and further apart in mountainous country. They should be built narrow and deep on a mountain ridge, and wide and shallow in valleys, with the overall perimeter maintained at a consistent twelve *zhang* [40 metres]'.[6]

A stele erected to record the establishment of the Huanghua command post, which is located near the reservoir of Huanghuacheng township, states: 'The Huanghua command post was built by the Autumn Roster in the seventh year of the Wanli reign [1579]. This section of wall, from the fortress designated serial number one to the fortress of serial number [text missing], where it meets with the section of Liangzhuo, is 150 *zhang* [500 metres] in length.' The names of officials and categories of workers are also recorded on this stele.

The most representative example of Ming era Great Wall construction can now be found at Jinshanling

Range, which is built across high mountain ridges. Many watchtowers built under the direction of Qi Jiguang can be found there. A stele commemorating the completion of the Huangyaguan fortress can be found at the Huangyaguan Museum of Great Wall History. Although much of the stele, which was erected around 1570, is missing, Qi Jiguang's official title can still be identified from several legible characters inscribed on the stone that read 'Commander in Charge of Training' (*zongli lianbing*).

The Huangyaguan Museum has another stele from Huangyaguan Pass that dates from the time when Qi Jiguang was supervising the building of walls within the area controlled by the Jizhou commandery. It bears the inscription 'Erected in the fourth year of Longqing' (1570). The characters of this stele are legible and include some of Qi Jiguang's titles at that time.

Where Qi Jiguang built watchtowers he also constructed beacon towers at half a kilometre or one kilometre intervals, the distance at which drum signals could be heard. A squadron of five soldiers was stationed at each beacon tower; each squad was reasonably well equipped with five cannon (*huochong*), one *sanyan* cannon, sixty bundles of dried vegetation for lighting signal fires and five lengths of fuse. Thus a message could be relayed by a number of different means along the entire length of the Great Wall under the Jizhou regional command, a distance of over 1000 kilometres, in about three hours.

After Qi Jiguang took up his post as commander of the Jizhou commandery, he discovered that some battalions were not training regularly and that the soldiers were unfit, incapable of marching in formation, had low morale, were unable to use their firearms and were poorly disciplined. He personally took charge of drilling and training the troops. This training included instruction in the use of a particular kind of sabre, which had a blade 89 centimetres long and which bore an inscription on its handle that read 'Wanli 10th year, Qi of Dengzhou' (see p 203). Qi drilled his men, bolstered their courage, rehearsed them in tactical movements and trained them in the use of firearms. Working with the existing infantry and cavalry battalions, he created a new combined force, consisting of infantry, cavalry, combat and supply battalions, that was well trained and familiar with the local terrain.

Infantry battalions

The infantry battalions were organised into a six-tiered structure. A battalion, which had a total of 2700 men, consisted of three divisions of two batteries each. A battery consisted of four platoons, with each platoon headed by a platoon commander. Each platoon had three banners, each headed by a banner commander. Each banner was made up of three squads, consisting of twelve soldiers and a squad leader. Each battalion was armed with 1080 fowling pieces and a number of bronze cannon.[7] In 1965, during the building of the road between Beijing and Chengde, in Hebei, a bronze cannon was discovered in a fortress to the west of the river at Huangyaguan Pass. It was inscribed 'Made by the Armaments Bureau in the second year of the Wanli reign [1574]', which indicates that it was used when Qi Jiguang was in command of the area.

The infantry battalions were also issued with stone bombs for use in defending fortified garrisons. These high-powered explosive devices were inexpensive to make. Their dimensions differed, depending on the type of stone used. A bomb was made by gouging a cavity out of a large stone and packing it with gunpowder and a fuse. They would be stacked in front of the crenellations along the walls. When the enemy approached, the bombs would be lit, then rolled down the wall to explode among the enemy below. Many such stone bombs can still be found in the gate tower of Shanhaiguan Pass.

The infantry battalions were also issued with 32 400 gunpowder tubes, 2160 kilograms of gunpowder, 216 000 rounds of lead shot, 3240 lengths of fuse, 6480 gunpowder projectiles and a number of 'Portuguese cannon'. 'Portuguese cannon' were introduced to China in the early Ming period and came in many varieties, all characterised by a long barrel with wide girth and a directional mounting on its upper side, and set upon a base that allowed free rotation. In Chengziyu, Funing county, Hebei, there is a fortress with a small 'Portuguese cannon' that is inscribed 'Transported from Beijing in the fourth year of Longqing [1570]', which indicates that it was transported to Chengziyu for use in defending the wall.

Firearms comprised a relatively large proportion of the infantry's weaponry. Useful for their long range and destructive power, they were employed in combination with regular arms for hand-to-hand combat and self-defence. The infantry battalions were also fitted with regular arms, such as long and short lances, spears, bows and arrows and clubs.

Cavalry battalions

Qi Jiguang placed great importance on cavalry: defending the northern frontier meant regularly engaging with Mongol soldiers who were highly skilled at shooting from the saddle. Like infantry battalions, cavalry battalions were arranged as six-tiered military structures. A battalion was divided into three divisions, formed from two batteries of four platoons. A platoon comprised three banners of three squads of twelve soldiers each. This amounted to 2700 officers and soldiers, including 432 musketeers carrying fowling pieces and triple-barrelled muskets or *sanyanqiang* (the latter being the most formidable weapon employed by the cavalry) and 432 soldiers operating hand cannon. Regular supplies included 3321 kilograms of gunpowder, 4752 lengths of fuse and 25 840 rocket arrows, as well as regular arms such as bows and arrows, spears, knives, lances and clubs.

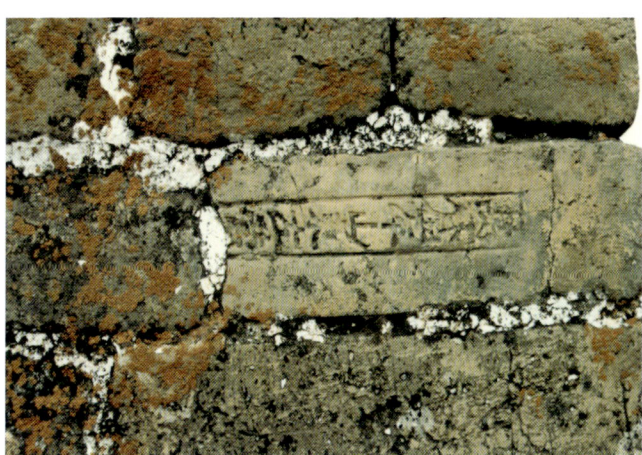

Close-up of a brick in the Great Wall: 'Made by the Left Battalion of Shandong in the fifth year of the Wanli reign [1577]'.
Photo: Luo Zhewen

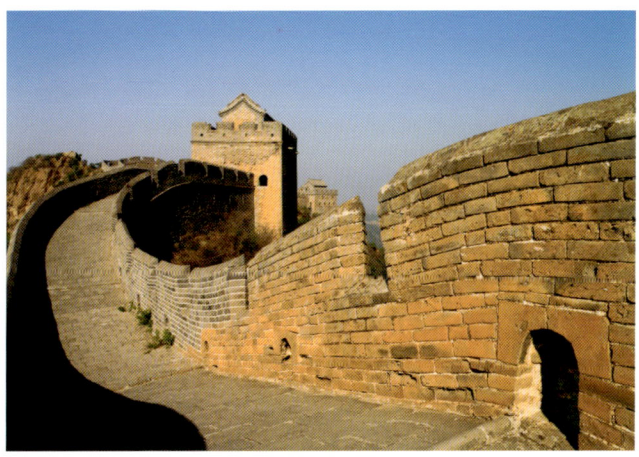

Original and restored brickwork and holes for stone bombs, eastern section of the Great Wall at Jinshanling, Luanping, Hebei.
Photo: Jean-Francois Lanzarone

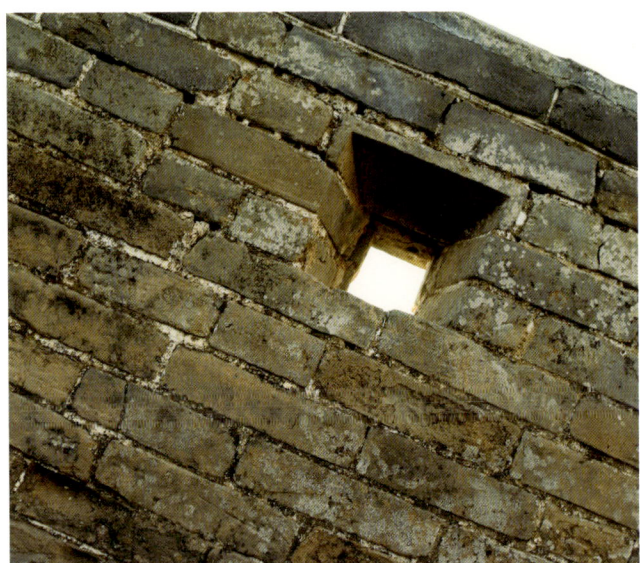

Original brickwork, showing a shooting hole, in the eastern section of the Great Wall at Jinshanling, Luanping Hebei.
Photo: Jean-Francois Lanzarone

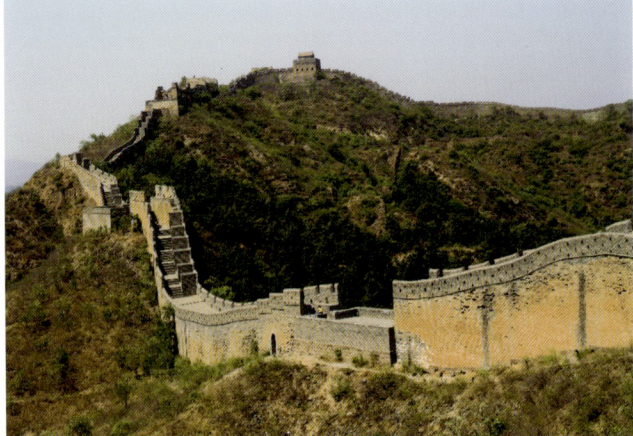

Barrier walls on the Ming dynasty Great Wall at Jinshanling, from which enemy troops that had successfully scaled the walls were attacked.
Photo: Jean-Francois Lanzarone

In addition, each battalion was issued with sixty crouching tiger cannon, which are small mortars shaped like a crouching tiger, around 2 *chi* [0.65 metres] long and weighing 60 *jin* [one Ming dynasty *jin* equals 590 grams]. Each round was capable of firing fifty to 100 pieces of lead shot. The crouching tiger cannon was a high-powered yet highly manoeuvrable weapon, suitable for close fighting in forests or fields and greatly effective in defending the Great Walls. It took three men to operate this cannon, which accounted for a further 180 men, amounting to a total of 1044 soldiers specialising in the use of artillery and firearms.

Combat-wagon battalions

Qi Jiguang designed the combat-wagon battalions specifically for use against Mongol cavalry in the narrow steep passes around the Great Walls in the Jizhou and Changping districts outside of Beijing. A combat wagon battalion was made up of two divisions, formed from four batteries of four platoons each. A platoon had two companies made up of two combat wagons, each mounted with two 'Portuguese cannon' and manned by twenty soldiers. There were 1301 soldiers in these battalions, which had 128 wagons, 256 'Portuguese cannon' and 2304 minor cannon. Each battalion was issued with 512 iron rods, 7680 *jin* [3840 kilograms] of gunpowder, 256 000 rounds of lead pellets and 1280 lengths of fuse. Apart from the combat wagons, there were two drum wagons, four wagons carrying rocket arrows, three wagons with seating and eight wagons for generals.

Ordnance battalions

Battles with Mongol forces in northern China would often involve long treks of several hundred kilometres across mountains and desert. To be successful, campaigns required a reliable supply of grain and fodder, gunpowder and shot. The senior officers of the supply battalions were each responsible for their own vehicles. Each adjutant commanded 1660 soldiers, with eighty combat wagons, 160 'Portuguese cannon' and 640 fowling pieces. Aside from the combat wagons, there were also vehicles for the adjutant and for battle drums. Each battalion was required to transport three days of food rations for 10 000 men and horses, as well as keep the forces on the front-line supplied with weapons and ammunition. These supply battalions transported all weapons and grain under guard, with a battle-ready combat team to defend them when necessary.

Under Qi's command

Qi Jiguang made heavy demands of his troops. He would first work with individual battalions, paying special attention to their use of firearms, then work with two to five battalions in combined manoeuvres, conducting various military exercises.

When combat-wagon battalions were deployed in the field, Qi ordered them to stay in the front-line so as to inflict maximum damage on enemy cavalry. The combat-wagon battalions would initially bombard the enemy with 'Portuguese cannon' and fowling pieces. At medium range they would deploy their guns and crouching tiger cannon, and at close range they would use triple-barrelled muskets and regular weaponry. This strategy emphasised the use of firearms and made improvements in the deployment of different forces. The coordinated use of light and heavy weapons among the infantry, cavalry and combat-wagon battalions allowed for strategic offensive and defensive manoeuvres, to fatal effect.

In more static battle situations, the actual fortifications and manning of the wall were crucial. Each of the watchtowers had a leader in charge of thirty to fifty soldiers, with eight 'Portuguese cannon', eight barrels of gunpowder, fifty stone cannons and 500 rocket arrows. The entire area between two adjoining towers could be covered by arms fire from both sides. One of Qi Jiguang's fortresses is preserved at the Jinshanling Range section

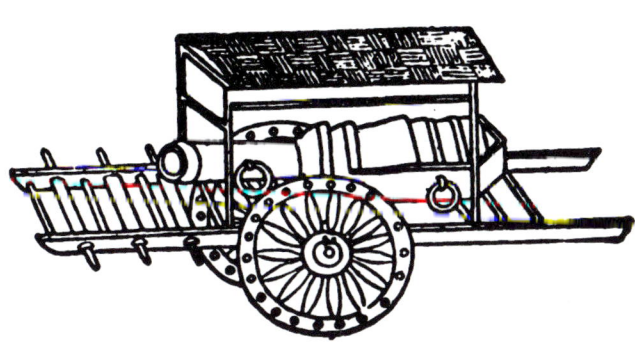

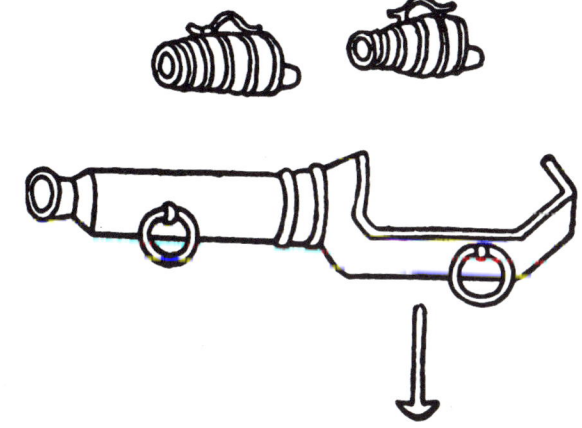

Woodblock print of 'Portuguese cannon'.
Reproduced from *Notes on military training* (Lianbing shiji zaji), 1937 reprint

of the Great Wall outside Beijing. The roof of the fortress has a parapet with crenellations for use in discharging cannon, and an internal staircase as well as rope ladders to allow people free movement between the two levels.

Qi Jiguang's troops were subject to extremely strict discipline. Troops in the vicinity of their home fortress would obey the orders of their leader. Away from the fortress, they would obey the nearest company commander. Orders issued within the army would be proven legitimate by the display of a metal permit inscribed with the character for 'authorization' (*ling*). Each soldier was issued with an identification permit worn at the waist.[8] Those travelling to or from their post were required to show this permit as proof of identity. The Ming dynasty employed a system of travel permits fashioned from bronze, an example of which is the 'bronze plate of the head of the Yongchang commandery for the night watch' (see p 205).[9]

If a guard detected enemy troop movements, a torch was raised immediately at a beacon platform, and the signal was relayed from platform to platform in both directions.

The infantry and cavalry of each circuit are to prepare their weapons upon receiving the signal, and either set out immediately or await further reports, or if the signal is received from the western sections of wall, to redeploy troops to defend that area. The troops of the entire garrison defending the walls responded in unison to the alarm. Soldiers on duty on top of the wall must remain vigilant day and night, and should be prepared to fall into rank immediately upon command and respond promptly to orders to advance or retreat.[10]

To further motivate his forces, Qi Jiguang transferred 3000 well-trained soldiers from his former command in Zhejiang in southern China to Jizhou. When they arrived it was raining heavily. Yet his soldiers stood in ranks outside in the rain and did not move all day until the order was given to do so. The Jizhou forces were said to have been profoundly impressed by this display of strict discipline.

As a result of Qi Jiguang's contribution to the construction and strengthening of the Great Wall defences, and to the discipline of his army, the Mongol soldiers had great difficulty in breaching them. In the spring of 1573, the leader of the Uriyanghkha Toghon Mongols, Dong Huli, together with his nephew Chaghan, charged the pass at Xifengkou and embarked on a campaign of pillage. Qi Jiguang raised his army and defeated them. But it was not long before Dong Huli again led his troops in another raid. This time, Qi captured the Mongol leader.

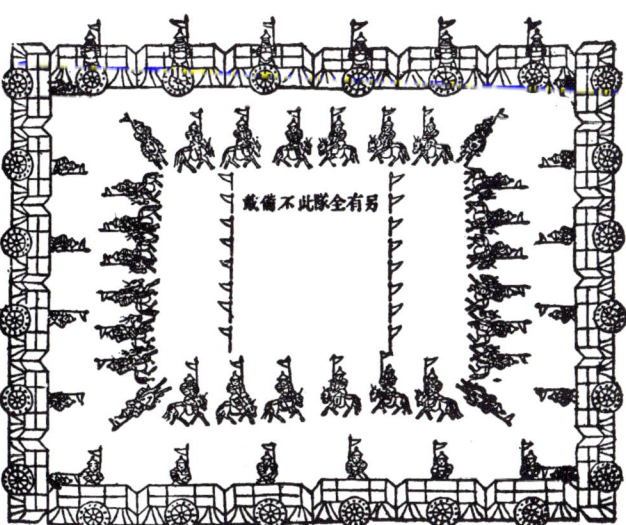

Illustration of the cavalry formation devised by Qi Jiguang.
Reproduced from *Notes on military training* (Lianbing shiji zaji), 1937 reprint

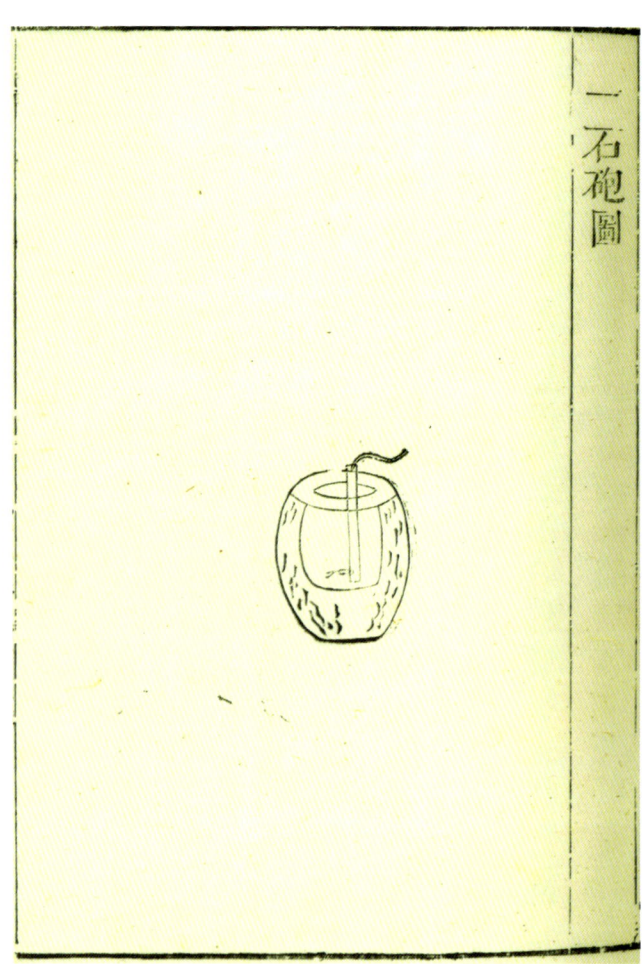

一石砲圖

Woodblock print of a stone bomb.
Reproduced from *Notes on military training* (Lianbing shiji zaji),
1937 reprint, courtesy the National Museum of China

Qi Jiguang released Dong in an attempt to sway the Mongols. But Dong Huli and Dong Changtu (Toghto) again banded together to raid Ming territory with their cavalry. They mounted a sudden attack on the Great Walls, but Qi Jiguang was waiting for them with his army. Dong Huli and Toghto were surprised when Qi's men, brandishing sabres, ambushed them and cut off their retreat. Toghto fled northwards with tens of thousands of his followers, but in the confusion there was a stampede in which men and horses were trampled or pushed into an abyss, leaving him with only a handful of survivors. At this point, another division of Qi's army charged from behind a mountain and took Toghto captive. Dong Huli approached the foot of the Great Wall. He pleaded with Qi Jiguang to release Toghto and promised they would never again attempt to breach the Great Walls. Qi Jiguang released Toghto. The two Mongol leaders, moved by Qi's act, returned both hostages and loot from previous raids. From this time on, Mongol forces never again breached the Ming borders.[11]

In 1582, Qi's patron at court, Zhang Juzheng, passed away. Qi Jiguang was relieved of his post and relocated to Guangdong. Unable to see his vision for the Great Walls fully implemented, he returned to his ancestral home of Dengzhou and, dejected, died three years later.

TRANSLATED BY ANTHONY GARNAUT WITH BRUCE GORDON DOAR

The emperor's call north

INTERVIEW WITH YANG JIANLI BY SANG YE

In 1644, the Manchu armies moved through the Great Wall to occupy Beijing, making it the capital of the Qing dynasty, which lasted until 1911. Before 'entering the pass', the Manchus had joined forces with Mongol clans. During their rule as the Qing, they expanded this coalition, both through diplomacy and under force of arms, to incorporate modern-day Xinjiang. During this last dynastic period, the Great Wall served no particular strategic function.

However, in the Qing dynasty conflicts outside the wall did continue, and during the years 1690 to 1755 the imperial rulers carried out a series of campaigns against the Zhungar [also known as the Dzungar, Zunghar, Junggar] empire of the Oirat Mongols, north of the Tianshan Mountains. During this war, instead of building new walls they constructed fortified garrison towns and filled them with imperial troops. Manchengzi, 'the Manchu walled city', outside the city of Wuwei in Gansu province, is one of these fortified garrisons.

Yang Jianli is a twenty-year old soldier in the fifty-fourth motorised brigade of the People's Liberation Army.

Originally, this castellated town of Manchengzi was a military barracks, and that's still what it is today. During the Qing dynasty it housed soldiers with queues. In the days of the Nationalists, the warlord Ma Bufang's troops were stationed here. They were good fighters and captured a lot of Red Army soldiers. Just think, those old Red Army men managed to survive the 25 000-*li* [12 500-kilometre] Long March only to be captured and killed here by Muslim soldiers. It doesn't seem fair. After liberation in 1949, this became a school for People's Liberation Army infantry and artillery troops. During its years as an artillery school it served for a time as a strategic missile base. Later the missiles were removed and eventually even the artillery left. That's when our motorised infantry brigade moved in.

I had a hint of what it was like to be a soldier even before I joined up. I had long hair then and my recruiting officer said, 'Get a crew cut. And don't say you can't afford it. If you don't have the money, I'll give you …' I thought he was going to say, 'I'll give you the money for it.' Instead he said, 'I'll give you a haircut myself.' It was really in your face.

I'd heard people say, 'In the vast desert the smoke rises in a straight line', so naturally I thought Wuwei would be a very desolate spot. But the commander who met our train said there were high-rise buildings, supermarkets and nightclubs. He told us we'd be stationed in the New City compound — that's what they'd renamed Manchengzi after liberation — on the edge of the city. And there were lots of girls in the communications corps as well. It was a veritable garden for the blossoms of the army.

When I got to Wuwei I discovered that what the commander said was true. The town was flourishing. But our compound was on the outskirts, surrounded by chaos and filth. It was like being next to a garbage dump. Sure, there were quite a few women soldiers around but, like that bustling centre of Wuwei itself, they had nothing to do with us.

One look at New City and my heart sank. The south gate is pretty modern, but the east and west gates are the original structures and the surrounding wall is made out

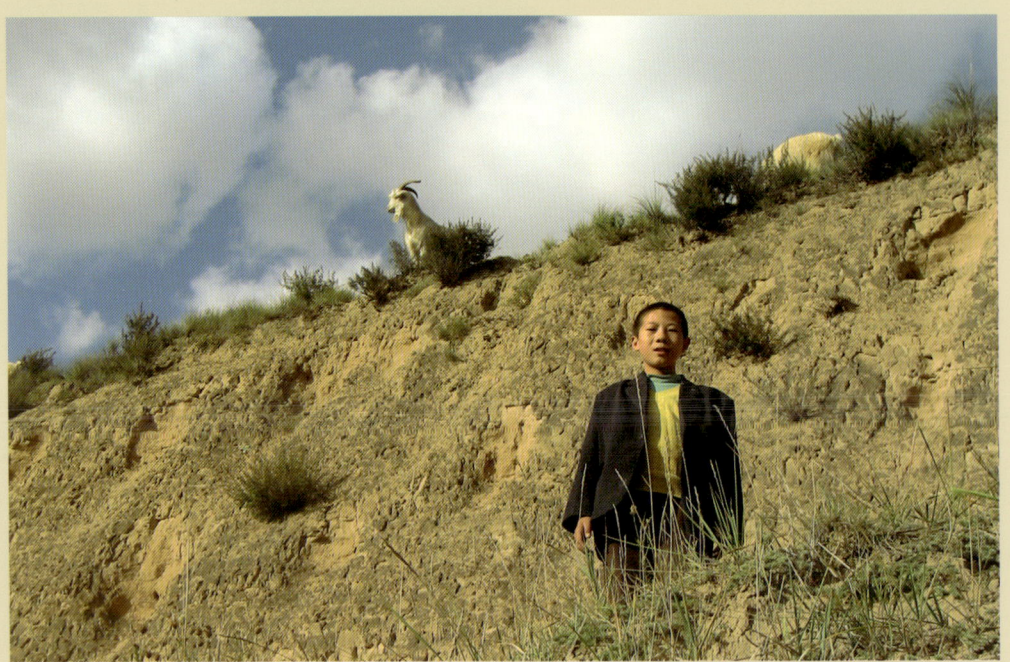

When his photo was taken, Kou Guiwen's mother had just died of heart disease because the family had no money to treat her illness. He is thirteen years old and has a strong sense of duty to his family. He was set to begin Year Seven at school but because tuition and board were very expensive, he decided to give up his schooling and to tend to the goats.
Photo: Yin Huairong; location: Xiangjiagou village, Shanxi province

of tamped earth. It's really solid and so wide that you could have men marching four abreast and still have room to move. You'd have to see it to believe it. So apart from being depressing, it's also pretty amazing, this 10-metre high old earthen walled city, like a castle from a children's story. It wasn't until later that I learned even Qianlong was still a boy when it was built.[1] That makes Manchengzi nearly 300 years old. For a moment, I went all romantic about this, suddenly recalling a poem our teacher made us learn as kids: 'The Son of Heaven orders me north to the wall'. It dates from the Zhou period, about 2700 years ago, and then there's this castellated city that's a few hundred years old, and you find you've walked into the tides of history. But I quickly learned that a soldier is just that, and there's no room for petit-bourgeois romanticism. As they say, a soldier has to 'be politically and militarily tough, outstanding in their work and rigorous in discipline, reliable and ready.' You have to 'pack your hopes in your rucksack, and become a brick in the Great Wall.'

There are lots of slogans like that in the army. Old soldiers come out with them at the drop of a hat: 'In the army, you must skill up. If you don't, you're out of luck.' 'The more you sweat in training, the less you'll bleed in fighting.' 'Sweat and bleed, but never weep. Lose skin and flesh, but your comrades keep.' Being a soldier is about making these slogans reality. But some of it is just hot air: when you're marching in formation you chant, 'Use me in the first battle, use me for victory.' The reality is that in modern warfare the first battle is a long-distance attack with missiles and airplanes. Our turn comes later.

When you first join a battalion, apart from marching 'one-two-one', you learn how to drop down and crawl. It's hard enough crawling over the parade ground, but when you start training out in the wild, crawling through the tussock and dirt, it's like you're using your clothes to wipe the ground. You pick up every bit of cow dung and horse manure you come across and feel like it can't get any harder. But there's worse because then they take you out to the Qilian Mountains in the Gobi Desert where you spend all morning dragging yourself back and forth across broken rocks. Your nose and mouth fill with sand until you don't even look human any more. At lunchtime you huddle in a group to eat your dry rations and then you spend the afternoon crawling through the dust and rocks again. Your hands, elbows and knees get shredded and you end up caked in mud made of blood, sweat and dirt. A soldier has to be prepared to bleed. 'Your suffering is nothing compared to the Red Army on the Long March. Your weariness is naught compared to the Old Revolutionaries.' You're covered in scars.

Marching in formation isn't hard, but they think of every way to torture you while you're doing it. The squad leader shouts out 'One!' and you put your right foot forward. It's still in mid-air when you realise that he hasn't shouted 'Two!' So you have to keep your leg in the air. They tell you it's about strengthening your will, but it's cruel. And they hit you. That's part of the training as well. Every enlisted man gets beaten. The squad leader is only a level-three officer, the lowest rank a volunteer soldier can be. As he hits you he says, 'You'll never grow up if you don't get walloped. It's my duty to beat you into shape. When you're squad leader you'll get to beat up the new recruits.' It's not that he hits that hard, but you're not allowed to give him one back and that's humiliating. But the squad leader's whistle is even worse. If he blows it in the dead of night, still half asleep, you have to jump out of bed and fall in. Then he makes you run a circuit around the parade ground before ordering you back to bed. Just when you're sound asleep again, the whistle could blow again. Since you decided to join up, you don't ask why. All an enlisted man has the right to say is: 'Here', 'Yes' and 'I understand'. When you've learned that, you're considered fit to be a soldier.

Apart from training and war games, you have to help reforest the Silk Road, do good deeds for the local people, and a ton of other things, big and small, designed to make you a better soldier. For example, on Sundays, just as you're having lunch, the squad leader might say, 'There'll be no break this afternoon. Hurry up with your meals because we've got work to do. The whole squad is going to collect nightsoil.' That means you're going to the local water plant to clean out the septic tank. No tools — you have to jump in barefoot and, with shit up to your knees, use your own washing basin to scoop out the muck. You end up with filth all over your arms, body and face. I'll never forget the stench and that sticky feeling. Collecting compost for fertiliser is fine, but why do it this way? No one can say. All we know is that you do 'what you're told and don't ask why. Take what you're given and never try and pass it by.'

The regulations stipulate that you get 6.2 yuan [$A1] for food every day; add to that what we grow ourselves and that amounts to about 8.2 yuan [$A1.40] daily. Is that a lot? No way! But things have improved. They don't just try and fill us up — the meals are actually nutritious as well. Volunteers get free food and clothing; the money you get paid on top of that is called an allowance. During your first year it comes to 80 yuan [$A13.50] a month, and goes up to 95 yuan [$A16] a month in your second year. Is that a lot? No way! Our commander says it's for buying things like toothpaste, stamps, various odds-and-ends and chewing gum. He says we should still be able to save, but he knows full well that it's not enough. Every soldier these days has to have enough to cover what we call stuff to eat, wear, rub, talk, wash, drink and drag.

'Eat' means snacks and the occasional meal out. As for 'wear', although you're normally in uniform, when you've got leave and want to go out looking good you need a few brand-name clothes to wear. Even guys need some inexpensive toiletries to 'rub' on. 'Talk' means long-distance calls, and they're not cheap. Training leaves you exhausted, so we get the laundry to wash our clothes.

Soldiers aren't allowed to drink, but nothing stops us from getting together on days off. As for 'drag' — what guy doesn't want to have a few cigarettes?

As a result, some guys end up borrowing money. They don't worry about paying back their debts because when you leave the service after two years your local government gives you a payout, about 3000 [$A500] a year. If you're in the service for five years that amounts to 15 000 yuan [$A2500]. So if borrowing a bit of money makes life easier, that's fine. My local government gives 3000 a year — more economically developed areas give a bit more. It's a market economy. If local governments didn't pay, they wouldn't be able to fill their quota of soldiers for the army. Without any incentive, who'd sign up?

After training like we do, everyone serving in Manchengzi becomes brothers, even the squad leader who hit me and the officers who don't even know my name. The Son of Heaven orders me north to the wall, and here together we stand or fall.

There are 206 large poplars in the centre of the compound. They're quite odd, because if you cut a branch you'll see there's a faint red star in the cross-section. They're called red star poplars. They say that one grows for each of the 206 Red Army soldiers killed by the Muslim troops. They're buried here and their spirits live on in the trees. It sounds far-fetched but cut any branch and you'll see that little red star. We've spilled our blood here too and we've become part of the Great Wall. It's like we're connected to those red stars. Just knowing that is enough. The army doesn't need anything more special than that from us. 'If you don't have to go to war, just behave yourself and be a good soldier for two years and that in itself is an outstanding contribution to the motherland.' Our political commissar says that all the time.

I feel as though my time here in Manchengzi has transformed me entirely. After high school I couldn't get into college. I was hanging out all the time at internet cafes playing computer games and my dad worried that I'd get into trouble. He insisted I join the army. After all that training I've learned to be a soldier. No one needs to worry about me anymore. Computer games are bullshit — I want to fight a real war, to see some action … I'll be demobbed in another year. I'll decide what to do after that. Maybe I'll be a pharmaceutical company rep. One of my classmates has made a fortune doing that. I'm sure I'd be even better at it than he is. After all, isn't it just a matter of selling pills? I'll shout our army slogan at every doctor I meet: 'I have what others don't! I'm better than the rest! Others are good but I'm the best! I'm the very best!'

TRANSLATED BY GEREMIE R BARMÉ

Ming dynasty

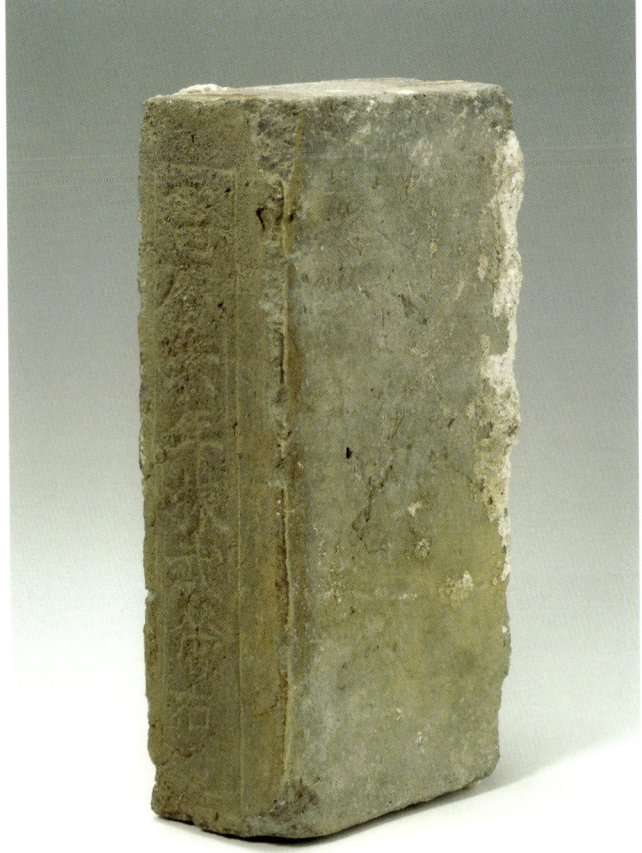

These bricks, made to a standard size and weighing about 12.5 kilograms, are typical of the bricks used in construction of the Ming dynasty Great Wall at the mountainous Jinshanling section. One is inscribed: 'Made by the Valiant Battalion in the sixth year of the Wanli Reign [1578]'. The inscription on the other reads: 'Made by the Border Cavalry Battalion in the sixth year of the Wanli Reign [1578]'. Bricks used in the Ming dynasty walls were thought to have been made in brick kilns built at many places near the walls, using locally quarried clays. Inscribed bricks provide valuable historical information about the date of construction and organisation of workforces engaged in building sections of the Great Walls.

Bricks from the Great Wall
Ming dynasty (1368–1644),
dated 1578
From the Jinshanling
section of the Great Wall
Terracotta
Above 9.5 (h) x 18.7 (w) x 37 (l) cm;
Right 9.5 (h) x 8.5 (w) x 37.5 (l) cm
Collection of the National Museum
of China (C9.343, C9.347)

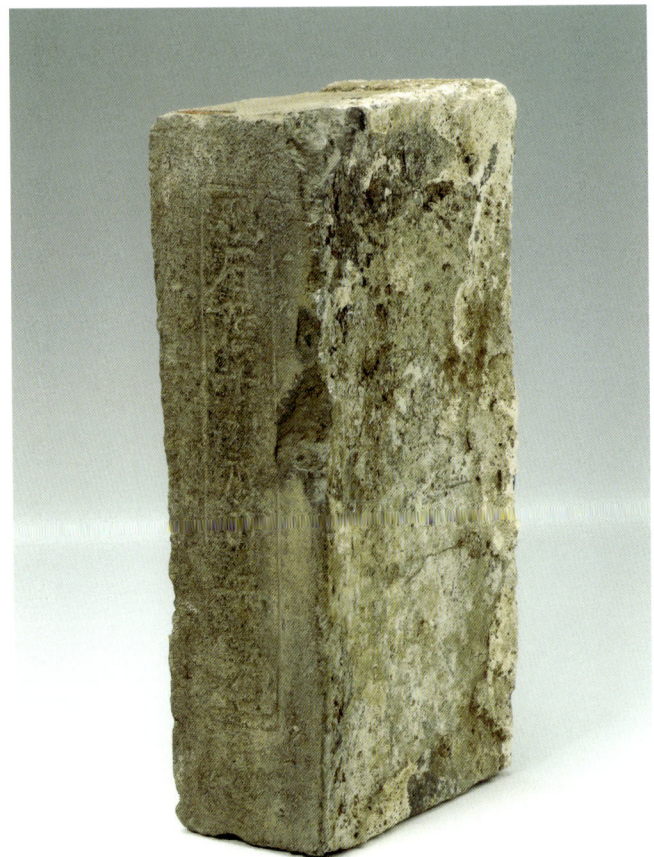

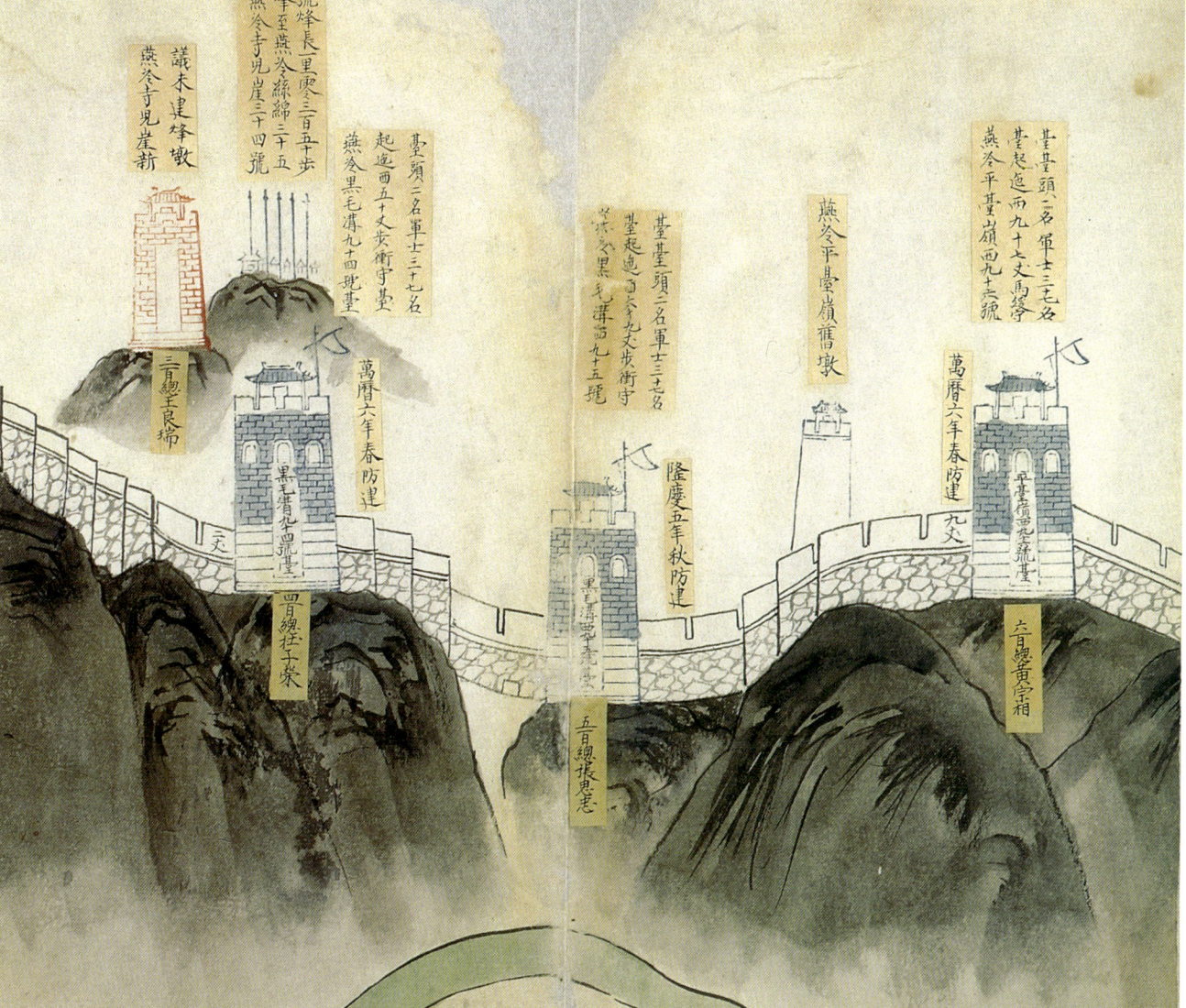

Plans of the Jizhou commandery, folded leaves
Artist unknown
Ming dynasty (1368–1644)
Painted and stamped,
ink and colour on paper
19.1 (h) x 332 (l) cm
Collection of the National
Museum of China (C14.2142)

Detail above
Full scroll following pages

The *Plans of the Jizhou commandery* (Jizhen changcheng tu) were originally folded in accordion form. The *Plans* have more than 670 sections depicting the territory of eleven passes on the twelve circuits in the Jizhou commandery. Jizhou was one of the nine regional commanderies established along the Great Wall in the Ming dynasty, each in charge of a section of the wall. The orientation of the *Plans* differs from that

of *The nine commanderies* scroll produced in the same period (see pp 198–99); it looks towards the equator with the south in the upper part and the north in the lower half. The locations of watchtowers, mountains, camps and fortresses are represented using a stamping technique, and the mountain, rocks, and hills are rendered in brush and ink using traditional Chinese landscape painting techniques. The techniques used indicate that the plans were made for practical, not decorative, purposes.

The characters written in ink on labels provide a record of military deployments along this section of the Great Wall, and suggest that the *Plans* were painted during the Wanli reign of the Ming dynasty (1573-1620). The section of the Great Wall under the Jizhou commandery served as an important barrier safeguarding the Ming capital in the north. Illustrated here are two of eleven sections of the plans.

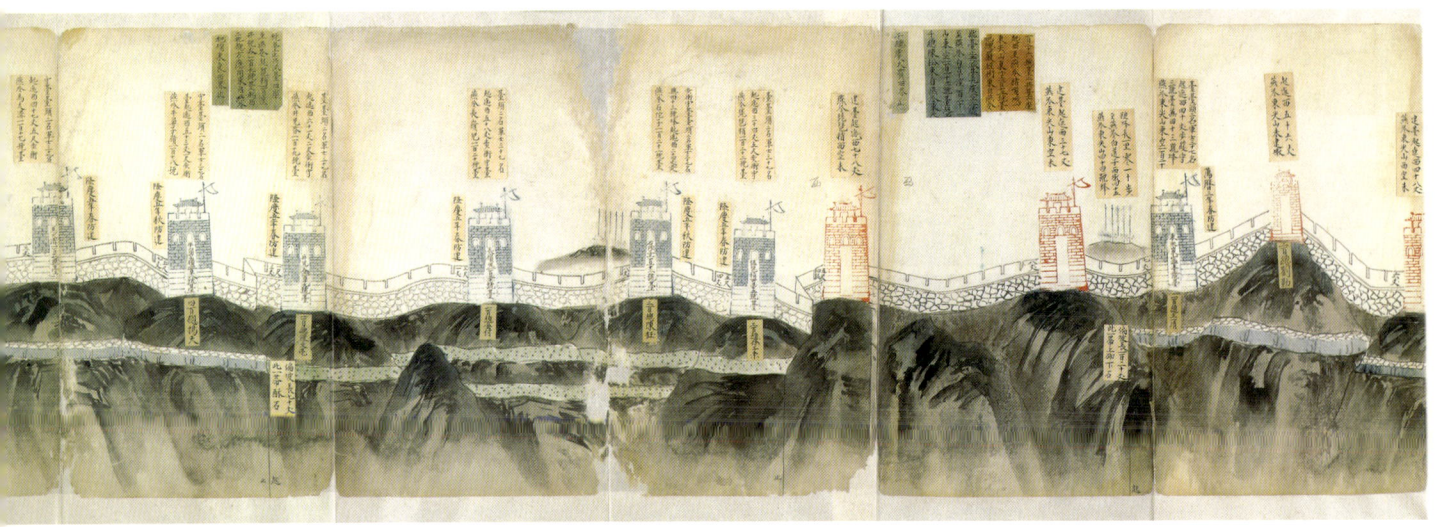

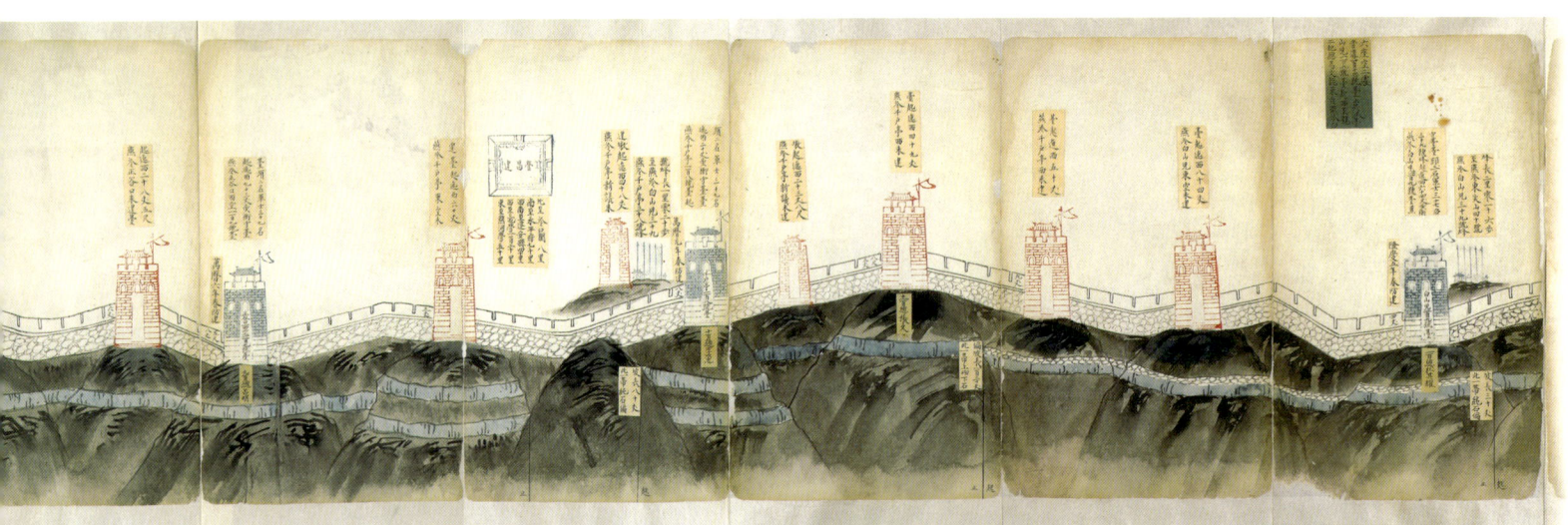

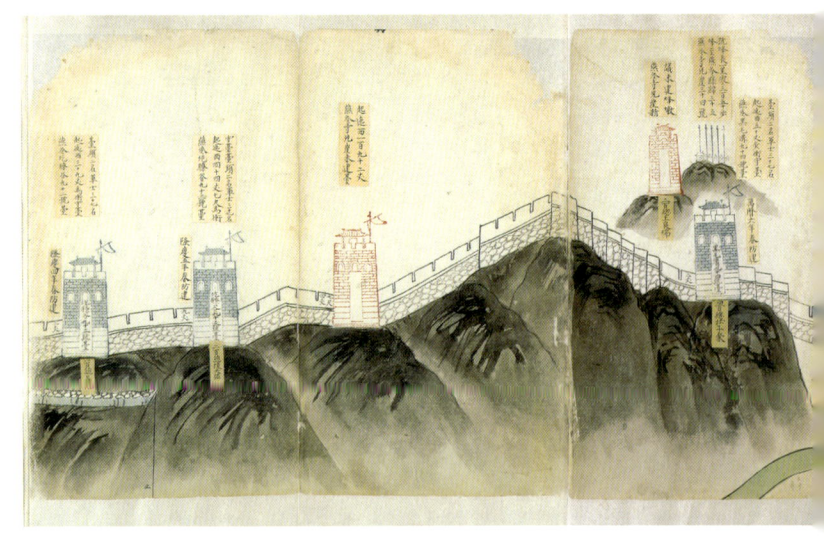

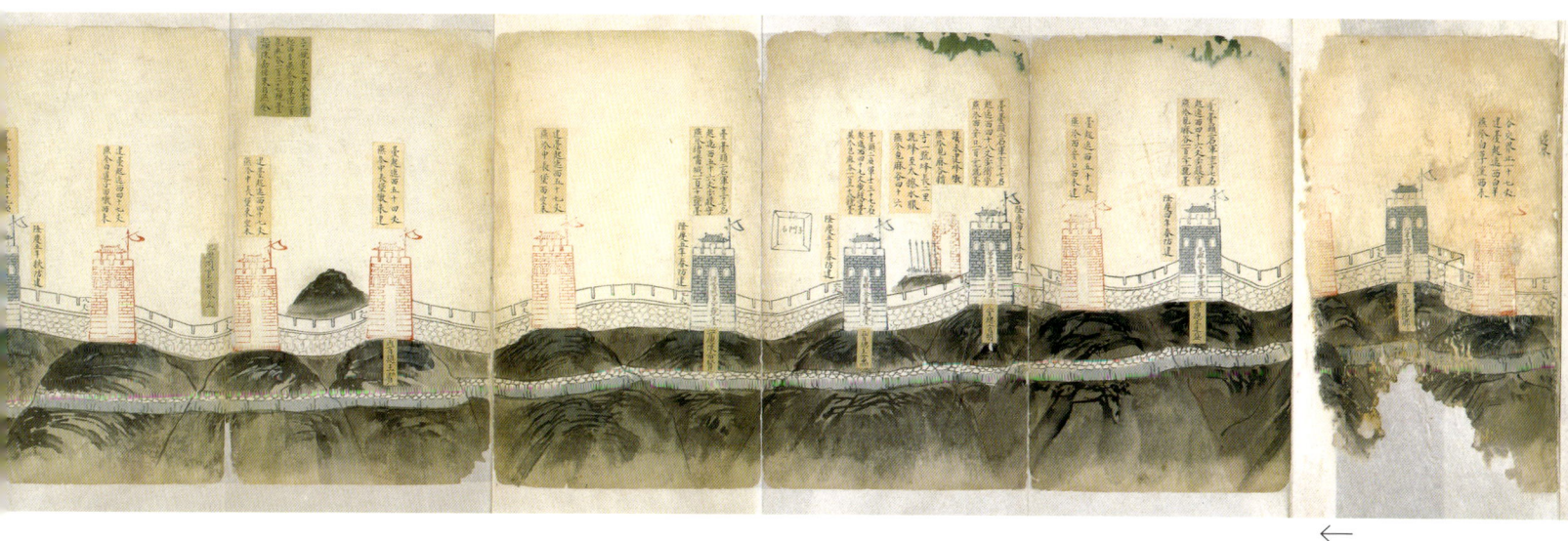

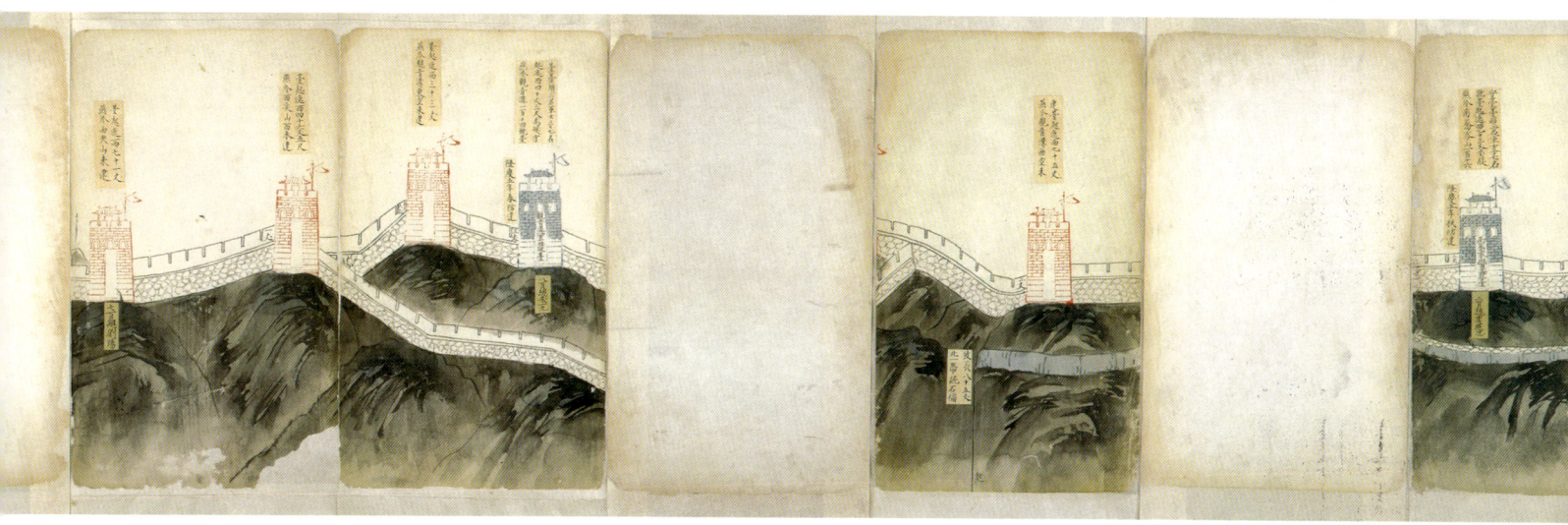

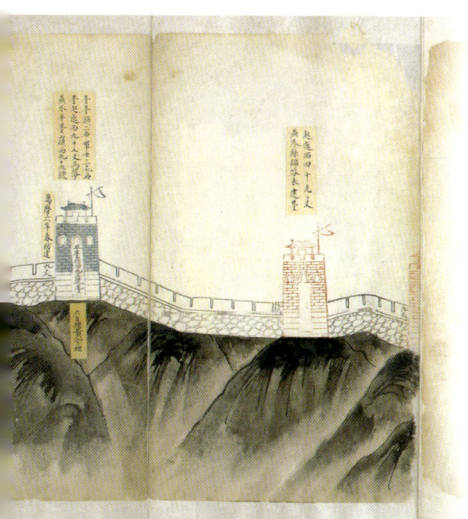

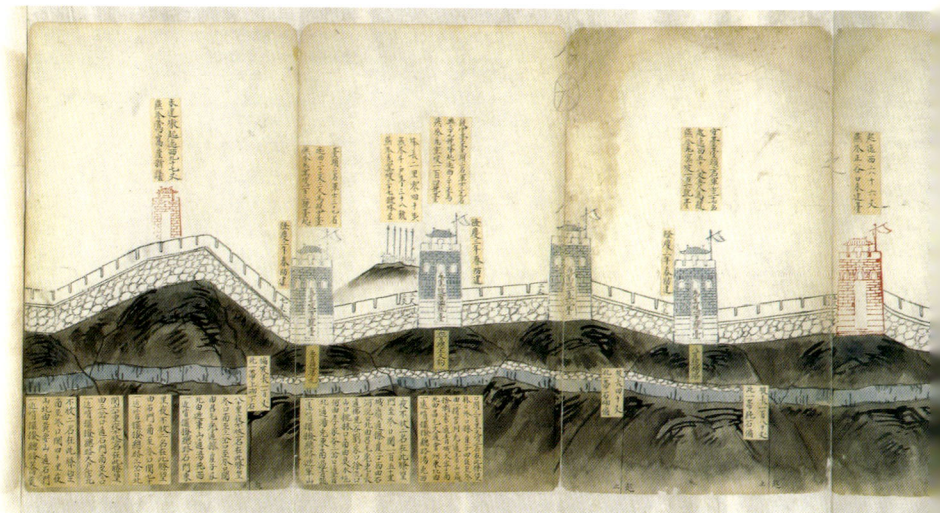